QUANTIFYING ARCHAEOLOGY

for Sue

(Quantifying
ARCHAEOLOGY)

STEPHEN (SHENNAN)

**EDINBURGH
UNIVERSITY PRESS**

ACADEMIC PRESS, INC.
Harcourt Brace Jovanovich, Publishers

© Stephen Shennan 1988

Published in Great Britain by
Edinburgh University Press
22 George Square, Edinburgh

Printed in Great Britain by
J. W. Arrowsmith Ltd, Bristol

British Library
   Cataloguing in Publication Data
Shennan, Stephen
Quantifying archaeology
1. Mathematical statistics
2. Archaeology—statistical methods
I. Title
519.5′02493   QA276
ISBN 0 85224 460 6 cloth
     0 85224 473 8 paper

Published in the
United States of America by
Academic Press, Inc.
Harcourt Brace Jovanovich, Publishers
San Diego, California
ISBN 0-12-639860-7

QA
276
.553

Contents

v

Preface

As chapter one of this book makes clear, quantitative methods have become increasingly important in archaeology in recent years, and indeed considerable progress has been made in terms of the degree of sophistication of the analyses and of the matching between archaeological data and appropriate mathematical methods. The specialists in any sub-field of a discipline, particularly when that sub-field involves mathematics, are always going to be working at a level which non-specialists cannot match, but it is important for the general health of the discipline as a whole that its practitioners should have some awareness of the sub-field and its wider implications. Archaeology now has a small group of impressively competent mathematical specialists but the bulk of the people practising the discipline do not even understand what they are talking about, never mind its implications. This is a dangerous state of affairs because it leads on the one hand to the outright dismissal of methods which may be useful, and on the other to an excessive gullibility with regard to claims backed by mathematical arguments and analyses. If you can't actually evaluate the arguments, what choice is there? This situation contrasts with what I believe is a much more healthy situation in geography, where the body of mathematical and statistical specialists is at the apex of a broadly based pyramid of practitioners with basic mathematical and statistical knowledge.

The difference lies in the educational process in the two disciplines. Quantitative methods were quickly integrated into the education of geographers as a result of the quantitative geography revolution of the 1950s and 1960s. Comparable developments in archaeology were never incorporated into the education of archaeologists to anything like the same extent, for reasons which, I suspect, have more to do with the sociology of the discipline, especially within the universities, than with anything else. Correspondingly, textbooks on mathematics and statistics in geography have proliferated, while

vii

it would be true to say that archaeology has had nothing comparable.

This book aims to fill that gap. It fits between *Mathematics in Archaeology* (Orton 1980) on the one hand, and *Mathematics and Computers in Archaeology* (Doran and Hodson 1975) on the other. Orton's book is a very clear, indeed excellent, account of how quantitative methods can be of assistance to archaeologists, but in no sense is it a textbook. Doran and Hodson's book is basically more advanced than this one. Its brief coverage of elementary methods, while in many ways a model of elegant conciseness, is too compressed for people who don't know the material already.

This book arises from a course in quantitative methods of data analysis which I have given over a number of years in the Department of Archaeology, University of Southampton. As time has gone on the course has changed considerably from the earliest version, in response to student feedback and developments in the field. (Statistics itself is a fast changing discipline, a fact which outsiders tend not to appreciate.) Indeed, some discussion and explanation is appropriate at this point, concerning what the book contains and what it doesn't.

First, it is about data analysis in *archaeology* and is thus oriented more towards studies of objects, excavations and archaeological data from surveys than towards more laboratory based studies, such as soil properties, chemical analyses, etc.; in general such studies have their own mathematical and quantitative tradition, derived from the discipline where the techniques originate.

This orientation has undoubtedly influenced the selection of material to present here. And indeed my next point concerning the book's content is precisely that it is not comprehensive, in the sense of covering all the quantitative techniques which have been used or could be useful to archaeologists. To do that would have taken a book far longer than this one. The intention has been to give an impression of the kinds of things which can be done at different levels; how the archaeological topic becomes translated into statistical terms, and the problems associated with this; and to provide a technical grounding in some of the most important techniques. In a textbook such as this it is natural that the latter should take up most of the space.

The aim of the first part is to show students how to carry out some of the most basic techniques for themselves; the aim of the second part is to give an intuitive understanding of some of the more complex methods, based on a geometric approach and archaeological examples, as a basis for understanding the literature. Familiarity with the material presented here in the context of archaeological examples will make it much easier for those who want to use other techniques not covered here to understand statistical literature written for other audiences, such as geographers and sociologists.

At the basic statistics level the most obvious omission is the *t*-test, and more generally a lack of discussion of distributional theory, except rather briefly in chapters 8 and 14. This was not done without considerable thought. In fact, such material was covered extensively in the early versions of the course from which this book originates. It was dropped because the amount of complex technical detail which had to be covered at a fairly early point in the proceedings was proving to be a major obstacle both to understanding the quantitative methods themselves and to seeing any relevance of them to archaeology. Not including them proved to be a lot more satisfactory: the gain far outweighed the loss.

Another obvious omission is spatial analysis. Hodder and Orton (1976) still provide a good introduction for archaeologists here, backed up by the many geographical texts. In this light it was felt that the desirability of including something rather more elementary than Hodder and Orton on spatial analysis was outweighed by the significant increase in size of this book which it would have involved.

The introductory intention of the book precludes examination of the more advanced techniques now being used in archaeological research, such as those based on computer simulation, but there is a brief discussion of these in the final chapter. One or two sections of the book, however, are more advanced than the rest and many people will want to skip them on the first time through. This is especially the case with the last section of chapter 7 and, to a lesser extent, parts of chapter 10 and 11. They are included to show what detailed data analysis can involve and how it may be done. They are examples, as are others in this book, of the realisation of a sceptical approach to data and data patterning. Indeed, if I have one hope for this book, it is not that readers will retain a memory of the details of the statistical techniques it covers, but that they will have acquired an informed, sceptical and questioning attitude to the quantitative analyses of themselves and others. In this way things can only improve.

Over the years, in teaching quantitative methods and preparing this book I have incurred a number of debts which must be acknowledged. First, and most important, I have to thank the students who have taken my courses, especially Todd Whitelaw, Hans-Peter Wotzka and Nick Winder. Their critical questioning has meant that I could never get away with anything and I've benefited enormously as a result! I'm also grateful to Professor Colin Renfrew for his early encouragement and support for the teaching of quantitative methods at Southampton, and to Archie Turnbull of Edinburgh University Press for encouraging me in the writing of this book and offering many constructively critical comments on an earlier draft. Finally, I owe a special debt of gratitude to Dr Nick Fieller, Department of Probability and Statistics, University of Sheffield, for his invaluable assistance in reading the manuscript with an expert eye; and to Professor R. Barry Lewis, Department of Anthropology, University of Illinois at Urbana-Champaign, who made many helpfully blunt comments and suggestions. Neither they nor anyone else except myself is responsible for the inadequacies that remain.

One

Introduction

The aim of this text is to make students familiar with some of the basic quantitative methods currently used in archaeology. Of course, these techniques are not specific to archaeology, being used in a great variety of fields, but experience has shown that archaeology students do not gain a great deal from attending statistics classes for sociologists or biologists because, although the statistical theory and methods are the same, the examples used are alien. To the student of archaeology such examples are boring and often incomprehensible. To most people quantitative methods tend to be sufficiently forbidding to need no handicaps of this kind. Teaching in such an alien framework is particularly unfortunate because many non-mathematically inclined people find that they can best get an initial grasp of a topic not by learning about the theory behind it, but by following through a worked example. For these reasons a specifically archaeological introductory text seemed worthwhile.

It is hoped that by the end of the book students will themselves be able to use the simple techniques described, will have some feel for the way archaeological questions can be translated into quantitative terms, and will have a basis for talking to statisticians, in their own terms, if problems are more complex. This last point is of some importance. If you turn to a statistician for help and neither of you knows what the other is talking about, you will probably end up with the wrong answer to the wrong question.

The text assumes very little in the way of prior knowledge. Only the most basic mathematical operations of addition, subtraction, multiplication and division, together with roots, powers and logarithms are needed. Calculus and matrix algebra are not required.

WHY QUANTITATIVE METHODS?

This question must be considered before we go further. In fact, it is possible to divide it into two rather different questions: why should

students concern themselves with quantitative methods in archaeology, and why should archaeology, as such, concern itself with
quantitative methods.

One answer to the first of these questions is that the archaeological literature is increasingly given over to papers whose arguments
depend on the application of such methods. A knowledge of them
is therefore essential if their arguments are to be understood and
evaluated. This is certainly true, but it does not answer the second
and larger question. The most cynical view would be that archaeology has become involved with quantitative methods purely as a
result of disciplinary fashion. The last thirty years have seen the
biological sciences, geography and many of the social sciences
become increasingly quantitative; it is now a matter of prestige for
a discipline to appear to be 'scientific', an endeavour in which
quantitative methods have a key role. Archaeology has simply
followed this trend, adopting the 'archaeologists in white coats'
image, and in the process has carried out a successful piece of
disciplinary imperialism, expanding its influence, its manpower and
the resources allocated to it generally. In due course, such an
argument might go, such approaches will become less fashionable,
indeed perhaps are already becoming so, and will gradually fade
from significance. I think it would be foolish to try to deny altogether this aspect of the 'quantitative revolution' as it has been
called in geography, but such arguments from the sociology of
science are certainly only part of the story.

One key factor has been the rise of the computer. As we are well
aware, computers now have a great variety of roles in archaeology.
In the last decade they have become increasingly widely used as
data management tools for such tasks as the recording of excavation
data and the building up of regional data banks of archaeological
information, the former development in particular greatly en-
hanced by the advent of microcomputers (Richards and Ryan 1985,
Gaines 1981). The use of computers in archaeological model-building has also become important: computer programs have been
written to simulate processes as diverse as the collapse of Maya
civilisation (Hosler *et al.* 1977) and tool manufacture and discard in
Australian aboriginal subsistence-settlement systems (Aldenderfer
1981); numerous examples are to be found in books edited by
Hodder (1978), Renfrew and Cooke (1979) and Sabloff (1981).

Here I want to consider only their use as tools for carrying out
data analysis, which is in fact the purpose for which computers were
first introduced into archaeology, and indeed into many other sub-

jects. Prior to the development and first application of computers in the 1950s and early 1960s uses of mathematics and statistics were largely restricted to the 'hard sciences'. This was at least partly because the solutions to many problems of interest could be obtained by means of elegant methods of mathematical analysis which did not require enormous numbers of calculations. Similarly, the statistical techniques which for the same reason were practically possible, proved very useful in many scientific, technological and industrial applications, but less so with the more intractable data of geography, archaeology or the social sciences. Only with the development of a means of carrying out enormous numbers of calculations at very high speeds did it become possible to apply methods appropriate to the kind of problems which the data from such disciplines presented.

It might be said that such an exciting new toy as the computer was eventually bound to be tried by archaeologists, and that the involvement of archaeology in quantitative methods simply stems from an attempt by archaeologists who like such toys to find a use for them. This cannot altogether be excluded.

However, it still does not take us to the heart of the matter, which lies not in fashion, nor in the availability of computers, but in the fact that quantitative reasoning is central to archaeology, and that a better grasp of this fact might well improve our work as archaeologists. Clive Orton's book *Mathematics in Archaeology* (1980) provides an excellent demonstration of why this is the case, by taking some of the standard questions which archaeologists ask, such as 'What is it?', 'How old is it?', 'Where does it come from?' and 'What was it for?', and showing how a quantitative approach can help to provide the answers. It follows, therefore, that quantitative methods should be seen, not as a distinct scientific specialism within archaeology, like pollen analysis, for example, or the various techniques of artefact characterisation, but as part of every archaeologist's mental tool-kit. Statistical, mathematical and computer specialists may often be required to cope with particular problems, but archaeologists must have sufficient quantitative awareness to recognise when problems arise which can be helpfully tackled in a quantitative fashion. No one else can do this for them.

Given that this is the case, it remains to be specified exactly where the mathematics and the archaeology come together. Part of the answer is in the simple description of the archaeological record: *numbers* of potsherds of different types, *sizes* of pits, and so on. Such quantitative information is an essential part of all modern archaeological reports, and simple quantitative description is the first topic we will consider.

Much more important than this, however, is the link described by Orton (1980). The archaeologist makes his inferences about the past on the basis of patterning and relationships in the archaeological record. Mathematics is an abstract system of relationships. The possibility then exists that mathematics may help us to recognise patterning in the archaeological record and to specify its nature. The area where mathematics meets the messier parts of the real world is usually statistics. It is precisely this fact that makes statistics in many ways a tricky subject, because mathematical and factual considerations are both involved, and because the relationships which we look at are almost never perfect ones.

Orton shows very clearly that all interpretation of the archaeological record is concerned with identifying patterning and is capable of benefiting from a quantitative approach. It is nevertheless a historical fact that the main impetus for the introduction of quantitative methods of archaeological data analysis came from the North American 'New Archaeology' tradition of the 1960s, and as a result of this 'New Archaeology' and the use of quantitative methods became inextricably associated in the general archaeological consciousness, both being labelled as 'anti-humanistic' (Hawkes 1968). Doran and Hodson (1975) were at pains to point out, correctly, that there was no necessary connection between the two, and that quantitative approaches could be used to tackle traditional archaeological problems. However, it is still the 'New Archaeology' tradition, now known, twenty-five years on, as the 'processual' school, that has made the greatest use of such techniques and it is worth asking why quantitative analysis has been, and remains, one of its distinguishing features, despite the fact that some applications of such methods have since been shown to be classic examples of misuse and misinterpretation (Thomas 1978).

I believe there are several reasons for this. First, least praiseworthy and probably least important: quantitative methods are regarded as 'scientific' and the New Archaeology specifically set out to adopt a scientific approach to the subject, making the use of quantitative methods ideologically necessary. Second, New Archaeology emphasised explicitness and objectivity, both of which are considerably aided by the rigour of quantitative analysis, which has a vital role to play in removing at least some potential sources of self-deception. Third, it advocated a hypothetico-deductive approach to the study of the past, in which hypotheses are gener-

ated, ideally from a strong base in theory; archaeological implications of those hypotheses are deduced; and these are then compared with the archaeological record for their goodness of fit.
Whatever the merits or demerits of such an approach – and they
have been the subject of considerable debate – it remains the case
that testing for the goodness of fit between hypotheses and data is
one of the main tasks with which statistics concerns itself.

Finally, and probably most important, the New Archaeology
took a systemic view of the past. Rejecting the view that spatial
differences in the archaeological record stemmed from the spatially
varying norms of the population, and that change through time was
the result of changing norms arising from diffusion, or the replacement of one people by another, it argued that what mattered was
the adaptive context – how people related to the environment and
to other people. Within this framework the investigation of relationships between variables which could be measured in the
archaeological record attained a new and justified significance; the
only way to do it was quantitatively.

To sum up, inasmuch as the processual school has been more
concerned than any other school of archaeology with the formulation of explicit hypotheses about relationships between features of
the archaeological record, it has inevitably been forced more frequently to depend on quantitative analysis. The demonstration of
the inadequacies of the normative approach and of the importance
of investigating systemic relationships has been a major advance,
and the quantitative consequences have to be faced.

Of course, in the last twenty-five years the processual school has
changed considerably. It has also been heavily attacked, particularly from the European side of the Atlantic, by critics who argue
that many of its most basic assumptions are invalid (e.g. Hodder
1982). It might perhaps be thought then that we are now in a period
when the use of quantitative methods in archaeology is going out
of fashion and declining in importance. Changes have certainly
occurred in the quantitative field. There is now less emphasis than
there used to be on statistical hypothesis testing in archaeology, a
situation which this book reflects. Furthermore, a greater awareness of the problems of interpreting the archaeological record as
evidence of past behaviour has also developed, and with it a rejection of the over-optimistic notion that quantitative data analysis
could somehow provide direct insights into the past which are
denied to more traditional approaches. However, I do not believe
that the theoretical changes which have been taking place within

the discipline as a whole will result in a decline in the use of quantitative techniques because the study of relationships between phenomena remains of fundamental importance, whatever the theoretical framework adopted, and in many cases the only way to investigate relational patterning in the archaeological record is quantitatively. Thus, for example, Tilley (1984, Shanks and Tilley 1982) makes extensive use of multivariate data analysis(see below, chapters 11 and 12) but rejects the theoretical basis of processual archaeology out of hand. The need for the methods arises because the archaeological record presents itself to us as an apparently largely disorganised mass of material, eloquent in its silence.

THE PLACE OF QUANTITATIVE METHODS
IN ARCHAEOLOGICAL RESEARCH

Before turning to the techniques themselves it is best to say something about the exact place of quantitative methods in the archaeological research process. Such analysis itself generally comes at a very late stage, but this is deceptive. At the research design stage the investigator should be deciding not just what to do but how to do it, including appropriate forms of analysis. Once these decisions are made they define the conduct of the research, and nowhere is this more important than in ensuring that the data collected and the method of their collection correspond to the requirements of the techniques it is proposed to use, including the theoretical assumptions the techniques presuppose. Discovering the problems at the analysis stage is too late.

Finally, and in a sense obviously, the techniques used have an effect on the results obtained and the archaeological conclusions drawn from them. In fact, as we shall see, the relation between the methods used and the patterns 'discovered' can be quite complex.

Research is not a linear process, of course; it is a loop, because the conclusions will inevitably send you or somebody else back to the first stage again, to design a new investigation.

THE EXERCISES: A COMMENT

The way in which the techniques used relate both to the initial research design and to the archaeological conclusions is obviously of considerable importance – indeed, in conceptual terms it is obviously more important than the details of the techniques themselves. These issues will inevitably be raised in this text, but its main aim is to make you familiar with the techniques, so it will be necessary to devote most attention to the details of how they are carried out. The importance of doing the exercises and problems cannot be over-emphasised. You may think you have understood everything you have read but you will only find out whether you have in fact done so by attempting and solving the problems. It is only by this process that you will achieve a degree of numeracy and, as Colin Renfrew has said, 'The days of the innumerate are numbered'.

Two

Quantifying Description

Collections of archaeological material do not speak for themselves; it is necessary for archaeologists to specify aspects which they are interested in, and these will be determined by their aims. The process of going from aims to relevant aspects of one's material is by no means simple. Some archaeologists, Lewis Binford in particular, would say that it has rarely been done successfully and that consequently most archaeological reconstructions of the past are no better than fictions (Binford 1981).

Let us consider an example. Suppose one is interested in studying social stratification through time in a given area. The next step might be to look at the archaeological record of that area and to decide that the best aspect for giving us an indication of changing social stratification would be the variation, through time, in the quantity of metal grave goods deposited in the richest graves in the area. A diachronic picture showing the changing quantities of metal could then be drawn. However, if the quantities of metal deposited related not to the wealth of the individuals but to changes in mining technology or in the trade contacts of the area, then the picture would reflect, not changing social stratification at all, but something else. If, after we had mistakenly argued that metal deposition related to social stratification, we then went on to try and explain the reasons for growing social stratification, we would be making matters even worse, because we would be trying to explain something that never occurred! Presented in this stark form, the pitfalls seem obvious enough, but they are very easy to fall into in practice, and much recent work has been devoted to improving our understanding of the processes which produce the archaeological record.

For the purposes of this text we will have to skirt round this problem most of the time and to assume that we have selected for investigation an aspect of our material which is appropriate to our interests. In practice, particularly at the level of describing material, such as that recovered from an excavation, there is broad agreement about what categories of information should be recorded and presented, so that, for better or worse, we do not have to agonise too much. Nevertheless, the problem sketched above is a very real one, basic to archaeology, and it will be necessary to return to it later.

Once we have defined the aspects of our material in which we are interested, it is necessary to prepare a record of them ready for analysis. When data are being collected, the process of assigning a value or score to the material in which we are interested constitutes the process of measurement. This is a much more general definition than simply measuring things with a set of calipers or weighing them on a pair of scales – measurement can be of many different kinds. If we are studying a collection of pottery, for example, there are many aspects in which we could be interested: the height or volume of the vessels, the decorative motifs used on them, the fabrics of which they are made, or their shapes. For each vessel in our collection we need to record the information in which we are interested. The result of this work will be a large table of scores and values for each aspect of interest to us (table 2.1). The aspects of our material in which we are interested in a given study are often referred to as the *variables* of interest.

Table 2.1. Example of the information recorded for a group of ceramic vessels.

	Height (mm)	Rim diameter (mm)	Fabric type	Rim type	Motif in position 1	Motif in position 2	...
Vessel 1	139	114	1	1	16	11	...
Vessel 2	143	125	2	1	12	9	...
⋮							
Vessel *n*	154	121	4	3	21	15	...

The process of measurement, especially the coding of such things as pottery descriptions, is by no means always a straightforward one and requires a lot of clear thinking (see Richards and Ryan 1985, Gardin 1980 for further discussion of this topic). More often than not it is carried out as a preliminary to entering the data into a file on a computer, prior to detailed analysis. It is very important that the data are coded in a form relevant to the intended analyses, otherwise a great deal of time may be wasted in juggling with the data in the computer files in order to put them into the right form.

The precise form in which the coding problem arises is now beginning to change as archaeologists increasingly use special database management programs for the input and handling of their data, as opposed to inputting them directly into specific data analysis programs with very precise data format requirements. This new development gives a welcome extra degree of flexibility but it does not remove the substantive problem of data description, as Gardin (1980) emphasises.

Other questions are raised by the coding process itself: it is important to avoid ambiguities and logical inconsistencies. Coding pottery decoration can be especially difficult since it can involve making decisions about what are the basic units of the decorative scheme, what are simply variations within the basic structure, and many others such; the matter is well discussed by Plog (1980).

A general question which often arises is what to include and what to omit from the description, even when you know what your aims are. For example, if studying a cemetery of inhumation burials containing grave goods and trying to make inferences about the social organisation of the community which deposited the burials, do you include information on the position of each of the grave goods in the grave as well as what they are? Perhaps the exact position of the limbs of the skeleton is significant in some way? The usual answer is to err on the side of inclusion rather than omission, but in a very large study this may involve an enormous amount of work which may not prove relevant and which may have cost an enormous amount of money, especially if it is fieldwork. A solution here is to carry out a pilot study: a preliminary analysis of a small part of the data is made using the full description and any variables which do not seem to vary are not recorded for the full data set. It is no exaggeration to say that decisions taken at the coding stage can have a major effect on the outcome of the subsequent analysis.

Once we have produced the table of data, all the information is there but it is not yet very accessible to us. We are not usually interested in the characteristics of each individual item, but in the assemblage of material as a whole, so that when we ask questions such as, 'How common are the different pottery fabrics?', 'Are the vessels a standard size?', answers are not immediately available from the table. We need to summarise our data (the values of our variables) in some way. Pictures are one of the best ways, but in order to produce appropriate ones we first need to consider the measurement characteristics of our variables, or what are known as *levels of measurement*.   What are these levels, or scales? They are, in order of their mathematical power, *nominal, ordinal, interval* and *ratio*. To start with the lowest, the nominal scale is so-called because it involves no more than giving names to the different categories within it. You might not think of this as measurement at all, but as the process of *classification*: placing things in groups or categories, a basic first step in virtually any investigation. Suppose we were studying British bronze age funerary pottery and we were dividing up the pots into collared urns, globular urns, barrel urns and bucket urns. This would represent a nominal scale, appropriate for this particular set of pots, in which there were four categories. In this case the process of measurement would consist of assigning one of these categories, or values to each of our pots. There is no inherent ordering among the pots implied by categorising them in this way. We could assign numbers to the categories, e.g.

1 = collared urn
2 = globular urn
3 = barrel urn
4 = bucket urn

If we did this we would be using the numbers merely as symbols that are convenient for us for some reason – perhaps as a shorthand notation. It would be meaningless to add or multiply these numbers together.

If it is possible to give a rank order to all of the categories, according to some criterion, then the ordinal level of measurement has been achieved. Thus, if we divided a collection of pottery up into fine ware, everyday ware and coarse ware, we could say that this was an ordinal scale with respect to some notion of quality. We could rank fine wares as 1, domestic wares as 2, and coarse wares as 3. Similarly, the well-known classification of societies into bands, tribes, chiefdoms and states (Service 1962) is a rank-ordering of societies with respect to an idea of complexity of organisation. Each category has a unique position relative to the others. Thus, if we know that chiefdom is higher than tribe and that state is higher than chiefdom, this automatically tells us that state is higher than tribe. On the other hand, we do not know *how much* lower chiefdom is than state, or tribe than chiefdom, we simply know the order – it is lower. It is this property of ordering which is the sole mathematical property of the ordinal scale.

In contrast to the ordinal scale, where only the ordering of the categories is defined, in interval and ratio scales the distances between the categories are defined in terms of fixed and equal units. The difference between these two, however, is rather less obvious

than the others we have seen so far, and is best illustrated by an
example. Is the measurement of time in terms of years AD or BC on
an interval or a ratio scale? It is certainly more than an ordinal scale
because time is divided into fixed and equal units – years. The
distinction between the two depends on the definition of the zero
point – whether it is arbitrary or not. Defining chronology in terms
of years AD or BC is an arbitrary convention. Other different but
perfectly valid chronological systems exist, with different starting
points, for example the Jewish or Islamic systems. If, on the other
hand, we consider physical measurements – such as distances, volumes or weights – then the zero point is not arbitrary; for example,
if we measure distance, whatever units of measurement we use, a
zero distance is naturally defined: it is the absence of distance
between two points; and the ratio of 100 mm to 200 mm is the same
as that between 3.94 inches and 7.88 inches, i.e.1:2. This is not true
of our chronological systems: the ratio of 1000 AD to 2000 AD is 1:2,
but if we take the corresponding years of the Islamic chronology
378 and 1378, the ratio is 1:3.65. Chronology then is an example of
an interval scale but physical measurements are examples of ratio
scales. In practice, once we get beyond the ordinal scale it is usually
ratio scale variables that we are dealing with in archaeology –
physical measurements of the various types referred to above, and
counts of numbers of items.

The reason for knowing about these distinctions is that they
affect the statistical techniques which we can use in any particular
case, whether we are using complex techniques of multivariate
analysis or merely drawing diagrams. In the chapters which follow,
as the different techniques are presented, one of the first considerations will always be the level of measurement of the data for which
the methods are appropriate. It is particularly easy to slip into
applying inappropriate methods when you are using a computer
since it will take the numbers you give it at face value and not
question what you ask it to do with them.

MOVING FROM ONE LEVEL
OF MEASUREMENT TO ANOTHER

The discussion so far has emphasised the distinctions between the
various levels of measurement, but it may be worth finishing by
looking at the possibilities of making the transition from one level
to another, for the scale of measurement for a particular property
of a set of data is not necessarily immutable.

Let us return to our example of dividing a pottery assemblage into fine ware, everyday ware and coarse ware, an ordinal scale based on an idea of fineness or quality. In principle there is no reason why we should not quantify the fineness of the pottery fabric, for example in terms of the mean grain size of the tempering material, or the ratio of inclusions to clay. We would then have a ratio scale of measurement of fineness and we could place each sherd or vessel at some specific point on the line from fine to coarse, measured in terms of fixed and equal units.

Some people see the prevailing level of measurement in a discipline as a measure of its scientific sophistication. Thus, a discipline in which many of the variables are measured on a ratio scale is more advanced than one in which the majority are only nominal scale variables. Whether one accepts this view or not, it is certainly the case that ratio scale variables, as in our pottery fabric example, contain more information about the property in question than ordinal scales, such as fine, medium and coarse.

There is, of course, no reason in principle why we cannot reverse the process. Starting with measurements of grain sizes in our pottery fabrics, for example, we could then categorise them as fine, everyday and coarse. If we do this, however, we are neglecting information, which is generally not a good thing to do. Nevertheless, the argument is not completely straightforward and controversies have raged in the archaeological literature about when and whether it is appropriate to categorise ratio scale variables (see the contributions to Whallon and Brown (1982), particularly those of Hodson and Spaulding).

The best guide is to make use of the level of measurement that will provide an answer to the question being investigated for the least cost. To refer again to the pottery, if our investigation requires no more than a distinction between fine ware, everyday ware and coarse ware, it is a waste of time and money to produce a detailed quantified description of every vessel's fabric. However, we may want to analyse a few samples of each fabric type to demonstrate to others that our distinctions between the fabrics are not purely subjective.

EXERCISES

2.1. Look at the series of decorated ceramic vessels from the German neolithic in figure 2.1, p.14 (after Schoknecht 1980), and devise a coding system that you think provides the basis for an adequate description of them. Code each of the vessels using your system (scale 3:16). What problems arose in coding, if any?

Figure 2.1

2.2. Try the same exercise with the set of illustrations of grave plans and their contents from a late neolithic cemetery in Czechoslovakia which appear in figures 2.2 to 2.7, pp. 16–21 (after Buchvaldek and Koutecky 1970). The contents of the graves are also listed since the nature of the objects is not always clear from the drawings and not all of them are illustrated. Scale: plans 1:27, pottery and grindstone 1:4, other items 1:2.

Grave 1	1. Amphora
	2. Decorated beaker
	3. Flat axe
	4. Flint blade
	5. Grindstone
Grave 2	1. Base sherds of beaker
	2. Decorated beaker
Grave 3	1. Decorated beaker with handle
	2. Decorated amphora
	3. Flint blade
	4. Piece of a copper spiral
Grave 4	1. Piece of flint blade
	2. Sherds probably from two vessels
Grave 5	1. Amphora
	2. Decorated amphora
	3. Mace head
	4. Flint blade
Grave 6	1. Quartzite scraper
Grave 7	1. Amphora
	2. Decorated beaker with handle
	3. Decorated jar
	4. Cylindrical beaker with lug
Grave 8	1. Amphora
	2. Decorated amphora
	3. Decorated beaker with handle
	4. Hammer axe
	5. Flint blade
Grave 9	1, 2. Decorated beakers
	3. Jug
	4. Decorated beaker
	5. Jar
	6. Decorated amphora
	7. Amphora
	8. Flint blade

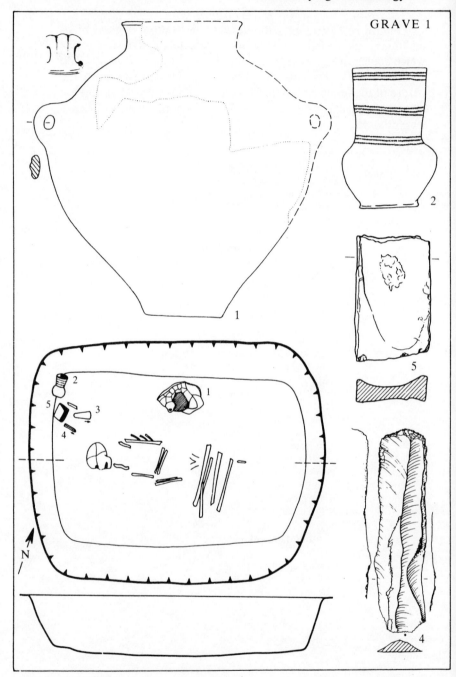

GRAVE 1

Figure 2.2

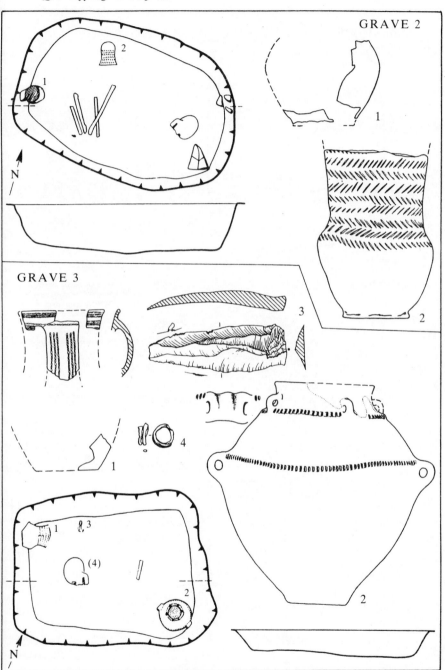

Figure 2.3

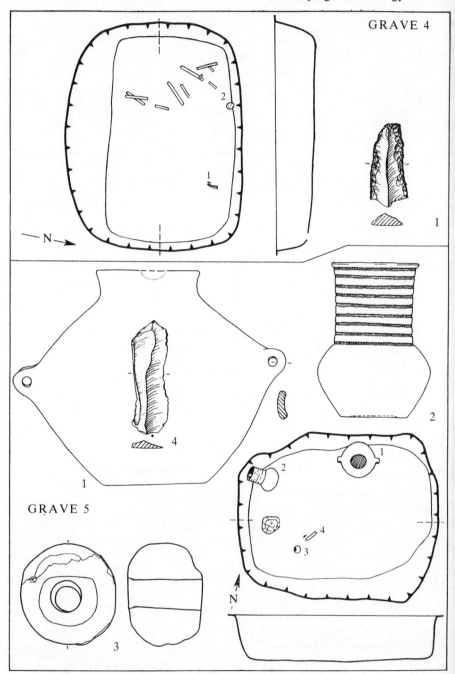

GRAVE 4

GRAVE 5

Figure 2.4

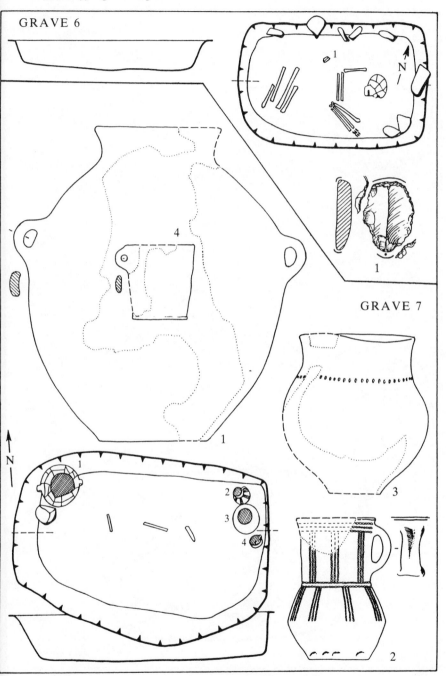

Figure 2.5

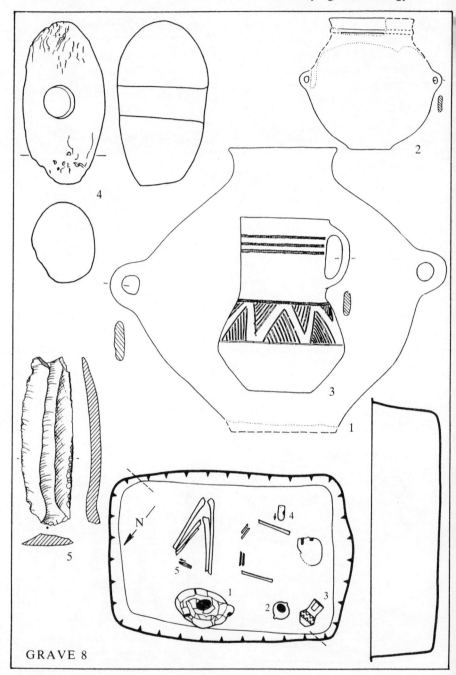

GRAVE 8

Figure 2.6

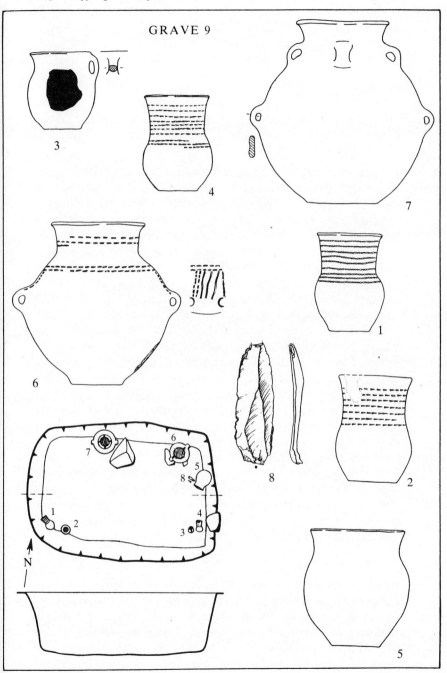

GRAVE 9

Figure 2.7

Three

Picture Summaries
of a Single Variable

In using quantitative methods in archaeology it is possible to get a long way simply by devising some pictorial means to represent your data. Once data are represented visually the power of the human eye and brain to detect and assess patterns can be immediately employed, and some very complex methods of quantitative analysis boil down to little more than ways of obtaining the best possible picture of a complicated data set. Conversely, however, the human eye can see patterns when none are really there, and this is a point to which we will return later.

The use of graphs and charts to display information has always had an important role to play in statistics, but essentially as a preliminary to the use of numerical summaries of the data, usually followed by the use of statistical inference (see below). Recently, an approach has been developed which pays less attention to the traditional methods of inferential statistics; it is known as the *exploratory data analysis* approach, and its hallmarks are a far greater concern with visual displays of data than with summary statistics derived from them, and a far lower emphasis on statistical significance tests (see Hartwig and Dearing 1979, Mosteller and Tukey 1977, Tukey 1977; for an archaeological discussion see Clark 1982, Lewis 1986). Rather, the aim is to explore the data set to hand, defined as relevant to some problem, to see what there is in the way of significant patterning. The idea is, to use the jargon of exploratory data analysis (or E D A as it is known), that

data = smooth + rough

In other words, a given set of observations can be divided into two components, a general pattern, the 'smooth', and the variations from that pattern, the 'rough'. The task of the data analyst then is to distinguish the smooth from the rough in the most objective kind of way, being continuously sceptical as he does so.

As Tukey (1980) has explained, the idea is not to reject traditional statistical inference methods, such as significance testing (see chapter 5), but to put them in their place, as only one part of the research loop, the continuing interplay between ideas and data. Just as important as the traditional role of statistics in testing ideas (what Tukey calls *confirmatory data analysis*) is its role in developing them, since they often arise from previous exploration of data rather than being 'bolts from the blue'. Visual display of the data is a good means to this end, not an end in itself.

This chapter will be concerned with the various visual means of representing the distributions of single variables, including methods which have become well-established in archaeology over the years and one which has seen relatively little use in archaeology, the stem-and-leaf diagram. Whatever the technique, however, the idea is to reduce the data to some kind of order, so that it is possible to see what they look like, to obtain an initial impression of the 'smooth' and the 'rough'. In general, this involves the presentation of *frequency distributions,* in which the observations are grouped in a limited number of categories.

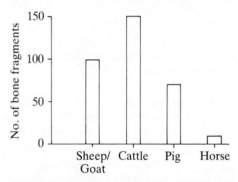

Figure 3.1. Bar chart of the number of bone fragments of different domestic animal species from a hypothetical British iron age site.

Probably the best known of these are simple *bar charts* or *bar graphs,* which are familiar from everyday life and whose use in archaeology is long established. These permit a distinction in terms of whether the categories are simply at the nominal scale, or whether there is an inherent ordering of the bars. An example of the former would be figure 3.1, which is a summary of the numbers of bone fragments of different types from a hypothetical British Iron Age site. There is no particular significance in the ordering of the species on the horizontal axis; it could be changed to any one of the different possible ways and the information contained within it would stay the same. The problem of having to commit yourself to a specific ordering which you automatically tend to read from left to right, can be circumvented by the use of the *pie chart* or *circle graph*. This requires the absolute numbers involved to be converted into relative proportions, and thus represents a gain in information in one sense and a loss in another: an idea of the total number is lost but the relative proportions emerge more clearly.

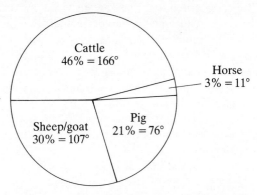

Figure 3.2. Pie chart of the relative proportions of bone fragments of different domestic species using the data from figure 3.1. Number of bone fragments = 330.

If it is felt to be important to present an indication of the number of cases involved rather than just the proportions, then this can be indicated in the key to the diagram; it is probably good practice to do this in any event. If a number of pie charts are being displayed together an idea of the relative sizes of the different samples can be given by making the area of the circles proportional to the sample size. In the case of the example using animal bone fragments just given, the pie chart would come out as figure 3.2, where the angle of the appropriate sector at the centre of the circle is the corresponding percentage multiplied by 360/100. Thus, if the cattle percentage was 46% this would give $46 \times 360/100 \simeq 166°$.

The pie chart is a very helpful mode of data presentation when the aim is to illustrate relative proportions of unordered categories, but it can be confusing if there are numerous categories, or categories with zero or very small entries, when the small entries have to be grouped together. Some authors, however, object to pie charts altogether (e.g. Tufte 1983), arguing that, for the relatively small quantities of data that can be contained in them, tables showing the actual percentages are more satisfactory.

With an ordinal scale the ordering of our categories is fixed by reference to some criterion, so here the horizontal ordering of the bars in the bar graph does mean something. At a higher level of measurement again not only is the ordering significant but so is the interval between the bars; an example is given in figure 3.3, where each bar is a count of one away from those adjacent to it.

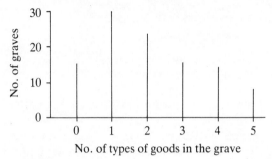

Figure 3.3. Bar chart of the number of graves containing different numbers of grave-good types for a hypothetical central European bronze age cemetery.

Here we have a bar graph summarising the numbers of graves in a bronze age cemetery which have particular numbers of types of grave goods. This time we are dealing with a ratio scale – zero here means a lack of grave goods. But the scale shown here has one particular characteristic to which attention needs to be drawn: it can only take countable whole number, or *integer* values. For a grave to contain 3.326 types of grave goods is simply impossible.

Other interval or ratio scales can take any value, and these are referred to as *continuous numeric* scales (often referred to as *real* values). Suppose we are measuring, for example, the heights of pots or the length of bones, then we might have measurements of 182.5 mm, 170.1 mm and 153.6 mm. Although the particular set of pots or bones which we measure will take a particular set of values, there is no theoretical reason why they should not take any decimal point value, the number of places after the decimal point simply being determined by the accuracy to which we are willing or able to take our measurements.

When we want to represent the frequency of different measured values of some continuous numeric variable like height, length or weight, then we are in a different situation from any of those looked at so far. We cannot have a separate category for 182.5 mm,

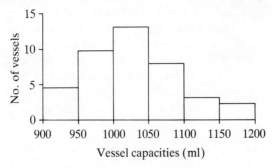

Figure 3.4. Bar chart of the distribution of vessel
capacities for a group of 40 bell beakers.

another for 170.1 mm and another for 153.6 mm; probably at most
one of our objects of interest will have exactly these values. What
we have to do is divide our variable up into a number of intervals,
whose width has been chosen by us, and then count the number of
observations falling into each interval. For example, figure 3.4
shows the frequency distribution of the capacities of a number of
bell beaker pots. Into each of the intervals are placed all the observations which fall within it. The decision on the number of intervals
to use is an arbitrary one, but should not be made without some
thought. We do not want to have so few intervals that any patterning in the distribution disappears altogether. On the other hand, if
we have very narrow intervals there will be lots of gaps and holes in
the picture. This will make it difficult to spot any trends in the
distribution, when one of the reasons for drawing the picture in the
first place was to pick up such patterns. In general, it is never good
to have more than twenty intervals because the picture then becomes too confusing. One useful rule-of-thumb which generally
produces a reasonable picture is to make the number of intervals
roughly equal to the square root of the number of observations; so,
for example, if our data are the volumes of forty pots then we would
divide volume into six intervals.

Because the variable is continuous it is important to be clear
exactly what the bar chart category intervals are. First, they must be
exhaustive, in other words the range must include all the observations; this is straightforward enough. Secondly, they must also be
mutually exclusive. If one of the capacity intervals was 900–950 ml
and the next 950–1000 ml then there would be ambiguity, since a
value of 950 would fall into both classes. We should be clear that the
range for the first interval is 900–949.9 ml, and for the next 950–

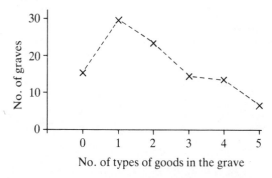

Figure 3.5. Frequency polygon of the data in figure 3.3.

999.9 ml, and so on.

Another way of expressing the information in an ordered bar graph is by means of what is called a *frequency polygon*. Figure 3.5 shows the grave-goods example illustrated above (figure 3.3) as a frequency polygon. This sort of presentation is frequently used for documenting change through time, with a time scale as the horizontal axis and some quantity as the vertical.

The methods outlined above are the traditional means of representing the distribution of single variables in diagrammatic form. The problem with them is that the only real 'truth' in a set of observations is the scores of the observations themselves. Once we try and summarise them, even in the form of a display like those above, we start losing information. (This is not necessarily a bad thing. As we have seen already, we often need to lose detail to gain in knowledge, to see the wood for the trees. However, there is no point in losing it if you don't have to.) Worse still, there is no single 'correct' picture. The shape of a histogram can vary considerably, depending on the width of the intervals and the exact starting point selected. On the other hand, a simple list of the data values is usually not conducive to pattern detection.

The integration of exact data values into a histogram can be achieved by means of a graphical method known as a *stem-and-leaf display*. It may be illustrated by means of data on the diameters of a sample of thirty-five post-holes from the late neolithic henge monument of Mount Pleasant, Dorset, England (from Wainwright 1979); these are listed in table 3.1. To produce the stem-and-leaf the first digits of the data values (here the post-hole diameters) are separated from the other(s). These first digits are then listed vertically down the left-hand side of the diagram in order, and form the

Table 3.1. Diameters (in cm) of 35 post-holes
from the late neolithic henge monument of
Mount Pleasant, Dorset, England.

48	57	66	48	50	58	47
48	49	48	47	57	40	50
43	40	44	40	34	42	47
48	53	43	43	25	45	39
38	35	30	38	38	28	27

stem (figure 3.6). The remaining digit(s) for each score is then
placed in the row corresponding to the first digit, in ascending
order, to form the leaf (figure 3.7). This gives us a picture that loses
none of the initial information.

```
2
3
4
5
6
```

Figure 3.6. The 'stem' of a stem-and-leaf
diagram of the Mount Pleasant post-hole
diameters listed in table 3.1.

```
2 | 5 7 8
3 | 0 4 5 8 8 8 9
4 | 0 0 0 2 3 3 3 4 5 7 7 7 8 8 8 8 8 9
5 | 0 0 3 7 7 8
6 | 6
```

Figure 3.7. Stem-and-leaf diagram of the
Mount Pleasant post-hole diameters listed
in table 3.1.

If, on inspection, we felt that it would be helpful to make the
intervals narrower, by making them five units wide rather than ten
units, this is easily done; we simply have two rows for each first
digit, one for second digits 0–4, the other for second digits 5–9
(figure 3.8).

One further useful point about this form of display is that it
enables one to see very easily exactly which are the aberrant values
in a distribution, and to investigate them further if necessary; in
fact, any peculiarities in the distribution will be easily visible.

```
2 |
2 | 5 7 8
3 | 0 4
3 | 5 8 8 8 9
4 | 0 0 0 2 3 3 3 4
4 | 5 7 7 7 8 8 8 8 8 9
5 | 0 0 3
5 | 7 7 8
6 |
6 | 6
```

Figure 3.8. Stem-and-leaf diagram of the
Mount Pleasant post-hole diameters listed
in table 3.1 with stem intervals 5 units wide
instead of 10.

Rather different is the *cumulative curve,* which does not give the same kind of picture at all but can in many circumstances give us a clearer representation of our data than is obtainable by other graphical means, especially when we want to compare one set of data with another. In general, cumulative curves are based not on the actual numbers in our categories or intervals but on those numbers expressed as a proportion or percentage of the total number of observations. How they work may be illustrated once again with the grave-goods example, which is first presented in the form of a table (table 3.2).

Table 3.2. Number of graves
containing different numbers
of grave-good types from a
hypothetical central European
bronze age cemetery.

No. of types of goods	No. of graves	Percentage of graves
0	17	15.6
1	30	27.5
2	26	23.9
3	17	15.6
4	13	11.9
5	6	5.5
	109	100.0

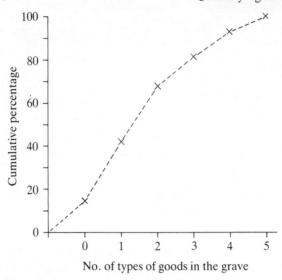

Figure 3.9. Cumulative curve of the data on numbers of grave-good types presented in table 3.2.

A new graph may now be drawn, with the horizontal scale as before indicating the number of types of grave goods in the grave but with the vertical scale a percentage scale ranging from 0 to 100. We note first that 15.6 % of the graves are in the zero grave-goods category, so we mark that on the graph. Now when we come to the 27.5 % of graves in the one grave-good category we add or accumulate these onto the 15.6 % in the zero category, so we have 15.6 + 27.5 = 43.1 %, which is the value for the one grave-good category, which can also be marked on the graph. The value tells us that 43.1 % of the graves have one grave good or less. We do this for all the categories in turn until the full 100 % of graves has been accumulated:

$$43.1 + 23.9 = 67.0$$
$$67.0 + 15.6 = 82.6$$
$$82.6 + 11.9 = 94.5$$
$$94.5 + 5.5 = 100$$

When the points have all been put in on the graph we can join them up and the resulting line is the cumulative curve shown in figure 3.9. This represents the shape of the cumulative distribution.

Simply as a means of representing the shape of the distribution of a single variable it may seem rather complicated and unnecessary. Why not use a bar chart? The answer is that it really comes into its own in making comparisons between distributions. Bar charts, with their varying patterns of bar heights, are rather difficult to compare visually. With the continuously rising line of the cumulative curve, similarities and differences between distributions are much more readily apparent.

This form of presentation is obviously truly meaningful only if there is a real ordering on the horizontal axis, that is, if we are dealing with data measured at an ordinal scale or above. If the level of measurement is nominal, any ordering will be arbitrary, as we have already mentioned, and the shape of a cumulative curve based on any such orderings equally arbitrary; it would be possible to play around with the data to produce a curve of some desired shape. Nevertheless, if a fixed order of presentation of the categories is adopted when comparisons are being made, cumulative curves can and have proved helpful in the presentation of nominal data such as paleolithic assemblages described in terms of numbers or percentages of particular artefact types: they should simply be used and viewed with caution.

The techniques described in this chapter have provided you with the basic tools for describing data distributions by pictorial means. As such, they may be used whenever we want to present a summary account of some results, or to have a first look for any patterning present in the data. Study of such distributions and their implications is also a prerequisite step before the use of many of the statistical methods to be described in this book.

EXERCISES

3.1. The following are the figures for the number of sherds of different pottery types from the henge monument at Mount Pleasant, Dorset, England (data from Wainwright 1979). Represent them by means of a bar graph and a pie chart and say which you prefer.

Neolithic plain bowl	391
Grooved ware	657
Beaker	1695
Peterborough ware	6
Bronze Age	591

3.2. The sizes (in hectares) of a number of Late Uruk settlement sites in Mesopotamia (data from Johnson 1973) are as follows:

```
45.0  37.0  34.8  52.0  75.0  86.0  59.7  74.0  32.0
57.7  65.0  86.0  37.0  38.4  90.5  45.0  67.0  50.0
33.0  30.0  43.2  32.0  35.2  54.5  43.1
```

Use an appropriate graphical method to represent these data. Does there seem to be any pattern in the distribution of settlement sizes? Does it change if you use a different width interval?

3.3. Draw a cumulative percentage frequency distribution of the following data on the age at death of the individuals buried in a prehistoric cemetery.

Age category	No. of burials
Infans i	10
Infans ii	16
Juvenilis	10
Adultus	32
Maturus	34
Senilis	4

Four

Numerical Summaries
of a Single Variable

The last chapter examined methods of *graphical* representation for distributions of observations measured at different levels. This one considers *numerical* summaries of information. I would be the first to agree that this is not intrinsically a very exciting topic, but there are two main reasons why it cannot be neglected. The first is that such summaries are becoming an increasingly important element of published descriptions of archaeological work. Modern excavations, for example, often produce so many finds of certain categories that the only way in which the information may be presented in a form sufficiently compact to be published, is in some kind of graph, with an associated numerical summary. Presenting information in this form is not to dehumanise archaeology but simply to offer in a publishable and comprehensible fashion the information on which inferences have been based, so that readers may have an opportunity of evaluating it. This presupposes, of course, a readership sufficiently educated to do so, a requirement which is vital for the future progress of archaeology.

The second reason for a concern with numerical description is that, on the whole, the methods to be described later in this book, which are concerned with the much more interesting questions of identifying patterns and relationships between variables, depend on the use of the descriptive measures now to be introduced.

It is important to remember that what we were doing with our graphical methods was summarising data; we were forgetting about individuals, individual sherds, pieces of chipped stone or whatever, and attempting to obtain some kind of overall picture of general trends in the data distribution. Although a picture or diagram of some kind may very often give us the summarised information we want, it is sometimes useful to reduce a data set still further, simply to one or two numbers, or *descriptive statistics*. This will be particularly useful when we want to make comparisons, for example between sets of data from different sites. On the other hand, reduction to one or two simple numbers can be potentially risky. When a lot of information is reduced to one or two numbers there is a greater danger of being misled, than when you have a graphical picture of the data in front of you. The conclusion to be drawn from this is that even if you are summarising data numerically you should always look at them graphically as well.

For nominal scale variables the matter of numerical summary is essentially trivial. We have our different categories, for example animal bones classified by species, or pots divided into types, and we can express the relations between the categories in terms of the percentages of the different categories in the assemblage; we might refer to the most common, or modal, category. Once this has been done there is little more to be said as far as summary description is concerned.

When we consider variables measured at interval scale and above, and require a best numerical summary of the information at our disposal, a number of different questions may be asked. To summarise the information fully, in fact, we need to measure four different aspects of the bar graphs or histograms that we have seen. These are:

i) *Central tendency,* or what is a typical individual?

ii) *Dispersion,* or how much variation is there? In a picture like figure 4.1(a) a typical individual is much more representative than in a distribution like figure 4.1(b).

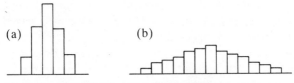

Figure 4.1. Two distributions in which there is
(a) very little, and (b) a great deal, of dispersion
round the central value.

iii) *Shape,* which has two aspects:
(iiia) is the distribution symmetrical or not? Figures 4.2(a), (b)

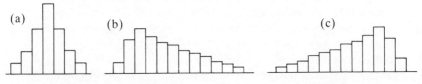

Figure 4.2. Examples of distributions of different shapes.

and (c) indicate some of the possibilities. In both the latter two cases the distribution is said to be *skew*. In (b) it is skew to the right – it has a long tail extending to the right. In (c) it is skew to the left – the tail is to the left.

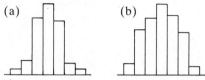

Figure 4.3. Examples of distributions with different length tails.

(iiib) The second aspect of shape concerns the length of the tails of the distribution, illustrated in figures 4.3(a) and (b). The degree of dispersion of these two distributions is fairly similar, but one has longer tails than the other. The length of the tails of a distribution is referred to as its degree of *kurtosis*. Distributions with long tails are *leptokurtic* and distributions with short tails are *platykurtic*.

In fact, the measures of shape figure much less prominently than the measures of central tendency and dispersion in most statistical applications, although the question of skewness is of great significance, usually as a problem to be overcome (see chapter 8). However, one area where measures of skewness and kurtosis are of interest in their own right is in the field of particle size analysis. An example of such analysis in the field of archaeology would be the description and comparison of pottery fabrics in terms of the distribution of different sizes of inclusions (e.g. Peacock 1971).

MEASURES OF CENTRAL TENDENCY

Now that these descriptive characteristics have been listed we can look at the question of central tendency in more detail. There are several ways of measuring this, and the same is true for dispersion. The best known and most commonly used measure of central tendency is the *arithmetic mean,* defined as the sum of the scores divided by the total number of cases.

Let us take as an example the diameters of seven of the Mount Pleasant post-holes listed in the previous chapter.

$$48 + 57 + 66 + 48 + 50 + 58 + 47 = 374$$

There are seven post-holes here so we divide 374 by 7 to give 53.4 cm as the mean diameter for this set of post-holes. We are, in effect, saying here that a typical post-hole is 53.4 cm in diameter. No post-hole is really 53.4 cm in diameter but this value is somewhere in the middle of all of them. In fact, the mean represents the centre of gravity of the distribution and has the specific property that the sum of the deviations of the individual scores from the mean is always zero. That is, if we take each of our observations, subtract the mean from each in turn and add up all the resulting differences, the answer will be zero. Thus:

$$(48 - 53.4) + (57 - 53.4) + (66 - 53.4) + (48 - 53.4)$$
$$+ (50 - 53.4) + (58 - 53.4) + (47 - 53.4)$$
$$= (-5.4) + 3.6 + 12.6 + (-5.4) + (-3.4) + 4.6 + (-6.4)$$
$$= 0.2$$

(This result is not exactly zero because of rounding error in the calculations.)

Here it is necessary to digress slightly. A verbal description has just been given of how to obtain an arithmetic mean, and the property which characterises it; this description has been supplemented by a numerical example. However, if we want to specify general rules for doing operations on numbers it is much more convenient to use mathematical symbolism. Symbols are an essential part of mathematics and they are probably the single most off-putting factor for people not naturally attracted to the subject. The main thing to remember about symbols is that they are simply a form of short-hand notation which can be easily manipulated.

Let us now have a look at the symbolism that relates to the arithmetic mean, which is conventionally expressed by $\bar{x}$ (called x-bar). We can say in general that:

$$\bar{x} = \frac{x_1 + x_2 + x_3 + \ldots + x_n}{n}$$

where x_1 is our first observation, x_2 the second observation, and so on. In the particular case of the post-holes:

$$x_1 = 48 \qquad x_2 = 57$$
$$x_3 = 66 \qquad x_4 = 48$$
$$x_5 = 50 \qquad x_6 = 58$$
$$x_7 = 47$$

There are seven observations here, $n = 7$, and the last observation is the seventh; so here $x_n = x_7 = 47$.

But we can summarise conveniently still further and say

$$\bar{x} = \frac{x_1 + x_2 + x_3 + \ldots + x_n}{n} = \frac{\sum_{i=1}^{n} x_i}{n}$$

Here x_i stands for any of our x values. Σ is the upper case Greek letter sigma and stands for summation. So we are being told to add up some x's. Which x's? The subscript and superscript of the Σ tell us which ones; they give us the range over which we are summing, from the first x to the nth x, or $i = 1$ to n. In the post-hole example there are seven x values which we want to add up, so we have

$$\sum_{i=1}^{7} x_i$$

When we have done the addition we divide by the number of observations n, again 7 in the example, to arrive at our value for $\bar{x}$.

If the numbers which we have to add up – the range of summation – is obvious then we might leave out the subscript and superscript and simply write

$$\Sigma x_i$$

You will meet this notation all the time in statistics and it is very important not to be put off or intimidated by it. Notation and symbolism are only a convenience, to make things easier for you. We can now return to the main theme, making use of this symbolic notation.

Calculation of the mean in the way just described is an easy matter when you have only small numbers of observations. Once you have large numbers of observations it becomes tedious even if you use a calculator, because you have to enter so many numbers; furthermore, the probability of making mistakes in data entry also rises. When you want to calculate a mean and have a large number of observations, it is generally best to group the data into a frequency distribution, as you probably have done anyway to produce a histogram or bar graph. The formula for the mean then becomes

$$\bar{x} = \frac{\sum_{i=1}^{k} f_i x_i}{n}$$

where f_i is the number of cases in the ith category, $n = \Sigma f_i$, x_i is the value of the ith category, and k is the number of categories.

As an example, let us suppose once again that we are concerned with graves and grave goods and want to find the average number of grave-good types in a group of graves. The data are shown in table 4.1, whence $x = 215/67 = 3.2$. Thus the average number of goods types per grave is 3.2.

When dealing with a set of continuous numeric values the situation becomes slightly more complicated, because observations with differing values will have been grouped together to form the bars or

Table 4.1.

No. of goods types in graves (x_i)	No. of graves in category (f_i)	$f_i x_i$
1	1	1
2	22	44
3	15	45
4	20	80
5	9	45
$k = 5$	$\sum_{i=1}^{5} f_i = 67$	$\sum_{i=1}^{5} f_i x_i = 215$

categories of the frequency distribution. In this case the x value for each category is given by the midpoint of that category. The figures for the vessel-capacity data illustrated in the previous chapter are shown in table 4.2, whence $x = 41100/40 = 1027.5$. The mean capacity for this group of vessels is 1027.5 ml.

Table 4.2.

Boundaries of capacity classes (ml)	Midpoint of capacity classes (ml) (x_i)	No. of vessels in class (f_i)	$f_i x_i$
900-949.99	925	4	3700
950-999.99	975	10	9750
1000-1049.99	1025	13	13325
1050-1099.99	1075	8	8600
1100-1149.99	1125	3	3375
1150-1199.99	1175	2	2350
k (no. of categories) = 6		$\sum_{i=1}^{6} f_i = 40$	$\sum_{i=1}^{6} f_i x_i = 41100$

That completes our account of the arithmetic mean, but there are other measures of central tendency of a distribution to be considered. One important one is the *median*, which plays a vital role in the exploratory data analysis approach to the numerical description of distributions presented later in this chapter. The median is the value such that half of the observations are above it and half below it. Obviously, if we want to find such a value we have to arrange our observations in ascending or descending order of size, in other words in rank order; it is therefore possible to calculate the median for ordinal as well as interval and ratio data.

Let us look again at the post-hole diameters, which were as follows: 48, 57, 66, 48, 50, 58, 47 cm. The first step is to put them in order, smallest to largest (or the reverse): 47, 48, 48, 50, 57, 58, 66 cm. If we are interested in the value such that half the observations are above it and half below, then obviously we want the middle value. Here we have seven observations. If we count along to the fourth one, from either end, we find 50, which is the median and has three observations below it and three above. If the number of cases is odd then the median will be the score of the middle case. If the number of cases is even then clearly there will not be a middle case, so the median is taken to be the mean of the two middle cases.

Suppose there were just six post-hole diameters: 48, 48, 50, 57, 58, 66 cm. In this case the median would be between 50 and 57, the mean of which is $107/2 = 53.5$ cm. For ordinal scale data the median rank may be calculated.

Finally, the *mode* should be mentioned. This is simply the most common or frequent value and obviously applies to nominal scales as well. In the grave-good example above (table 4.1) the modal value is 2, in the vessel-capacity example (table 4.2) it is the class 1000–1049.99 ml. It is clearly impossible for a mode to exist unless we already have a frequency distribution of some sort, a point which is particularly relevant to continuous numeric data, where two observations will hardly ever have the same value.

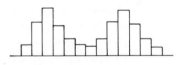 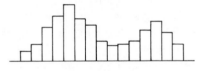

Figure 4.4. An example of a bimodal distribution.

Figure 4.5. A distribution with a main and a subsidiary mode.

It is possible for a distribution to have more than one mode (figure 4.4) or to have a main mode and a subsidiary one (figure 4.5). It is perhaps worth emphasising that if a distribution is bimodal, or has a mode and a major subsidiary mode, then providing a single measure of central tendency or dispersion for it is meaningless and totally inappropriate. You must either give the two modes or, preferably, split the distribution into its constituent parts and calculate the relevant measures for each part separately (see Mellars and Wilkinson 1980 for an example of the analysis of bimodal data in archaeology).

In the case of the post-hole diameters we might be particularly interested to see if there was more than one mode in the data since that might suggest that different thicknesses of posts had different functions. If we simply had variation around a single mode it might merely indicate the degree of success the builders had in finding timber of the right size for one single purpose, or the flexibility of their specifications.

How do these different measures of central tendency compare with one another? To some extent the one we will use will depend on what we are trying to do; but in general, if we have nominal or ordinal data then we do not have much choice, while for interval and ratio data the most frequently used measure of central tendency is the mean.

The mode simply gives us the most common value, but does not tell us where it lies in relation to the other values. The mean uses more information than the median, in the sense that all the exact scores are used in computing it, whereas the median uses only the relative positions of the scores. Very often it is desirable to make use of all the information available, so the mean is to be preferred. In fact, if the distribution is symmetrical, the mean, the median and the mode all coincide. If the distribution is very skew, however, the situation changes significantly. Suppose, for example, that in the case of the vessel capacities illustrated in figure 3.4 one of them had a volume of 2500 ml. Such a distribution would be skew, with one observation a long way over to the right. In this case the mean vessel capacity would change considerably; it would be pulled over to the right and move away from the bulk of the observations, and as a result it would not be very representative. The median on the other hand would hardly be affected at all in such a case; it would be much more representative of the mass of observations.

From this you can see that we cannot consider the question of central tendency – what is a typical individual – in isolation, but we have to think about the shape of the distribution as well. It is always helpful to know what the frequency distribution of your data looks like, not least if you intend to go on to use complex statistical methods, because if the distribution has any peculiarities of shape or dispersion you need to know about them.

MEASURES OF DISPERSION

If data are widely dispersed then a simple measure of central tendency will not be such a 'typical' value as it is when data are narrowly dispersed; this point was illustrated in figure 4.1.

There are several ways of quantifying dispersion. The simplest is the *range,* the difference between the highest and the lowest scores in the data under consideration. Its disadvantage is that it is based on only two cases and those the two most extreme ones. Since extremes are likely to be the rare or unusual cases, almost by definition, it is usually a matter of chance if we happen to have one or two very extreme observations in our sample. For this reason the range is not particularly satisfactory as a measure of dispersion.

More useful is a quantity known as the *inter-quartile range.* Just as we can specify the median of a distribution as that value such that 50 per cent of the observations fall below it and 50 per cent above it, so one can define the first and third quartiles of a distribution of data values measured at an ordinal scale or above. The first quartile is that value which has 25 per cent of the observations below it and 75 per cent above it, while conversely the third quartile is that value which has 75 per cent of the observations below it and 25 per cent above it. The difference between the value of the first and third quartiles, the middle 50 per cent of the distribution, is known as the inter-quartile range. Obtaining it is clearly directly analogous to obtaining the median, and its properties likewise, in the sense that only the rank order of the observations is taken into consideration and the existence of very large or very small values at either end of the distribution will not make any difference. We will look again at the inter-quartile range below (p. 44) but can note for the moment that it has found occasional use in the archaeological literature (e.g. Ottaway 1973).

Since the inter-quartile range only makes use of the rank-order of the observations, if the data are measured at an interval scale, or above, information is being lost – the exact scores of the observations are not being used. It has been usual to take the view that it is preferable to make use of all the information available when calculating a measure of dispersion, in the same way as when using the mean as a measure of central tendency; but, as with the mean, there are occasions when using all the information can give a positively misleading result, depending on the shape of the distribution (see p. 44). However, if we are using the mean as the measure of central tendency the obvious thing to do is to take the sum of the deviations of the observations from the mean as a basis for measuring dispersion. Unfortunately, as we have already seen, this will always be zero, since the positive and negative differences cancel out one another. There are two ways round this problem: either we can ignore the sign and take the absolute value of the differences;

or we can square the differences, remembering that a minus times a minus equals a plus so that all quantities become positive ones.

In fact, the second solution is much more often adopted: the measure of dispersion is based on squaring the differences between the mean and the values of the individual observations and is known as the *standard deviation, s*:

$$s = \sqrt{\frac{\sum_{i=1}^{n}(x_i - \bar{x})^2}{n-1}}$$

In words, we take the deviation of each score from the mean, square each difference, sum the results, divide by the number of cases minus one, and then take the square root. The result is that the greater the dispersion in the distribution, the larger the standard deviation. If we stop before taking the square root we have the variance, s^2, the average (or mean) of the squared differences between the mean and the data values. Because the variance is a squared quantity it must be expressed in units which are the square of the original units of measurement. More often than not when describing a distribution it is desirable to have the dispersion measured in the same units as the original measurements, so the standard deviation tends to be intuitively more meaningful than the variance. For instance, if we wanted to know the degree of dispersion around the mean value of the length of a set of flint blades, then if we were measuring them in millimetres we would want dispersion measured in millimetres and not square millimetres.

The variance/standard deviation plays an extremely important role in many statistical tests and for that reason is the most important measure of dispersion for sets of data for which it is an informative measure, that is to say, distributions which are unimodal and symmetric. Some of the problems with it will be considered below but before turning to them it is necessary to look again at how to calculate it because the formula given above is laborious to use if you have many observations. Such difficulties present less of a problem nowadays because of the sophistication of modern calculators but it is probably still worth giving one of the versions of the formula that are easier to compute:

$$s = \sqrt{\frac{\sum_{i=1}^{n}x_i^2 - [(\sum_{i=1}^{n}x_i)^2/n]}{n-1}}$$

Let us work out the standard deviation of the seven post-hole diameters, using both versions of the formula.

We have already seen that

$$\bar{x} = 374/7 = 53.4$$

Using the first formula the sum of the squared deviations is

$$(48 - 53.4)^2 + (57 - 53.4)^2 + (66 - 53.4)^2 + (48 - 53.4)^2$$
$$+ (50 - 53.4)^2 + (58 - 53.4)^2 + (47 - 53.4)^2 = 303.71$$

$$s = \sqrt{\frac{303.71}{7-1}} = 7.1$$

Before illustrating the second method, and making sure we get the same result, it is important to be clear about the difference between the terms Σx_i^2 and $(\Sigma x_i)^2$ in the formula. In the first case we are being told to take each x value, square it and sum all the squared values. In the second case we are being told to sum the x values and square the total. These give different results! Now

$$s = \sqrt{\frac{20286 - [(374)^2/7]}{7-1}} = \sqrt{\frac{303.71}{6}} = 7.1$$

If we are dealing with grouped data the formula for the standard deviation is

$$s = \sqrt{\frac{\sum_{i=1}^{k}(x_i - \bar{x})^2 f_i}{n-1}}$$

where x_i is the value of the ith category, f_i is the number of observations in the ith category, k is the number of categories and n is the total number of observations.

The precise significance of the standard deviation as a measure of dispersion will be considered in chapter 8 when we turn to the 'normal' distribution, a special bell-shaped distribution that statisticians have found very useful; for the moment, however, we can note that, given a unimodal symmetric set of data, it tells us what is a 'typical' deviation from the data mean. In the case of our postholes a typical deviation from the mean is 7.1 cm.

Sometimes we may want to make comparisons between sets of data in terms of their dispersion. For example, if we were studying standardisation of lithic core production in prehistoric quarries we might want to know if the sizes of cores from one quarry were more variable than those from another, perhaps to try and make inferences about different degrees of craft specialisation. Very often, the larger the mean, the larger the standard deviation, so that if one quarry produced large cores and the other smaller ones, the distribution of core sizes from the former might well have a larger standard deviation for this reason, rather than because production was less standardised. We can get rid of this effect by using the *coefficient of variation*, simply the standard deviation divided by the mean; sometimes the result is multiplied by 100 to make it a percentage. This gives us a standardised measure of dispersion.

THE EXPLORATORY DATA ANALYSIS VIEW OF NUMERICAL SUMMARIES: ROBUST DESCRIPTIONS OF CENTRAL TENDENCY AND DISPERSION

Traditional mean-based numerical summaries are regarded with some suspicion by the exploratory data analysis approach, which, as we have seen, places considerable emphasis on the importance of good visual displays. Since such summaries are often convenient and necessary, however, the emphasis is on their being as *robust* as possible. In other words, they should do what they purport to do, give accurate summaries in a wide variety of different situations, not just under a very restricted set of assumptions; in particular, they need to be resistant to changes in just one or two values in the distribution as a whole. If we are seeking robust summaries of central tendency and spread of a distribution, the mean and standard deviation are not very satisfactory, since their usefulness is restricted to distributions which are unimodal and symmetrical. In other circumstances the median and the inter-quartile range are likely to give a better indication of the value of a typical observation and the degree of dispersion around that value. This is the view taken by the EDA approach, although many of its advocates prefer to use the term 'midspread' rather than inter-quartile range, and refer to the lower quartile value as the 'lower hinge' and the upper quartile value as the 'upper hinge' of the distribution.

The use of the median and inter-quartile range can be extended to produce a numerical summary of a distribution consisting of the values of the median, upper and lower hinges and maximum and minimum values of the distribution, together with a note of the intervals between them. For the 35 post-hole diameters it would look like this:

	Min	Lower hinge	Median	Upper hinge	Max
	25	38.5	44	48	66
Intervals		13.5	5.5	4	18

To this we can also add the distances between the minimum and the median (the 'lowspread'), between the lower and upper hinges (the inter-quartile range or midspread), and between the median and the maximum value (the 'highspread'), thus:

25		38.5		44		48		66
	13.5		5.5		4		18	
		19		9.5		22		

We can now see at a glance, for example, that the size difference between the smallest post-hole (25 cm) and the lower hinge value (38.5 cm) is 13.5 cm, while from the lower hinge to the median (44 cm) it is only 5.5 cm; the difference between the minimum and median is therefore a total of 19 cm.

To find out whether the distribution is approximately bell-shaped or not, and therefore, for example, whether it might be appropriate to go on to use the normal-theory-based statistics discussed in chapter 8 and later chapters of this book, we can do a few quick checks on these numbers (Hartwig and Dearing 1979, 23). If the distribution is symmetrical and bell-shaped:

1. The lowspread and the highspread will be equal.

2. The distances from the lower hinge to the median and from the upper hinge to the median will be equal.

3. The distances between the lower hinge and the minimum value and between the upper hinge and the maximum value will be equal.

4. The distances from the median to the hinges will be smaller than those from the hinges to the extremes because of the concentration of the cases in the middle part of the distribution.

On the basis of these criteria it would seem that the post-hole distribution is quite close to 'normality', as indeed it appears from the shape of the stem-and-leaf histogram of these data (see figure 3.7) but, as we shall see, this form of *numerical* summary does not give as much weight as it might to the distribution tails and these need to be investigated as well.

Numerical summaries of the kind we have just seen may be contrasted with *visual summaries* of a distribution, as opposed also to the more complete visual representation of the stem-and-leaf diagram. When distributions are of an unusual shape this is very often particularly apparent in the tails, and may be revealed by the form of visual summary known as the *box-and-whisker plot*.

A box-and-whisker plot for the Mount Pleasant post-holes is illustrated in figure 4.6. The left-hand side of the box is at the lower hinge of the distribution, the right-hand side at the upper hinge, and the vertical line marks the median. The box thus contains half the cases in the distribution. The crosses mark the cases furthest

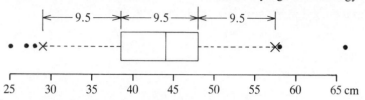

Figure 4.6. Box-and-whisker plot of the diameters
of 35 Mount Pleasant post-holes.

from the box at either side but still within one* midspread of the
nearest hinge. Beyond this, cases are marked individually.

In a normal distribution 95 per cent of all cases will lie within the
range defined by the endpoints (crosses) of the whiskers, so a
distribution with much more than five per cent of the values outside
this range is beginning to depart from normality (see Hartwig and
Dearing 1979, 24). In the case of the Mount Pleasant post-holes
(figure 4.6) we see that 5 out of the 35 observations, or just over 14
per cent, fall outside this range, which suggests that the picture they
present us with is not after all completely straightforward. In this
case there are 3 post-holes which are extremely small and 2 which
are extremely large, in relation to the rest of the distribution. In a
real study an obvious next step would be to identify these on the site
plan and investigate whether they appear to have to have any
special functional role.

Stem-and-leaf displays and box-and-whisker plots are both available on the MINITAB statistical package (see appendix 2), which
certainly provides one of the easiest ways of obtaining them. As you
have seen, the two techniques differ in that stem-and-leaf displays
give a complete visual picture of the data, while box-and-whisker
plots sacrifice this for the sake of applying, as it were, a magnifying
glass to the distribution tails to see if they depart from normality.
Box plots can be particularly useful when making comparisons
between different sets of data because it is possible to see immediately if there is any asymmetry in the main bulk of the observations,
and whether some sets have more extreme observations than
others. The reasons for the differences can then be followed up.

A combination of stem-and-leaf displays, number summaries
and box-and-whisker plots will soon reveal any peculiarities of
distribution shape. When such shape peculiarities as skewness,
multiple peaks or the presence of outliers (values very different

---

* On MINITAB the ends of the whiskers are at 1.5 midspreads
from the nearest hinge.

from the bulk of the observations) do exist, the shape of the distribution, rather than its central tendency or dispersion, is likely to be its most important characteristic; relying simply on central tendency and dispersion as summary measures of a distribution can cause you to miss the most important characteristic of a set of observations. Furthermore, if you do not know about the distribution shape, then it is impossible to tell whether, or in what way, the measures of central tendency or dispersion are misleading; shape is relevant to the choice of appropriate measures for these. Finally, remember that shape is best perceived visually.

The importance of considering the shape of the distribution cannot be emphasised too strongly. It is surprising how many people go astray by ignoring the basic rules of studying the visual and numerical summaries of the individual variables they are studying even when they actually know them.

EXERCISES

4.1. Refer to the data on Uruk settlement sizes in exercise 3.2. (a) How would you describe the shape of the frequency distribution of these data? (b) What do you think would be the most appropriate measures of (i) central tendency, (ii) dispersion? (c) Calculate these measures.

4.2. Below is a list of the lengths (in metres) of some neolithic burial mounds from southern England. Analyse this distribution using the techniques described in this chapter and the preceding one and discuss your conclusions.

33	30	36	60	70	95	75	63	60
34	58	72	70	44	35	71	51	36
60	98	49	70	61	81	74	64	51
95	69	56	37	31	58	51	51	52

Five

An Introduction to Statistical Inference

Now that we have covered some of the basics of descriptive statistics we can start looking at statistical inference and the use of statistical methods of comparison in archaeology. It should be said right at the start that statistical inference is by no means conceptually straightforward, and that the issues raised by its role in archaeology are controversial ones (see e.g. Cowgill 1977). There are two rather different contexts in which these topics impinge on archaeology and it is worth trying to keep them notionally separate from one another to start with, even though they are closely related.

First, and conceptually more straightforward, is the case where the archaeologist is in control, actually carrying out a selection process in the course of an archaeological project. Rarely do archaeologists have the resources to investigate everything in which they are interested, whether whole regions, complete sites, or total assemblages of artefacts. Normally they can investigate only part of their population of interest and would like that part to be representative of the total if at all possible. Provided that aims are clearly formulated, concepts of statistical inference can be extremely useful in the selection of a sample which will provide results whose reliability and precision we can assess. There is a relatively well-defined set of problems involved here, usually included under the heading of *sampling* in archaeology, and for the most part left to be discussed below in the chapter which deals with this topic.

The second main context in which statistical inference can be relevant arises from the process of comparison. Is the density of sites in area A the same as that in area B? Is the proportion of pottery type X the same at site Y as at site Z? Do rings of type S tend to occur more often in female burials than in male burials at cemetery T? Archaeological questions are quite often of this form, either comparisons between different sets of data, as in the examples just given, or comparisons between an observed set of data and the expectations derived from a theoretically-based model: for

48

example, whether a distribution of sites differs from randomness or not.

In the instances just listed it is unlikely that the two sites, regions and sexes will have exactly the same values in each case for the variable concerned. In any comparison between two cases there will almost always be some difference between them, however slight. The question which then arises is, how great does the difference have to be before we start taking it seriously and acting on the assumption that it is a 'real' one? This seems to be a perfectly valid question to ask and the discipline of statistics appears to provide a way of answering it in any given case, by means of *significance testing*. In order to see how this works it will be necessary to describe the theory behind it, in the abstract, before going on to look at its use in archaeology. It may be as well to state here, however, that I think significance testing does have a role, but it is by no means the only or even the main justification for the application of quantitative methods in archaeology.

SAMPLES AND POPULATIONS

Statistical inference concerns the problem of making decisions in the face of uncertainty; this uncertainty is quantified by means of probability theory. The inferences are about 'populations' and the uncertainty arises because they are made from samples of those populations. Precisely what the populations are in the case of archaeology is a matter for discussion (see below). There are two main aspects of statistical inference, hypothesis testing and estimation (see Cowgill 1977). There is in fact quite a close connection between the two, but in general terms the first involves testing some idea about the population, the second involves estimating the value of some characteristic of the population on the basis of the sample data, or providing upper and lower limits within which the value may be expected to lie. The presentation of radiocarbon dates is the classic example in archaeology of this latter procedure. In both cases what we want to do is in effect to say something about some aspect of a population on the basis of a sample drawn from it.

The characteristics of a population are known as *parameters*; the characteristics of a sample are known as *statistics,* and it is important to make a clear distinction between the two. Population characteristics are generally given as Greek letters, sample statistics by ordinary lower case letters. Thus the population mean is designated by Greek μ (mu) and the sample mean by $\bar{x}$; the population standard deviation by σ (sigma) and the sample standard deviation by s.

Parameters are *fixed* values referring to the population and are generally *unknown*; for example, the mean rim diameter of all vessels of type Y from site X. Statistics on the other hand vary from one sample to the next and are known or can be obtained; for example, the mean rim diameter of the vessels from trench A or trench B at site X. On the other hand *we do not know* how representative the sample is of the population, or how closely the statistic obtained approximates the corresponding unknown parameter, and our goal is usually to make inferences about various population parameters on the basis of known sample statistics.

In tests of hypotheses we make assumptions about the unknown parameters and then ask how likely our sample statistics would be if these assumptions were actually true. We attempt to make a rational decision as to whether or not our assumptions about the parameters are reasonable in view of the evidence at hand, so hypothesis testing is a kind of decision-making. The two types of questions most commonly found in hypothesis testing are:

1. What is the probability that two (or more) samples are drawn from different populations?

2. What is the probability that a given sample is drawn from a population which has certain defined characteristics?

This is clearly a rather restricted sense of the general idea of hypothesis testing. In particular, as both these questions indicate, hypotheses are statements which are defined in terms of clear expectations about the data and are therefore potentially rejectable. We reject or fail to reject the hypothesis realising that since our judgement is based only on a sample, we have always to admit the possibility of error due to the lack of representativeness of the sample. Probability theory enables us to evaluate the risks of error and to take these risks into consideration.

In general we start off by testing what is called the *null hypothesis*: the hypothesis of no difference. To refer back to the two questions above, we start with the assumption that our two or more samples are in fact drawn from the same population; or, that our sample really is drawn from a population with the characteristics which we have specified. Clive Orton (1980) presents this in the form of the question, 'Is there a case to answer?' What is at issue is best illustrated by a straightforward example. Suppose we want to compare the densities of archaeological sites in two different areas: are they different or not? The usual procedure is to set up a null hypothesis stating that there is no difference between the two areas in their average densities of sites; one then proceeds to examine the evidence against this hypothesis of no difference.

If we imagine our two areas divided into one-kilometre squares then it is highly unlikely that every square in each of the two areas will have an identical number of sites. There will be considerable differences from one to the next, so that if one randomly picked ten squares from one area and calculated the mean density of sites for those ten squares, and did the same for ten squares from the other area, the means of these two samples could be quite different from one another even if the population mean densities (the mean densities for all the squares in each of the two areas) were identical. This would happen if, by chance, one picked ten squares from a thinly occupied part of one of the areas and ten squares from a densely occupied part of the other. Such chance or *stochastic* sampling effects are explicitly built into statistical tests and are therefore taken into account when we make our decision, on the basis of the test, about whether or not the population (as opposed to the sample) mean densities really are different from one another.

Usually, the null hypothesis, H_0 as it is designated symbolically, is compared to the alternative hypothesis, H_1. For the moment we can say that this alternative hypothesis is simply the hypothesis that there is *a* difference, it says nothing about what size or type of difference exists, although this point will have to be qualified below. It is commonly but not invariably the case in statistical analysis that we wish to reject the null hypothesis and accept the alternative, although occasionally the null hypothesis is set up in the hope that it is true.

If we are going to make a decision about whether or not to reject the null hypothesis, what criterion do we use as the basis for making it, bearing in mind the chance effects that can arise when samples are selected from populations? Essentially, we look at the values for our two samples, note the difference between them, and ask how probable it is that a difference this large could occur if they were really two samples from the same population. If the probability of the difference being as large as it is, is very small (on the assumption of no difference), we reject the assumption and infer that there *is* a difference. This probability is known as the *level of significance,* denoted symbolically by the Greek letter α (alpha).

It is up to the investigator to decide on the level of significance which is acceptable. This means deciding how improbable a result has to be under the assumptions of the null hypothesis (the hypothesis of no difference) before that hypothesis is rejected. Normally, before we go as far as rejecting the null hypothesis we want the probability of it being valid, given the results, to be very small, so that some confidence can be placed in our rejection of it.

By convention the two most commonly used significance levels are $\alpha = 0.05$ and $\alpha = 0.01$. When we select a significance level of 0.05 it means that we have decided to accept the null hypothesis as true unless our data are so unusual that they would only occur five times out of 100, or less, if the null hypothesis (the hypothesis of no difference) were true; in which case we would reject it. In other words, if we drew 100 pairs of samples from two identical populations and noted the difference between their values, only five of the differences, on average, would be as large as that observed. In these circumstances we would decide that the results are such that it is highly improbable that the null hypothesis is true. Similarly for the 0.01 significance level, except that this time we are asking for the results to be so unusual that they would only occur once in 100 times, or less, under the null hypothesis before we would decide to reject it; that is to say, if the hypothesis of no difference is true then we would expect such a result only once in 100 or less.

Of course, it is perfectly reasonable to use other levels of significance. If the decision is one of critical importance you may only want to take the chance of being wrong once in 1000.

On the basis of this discussion you may think that the obvious thing to do is always to go for very conservative levels of significance – only rejecting the null hypothesis if the probability of it being valid is one in 1000 or less. But there is a catch to doing this, because if you insist on only rejecting the null hypothesis under very extreme circumstances, then you run a considerable risk of *accepting* the null hypothesis when it is in fact *false,* the converse error of the other.

Rejecting the null hypothesis when in fact it is true is known as a 'type I error'. This is a 'sin of commission' in statistical terms because it means that a significant relationship or difference is being claimed when none really exists. Accepting the null hypothesis when it is false is known as 'type II error', and represents a failure to identify a significant relationship or difference where one actually does exist. In most circumstances it is more serious to make a type I error – claim a relationship when none exists – than to fail to identify a significant relationship.

In setting a significance level you decide on the probability you are prepared to accept of making a type I error. It is the seriousness attached to type I errors – claiming something is going on in the data when it is not – which leads statisticians to set fairly demanding standards before they are prepared to reject the null hypothesis. This presupposes that we wish to reject the null hypothesis, which, as we have seen, is the usual case. If, on the other hand, we really hope that the null hypothesis is true, we should be trying to mini- mise the probability of making a type II error, the probability of accepting H_0 when it is actually false.

SIGNIFICANCE TESTING IN ARCHAEOLOGY

The preceding discussion of samples and populations, null hypo- theses and levels of significance has given some indication of what is involved in carrying out a significance test, but it has not con- sidered the assumptions required if such a test is to be satisfactorily carried out, nor how archaeological data relate to those assump- tions; the specific archaeological example used as an illustration above was in fact carefully defined to meet all the necessary assump- tions. It is now necessary to raise the various issues involved in using significance tests in an archaeological context and the clearest method of doing this is to follow through a hypothetical example and consider its implications.

For example: a study is being made of a hypothetical bronze age cemetery in Czechoslovakia and it has been noted that the female burials can be divided on the basis of the grave goods they contain into two groups, which we have labelled 'rich' and 'poor'. The question arises whether or not the distributions of ages at death of the individuals in these two groups are different from one another; the answer we obtain to this question will have a considerable bearing on how we interpret the cemetery. The relevant informa- tion is given in table 5.1.

The question then is of the type noted at the beginning of this chapter: are these two distributions the same or not? Given that they are not exactly the same, is the difference big enough to say that they really are different? It is Clive Orton's question, is there a case to answer? The question is a fairly important one, since if we infer that there is a real difference we have something which needs to be explained. If, on the other hand, we infer that the difference is not large enough to be taken seriously then there is not much more to be said.

If we want to use a significance test as a basis for making a decision about whether or not to take the difference seriously, the first thing to do is set up a null hypothesis and its alternative:

H_0: there is no difference between 'rich' and 'poor' female burials in their distribution of ages at death.

Table 5.1. The distribution of ages at death of
a group of female burials from a hypothetical
bronze age cemetery in Czechoslovakia for
which the burials have been divided into
'rich' and 'poor' categories on the basis of
their associated grave goods.

Age category at death	'Wealth' category	
	'Rich'	'Poor'
Infans I	6	23
Infans II	8	21
Juvenilis	11	25
Adultus	29	36
Maturus	19	27
Senilis	3	4
Total	76	136

H_1: there is a difference between 'rich' and 'poor' female
burials in their ages at death.

Let us suppose that in this case we will follow convention and select
a significance level of 0.05; that is to say, we will reject H_0 if, on the
assumption that it holds, the results observed would only occur five
times out of 100 or less.

In carrying out any test it is necessary to make a number of
assumptions, about the population in which we are interested and
also about the sampling procedures used. These assumptions can
be divided into two categories: those we are willing to accept, and
those we are dubious about and therefore interested in. The null
hypothesis is the assumption about which we are dubious and which
therefore interests us. From the point of view of the statistical test,
unfortunately, all assumptions have the same logical status: if the
results of the test indicate rejection of the assumptions, all we can
say on the basis of the test is that at least one of the assumptions is
probably false. Since the test does not indicate which of the assumptions are erroneous, it is obviously vital, if results are to be meaningful, that only one of the assumptions should be really in doubt; this
can then be rejected as the invalid one. Thus, when you are selecting a test, it is important to select one that involves only a single
dubious assumption, the null nypothesis.

One of the first things to be taken into account when selecting a
test is the level of measurement of the data. Tests for data measured
at interval or ratio level are not appropriate to data measured at a

very low level. On the other hand, if we use a test appropriate to data measured at a very low level on higher level data then we are wasting information and not using as powerful a test as we might. In the present case we can say that the age categories represent an ordinal scale.

As we will see later, many statistical tests require specific assumptions to be made about the form of the distribution under investigation, but this is by no means true for all of them. One test appropriate for comparing two ordinal scales which specifies very few such assumptions is the *Kolmogorov–Smirnov test*. This requires that the observations should be divided into at least two mutually exclusive categories and that they should be measured at the ordinal level or above. The test is based on the difference between the two cumulative distributions of interest; for the version described here both the samples should be greater than forty in size.

The first step is to convert the original counts into proportions of their category total. Thus, for example, there are 76 burials in the 'rich' category; 6 of the 76 belong in the Infans I age category, which proportionally is $6/76 = 0.079$, on a scale from 0 to 1, or 7.9 % on a scale from 0 to 100. In the 'poor' category $23/136$ burials are in the Infans I age group, 0.169 on a scale from 0 to 1, or 16.9 % on a scale from 0 to 100. This operation is performed on each of the age categories in each of the 'wealth' classes, to give table 5.2.

Table 5.2. Numbers and proportions of burials by wealth and age categories.

Age category	'Wealth' category			
	'Rich'		'Poor'	
Infans I	6	0.079	23	0.169
Infans II	8	0.105	21	0.154
Juvenilis	11	0.145	25	0.184
Adultus	29	0.382	36	0.265
Maturus	19	0.250	27	0.199
Senilis	3	0.039	4	0.029
Total	76	1.000	136	1.000

The proportions are then accumulated for each age category within each of the 'wealth' classes, in the way we have already seen when producing a cumulative curve. Thus, the proportion of 'rich' burials in the category Infans II or younger is $0.079 + 0.105 = 0.184$; in the category Juvenilis or younger it is $0.184 + 0.145 = 0.329$; and so on. The result of this operation is given in table 5.3.

Table 5.3. Cumulative proportions of
burials by wealth and age categories.

Age category	'Wealth' category	
	'Rich'	'Poor'
Infans I	0.079	0.169
Infans II	0.184	0.323
Juvenilis	0.329	0.507
Adultus	0.711	0.772
Maturus	0.961	0.971
Senilis	1.000	1.000

The test is based on an assessment of the largest difference
between these two distributions of cumulative proportions, so the
next step is to calculate the differences between them for each age
category and to note which is the largest (without regard to whether
the difference is positive or negative); see table 5.4.

Table 5.4. Cumulative proportions of burials
by wealth and age categories and differences
between them.

Age category	'Wealth' category		
	'Rich'	'Poor'	Difference
Infans I	0.079	0.169	0.090
Infans II	0.184	0.323	0.139
Juvenilis	0.329	0.507	0.178
Adultus	0.711	0.772	0.061
Maturus	0.961	0.971	0.010
Senilis	1.000	1.000	0.000

On the basis of this we can see that the largest difference lies at
the Juvenilis category and is 0.178. Before considering what to do
with this number, and how it relates to our declared significance
level, it is worth noting that we can, of course, present these
distributions graphically to obtain an intuitive feeling of what they
look like and what the difference between them represents (figure
5.1); the largest difference between the two curves is indicated on
the figure.

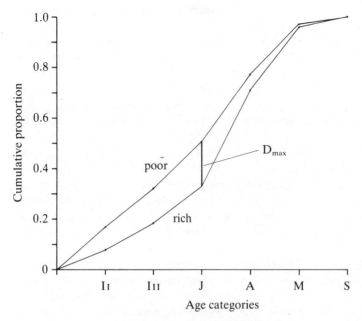

Figure 5.1. Plot of the cumulative age distributions of 'rich' and 'poor' burials using the data from table 5.1.

What Does it Mean to Carry Out a Significance Test on Such a Problem?

Given that there is such a difference between the two distributions, is it 'real' or not? Using a significance test to answer the question, *are these two distributions different from one another,* presupposes the rephrasing of the question to read, do the two sets of sample data we have come from identical populations? As we have seen, statistical inference is all about making inferences about populations on the basis of samples. But what is the population of which our data can be regarded as a sample?

This question brings us to the key assumption of the Kolmogorov–Smirnov test, indeed of all significance tests, which has not yet been mentioned. They presuppose that we have a sample of a population and that there is independence of selection within the sample, in other words, that the selection of one individual has no effect on the choice of another individual to be included in the sample. The method usually adopted to try and meet this specification is *random sampling.* A random sample has the property not only of giving each individual an equal chance of being selected but of giving each combination of individuals an equal chance of selection.

It is obvious that no archaeological sample can be considered a random sample of what was once present. It is true, however, as we noted at the beginning of this chapter, that sometimes archaeologists are in a position to select random samples of the archaeological record, the problems of which are considered in the later chapter on sampling. On the other hand, in most cases, and certainly in that considered in our example, we are dealing with a set of data which has not been collected in this way. Furthermore, if the hypothetical cemetery from which the burials of our example are derived has been totally excavated, then in one sense at least we are dealing with a population and not a sample at all. If we are dealing with a population, where does the sampling variation come from which is supposed to account for the differences between the samples?

It is perhaps worth noting at this point that this problem is by no means peculiar to archaeology but occurs in most social sciences where statistics are used, including geography and sociology, and in no case does it seem to be properly resolved. For some the line of reasoning just indicated leads to the conclusion that standard statistical inferential procedures such as significance testing are simply irrelevant except in very restricted situations. Others, whose viewpoint I share, suggest that in many circumstances we can postulate a hypothetical or ideal population of which we can consider our data a sample. This may seem a distinctly dubious argument, invoking a population 'which can be loosely if unkindly defined as the population that we need in order that our sample may be considered random', as Orton (1982) has argued in a slightly different context. It is not necessarily as bad as it seems.

There are two slightly different ways of considering how such hypothetical populations arise. One of these stems from the concept of *randomisation*. It may be illustrated with our example of the distribution of ages at death in the two groups of burials. We can take as given the fact that there are 76 burials in the 'rich' category and 136 in the 'poor' category. We can also take as given that there is a total of $6 + 23 = 29$ burials in the Infans I category; $8 + 21 = 29$ burials in the Infans II category; and so on. This information is fixed for the set of data under consideration and what is at issue is the way the burials in each of the age categories are distributed across the two 'wealth' categories. Is the distribution of the ages of the two wealth categories different or not? If the distributions are not different then the ratio of 'rich' individuals to 'poor' individuals in each age category should be the same as it is for the population as a whole. Thus, in category Infans I, on the basis of a distribution corresponding to 76:136, there should be 10 burials in the 'rich' category and 19 in the 'poor' category. If we imagine carrying out a large number of experiments in which we randomly assign burials to the 'rich' and 'poor' categories according to the ratio 76:136, for each of the age categories; and if, each time we do it, we plot the cumulative curve for the two distributions and note the largest difference between them; then, after a large number of such experiments we will have a large number of largest differences, experimentally generated, with which to compare the difference between our two real distributions, and on the basis of which we can decide whether it is an unusual one or not. If it is sufficiently unusual we will decide to reject the null hypothesis and decide there is a 'real' difference between the distributions.

This is one way then in which we can obtain a population to which we can relate our sample. In some circumstances it is necessary actually to generate the randomised population using computer methods; in others, such as the case being considered in our example, the standard test is such that its use can be regarded as equivalent to the randomisation process.

Randomisation is probably the most straightforward way of conceptualising, and indeed realising, the idea of a hypothetical population. Another way is to conceive of the archaeological evidence in a given case as one specific empirical outcome of a system of behaviour based on social rules. Any given act or example of behaviour producing archaeological evidence will be based on the rules but is likely to be affected by all sorts of contingent circumstances, so that variation is introduced which is in fact random or chance variation, in the sense that it is not systematically related to the rules generating the behaviour. Such a line of argument in fact has been pursued most consistently not in relation to significance testing as such, but in the identification and definition of archaeological types by one particular school which believes that in defining types we should be discovering those in the minds of the makers of the artefacts and establishing the rules by which they were produced (for a recent discussion of these issues see Whallon and Brown 1982).

The whole argument is clearly more appropriate to some archaeological circumstances than others, and in particular to cases where we know we are dealing with the results of intentional behaviour, and that our observations are not being biased in some way by recovery factors. In order to use such an approach in the case of our burial example we would have to be aware of two limitations. First, the results only apply to the burials in this particular cemetery; they do not take into account the fact that 'rich' and 'poor' individuals in any or all of the different age categories may have been buried elsewhere, or may not have been buried at all in an archaeologically recognisable fashion. Secondly, it would have to be shown that any relationship between 'wealth' category and age distribution was not the result of some other factor, such as variation in preservation conditions. With these stipulations, it could be argued that any patterning in the relation between age at death and 'wealth' category was the result of rule-bound social behaviour but that for all sorts of reasons there will have been variation in the closeness with which the rules were followed, producing a distribution of behaviour with a mean value and variation around it, as Barth, for example, has argued (1967). Where such behaviour has an archaeological outcome, the particular set of behaviours whose evidence we recover will be just one of a range of possibilities.

The arguments just presented are quite complex ones and are in many ways at a deeper level than the straightforward presentation of methods which occupies most of this book. Nevertheless, they are important ones, since they are at the heart of discussions about the appropriateness of statistical inference in archaeology, as in other disciplines, and therefore cannot be neglected.

The Kolmogorov–Smirnov Test Completed

After this long but important digression it remains to complete the example significance test we have been following through. We have found that the largest difference between the cumulative curves of age at death for our two 'wealth' categories is 0.178, at the Juvenilis category. The question is: do we regard this as an unusually large difference between the two curves on the null hypothesis that they both represent samples from identical populations whose differences arise from chance variation. To find this out the observed difference is compared with an expected distribution of differences derived theoretically. Such distributions are often presented in the form of statistical tables, and we will see an example of this in the next chapter. The Kolmogorov–Smirnov test is slightly different in that the minimum difference between two cumulative distributions which will be significant at a given level is obtained by evaluating a formula. If the observed difference is equal to or greater than this then it is statistically significant at the set level. In this case we have set the significance level at 0.05 and the appropriate formula is

$$1.36\sqrt{\frac{n_1 + n_2}{n_1 n_2}}$$

where $n_1 =$ the number of individuals in sample 1 and $n_2 =$ the number of individuals in sample 2. Here

$$1.36\sqrt{\frac{76 + 136}{76 \times 136}} = 0.195$$

1.36 is the theoretically derived multiplication factor appropriate to the 0.05 level. If the 0.01 level is required, the coefficient is 1.63; if 0.001 it is 1.95.

Having obtained the minimum required difference for H_0 to be rejected at the given significance level we see that the observed maximum difference ($Dmax_{obs}$) at 0.178 is not as great as the minimum required difference for the 0.05 level ($Dmax_{.05}$), at 0.195. Since the observed difference is less than the minimum required to reject H_0 at the 0.05 level, we cannot reject the null hypothesis. There is not a significant difference in the distribution of age at death between the 'rich' and 'poor' categories.

It is important to note that *this does not mean that the distributions are the same.* It simply means that there is insufficient evidence to suggest that they are different; there does not appear to be a 'case to answer'. We cannot be very sure that there is anything here to be explained.

OTHER TESTS FOR DIFFERENCES BETWEEN TWO ORDINAL SCALE DISTRIBUTIONS

The main intention of describing the Kolmogorov–Smirnov test in this chapter was to give an idea of what is involved in statistical inference, but it is worth noting that this is by no means the only technique for testing whether two ordinal scale variables are different from one another. The *Mann–Whitney test* and the *runs test* may also be used in such circumstances. These are not described in detail here but may be found in many of the standard statistics textbooks (e.g. Blalock 1972). However, a brief indication of what is involved in these tests will be presented, to give an idea of when they are appropriate.

Imagine that we have survey data for the sizes of 20 early neolithic settlements on two different soil types in southern Italy. Estimating site size from survey data can be problematical and is very often imprecise. In this case we do not feel justified in stating the precise area of each site but do feel that we can rank them according to size. Do larger or smaller sites tend to be on one soil type rather than the other?

We can rank the sites in order of size, indicating for each site the soil type (A or B) on which it lies (largest to smallest, left to right). We might obtain an ordering like this:

AABABBBABAAABBABBAAB

or like this:

BBBBBABBBABBAAAAAAAA

In the first case there are very short runs of sites on the same soil type mixed in with short runs of sites on the other soil type; i.e. sites on the two soil types are intermixed in terms of size. In the second case the number of runs is much smaller: there is a predominance of sites on soil B at one end of the size range and of soil A at the other. The runs test will tell us whether the number of runs we have in a particular case is more or less than we would expect if the two distributions were randomly intermixed.

The Mann–Whitney test is very similar, and to illustrate what is involved we can stay with the same example. Again we rank the sites in order of size. We can now focus on all the sites on one of the soil types. Here it doesn't matter which since there are ten on each, but if the numbers weren't equally balanced we would choose the soil type with the smaller number of sites. We then note for each of our sites, say those on soil B, how many of the sites on soil A rank lower than it. Thus, for the first of the two orders given above we see that the highest ranked soil-type B site is third, with eight soil-type A sites below it. The next highest ranked soil B site is fifth, with seven type A sites below it, and so on. In the second case above, each of the first five B sites has ten soil A sites below it. We add up the number of A sites below B sites for all the B sites. If in general the B sites are smaller than the A sites they will have very few A sites below them; if they are larger they will have very many below them; while if the site sizes on the two soil types are randomly intermixed the number of A sites below B sites will be somewhere in the middle. We use the Mann–Whitney test to find out if the numbers in our particular case do differ significantly from random intermixing.

CONCLUSION

This chapter has only attempted to deal with the significance test aspect of statistical inference; estimation will be considered in the chapter on sampling. The aim has been to discuss the issues involved in using such tests in the context of a specific example. As I have already emphasised, however, significance tests are by no means the only, or the most important reason for the use of quantitative methods in archaeology. In fact, as we will see in later chapters, *statistical significance* and *substantive significance in archaeological terms* are not necessarily the same thing at all: questions of the strength and the form of the relationship between variables are usually far more interesting and important than questions of statistical significance.

5.1. On one side of a prehistoric settlement is a cemetery of megalithic tombs. Among other aspects interest is focused on the significance of the spatial distribution of the tombs and it occurs to the investigator that the proximity of the tombs to the settlement may be relevant in some way. The tombs and their contents vary in a number of different respects and in particular it has proved possible to divide them on the basis of their morphology into an 'elaborate' category and a 'simple' category. The cemetery has been divided into a number of bands of approximately 200 m width, although varying somewhat as a result of the local topography. Band A is the closest to the settlement and the distances of the bands increase up to band F, which is the furthest. Given the information below, is there any indication that distance from the settlement and tomb elaboration are related?

Band	Number of tombs: Elaborate	Simple
A	12	6
B	8	6
C	17	10
D	7	16
E	13	19
F	14	18

Discuss the assumptions that you are making in your analysis.

5.2. In a study of social organisation at a hypothetical Formative site in Mexico an investigation of the burials was carried out. Some of them were in ordinary graves whereas others were in built tombs. The question arose whether any biological characteristics of the individuals in the cemetery were associated with the difference in burial mode.

Below is information on the numbers of individuals in each of a series of age categories, divided according to whether they were buried in ordinary graves or built tombs. Are the age distributions of the buried populations different for the two burial types?

	Age Categories					
	1	2	3	4	5	6
Graves	25	18	29	14	24	9
Tombs	8	4	6	18	40	5

5.3. Below is information on the length of bone fragments from two pleistocene caves in southern England (data from Boyle 1983). Do you think that the length distributions of the fragments at the two sites are different from one another?

Length category (mm)	No. of fragments: Cave 1	Cave 2
0-9	1	0
10-19	21	6
20-29	15	11
30-39	5	11
40-49	7	6
50-59	1	6
60-69	2	6
70-79	3	4
80-89	3	2
90-99	0	5
100-109	2	9

Six

The Chi-Squared Test

The previous chapter used the Kolmogorov–Smirnov test to demonstrate what is involved in carrying out a significance test and the kinds of assumptions which have to be made. Although it is very useful, there is a restriction on the use of the test, in that the level of measurement presupposed is ordinal or higher. The chi-squared test does not have this restriction. It can be used with data measured at the nominal scale, in other words, simply classified into categories; it is also easy to calculate, although this last point is less important these days with the wide availability of calculators and computers. Because of this lack of restrictions the chi-squared test can be used to assess the correspondence between distributions in a wide variety of different situations and as a result is applied very extensively. The test is being presented here for several different reasons; first, because it is so commonly used and useful; second, because it provides a further illustration of how significance tests may be set up in an archaeological context; and third, because it provides a convenient bridge from concepts of statistical significance to concepts of the *strength* of the relationship between variables.

There are two slightly different versions of the chi-squared test, although obviously the principle in both is the same. The first, perhaps less familiar to archaeologists, is the one-sample test, in which a sample is compared to a specified theoretical population and a test is made of how good the correspondence or 'fit' is between these two distributions; the idea is clearly important when we are testing theoretically-derived models.

In describing the test it is easiest to begin with an example. A question frequently of interest is the distribution of settlement in relation to soil differences; were certain areas more attractive than others to early settlement?

Suppose we have an area in eastern France with three different soil types: rendzina, alluvium and brown earth. There are 53 late neolithic settlements in the area and a look at the map suggests the possibility that the rendzinas may have been preferred. The question is whether or not it is possible that the distribution of settlements with regard to soil could be a matter of chance. If all three soil types were equally attractive to settlement then it would be reasonable to assume that we should find approximately the same density of settlement in each. In other words, the distribution of settlements would be roughly evenly spread over the landscape and variations would not relate to soil but to such factors as small local differences in topography, or the whims of the founding settlers. In this context we can use the chi-squared test.

Table 6.1. Numbers of late neolithic settlements on different soil types in eastern France.

Soil type	No. of settlements
Rendzina	26
Alluvium	9
Brown earth	18
	53

The first thing we can do is to note the numbers of settlements on each of the soil types (table 6.1). How do we calculate the theoretically derived expected frequencies to compare with these? We have already seen that if we postulate that all three zones were equally attractive to settlement, we should expect the same density of settlements in each. This represents our theoretically-derived null hypothesis for calculating expected frequencies. Thus, it is reasonable to assume that if rendzinas make up 32% of the area, as we will suppose they do, then 32% of all the settlements should be on rendzinas; similarly if we suppose 43% of the area to be brown earth and 25% alluvium. In other words, we calculate the expected number of settlements for each soil type by allotting the same proportion of the total number of settlements to that soil type as it occupies of the total area (table 6.2).

If we compare the observed and expected values in this table for the number of settlements on each of the soil types, there are some obvious differences between the distribution anticipated if all areas were equally attractive to settlement and what we actually observe. The question is, are the differences so great that the probability of their being the result of chance variation is acceptably low? This is where the chi-squared test has its role.

Table 6.2. Observed and expected numbers of late neolithic settlements on different soil types in eastern France.

Soil type	Observed no. of settlements	% of area	Expected no. of settlements
Rendzina	26	32	17.0
Alluvium	9	25	13.2
Brown earth	18	43	22.8
	53	100	53.0

The one-sample chi-squared test presupposes a set of observations divided up into a number of mutually exclusive categories. A comparison is then made between the distribution of observations across the categories and the distribution to be anticipated under some theoretically derived expectation, specified by the null hypothesis. The differences between the two distributions for each category are noted and a chi-squared value is calculated, based on the sum of the differences. The calculated value is then compared with the minimum value required to reject the null hypothesis at the level of significance which has been set. In effect, in setting the situation up as a significance test we are asking whether our observations could be a random sample of a population which has the characteristics specified in the null hypothesis.

Carrying out the test requires a number of assumptions. As always, it is necessary to specify a null hypothesis and set a significance level, and to be able to specify some population of which we can regard our observations as a sample in the way discussed in the previous chapter. As we have already noted, the level of measurement required is not at all demanding, simply a nominal scale with at least two mutually exclusive categories into which the observations have been divided; the observations themselves must be *counts,* not percentages or other forms of ratio.

The formula for chi-squared is given by

$$\chi^2 = \sum_{i=1}^{k} \frac{(O_i - E_i)^2}{E_i}$$

where k is the number of categories, O_i is the observed number of cases in category i, E_i is the expected number of cases in category i, and χ^2 is the symbol representing chi-squared, using the Greek letter 'chi'.

In words this formula reads as follows: for each category subtract the expected value from the observed value, square this difference, and divide the result by the expected value; once this has been done for each category, sum the results for all categories. The result is a calculated chi-squared value.

Once we have computed a value for chi-squared we need to test it for statistical significance. In the case of the Kolmogorov–Smirnov test this was done by comparing the observed largest difference with a value obtained by substituting sample size numbers into an appropriate formula giving the size of the difference required for the result to be statistically significant. In the case of chi-squared, tables have been produced which provide the values with which to compare the calculated value (see appendix 1, table A). In order to find the relevant value in the table with which to make the comparison it is necessary to know two things: the level of significance which has been decided – straightforward enough – and the number of *degrees of freedom* associated with the sample.

What is meant by the number of degrees of freedom is not so straightforward. Essentially, the form of the theoretical chi-squared distribution, which is tabulated in the chi-squared table, varies according to the number of categories into which the observations are divided. The greater the number of categories, then the larger the value of the chi-squared statistic obtained from the data needs to be, in order to reach a given level of significance. This makes sense, since it is clear from the formula for the chi-squared statistic that the number of quantities being summed depends on the number of categories, so the larger the number of categories the bigger the sum, which is the calculated chi-squared, is likely to be. In the case of the one-sample test, however, the number of degrees of freedom is not equal to the number of categories but to the number of categories minus one; in symbols:

$$\nu = k - 1$$

where ν (Greek letter 'nu') is the number of degrees of freedom and k is the number of categories.

Why should this be the case? This is best illustrated by referring to our example, where there are 53 observations (settlements) divided into three categories (soil types). Given that there is a total of 53 observations altogether, and that $26 + 9 = 35$ are in the first two categories, then the value in the third category *has to be* $53 - 35 = 18$. In other words, the values in the first two categories are free to vary but the value in the last category is not; it is fixed by the requirement that the sum over all three categories should equal the total number of observations with which we started.

When you know the relevant number of degrees of freedom and the level of significance which has been fixed, it is possible to find the appropriate value in the table with which to compare the calculated value. In a chi-squared table the number of degrees of freedom is given down the left-hand side and the significance level across the top. Thus, if you have two degrees of freedom and are using the 0.05 significance level, then you find the row for $v = 2$, go across it until you reach the column for the 0.05 significance level and read off the number, in this case 5.99. This is the tabulated chi-squared value with which the calculated value obtained from the data must be compared:

If $\chi^2_{calc} \geqslant \chi^2_\alpha$, reject H_0

If $\chi^2_{calc} < \chi^2_\alpha$, accept H_0

Before turning to our example, however, one more point needs to be noted. The tabulated values in the chi-squared table only give the correct level of significance for samples above a certain size, although the restriction is not a very severe one. If the test has only one degree of freedom then no category should have an *expected* value less than 5; with larger numbers of categories this restriction can be relaxed considerably. In cases where this problem arises there are ways round it, for example by constructing a randomisation test.

Now that the general procedure for carrying out a chi-squared test has been described, it is possible to show its use in our example, which must first be set up in the appropriate form for a significance test:

H_0: settlements are equally distributed across all three soil types.

H_1: settlements are not equally distributed across all three soil types.

Selected significance level: $\alpha = 0.05$

There is no need to be extremely conservative in selecting the level. We are interested in whether or not we have an indication of a divergence from equality of distribution.

The data are measured at a nominal scale only, they are counts divided into categories and the categories are mutually exclusive. None of the expected values calculated above is less than 5. Use of a one-sample chi-squared test is therefore appropriate.

The expected values under H_0 have already been generated (table 6.2) so it is now possible to carry out the necessary calculations.

$$\chi^2 = \sum_{i=1}^{k} \frac{(O_i - E_i)^2}{E_i}$$

$$= \frac{(26-17.0)^2}{17.0} + \frac{(9-13.2)^2}{13.2} + \frac{(18-22.8)^2}{22.8}$$

$$= 4.76 + 1.34 + 1.01$$

$$= 7.11$$

This must now be compared with the appropriate tabulated value. Degrees of freedom are $k-1$, where k is the number of categories: here $3-1=2$. From the table the critical chi-squared value for two degrees of freedom and the 0.05 level of significance is 5.99. If $\chi^2_{calc} \geq \chi^2_{\alpha}$, reject H_0: here $7.11 > 5.99$, and therefore we reject the null hypothesis in this case.

But it is important not just to stop at this point. It is necessary to relate the result of the test to the archaeological problem. In this case we have to accept the alternative hypothesis that settlements are not equally distributed across all three soil types. To relate our data to a population in the way discussed in the previous chapter, we can say that if we carried out a large number of experiments randomly allocating 53 settlements to these three soil types on the assumption of an equal distribution, the distribution we have actually observed would be a very unusual one, and at the 0.05 level requires us to reject the assumption of equal distribution. There may be many reasons for this, and we will consider the problems of moving from statistically significant associations and correlations to inferences about causation below.

THE CHI-SQUARED TEST
FOR CROSS-CLASSIFIED DATA

Having looked at the case in which a sample is compared to a specified theoretical population, let us now turn to the use of chi-squared to test for independence of classification in cases where data have been classified in terms of two different criteria, again beginning with an example.

Suppose we are studying a north German iron age inhumation cemetery and we suspect there is a relationship between an individual's sex and the side on which that individual is lying in the grave. We have the information given in table 6.3, which is often referred to as a *contingency table*. Tables like this one are 2×2 (2 by 2) tables since there are only two rows – right-hand-side and

Table 6.3. Side on which individuals were placed in the grave cross-tabulated against their sex, for a north German iron age inhumation cemetery.

	M	F	
RHS	29	14	43
LHS	11	33	44
	40	47	87

left-hand-side – and two columns – male and female. The individual entries in the table, e.g. that for male, right-hand-side, are referred to as the cells. The numbers at the end of each row are the row totals and at the bottom of each column, the column totals. In the bottom right-hand position is the total number of observations, here 87.

Basically, the test for such tables is very similar to the one we have just seen, in that the data are counts divided into mutually exclusive categories. This time, however, instead of comparing the distribution of an observed sample with that of a theoretically specified population, we are asking whether two classifications of our data are independent of one another, in the sense that membership of a particular category of one classification is unrelated to membership of a particular category of the other. Nevertheless, in both cases we are testing for what statisticians call 'goodness-of-fit'.

The assumptions required in this case are again very similar to those for the one-sample test: nominal scale or higher level of measurement and no expected frequency less than 5 in the case of one degree of freedom (see p. 73 for degrees of freedom in contingency tables). Now, however, we have two distinct classification criteria, divided into at least two mutually exclusive categories. Thus, to refer to our examples, for the one-sample chi-squared test our settlements were categorised according to one variable alone, their soil type; for the contingency table our burials are categorised or classified in terms of two variables: their gender and the side on which they were lying in the grave.

The calculation of chi-squared is as before, based on the difference between the observed and expected values for each category. The number of categories is the number of cells in the table: in our example there are two gender categories and two side categories, so the number of cells, as you can see from table 6.3, is $2 \times 2 = 4$.

For the one-sample chi-squared test the expected values were generated by the theoretical population postulated by the null hypothesis. The idea is very similar here, in that we are asking in this case whether male and female burials have the same proportional division into left-hand-side and right-hand-side burials. Thus, if there are altogether 43 right-hand-side burials and 44 left-hand-side, then we would expect the 47 female burials and the 40 male burials to be divided into the right-hand-side and left-hand-side categories according to the 43:44 ratio. In fact, rather than actually carrying out this operation, the appropriate expected values for a given cell in the table may be obtained by multiplying the row sum corresponding to the cell by the column sum corresponding to the cell and dividing the result by the total number of observations. Thus, for the top left-hand cell of the table given above the expected value is $(40 \times 43)/87 = 19.8$.

It is possible to work out the expected values for the other cells of the table in the same way. However, since we know the marginal totals of the table and the expected value for the top left-hand cell, we can obtain the expected values for the other three cells by subtraction.

$$43 - 19.8 = 23.2$$
$$40 - 19.8 = 20.2$$
$$44 - 20.2 = 23.8$$

We then make out a table including the expected values in parentheses (table 6.4), and we may now set up the significance test for the burial data.

Table 6.4. Side on which individuals were placed in the grave cross-tabulated against their sex, with the expected values for each category shown in parentheses.

	M	F	
RHS	29	14	43
	(19.8)	(23.2)	
LHS	11	33	44
	(20.2)	(23.8)	
	40	47	87

H_0: the distribution of male and female burials across the two burial position categories, left-hand-side and right-hand-side is the same.

H_1: the distribution of male and female burials across the two categories is different.

Selected significance level: $\alpha = 0.05$

The data meet the required assumptions for a chi-squared test on cross-classified data, so the next step is to calculate the chi-squared value for the data, using the formula given above (table 6.5).

Table 6.5. Calculation table for obtaining chi-squared value from data in table 6.4.

Category	O_i	E_i	$(O_i - E_i)$	$(O_i - E_i)^2$	$\dfrac{(O_i - E_i)^2}{E_i}$
1	29	19.8	9.2	84.64	4.27
2	14	23.2	-9.2	84.64	3.65
3	11	20.2	-9.2	84.64	4.19
4	33	23.8	9.2	84.64	3.56
				$\chi^2 =$	15.67

The process of testing this calculated value for significance is the same as before, in that it is compared to the value in the chi-squared table which corresponds to the required level of significance and the appropriate number of degrees of freedom. For the test on cross-classified data, however, the number of degrees of freedom has to be calculated differently and is given by $v =$ (the number of rows in table -1)(the number of columns in table -1). For our example we have $(2-1)(2-1) = 1$.

This may be related to the observation above that once we had worked out the expected value for the top left-hand cell of the table, the expected values for the other cells were fixed and could be obtained by subtraction. If we now look up the tabulated value of chi-squared for one degree of freedom and the .05 level of significance we find that it is 3.84. $\chi^2_{calc} = 15.67$, $15.67 > 3.84$, and accordingly we reject H_0. We can note incidentally that a value of 15.67 for chi-squared would even be significant at the .001 level. It thus appears that male and female burials are not distributed in the same way over the two position categories.

One final calculation note. The method described above is the general way of calculating chi-squared, however many rows and columns there are in the table. In fact, for the case of a 2×2 table, a table with 2 rows and 2 columns, there is an alternative more convenient formula:

$$\chi^2 = \frac{n(ad - bc)^2}{(a + b)(c + d)(a + c)(b + d)}$$

where n is the sample size and a, b, c, d refer to the cells of a table labelled

a   b

c   d

HOW USEFUL IS THE CHI-SQUARED TEST?

It should be clear from what has been said about the chi-squared test that it can be extremely useful and informative, but it is appropriate to finish this chapter with a list of its limitations:

1. Chi-squared does not tell us about the strength of a relationship; it simply tells us about the probability of whether or not a relationship exists. This point will be amplified very considerably in the next chapter. For the moment we can note that even if the connection between the two variables is weak, we may still obtain a statistically significant result. Thus, to take the example we have just looked at, we might get a statistically significant result even if there was only a slight tendency for males to be buried on their right and females on their left. Even though slight the tendency could still be a real one (see the third point below).

2. It does not tell us anything about the way in which the variables are related; it simply measures departures of expected from observed values.

3. As with any test statistic, sample size affects the magnitude of chi-squared. For a given departure from independence its size is proportional to the size of the sample; this means that you can practically always obtain a significant relationship by making the sample size large enough. The difficulty then arises of distinguishing *statistical significance* from *substantive significance*.

What we need to do when we have cross-classified data is examine them in considerable detail; simply carrying out a chi-squared test is not enough; indeed, often you know ahead of time that the chi-squared result is going to be significant, so by relying solely on this you gain little new information. It is now necessary to examine these points in more detail.

EXERCISES

6.1. In an excavated cemetery of single inhumation burials 35% of the skeletons have been found to have bronze rings as grave goods.

A group of 15 graves has just been found, adjacent to but separate from the rest, and 10 of them contain bronze rings. Is this group of graves different from the rest of the cemetery with regard to the deposition of rings?

6.2. Work on the analysis of prehistoric rock art is often concerned with the identification of recurrent patterns of association between motifs. In the case considered here there were 9 different motifs. 21.2% of the individual occurrences of the motifs were involved in superimpositions with other motifs. 15 out of 24 occurrences of the 'sheep' motif and 13 out of 127 occurrences of the 'human' motif were involved in superimpositions. Do these patterns appear to be different from those for the population as a whole?

6.3. In an analysis of spatial patterns in local exchange in Mesopotamia a particular type of centrally produced pottery is examined (data from Johnson 1973). Examination suggests that the width of the painted lines used in decoration differs between the two centres of manufacture; study of a bar graph of line widths from the pottery suggests that the lines can be divided into two categories, heavy and fine. Settlements in the study area divide into two groups, eastern and western. Is the pottery with the two line types differentially distributed with regard to the east-west division, given the information below?

	Eastern area	Western area	
Heavy line	42	10	52
Fine line	17	21	38
	59	31	90

6.4. We are studying a cemetery in which there are three different grave types: simple earth pits, graves with wooden chambers, and graves with stone chambers. We suspect there may be a relationship between the type of grave in which individuals were buried and their age at death; we can define three age categories by anthropological examination of the skeletons: less than 21, 21–40, over 40. Individuals are distributed as shown in the table on p. 76. Is there a significant relationship between age and grave type?

Exercise 6.4

	< 21	21-40	> 40
Simple pit	23	19	11
Wooden chamber	12	17	13
Stone chamber	10	16	15

Table 7.1. Side on which individuals were placed in the grave cross-tabulated against their sex.

	M	F	
RHS	30	14	44
LHS	10	34	44
	40	48	88

Table 7.2. Side on which individuals were placed in the grave cross-tabulated against their sex. Numbers in each category are half those in table 7.1.

	M	F	
RHS	15	7	22
LHS	5	17	22
	20	24	44

Seven

Beyond Chi-Squared:
Describing Association Between
Two Nominal Scale Variables

The limitations of chi-squared, listed at the end of the last chapter, can be construed more widely as limitations of the whole significance test approach: it does not usually take us very far in understanding the object of our investigation. Indeed, if it is used incautiously it can be positively misleading, since statistical significance may be taken more seriously than it deserves to be. This chapter outlines some methods which may be used to extract much more information from nominal scale data than simply subjecting them to a chi-squared test. But although the techniques described refer specifically to contingency tables, the approach behind them may be generalised to any kind of analysis and is not dissimilar from the EDA approach discussed in an earlier chapter; in fact, the role played by significance testing in the rest of this book is relatively small. The first stage in outlining this approach is to enlarge on the comments made at the end of the previous chapter.

It was suggested that for a relationship to be statistically significant, it is not necessary that it is significant in the sense of being strong; it is possible for a relationship to be significant statistically yet quite weak. This is because statistical significance arises from the combined effect of two different factors: the strength of the relationship and the size of the sample. Consequently, we *cannot* use the value of chi-squared or its associated probability level as a measure of strength of relationship, and say, for example, that a result significant at the .001 level indicates a stronger relationship than one significant at the .05 level.

The effect of sample size on the chi-squared value and significance level may be illustrated by looking again at the burial example from the previous chapter, altered slightly for the purpose of this illustration so that all the numbers are even ones (table 7.1). Here chi-squared = 18.33 with one degree of freedom, significant at much more than the .001 level. If we halve the numbers but keep the same proportional distribution across the categories, we have table 7.2.

Here chi-squared = 9.16 with one degree of freedom, significant at the .01 level. Similarly, if we doubled the original numbers, we could obtain a chi-squared value of 36.66. Thus, in general, if we keep the proportions in the cells constant and simply multiply the numbers by some factor k, then we multiply the resulting chi-squared by k.

All this makes sense. If we are asking the significance-test question – does a relationship exist or not? – we will have more confidence in our answer if it is based on a large number of observations. If the number of observations is very large, then even if only a very weak relationship exists between our variables, or only some very slight difference between our samples, we can have some confidence that it is 'real'. Conversely, if the number of observations is very small then for any difference or relationship to be regarded as 'real' it will have to be very marked indeed. Such marked differences or strong relationships are almost bound to be of interest to us, but the same is not necessarily true of weak ones: a very slight relationship or difference may be 'real', but does it matter?

The foregoing discussion shows that we need to measure strength of relationship separately from statistical significance, and that chi-squared at least is not an appropriate measure for doing this, except perhaps in those rare instances where our aim simply involves the making of comparisons across samples which are identical in size.

This question of comparison is an important one. Generally, we are not interested in a given single case where the strength of relationship is being measured. More often than not, comparisons are being made, for example with the same measure on other data sets. For this reason such measures need to be standardised. It is also convenient for such measures to have a well-defined upper and lower limit, conventionally 1.0 as the upper limit and either 0 or -1.0 as the lower limit. Most measures take a value of 1.0 or -1.0 when the relationship is a perfect one and a value of zero when there is no relationship between the variables.

Given that chi-squared is dependent on sample size one obvious thing to do is to divide the value of chi-squared by n, the number in the sample; this means that we will get the same result when the proportions in the cells are the same, regardless of the numbers. The coefficient obtained by dividing chi-squared by n is known as ϕ^2 (phi-squared); its value is zero when there is no relationship between the two variables. With 2×2 (or $2 \times k$) tables ϕ^2 has an upper limit of 1.0 which is reached when the relationship between the two variables is perfect, as shown in table 7.3. In this case $\chi^2 = 100$ and $\phi^2 = 100/100 = 1.0$.

Table 7.3. An example of a perfect relationship or association in a 2×2 table.

	M	F	
LHS	50	0	~~50~~
RHS	0	50	50
	50	50	100

In a 2×2 table, whenever two diagonally opposite cells are empty the chi-squared value for the table will be equal to the number of observations and ϕ^2 will therefore be 1.0; this is sometimes referred to as *absolute* association. Referring to this substantive case we could say that variation in the side on which individuals are lying in the grave is completely accounted for by their sex, or associated with their sex.

As we noted above, ϕ^2 has the convenient upper limit of 1.0 only when the table has two rows and/or two columns. This will hold true, for example, in a table of 2 rows and 20 columns, or 2 columns and 20 rows, but not in a table of 3×20, or even 3×3. For tables where the number of rows and columns is greater than two, ϕ^2 will have a higher upper limit than 1.0. In order to scale it down to have this limit for larger tables, ϕ^2 itself must be standardised. The best known of these standardisations is Cramer's V^2:

$$V^2 = \frac{\phi^2}{\min(r-1, i-1)}$$

where $\min(r-1, c-1)$ refers to either (the number of rows -1) or (the number of columns -1), whichever is the smaller. This takes a maximum value of 1.0 even when numbers of rows and columns are not equal, and for tables larger than 2×2 or $2 \times k$; in these latter two cases V^2 obviously reduces to ϕ^2.

Yule's Q is another measure of association or relationship quite frequently used, although it is only applicable to the 2×2 table:

$$Q = \frac{ad - bc}{ad + bc}$$

where *a, b, c, d* refer to the cell frequencies of a table labelled as follows:

    a b
    c d

Imagine a 2×2 table in which we plot the presence/absence of something, for example a particular grave-good type in a grave, against the presence/absence of something else, say another grave-good type. We can label the table thus:

	+	−
+	++ (a)	+− (b)
−	−+ (c)	−− (d)

The top left cell indicates joint presence, the bottom right joint absence, and the other two the cases where one is present and the other absent. The a and d cells are the cases where our two attributes *covary* positively: when one is present so is the other, when one is absent the other one is too. Thus multiplying the number of instances of joint presence (a) and joint absence (d) gives us a measure of the *positive covariation* between our two attributes. On the other hand, multiplying the number of instances where one is present and the other absent (b), and where one is absent and the other present (c), gives us a measure of the *negative covariation* between our two attributes: the extent to which the presence of one implies the absence of the other. If, when one is present, the other is sometimes present and sometimes absent then there is no systematic relationship between the two. The definitive example of no relationship is when ad (the positive covariation) is equal to bc (the negative covariation), and thus $Q = 0$. On the other hand, Q will have a limit of + 1.0 for perfect positive covariation or association and − 1.0 for perfect negative association. Thus, while ϕ^2 can only be positive, Q can also take negative values. However, the major difference between these two measures lies in the way that they treat association, a point best illustrated by an example.

In both tables 7.4 and 7.5 the value of one of the cells is zero. It is a result of the formula for Q that it takes a value of 1.0 in both of them, and indeed in any 2 × 2 table with a zero entry. In this case we can see that it reflects the perfect association between the male category and just one of the two side-lying categories – the right-hand-side. By contrast, in the first table female burials are equally split between the two sides, while in the second they tend towards the left, the opposite pattern to the males. In neither case are

Table 7.4. Comparison between Q and ϕ^2, example 1. Here $Q = 1.0$ and $\phi^2 = 0.375$.

	M	F	
RHS	60	20	80
LHS	0	20	20
	60	40	100

Table 7.5. Comparison between Q and ϕ^2, example 2. Here $Q = 1.0$ and $\phi^2 = 0.643$.

	M	F	
RHS	60	10	70
LHS	0	30	30
	60	40	100

females exclusively associated with the left-hand-side, which would be required for ϕ^2 to take a value of 1.0, but of course ϕ^2 does increase from the first table to the second as the distribution of females becomes more asymmetrical.

Q is a good coefficient for picking out fairly weak associations but once it has reached its upper or lower limit it can obviously go no further. It has therefore been criticised because it cannot make the distinction between what is sometimes called 'complete' association, when one cell takes a zero value, and 'absolute' association, referred to above, when two diagonally opposite cells take zero values and ϕ^2 reaches its upper limit. Nevertheless, Q can be very useful so long as this point is borne in mind.

OTHER MEASURES OF ASSOCIATION

Phi-squared, Cramer's V and Yule's Q are by no means the only measures of association for variables measured at a nominal scale. A number of others are also available but are not described here in any detail. The aim is not to be comprehensive but to present a number of coefficients that are useful in themselves and, more importantly, to give an idea of what is involved in measuring association. Now that you have seen the general idea you can look up some of these others, if you wish, in such textbooks as Blalock (1972).

You will find that many computer statistical packages include

Goodman and Kruskal's tau and lambda. Both these statistics relate association between variables to reducing the number of errors we will make in guessing the value of one variable if we use the value of the other variable to help us in the guess. Thus, to take the data from table 7.5, we know that there are 100 graves, 70 with right-hand side burials and 30 with left-hand side burials. Suppose we have to guess for each grave whether it is left-hand side or right-hand side. If we made 70 right-hand guesses and 30 left-hand guesses many of them would be wrong. If, on the other hand, we know the sex of the individual buried, we can improve our guess-work considerably because the individual's sex and the side on which they lie in the grave are related to one another. Thus, if we know that a grave contains a male we must guess that the burial is right-hand side, because there are no left-hand side male burials. If we know that the grave contains a female our best guess is that it will be a left-hand side burial, although we won't always be right. The stronger the relationship between the two variables the more successful will we be in using the value of a case on one to predict its value on the other. If there is no relationship between them, using one to predict the other won't be any help.

Goodman and Kruskal's tau and lambda use this general idea in slightly different ways, but both of them are asymmetrical. This is worth thinking about! To refer to our example in table 7.5 again: if we know that a grave contains a male we can predict with 100% success that the individual will be on his right-hand side; however, if we know that an individual is on its right-hand side we cannot predict with 100% success that it will be a male, because 10 of the 70 are female.

ASSOCIATION AND CAUSAL INFERENCES

Often, when we are looking at association in the way indicated above, we are thinking, as we have already implied, in terms of an *independent* and a *dependent* variable. Thus, in the case of the individual's sex and the side on which they are lying in the grave, it is possible to visualise the side on which the individual was deposited in the grave as *dependent* on their sex, but not their sex being dependent on the side on which they are lying. This is satisfactory as far as it goes. However, although we have talked in a statistical sense about one variable accounting for another or being associated with another, we cannot necessarily infer a causal relationship between the two. All statistics books warn of the danger of inferring causation from association, because of the possibility of spurious correlation.

Of course, causal relationships can never be disentangled by mere statistical analysis, but in the process of disentangling them statistical methods can be either extremely useful or positively misleading. If we simply take the first statistic we obtain at its face value we can easily be misled. It is important to be sure that any connection we infer between objects, events or processes is real and true, and it is generally suggested that the acid test of a real relationship is that it should not change regardless of the conditions under which it is observed; in other words, does the relationship between two variables persist or disappear when we introduce a third?

The process of investigating relationships between variables under a variety of different conditions is a very general and important one if valid inferences about those relationships are going to be made. We will see it recurring again and again. It is proposed to introduce the idea here, illustrating it by means of Yule's Q. We have seen how Q works in the simple 2×2 table case. The question now arises of what happens when we introduce a third variable, so that we have a $2 \times 2 \times 2$ table. The various possibilities are best illustrated by means of examples.

Table 7.6. Volume of grave cist tabulated against the sex of the individual buried.

	Volume of grave cist	
	$\leqslant 1.5\,m^3$	$>1.5\,m^3$
M	22	47
F	33	26

The Q coefficient simply between two variables, as in table 7.6, where

$$Q = \frac{572 - 1551}{572 + 1551} = -0.461$$

is referred to as a *zero-order* coefficient; it is not taking into account the effects of any other variables. In terms of some of the standard arguments about burial practice and social status we might conclude that we have evidence here for a lower status for women, less energy being put into digging their grave pits. What happens though if we take into account the height of the individuals in the graves, using estimates derived from long bone measurements? If we want to introduce an extra variable like this we have to split our original table into two (table 7.7).

Table 7.7. Volume of grave cist tabulated against
the sex of the individual buried and against the
individual's estimated height.

| | | Volume of grave cist | |
		$\leqslant 1.5\,m^3$	$> 1.5\,m^3$
Est. height	M	18	4
$\leqslant 155$ cm	F	30	6
Est. height	M	4	43
> 155 cm	F	3	20

How do we analyse this new table? What is of interest is what
happens when we 'control for' the third variable. This is an important concept which will recur frequently in what follows (see especially chapter 11), but what does it mean? The idea is that we look at
the relationship between our original two variables while taking
into account, or holding constant, the effect of the new one. We do
this by looking, in this instance, at the sex/grave-volume relationship for one height category, then for the other height category, and
finally amalgamating the two. This is in contrast to the original
zero-order coefficient, where we did not make any distinction in
terms of the individuals' heights. The new coefficient is not a zero-
order coefficient but a *partial* coefficient; it is a *first-order* partial
because we are only 'controlling for' a single variable, height in this
case.

To understand the effect of the third variable on a relationship we
compare the values of the zero-order and partial coefficients, because this gives the answer to the question, what happens to the
relationship when this variable is controlled. There may be no
change, it may get stronger, or it may become weaker. The first
thing we need to do then is calculate the partial for the table in the
example. Let us suppose a general table (table 7.8), where the
zero-order coefficient between x and y is given simply by amalgamating the two tables.

$$Q_{xy} = \frac{[(a+e)(d+h)] - [(b+f)(c+g)]}{[(a+e)(d+h)] + [(b+f)(c+g)]}$$

The partial, controlling for t, is given by

$$Q_{xytiedt} = \frac{(ad + eh) - (bc + fg)}{(ad + eh) + (bc + fg)}$$

Table 7.8. A general $2 \times 2 \times 2$ contingency table.

		y	not y
t	x	a	b
	not x	c	d
not t	x	e	f
	not x	g	h

If we do this calculation for the table of numbers in the grave pit-size example we have

$$Q_{xy\text{tied}t} = \frac{188 - 249}{188 + 249} = -0.139$$

It was indicated above that one of three options is possible when we compare the partial and the zero-order coefficient. 'No change' is when the partial is equal to the zero-order coefficient. It means that there is no difference in the relationship between x and y whether or not the third variable is controlled; in other words, the third variable has no effect on the original two-variable relationship. In the example, however, we see that the partial is smaller than the zero-order, that is to say, the relationship between x and y becomes weaker when the third variable is controlled. The conclusion to be drawn in this case is that *it is variation in the third variable which explains the existence of the* xy *relationship*. Thus, with reference to the example, the relation between sex and grave pit volume largely disappears when the height of the individuals is controlled. The zero-order relationship between sex and grave volume may be said to be spurious: it results from the fact that there is a relationship between the height of individuals and the volume of their grave pit, and that women tend to be smaller than men.

Let us now take another example, again based on analysing burials. Table 7.9, where $Q = -0.34$, indicates that women tend to

Table 7.9. Presence/absence of rings tabulated against the sex of the individuals buried with them for a hypothetical north German iron age cemetery.

	Rings in grave	
	Present	Absent
M	42	66
F	53	41

have rings more often than men. But let us also suppose that we have information which enables us to divide our cemetery into two phases: table 7.10, where $Q_{xytied_t} = -0.524$. In other words, we have a case here where the partial is greater than the zero-order. The strength of association between x and y is being suppressed when the third variable is not taken into account; when it is controlled the association is improved.

Table 7.10. Presence/absence of rings tabulated against the sex of the individuals buried with them, subdivided by phase.

| | | Rings in grave | |
		Present	Absent
Early	M	31	27
	F	25	5
Late	M	11	39
	F	28	36

We can actually gain some more insight by calculating Q for each of the two sub-tables separately. These two coefficients are known as *conditional coefficients*. One is the zero-order coefficient for those individuals characterised by one state of the third variable, the other is the zero-order for individuals characterised by the other state of the third variable.

$$Q_{xyt} = \frac{ad - bc}{ad + bc}$$

$$Q_{xynot_t} = \frac{eh - fg}{eh + fg}$$

In the case of our example the conditional for the early phase is

$Q = -0.62$

For the later phase it is

$Q = -0.47$

The partial is actually the average of these two conditionals, taking into account the different size samples on which each is based.

If we look at the sub-divided table for the example, we see that in the early phase the majority of women have rings whereas men are roughly equally divided into those with rings and those without. In the later phase women are more or less equally divided while less men have rings than do not. Thus, taking time into account makes a big difference to interpretation. The two conditionals, and consequently the partial, take the values they do because in the early phase there are very few females without rings, while in the late phase there are very few males with them. Both these situations have the same effect on the Q coefficient, of course, because the values of diagonally opposite cells are multiplied together.

Table 7.11. Presence/absence of beads tabulated against the rank of the individuals buried with them.

| | | Beads in grave | |
		Present	Absent
Rank	High	53	39
	Low	44	55

One further important possibility remains to be illustrated and considered. Staying with the cemetery analysis theme, let us suppose that on some reasonable criterion we have divided the burials into a 'high rank' and a 'low rank' group. The criterion did not involve consideration of presence or absence of beads in the grave and we now wish to see if this is related to rank. From table 7.11, where $Q = 0.25$, there appears to be a suggestion that presence of beads is slightly associated with high rank. Let us now try controlling for sex: table 7.12, where $Q_{xy\text{tied}t} = 0.35$.

Table 7.12. Presence/absence of beads tabulated against the rank of the individuals buried with them, subdivided by sex.

| | | Beads in grave | |
		Present	Absent
Male	High	9	33
	Low	15	28
Female	High	42	6
	Low	29	27

Comparison of the partial and zero-order Q coefficients suggests at first that we are dealing with a case of slight suppression; when we control for sex the strength of the relationship between beads and rank increases. But let us now calculate the conditionals for each of the categories of the control variable, sex.

$$Q_{xy\text{males}} = -0.32$$
$$Q_{xy\text{females}} = 0.73$$

Clearly they differ enormously, so that the partial coefficient of 0.35 obtained by averaging the two conditionals is completely misleading. There is obviously a very different relationship between rank and the presence of beads among males from that which exists for the females; few high-ranking males have beads, while most high-ranking females do have them. This outcome is called *specification* or *interaction*; the effect of the third variable is to specify which of two different relationships holds between the x and y variables. Further progress can only be made by dividing our sample into two groups on the basis of the specifying variable (here sex) and continuing the search for causal connections within each group separately.

So far, we have developed the techniques to examine relationships and we have looked at the effect which a third variable, t, may have on the relationship between x and y; thus, we can check, for instance, within the bounds of this three-variable system, whether or not a relationship is spurious.

We may also wish to observe the effect of y on the xt relationship and x on the yt relationship, to complete our investigation into the connections between all three variables. This amounts to being able to define the true causal connections within the three-variable system as opposed to the simple pairwise association. A moment's thought will show you that this is a complicated matter. For a start you have twelve different Q coefficients to cope with, and if you take into account the fact that relations may be positive or negative, dependence may be one way, the other way, or mutual, then you have an enormous number of different relationships.

It is clearly most sensible to investigate them by using your *a priori* knowledge to predict certain relationships – to hypothesise a set of causal assertions – and proceed to test them. If we are wrong, we reconsider the assertions and test a new model. Obviously, to do this we need to be able to predict the behaviour of the coefficients of association under our *a priori* assumptions. If the coefficients do behave as we expect them then we may provisionally consider the assertions as valid ones. To summarise the appropriate procedure:

1. Try to start with a well-thought-out hypothesis; simply applying Q (or any other coefficient) to see what happens is often a substitute for actually thinking about cause and effect relations.

Start by defining the variable most in need of explanation and select its most likely explanation; you can develop and expand the variables considered as you go on.

2. It is most important to control for other variables even if the association between the initial two variables in the analysis is a strong one: it may be spurious. On the other hand, a relationship that initially appears weak may be masked by something else, so again introducing control variables is essential.

3. When interaction, or specification, occurs, appropriate action must be taken. In general this means carrying out separate analyses of the relationship between the first two variables for each of the two categories of the third variable, and ensuring that it is clearly stated to which category any conclusions refer, since they will be different for each one.

A MODERN APPROACH TO INVESTIGATING RELATIONSHIPS BETWEEN NOMINAL SCALE VARIABLES: AN ELEMENTARY INTRODUCTION TO LOG-LINEAR MODELS

In fact, analyses of the relations between nominal scale variables are rarely approached today by means of the Q coefficient, or any of the other association coefficients we have seen, but by means of *log-linear modelling* and the closely related method of *logit regression* (and potentially also by means of the technique known as correspondence analysis, discussed below in chapter 13). The application of such models is a relatively recent development, dependent, like so many others in statistics, on the availability of computer power. Because of their usefulness and gradually increasing use in archaeology (see e.g. Clark 1976, Spaulding 1977, MacIntosh and MacIntosh 1980) it is important to be aware of what they do and how they work. Lewis (1986) provides a more extended account than is given here.

Conceptually what they involve is quite straightforward, although the notation can be a bit off-putting and the calculations are so tedious that in practice they require the use of an appropriate computer program.

The problems they solve are those that we have already seen in the previous section: how do we investigate the relations between more than two variables in a coherent fashion, within a single framework, so that we can assess which relations are the important ones, taking into account all the various possibilities and avoiding the kinds of situation illustrated earlier in this chapter, where the introduction of a third variable had varying but often disturbing effects on relations between the other two.

The modern approach takes us back to chi-squared. So far we have only seen this used to test a null hypothesis of no association between two variables, by looking at the discrepancy between the observed data values and those expected under the null hypothesis. In log-linear modelling we're not restricted to a null hypothesis. The essence of the technique is to build models of the possible relations between variables in the data set, to derive expected values for these different models, and to decide which model best fits the data by comparing the expected values produced by the models with the observed data values, with the stipulation that the model selected should be the simplest which shows a reasonable fit between observed and expected.

The log-linear bit comes in to the building of the models; the following discussion of what this involves is influenced by Lewis (1986). The simplest possible model is the one we've already seen: the null hypothesis of independence. When we have two variables we saw that in order to find the expected value for a given cell of the table we multiplied the row sum for the cell by the column sum and divided by the total number of observations.

$$\text{expected value} = \frac{(\text{row sum})(\text{column sum})}{\text{total number of observations}}$$

We obtained the expected value by a process of multiplication and division. If, however, we wanted the log of the expected value we could change this as follows:

$$\log(\text{expected value}) = \log(\text{row sum}) + \log(\text{column sum}) - \log(\text{total number of observations})$$

Because with logarithms addition corresponds to normal multiplication and subtraction to normal division, we now add and subtract instead of multiplying and dividing. As our expression for the expected value now only involves addition and subtraction it is said to be *additive,* or *linear,* in the logarithms of the original values.

Why on earth should we want to do this? As we will see when we come on to regression analysis, linear models are usually much easier to handle, and using them we can take our analysis of the relations between variables a lot further than simply testing for independence. Remember that the aim of log-linear modelling is to build models that fit the data, subject to the stipulation of parsimony noted above.

Suppose that having worked out the log of the expected value in the way illustrated it is considerably different from the log of the observed value. What this means is that modelling (or describing) the expected value in terms of the row sum, the column sum and the total number of observations is insufficient. Something is missing. If we now postulate that our two variables are related and *add* an extra term to our equation to take account of this relationship then, if we're only dealing with two variables, we will find that our new model fits perfectly. If we're dealing with *more than* two variables we can successively add extra terms to the equation, trying to improve the fit between expected and observed. Our choice between the various possible models will be determined by the goodness of the fit and the criterion of simplicity.

Table 7.13. The data of table 7.7; $n = 128$.

		Volume of grave cist $\leqslant 1.5\,\mathrm{m}^3$	$>1.5\,\mathrm{m}^3$
Est. height	M	18	4
$\leqslant 155$ cm	F	30	6
Est. height	M	4	43
>155 cm	F	3	20

As usual, what is involved is best illustrated by means of an example. Let us consider again one of the examples used to illustrate the use of the Q coefficient with three variables, from the previous section of this chapter: the example (table 7.7) in which we are trying to understand the relationship between the volume of the grave pits and the height and sex of the individuals buried in them, in an analysis of a hypothetical cemetery of single inhumation burials. The simplest model to test for this table is that the three variables are unrelated to one another; the most basic null hypothesis in other words, but now for three variables rather than two. We can write this model out as follows, for the top left cell in table 7.13, using the approach described above:

log(expected number of small males in small grave pits) =
    log(total number of males) +
    log(total number of small grave pits) +
    log(total number of small individuals) −
    log(total number of observations)

What it says is that the total number of small males in small grave

Table 7.14. Expected values added to
the data in table 7.13.

| | | Volume of grave cist | |
		$\leqslant 1.5\,\mathrm{m}^3$	$>1.5\,\mathrm{m}^3$
Est. height	M	18 (13.4)	4 (17.8)
$\leqslant 155\,\mathrm{cm}$	F	30 (11.5)	6 (15.3)
Est. height	M	4 (16.2)	43 (21.5)
$>155\,\mathrm{cm}$	F	3 (13.9)	20 (18.4)

pits is simply a function of the total numbers of males, small grave
pits and small individuals, taking into account the total number of
observations.

If this is a good model then the expected number of small males
in small grave pits which it produces will be very close to the actual
number. If it's not, then of course there will be a discrepancy. We
can model the expected numbers of all the cells of the table in this
way, and of course if there are a lot of discrepancies between
observed and expected values we will end up with a significant
chi-squared value. The expected and observed values for the example are shown in table 7.14 and the test for the difference between them can now be carried out. In fact, for reasons which will
become apparent below, the chi-squared statistic itself is not used,
but a statistic which is equivalent to it, known as G^2.

$$G^2 = 2 \sum \left[(\text{observed}) \log_e \left(\frac{\text{observed}}{\text{expected}} \right) \right]$$

where summation is over all the cells in the table. For the example
considered here we have

$$
\begin{aligned}
G^2 = &[18\log_e(18/13.4)] + [4\log_e(4/17.8)] + [30\log_e(30/11.5)] \\
&+ [6\log_e(6/15.3)] + [4\log_e(4/16.2)] + [43\log_e(43/21.5)] \\
&+ [3\log_e(3/13.9)] + [20\log_e(20/18.4)] \\
= &\ 87.54
\end{aligned}
$$

The statistical significance of the G^2 value may be obtained from
the chi-squared table, but of course this requires us to know the
correct number of degrees of freedom for our example: degrees of
freedom = (number of cells) − (number of quantities estimated
from the data). There are eight cells and we have had to obtain four
quantities from the data (number of males, number of small grave
pits, number of small individuals and the total number of observa-

tions), so here the number of degrees of freedom is four. With four degrees of freedom the G^2 value is very highly significant. The null hypothesis that the three variables are independent of one another must be rejected.

The traditional use of chi-squared would leave the matter here, very much as we saw in chapter 6. What we want to do, however, is improve our model. Since independence doesn't hold there must be relationships between sex, grave-pit size and individual height of which we haven't taken account, and which we need to include in our model. The possibilities here are quite considerable. First any single pair of these variables may be related:

    sex and grave-pit size
    sex and individual height
    individual height and grave-pit size

At a more complex level any two pairs may be related:

    sex and grave-pit size, and at the same time sex and height
    grave-pit size and sex, and grave-pit size and height
    height and sex, and at the same time height and grave-pit size

More complex again: all three pairs may be related:

    sex and grave-pit size, and sex and height, and grave-pit size
    and height

Finally, all three variables be simultaneously related to one another: thus sex may be related to grave-pit size not just directly, or pairwise, but indirectly via height as well, and this may be true of all three variables.

It is possible to see that as you work through the levels of complexity, each one includes the one below: so that if two pairs of variables are related this obviously implies that one pair was related at the previous step; similarly for three pairs to be related two pairs must be at the level before.

The idea is to start at the simplest level and work up the hierarchy of complexity, stopping with the simplest model that fits the data. At each successive level of complexity a degree of freedom is lost, since the data are being used to estimate the association between each pair of variables. Thus, on our model of independence or no association that we started with there were four degrees of freedom. By the time we get to the highest level of complexity, where all three variables are simultaneously related to one another, there are no degrees of freedom left at all. The expected numbers would correspond to the observed numbers and we would simply be reproducing the data we started with, so this final model, which is said in the jargon to be *saturated,* does not have much interest!

The discussion above is summarised in table 7.15 (based on Fienberg 1980), which lists the various models, the number of degrees of freedom associated with them and their descriptions in terms of mathematical symbols, using Fienberg's notation. You should note that for models 2 and 3 only one of the three possible options is listed.

Table 7.15. Possible log-linear models for the relationships between three variables.

Model	d.f.	Abbreviation	Symbolic description
1. No association	4	[1][2][3]	$\log E_{ijk} = u + u_1 + u_2 + u_3$
2. Association of 1 pair of variables	3	[12][3]	$\log E_{ijk} = u + u_1 + u_2 + u_3 + u_{12}$
3. Association of 2 pairs of variables	2	[12][23]	$\log E_{ijk} = u + u_1 + u_2 + u_3 + u_{12} + u_{23}$
4. Association of 3 pairs of variables	1	[12][23][13]	$\log E_{ijk} = u + u_1 + u_2 + u_3 + u_{12} + u_{23} + u_{13}$
5. Interaction between all 3	0	[123]	$\log E_{ijk} = u + u_1 + u_2 + u_3 + u_{12} + u_{23} + u_{13} + u_{123}$

To illustrate how the equations are to be read let us take that for model 3 in relation to our example, assuming that as above when we were testing for independence, we want the expected value for the number of small males in small grave pits, but now postulating that there is a relationship between sex and grave-pit size, and between grave-pit size and height.

log(expected number of small males in small grave pits) $[\log E_{ijk}]$
  = log(total number of observations) [u] +
    log(total number of males) $[u_1]$ +
    log(total number of small grave pits) $[u_2]$ +
    log(total number of small individuals) $[u_3]$ +
    log(interaction between sex and grave-pit size) $[u_{12}]$ +
    log(interaction between grave-pit size and height) $[u_{23}]$

Having already rejected the model of no association for our example we can now set up and test the various possible level 2 models, postulating an association between any one of the pairs:
  2a) sex and grave-pit size
  2b) individual height and grave-pit size
  2c) sex and individual height
Tables 7.16–7.18 show the observed values for the data, together

Table 7.16. Expected values for model 2a added to the data in table 7.13.

		Volume of grave cist	
		$\leqslant 1.5\,\text{m}^3$	$> 1.5\,\text{m}^3$
Est. height	M	18 (10.0)	4 (21.3)
$\leqslant 155\,\text{cm}$	F	30 (15.0)	6 (11.8)
Est. height	M	4 (12.0)	43 (25.7)
$> 155\,\text{cm}$	F	3 (18.0)	20 (14.2)

Table 7.17. Expected values for model 2b added to the data in table 7.13.

		Volume of grave cist	
		$\leqslant 1.5\,\text{m}^3$	$> 1.5\,\text{m}^3$
M	$\leqslant 155\,\text{cm}$	18 (25.9)	4 (5.4)
	> 155	4 (3.8)	43 (34.0)
F	$\leqslant 155$	30 (22.1)	6 (4.6)
	> 155	3 (3.2)	20 (29.0)

Table 7.18. Expected values for model 2c added to the data in table 7.13.

		Sex	
		M	F
$\leqslant 1.5\,\text{m}^3$	$\leqslant 155\,\text{cm}$	18 (9.5)	30 (15.5)
	> 155	4 (20.2)	3 (9.9)
$> 1.5\,\text{m}^3$	$\leqslant 155$	4 (12.6)	6 (20.5)
	> 155	43 (26.8)	20 (13.1)

Table 7.19. Summary of fit of log-linear models of relationships between sex, height and grave-pit volume.

Model	Abbreviation	G^2	d.f.
1. No association	[1][2][3]	87.54	4
2. Association of 1 pair of variables:			
a)	[12][3]	79.70	3
b)	[1][23]	11.38	3
c)	[13][2]	76.17	3

with the expected values under each of these models. The G^2 (chi-squared equivalent) values for these different models, and for the initial test of independence, are shown in table 7.19, where variable 1 = sex, 2 = volume and 3 = height.

All these G^2 values are significant at least at the .01 level, which means that it is highly improbable that any of these models fit the data values: the differences between the observed values and the values expected under the model are too great. Nevertheless it is clear that model 2b, presupposing a relationship between height and volume, produces a marked drop in the G^2 value and provides the best fit of any of the models tried so far.

Let us move up to the next level, and models which presuppose relationships between two pairs of variables.

    3a) sex and height are related and so are height and grave-pit size; sex and grave-pit site are not related

    3b) sex and height are related and so are sex and grave-pit volume; height and grave-pit size are not related

    3c) sex and grave-pit volume are related, height and grave-pit size are related, but sex and height are not related

Table 7.20. Expected values for model 3a added to the data in table 7.13.

| | | Volume of grave cist | |
		$\leqslant 1.5\,m^3$	$> 1.5\,m^3$
Est. height	M	18 (18.2)	4 (3.8)
$\leqslant 155\,cm$	F	30 (29.8)	6 (6.2)
Est. height	M	4 (4.7)	43 (42.3)
$> 155\,cm$	F	3 (2.3)	20 (20.7)

Table 7.21. Expected values for model 3b added to the data in table 7.13.

| | | Volume of grave cist | |
		$\leqslant 1.5\,m^3$	$> 1.5\,m^3$
M	$\leqslant 155\,cm$	18 (7.0)	4 (15.0)
	> 155	4 (15.0)	43 (32.0)
F	$\leqslant 155$	30 (20.1)	6 (15.9)
	> 155	3 (12.9)	20 (10.1)

Table 7.22. Expected values for model 3c added to the data in table 7.13.

		Sex	
		M	F
≤1.5 m³	≤155 cm	18 (19.2)	30 (28.8)
	>155	4 (2.8)	3 (4.2)
>1.5 m³	≤155	4 (6.5)	6 (3.5)
	>155	43 (40.5)	20 (22.5)

Table 7.23. Summary of fit of log-linear models of relationship between sex, height and grave-pit volume.

Model	Abbreviation	G^2	d.f.
1. No association	[1][2][3]	87.54*	4
2. Association of 1 pair of variables:			
a)	[12][3]	79.70*	3
b)	[1][23]	11.38*	3
c)	[13][2]	76.17*	3
3. Association of 2 pairs of variables:			
a)	[13][23]	0.36	2
b)	[12][13]	69.17*	2
c)	[12][23]	3.98	2

Tables 7.20–7.22 show the observed values for the data again, but now with the expected values for each of the three level 3 models. A look at these indicates immediately that the fit of model 3a is excellent, that of 3b is very poor while that of 3c is also very good. The G^2 goodness-of-fit values for these three models and all the others we have looked at are presented together in table 7.23, with all those marked which are statistically significant at the .05 level.

It is when we come to comparing the results in a table such as this that the use of G^2 rather than chi-squared becomes important. If we take, for example, the G^2 value for a level 2 model, say model 2b, and subtract it from the G^2 value for the level 1 model of independence, the difference between them is a measure of the improvement in goodness of fit. In this case $87.54 - 11.38 = 76.16$. Such comparisons can be carried out between models at any two different levels. We could, for example, obtain the difference between the level 1 G^2 and that for model 3a: $87.54 - 0.36 = 87.18$, the improvement obtained by predicting the cell values not on the assumption of independence but on the assumption of a relationship between variables 1 and 3 (sex and height) and 2 and 3 (height and grave volume).

Furthermore, the differences may be tested for statistical significance, using the number of degrees of freedom obtained by subtracting the number of degrees of freedom for the higher level model from the number for the lower level. Thus, for our second example above, the number of degrees of freedom for the level 1 model of no association is 4, the number for model 3a is 2, so we have a G^2 difference of 87.18 with 2 degrees of freedom, which we can look up in the chi-squared table to establish its statistical significance. If the more complex model produces a statistically significant decrease in G^2 then we can adopt it.

When we look at the results for the level 3 models we see that two of the three G^2 values represent a considerable improvement over those for level 2. The one which does not, model 3b, has a worse fit than model 2b, and this occasions no surprise because it leaves out the relationship between variables 2 and 3, pit size and individual height, which model 2b established as very important.

Clearly the best fitting model is model 3a, with a G^2 value of almost zero, indicating a virtually perfect fit between the expectations of this model and the data values. Is it significantly better than 2b? Let us compare the G^2 values: $11.38 - 0.36 = 11.02$ with one degree of freedom, which is highly significant. The appropriate model following the formulation of table 7.15 is:

$$u + u_1 + u_2 + u_3 + u_{23} + u_{13}$$

Again, if we want to relate this to the predicted value for a particular cell, and take as usual the cell representing small males in small grave pits, we have

> log(expected number of small males in small grave pits) =
>> log(total number of observations) +
>> log(total number of males) +
>> log(total number of small grave pits) +
>> log(total number of small individuals) +
>> log(interaction between grave-pit size and height) +
>> log(interaction between sex and height)

In other words, the grave-pit size is related to the individual's height and the individual's height is related to their sex, but sex and grave-pit size are not directly related. These relationships, which make intuitive sense, account for what is going on in the data, and there is no need to move to a higher level of complexity.

As you will have gathered, the only really complex part of log-linear modelling, the 'black box' in the account presented here, is the calculation of the expected values. That doesn't matter, however, because the calculations are not done by hand, but by computer. A number of statistical computer packages include log-linear modelling methods (see appendix 2).

The account presented here may be supplemented by reference to Fienberg (1980) and Lewis (1986), which is specifically archaeological in content. It also includes a description of the more restricted case in which we can postulate that one of our variables is a dependent whose variation we are trying to understand in terms of the effects of a number of independents: the logit model. In fact log-linear modelling, and particularly the logit model, together with regression analysis (chapters 9–11) and analysis of variance (not covered here; see, e.g., Blalock 1972) are all specific instances of what is known as the *generalised linear model* (Baker and Nelder 1978, Everitt and Dunn 1983), in which data values are accounted for in terms of the *additive* effects of a number of variables.

EXERCISES

7.1. Rim type and neck form were recorded for a group of sherds from a Mesopotamian settlement site, and the results are given below for both decorated and undecorated sherds.

No. of sherds	Rim type	Neck form	Dec/ undec
16	1	1	dec
9	1	2	dec
14	1	1	undec
32	1	2	undec
7	2	1	dec
14	2	2	dec
30	2	1	undec
18	2	2	undec

a) How strong and of what form is the overall relationship between neck form and rim type? Is this relationship significant? b) In what way does the introduction of the third variable, decoration, affect the relationship between rim type and neck form, both overall and conditionally?

7.2. An analysis is being carried out of the association between two
different motifs occurring on a particular set of ceramic vessels from
a central European iron age cemetery, based on the following data:

		Motif 1	
		Present	Absent
Motif 2	Present	29	17
	Absent	23	32

Do your conclusions about the relationship between the two motifs
change when independent evidence of the chronology of the graves
is used to divide the vessels into two phases?

		Motif 1	
		Present	Absent
Early phase			
Motif 2	Present	15	7
	Absent	9	11
Late phase			
Motif 2	Present	14	10
	Absent	14	21

Eight

Numeric Variables:
The Normal Distribution

The chapters immediately preceding this one have been concerned with nominal scale variables and in particular with ways in which relationships between them may be analysed. The chapters following will deal with such relationships between numeric variables measured at an interval scale or above; but before the necessary methods can be described it is necessary to go back to the topics, treated in chapters 3 and 4, concerned with describing the distributions of single variables, and to consider one distribution in particular, the normal or Gaussian distribution, already briefly mentioned in chapter 4.

Even if you have no idea what a normal distribution is, the odds are that you believe it to be important. In this you would be largely correct, both because a large number of observed distributions are found to be approximately normal, and also because of the theoretical significance of this distribution, in inductive statistics and as the basis for many statistical methods.

For these reasons many statistics textbooks give a central role to the theory of the normal distribution and its use as a basis for statistical inference, including significance testing. In this text it is played down, particularly its statistical inference role. There are a number of reasons for this. The tests based on it are conceptually difficult and they are not of central importance. As we have seen already, a great deal can be done without ever making use of the normal distribution, and even within the discipline of statistics generally its use is arguably becoming less important. When statistics was developing, normal theory provided a theoretical sheet-anchor for the development of statistical methods. With the increased availability and capacity of computers it has now become possible to simulate statistical distributions directly using numerical techniques. Furthermore, advocates of the exploratory data analysis approach make the point that normal theory based methods are often very sensitive to irregularities in the data; this point will be considered again in the next chapter.

Nevertheless, the normal distribution cannot be completely ignored, and the reason for turning our attention to it here is that, for
variables measured at an interval scale or above, the majority of
the currently used methods for investigating relationships between
them are actually based upon it. Furthermore, as we will see later
in this chapter, action can often be taken to make data distributions
correspond reasonably closely to normality even if they are not
normal to start with.

In what follows the intention is to look at the normal distribution
purely from a descriptive point of view, and in particular to consider
how the standard deviation (see chapter 4 for a description of the
standard deviation) relates to it.

THE NORMAL DISTRIBUTION

In considering the use of bar charts to display the frequency distributions of continuous numeric variables in chapter 3 it was noted
that the width of the intervals is important. In particular, if the
intervals of the distribution become narrower and narrower for a
given sample size, the distribution eventually starts to look very
irregular, with gaps and holes in it. If we increased the number of
cases, however, and kept increasing it as we made our intervals
narrower, then the distribution would become increasingly fine in
its divisions but still retain the same shape. Thus, in figure 8.1, it
would be possible to go from (a) to (b).

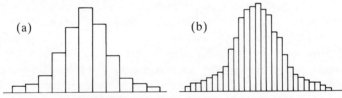

Figure 8.1. (a) Histogram with wide intervals; (b) histogram with very narrow intervals, based on a very large
number of observations.

Assuming that the distribution has the shape shown in figure 8.1,
if we imagine the intervals becoming infinitely narrow and the
number of observations correspondingly large, we end up with a
smooth bell-shaped curve (figure 8.2).

Just as the area within a bar chart can be calculated by summing
the areas of the individual rectangles, so the area under the smooth
curve can be calculated by summing the infinitely large number of

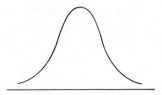

Figure 8.2. A normal distribution.

rectangles under the smooth curve; this is the calculus operation of integration.

The normal curve is a symmetrical smooth bell-shaped curve defined by a particular equation; one feature of it is that the two tails extend infinitely in either direction without reaching the horizontal axis. At the level of this text the equation is not of any interest. What is important is that regardless of what particular mean and standard deviation a given normal curve may have, there will be a constant proportion of the area under the curve, or a constant proportion of the cases in a frequency distribution of this form, between the mean and a given distance from the mean, expressed in standard deviation units (figure 8.3).

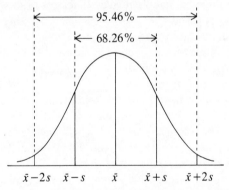

Figure 8.3. The percentage of the area under a normal curve within one and two standard deviations of the mean.

It is worth giving several examples of this to make it clear. Thus, the area under the curve between the mean and a point one standard deviation either greater or smaller than the mean will be 34.13% of the total area under the curve. Between one standard deviation less than the mean and one standard deviation more than the mean there will be twice 34.13%, or 68.26% of the area under the curve. The corresponding figures for two standard deviations are 47.43 % and 95.46 %, and for three standard deviations 49.86 % and 99.73 %.

Although these figures are based on the theoretically defined normal curve, many empirically obtained frequency distributions of data are sufficiently close to it for these rules about the proportion of the distribution within particular standard deviation distances from the mean to be applicable. For this reason these constant proportionalities can be put to use.

The fact that many real frequency distributions are quite close to normality, so that these theoretical results can be used, is not accidental. If the value of some variable is the result of the cumulative effect of a large number of other variables which are independent of one another, then it can be proved mathematically that the distribution of the values of that variable will be approximately normal. An example of such a variable in the field of biology, where the normal distribution saw early application, is body height. This is mainly determined by a large number of genetic factors, but also by such factors as nutrition and environment. These different factors will tend to act in different directions. The result is that the distribution of heights in a population will be a normal one, as indeed it is. There are many archaeological instances of ratio scale variables, particularly physical measurements such as lengths, breadths, weights, volumes and so on, which are likewise affected by a large number of different factors acting in different directions, with the result that the distribution of the variable values is a normal one, or at least not far from it.

It is now necessary to show how these constant proportionalities characteristic of the normal distribution may be used and interpreted in a specific archaeological case. This will inevitably be somewhat artificial since they are generally used as a means to an end rather than being an end in themselves, which is how we will have to treat them here. Let us suppose then that we are dealing with a large set of projectile points from the south-western United States. Their lengths are normally distributed, with a mean of 110 mm and a standard deviation of 20 mm (see figure 8.4). Initially we want to find out the proportion of their lengths which lie between 110 and 140 mm.

It is first necessary to work out how many standard deviations 140 is from 110; in millimetres it is 30 and the standard deviation is 20. If we divide the difference between the mean and the value in which we are interested by the standard deviation we obtain the figure we want: 30/20 = 1.5. The value 140 is 1.5 standard deviations away

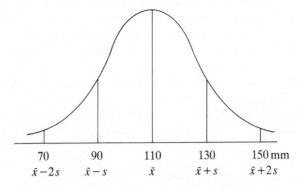

70	90	110	130	150 mm
$\bar{x}-2s$	$\bar{x}-s$	$\bar{x}$	$\bar{x}+s$	$\bar{x}+2s$

Figure 8.4. The distribution of lengths of a large number of projectile points from the south-western United States.

from the mean. When a quantity is presented in the form of a number of standard deviation units away from the mean of its distribution it is said to be in the form of a *Z* score (or standard score), where *Z* represents the deviation from the mean in standard deviation units. The general expression is

$$Z = \frac{x - \bar{x}}{s}$$

where $\bar{x}$ is the mean, *s* is the value of the standard deviation, and *x* is the value of the boundary of the interval in which we are interested.

How do we get from a value for *Z* to a value for the proportion of cases within the interval in which we are interested? The answer is that tables have been constructed to do this for what is known as the standard form of the normal curve, expressed in terms of *Z* scores (see appendix 1, table B). The table assumes that the area under the normal curve sums to 1.0, with 0.5 to the left of the mean and 0.5 to the right. The values of *Z* are given down the margins of the table and along the top. The first two digits of *Z* are obtained by reading down and the third by reading across. The left-hand page of the table is for negative *Z* values, i.e. values less than the mean, and the right-hand page for positive *Z* values, values greater than the mean. In this case we are interested in a *Z* value of +1.50, so we look down the left-hand column of the right-hand page for *Z* = 1.5, and across to the first column right, corresponding to *Z* = 1.50. Figures within the body of the table indicate the proportion of the total area under the curve which lies between the *Z* value and the extreme right-hand end of the curve. In this case we see that the value is 0.06681, or 6.7%. But we want to find the area not between $Z = 1.5$ and the right-hand end of the curve, but between the mean and $Z = 1.5$. We know that the proportion between the mean and the right-hand end is 0.5, so the proportion between the mean and $Z = 1.5$ must be $0.5 - 0.06681 = 0.43319$. Rounding the last two figures we have 0.433 or 43.3% of the curve lying between the mean and a line at $Z = 1.5$. Translating back into our example, we can say that 43.3% of the projectile-point lengths will be between 110 and 140 mm (see figure 8.5).

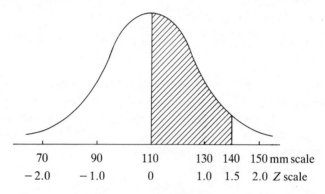

| 70 | 90 | 110 | 130 | 140 | 150 mm scale |
| -2.0 | -1.0 | 0 | 1.0 | 1.5 | 2.0 Z scale |

Figure 8.5. Distribution of projectile-point lengths with Z-scores corresponding to actual standard deviation values.

If we had been asked to find the proportion of lengths between 110 and 80 mm, or 1.5 standard deviations less than the mean, we would find the value in the table corresponding to $Z = -1.50$, which is 0.93319; that is to say, 93.3% of the total area under the curve is between a line at $Z = -1.50$ and the extreme right-hand end of the curve. We want the area between $Z = -1.5$ and the mean, so we have to subtract 0.5, to give 0.43319; unsurprisingly, exactly the same as between the mean and $Z = +1.50$. If the question had referred to the proportion of lengths between 80 and 140 mm, or within 1.5 standard deviations either side of the mean, we would simply double the answer for one half: $0.433 + 0.433 = 0.866$. Obviously, the proportion or percentage can easily be translated into real numbers if necessary so long as we know the total number of observations in our distribution.

If we had been asked to find the proportion of projectile points with lengths greater than 140 mm then the problem would have been less complicated. We would simply need to know the area between $Z = +1.50$ and the extreme right-hand end of the curve. We obtain this simply by reading off the value for $Z = 1.50$ in the table, as we already have done to work out the first question: 6.7% of the area under the curve is between $Z = 1.50$ and the extreme right of the curve, so that 6.7% of the points have a length greater than 140 mm.

For points less than 80 mm the procedure is similar to the first two cases we looked at. The area under the curve corresponding to $Z = -1.50$ is 0.93319, as we have seen already, so we have $1.0 - 0.93319 = 0.06681$, or 6.7%.

Not all tables of the standardised normal distribution are set up precisely as table B of appendix 1 is, but they are all very similar and it shouldn't be difficult to work out what to do.

The calculation of proportions of projectile-point lengths in specific intervals of the overall distribution of lengths might be of interest in itself if we had some specific hypothesis concerning the functional or cultural significance of projectile-point length, but the object here is to illustrate the way in which the standard normal distribution and real data relate to one another since an understanding of this is important in the chapters that follow.

In effect, what we are doing when we perform these operations is carrying out a standardisation of our original data. We start off with a particular normal distribution with a mean and standard deviation expressed in terms of the units in which the observations were made; millimetres in the examples just given. We then re-express the observations in terms of standard deviation units either side of the mean. The mean becomes zero and observations less than the mean are negative quantities, those greater than the mean are positive, thus the new distribution has a mean of zero and a standard deviation of one. No matter what the original units of measurement we can convert any normal distribution to this standard deviation unit form and it will have the properties which we have seen to characterise the normal distribution, in terms of the proportion of the area under the curve, or cases within the distribution, within a given interval, the information given in the Z table.

The most obvious way in which the normal distribution impinges on archaeology is in the presentation of radiocarbon dates, where the dates are given in the form of a mean and standard deviation (see Thomas 1976, Orton 1980 for a more extensive discussion of this matter). It is all too easy to forget that there is only a 68.26% probability of the date lying within one standard deviation of the mean. Conventional statistical practice indicates that we should not normally be satisfied with less than a 90 % or 95 % probability. The trouble is that time intervals of ± 2 standard deviations are generally so wide that, consciously or unconsciously, archaeologists prefer to overlook them and go for spurious precision.

WHAT DO WE DO IF THE DATA ARE NOT NORMALLY DISTRIBUTED?

The question naturally arises how we know whether or not our data are normally distributed. There are a number of ways of finding this out; one method is to plot the cumulative frequency distribution of the data on special graph paper known as *arithmetic probability paper* (see figure 8.6). As you can see, the horizontal scale is plotted in regular equal units for the range of the variable concerned, but the vertical scale records the cumulative distribution of observations (divided into 1000 parts) on a variable scale so that, for instance, the vertical distance from 50–60 % (500–600 on this scale) is similar to the vertical distance from 1–2 %. Note that the vertical scale is drawn from 0.1 to 999.9. This is because the normal curve is *asymptotic*, as we have already noted: it approaches zero at either end without actually ever reaching it, thus 0 % and 100 % (0 and 1000) are infinitely distant. The constant horizontal and variable vertical scale have the effect of turning the cumulative curve of a normal distribution into a straight line. Alternatively, programs exist for doing precisely the same thing on a computer.

Two other extremely useful methods of checking for normality have already been described in the exploratory data analysis section of chapter 4. Study of the intervals between the minimum value, the lower hinge, the median, the upper hinge and the maximum value will give a good idea of the overall symmetry and degree of concentration of the central values of the distribution. Use of the box-and-whisker plot brings out peculiarities in the distribution tails. This is particularly important because it may only be here that deviations from normality are obvious.

What happens if the data are not normal and we want them to be so for some reason, such as the application of a method which presupposes normal distributions? Can we and should we do anything about it? There is no doubt about our ability to do so, by means of transformations. The Z standardisation has already been described in this chapter, but that simply changed the original scale into a new one, without affecting the shape of the distribution in any way. Other transformations can be applied to data to actually change the distribution shape, by changing the relative lengths of

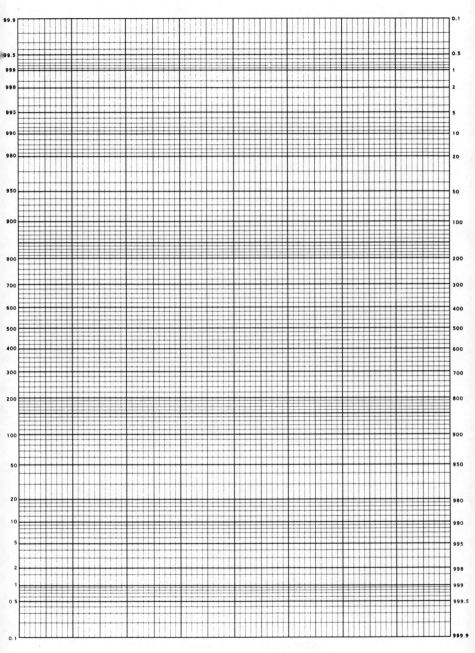

Figure 8.6. An example of arithmetic probability paper.

different parts of the scale.

In the past there has been a certain amount of debate about the utility and validity of transforming data, and some people have argued that it is simply 'fudging'. The view taken here is that transformations are a useful and valuable tool for data analysis, like any other; in fact, we have already seen their use in the previous chapter, where the log-linear modelling approach was based on the logarithms of the numbers in the tables, rather than the original values. The use of a transformation enabled us to go further with our understanding of the data than would otherwise have been possible. It is very often the case that patterns emerge more clearly in transformed than in untransformed data and the use of certain methods requires that the data be in a particular form. If a particular method that you wish to use presupposes a normal distribution then there is no reason not to transform it. Why should we privilege one form of numerical scale rather than another? The only proviso here is that the transformation should be interpretable, and we tend to feel more at home with the scales of measurement which have reality to us in our daily lives. However, that is no reason to carry such restrictions into our data analysis.

In practical archaeological situations one of the situations that arises most commonly is that distributions are positively skewed, with a long upper tail. In this case the possible transformations to normality are quite straightforward. What they need to do is 'pull in' the upper tail while leaving the rest of the observations largely unchanged. One way of doing this is to take the square root of each observation; a more drastic effect is produced by taking logarithms. What is involved is best illustrated by means of an example.

Let us suppose that we have been carrying out a field survey and have been collecting lithic artefacts over a wide area, using a grid system. As a result of this we have information on the number of lithic artefacts per square for each grid square. We want to carry out a correlation analysis on these data (see next chapter) and to do this it is preferable for the data to be normally distributed. We have plotted a histogram of the data and found that the distribution is positively skew so we want to carry out a transformation of the type just described. Rather than transform each observation we will transform the midpoint of each class interval; this is less laborious and easier to demonstrate. The untransformed distribution is given in figure 8.7.

If we try a square-root transformation we need a new horizontal scale in units of $\sqrt{x}$. To obtain this we look at the value of the class

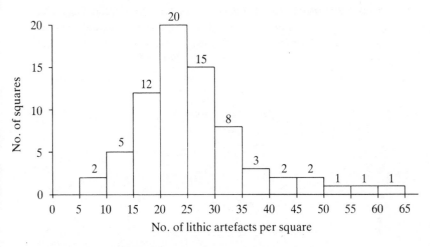

Figure 8.7. Distribution of numbers of grid squares containing different numbers of lithic artefacts: data from a hypothetical field survey.

midpoints in the original histogram, take their square roots and then put the cases from each original class into the correct square-root class. As you can see from figure 8.8, the data now show a much closer approximation to normality.

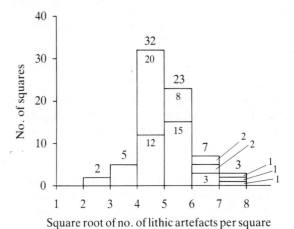

Figure 8.8. Distribution of numbers of grid squares containing different numbers of lithic artefacts: number of artefacts per square transformed to the square root of the original value.

If we were trying a log transformation we would need a new scale in units of log x (here log to the base 10). By analogy with the square-root example we take the log of each class midpoint, work out our scale and plot the histogram (figure 8.9).

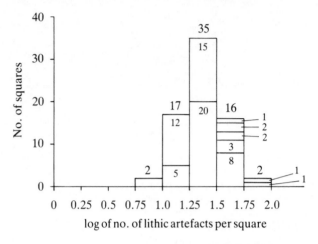

logs of class midpoints 0.875 1.096 1.352 1.511 1.759
                                 1.243 1.439 1.574 1.795
                                               1.628
                                               1.676
                                               1.720

Figure 8.9. Distribution of numbers of grid squares containing different numbers of lithic artefacts: number of artefacts per square transformed to the common logarithm of the original value.

In fact, as you can see, in this case the result comes out very similar for both transformations, the square root and the log. This is so because the positive tail in this case is not very large. Suppose the highest observation had been 1,000,000. The square root of this number is 1,000, but its logarithm is 6, so in this case the difference between the two is considerable. As a general guide, logarithms are appropriate for inherently positive data in which the values go close to zero (e.g. densities), while square roots are often used to transform frequency-count data.

EXERCISES

8.1. A group of pots is found to have a mean capacity of 950 ml with a standard deviation of 56 ml. The shape of the distribution of volumes is normal. (a) What proportion of the pots have a cubic capacity greater than 1050 ml? (b) What proportion have a capacity less than 800 ml? (c) What proportion of the capacities lie between 900 and 1,000 ml?

8.2. In the course of a study of a group of handaxes it is decided to investigate the relationship between handaxe weight and a number of other variables. The methods it is required to use presuppose that the handaxe weights are normally distributed. Compilation of a frequency distribution of weights produces the information below. Check whether it is normal and if it is not take appropriate action to make it so.

Interval (g)	No. of handaxes	Interval (g)	No. of handaxes
200-249	5	650-699	3
250-299	10	700-749	3
300-349	13	750-799	2
350-399	17	800-849	2
400-449	13	850-899	2
450-499	8	900-949	1
500-549	5	950-999	1
550-599	4	1000-1049	1
600-649	4		

Nine

Relationships between Two Numeric Variables: Correlation and Regression

METHODS OF VISUAL DISPLAY: SCATTERGRAMS

The investigation of relationships between two numeric variables has one great advantage over the study of relationships between nominal scale variables which we have seen in earlier chapters: the relationships can be presented in the form of a visual display, known as a *scatter diagram* or *scattergram,* where one variable is plotted against another. As always, such pictures can convey a great deal of information and prevent us from being misled, which can happen all too easily if we consider only numerical summaries of relationships.

Table 9.1. Quantities of New Forest pottery recovered from sites at varying distances from the kilns.

Site	Distance (km)	Quantity (sherds per m³ of earth)
1	4	98
2	20	60
3	32	41
4	34	47
5	24	62

For each observation we have a value for one variable and a value for another. Thus, suppose we are interested in the relationship between the quantity of pottery from the Romano-British kilns of the New Forest, in southern England, reaching sites at varying distances from the source. We might have the information shown in table 9.1. We can then produce a scattergram and plot in the points, with distance as the horizontal axis and pottery quantity as the vertical axis. Each site is placed at the appropriate point above the horizontal axis and opposite the vertical axis corresponding to its values on the variables (figure 9.1).

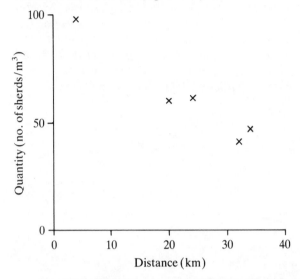

Figure 9.1. Plot of the quantity of Romano-British pottery from the New Forest kilns reaching various sites, in relation to the distance of the sites from the kilns.

This scattergram simply as it stands is extremely informative. We can see that the quantity of pottery decreases as distance from the source increases. We can also see that the relationship is roughly in the form of a straight line: an appropriately positioned straight line would pass very close to all the points. In other words, for a given increase in distance, there is a given decrease in pottery quantity, all along the distance scale, and all the sites more or less follow this relationship.

In this case we can say that one of these variables is an independent and the other a dependent. We imagine that pottery quantity is in some way affected by distance and therefore dependent on it, but the converse, that distance is affected by pottery quantity, does not hold. In such circumstances it is conventional to make the independent variable the horizontal axis, or *x* axis, of the graph, and the dependent the vertical or *y* axis.

It need not always be the case that we can specify dependent and independent variables. Suppose we are studying the dimensions of a group of neolithic beakers from Hungary and the relationships between them, in order to characterise the main aspects of variation in their shape (cf. Whallon 1982, for a study of Swiss neolithic vessels); we might plot height against rim diameter (figure 9.2). We can see that they match each other quite closely, so that the rim diameter and height are in fairly constant proportion to one another. In this example we can still plot the scattergram and it plays the same kind of role as the previous one in showing us the relationship between the two variables, but there is no intrinsic reason why one of them should be regarded as dependent on the other.

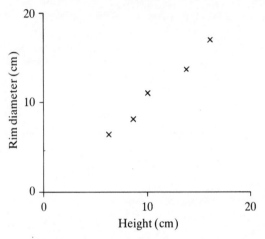

Figure 9.2. Rim diameter plotted against height for a hypothetical group of neolithic beakers from Hungary.

Scattergrams are the most important means of studying the relationships between pairs of variables. From them we can gain an idea first of the *direction* of a relationship: is it positive or negative? The height *v.* rim diameter plot is an example of the first: as heights become larger rims become larger. The pottery and distance plot is an example of the second: as distance increases, pottery quantity decreases.

The scattergram will also tell us about the *shape* of the relationship. Both those illustrated have clearly been straight line or *linear* relationships. By no means all relations between variables are of this kind. In fact, graphs of the quantity of some commodity against distance from its source are more commonly of the type shown in figure 9.3. This relationship is curvilinear, but it is still *monotonic,* i.e. throughout its range as distance gets larger, quantity gets smaller; it is not the case that for part of the distance scale pottery quantity decreases and then for the next part it starts to increase.

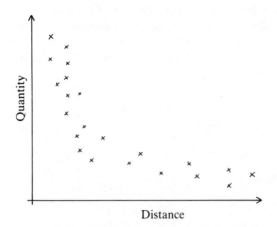

Figure 9.3. Plot of hypothetical quantities of a commodity reaching certain sites against the distance of these sites from the source, showing a curvilinear relationship.

An example of a *non-monotonic* relationship would be figure 9.4, which would be of interest to an archaeologist trying to estimate the ages at death of the animals whose bones he is studying. In this case the tooth increases in height as it grows after eruption and the animal's age increases, but as the tooth starts being used it gradually gets ground down and its height starts decreasing.

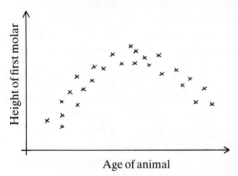

Figure 9.4. Plot of height of first molar against age at death for a number of sheep jawbones of known age at death.

The scattergram will also give us an idea of the strength of the relationship. Compare the two scattergrams of the relationship between weight and number of flake scars for two hypothetical groups of flint handaxes from the gravels of the Thames valley in southern England (figure 9.5). In one case the relationship is clearly much stronger than in the other because the points are much more narrowly concentrated together in a long thin band: they are generally much closer to any straight line we might draw through the scatter of points.

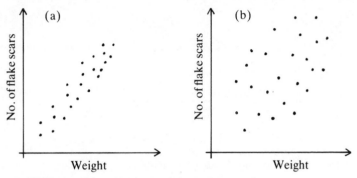

Figure 9.5. Scattergram of weight against number of flake scars for two groups of handaxes.

Scattergrams such as these, with two axes at right angles to each other, one for each variable, are by far the most common form of scattergram used in archaeology, as in other disciplines. Nevertheless, one other form does deserve mention, the *tripolar graph,* of which an example is illustrated in figure 9.6. As you can see, there are three axes at 60° to one another, forming a graph which is triangular in shape. Triangular or tripolar graphs can be used to plot not just two but three variables against one another in cases where the three variables make up a closed scale. By a closed scale we mean a scale with a fixed sum, like the percentage scale. Faunal assemblages from sites are often described in terms of the percentages of bones belonging to different species. Very often in a European or Near Eastern agricultural context only three species are of interest: cow, pig and sheep/goat. For a particular assemblage, if cow makes up 20% and pig 30%, then sheep/goat must make up 50%, otherwise the percentages will not sum to 100.

Figure 9.6 shows a tripolar graph for the faunal assemblages from the successive phases of occupation at the Bronze Age site of Phylakopi on the Aegean island of Melos (Gamble 1982). To show how to read it, let us take as an example phase o by weight. If we look along the sheep/goat scale we see that its value is about 76%, on the pig scale about 17% and on the cow scale about 7%. For

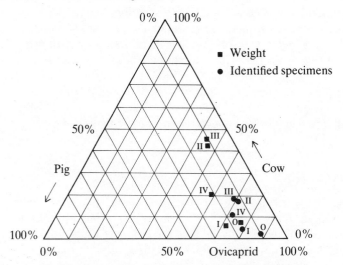

Figure 9.6. Tripolar graph of faunal percentages from the five city phases at Phylakopi: phases o, ɪ from the early bronze age; ɪɪ, ɪɪɪ from the middle bronze age; ɪv from the late bronze age (after Gamble 1982).

phase ɪɪɪ by weight we have 44, 11 and 45% respectively. By using the graph we have a ready means of tracing the temporal trends in faunal assemblage composition at Phylakopi.

In any study of relationships between interval scale variables, it is always essential as a first step to plot the scattergram and see what it looks like. But we may want to do more than this. We may want to describe the relationship in the scattergram mathematically, perhaps for the purpose of comparison with other similar data sets. Similarly, we may well want to define the strength of relationship mathematically: how good is the fit of the data to the proposed relationship?

DESCRIBING RELATIONSHIPS BY NUMBERS

a) *The Form of the Relationship*

The process of describing the relationship is called *regression* and that of measuring how well the data fit the relation is *correlation*.

Regression differs from other techniques we have looked at so far (with the exceptions of the methods described at the end of chapter 7) in that it is concerned not just with whether or not a relationship exists, or the strength of that relationship, but with its nature. For this reason it is important not just in standard statistics but also in model-building – it is concerned with prediction. We use an independent variable to estimate the values of a dependent variable.

The most general way of stating a hypothesised relationship mathematically is $y = f(x)$. This does not tell us a great deal: simply that the value of y (the dependent variable) at a particular point is a function of the value of x (the independent variable) there. It does not say anything about the specific nature of the relationship although it would be easy enough to put in some figures, e.g.

$$y = x \qquad (a)$$
$$\text{or} \quad y = 2x \qquad (b)$$
$$\text{or} \quad y = x^2 \qquad (c)$$

These may be worth spelling out. Thus, (a) tells us that the y value at a given point is the same as the x value of the point; (b) tells us that the y value is twice the x value of the point; (c) states that the y value of a given point is the square of the x value at that point. Such equations can be represented by lines on a graph; those for (a), (b) and (c) are shown in figure 9.7.

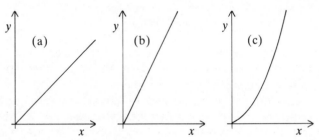

Figure 9.7. Graphs of the equations (a) $y = x$; (b) $y = 2x$; (c) $y = x^2$.

If our specification of the relationship between two variables by one of these functions was perfect, then from knowledge of x at a given point we could predict the value of y for that point with certainty. For example, if there was a perfect relationship in a particular case between the density of obsidian at a site and the distance of the site from the obsidian source, then from a knowledge of the distance of the site we could predict exactly its obsidian density; or, if there was a perfect relationship between height and rim diameter for a group of vessels, then from a knowledge of rim diameter we could predict height exactly (and vice versa in this case).

Of course, in most cases, indeed all cases outside the hardest natural sciences, things are never completely predictable. In some cases, again particularly in hard experimental sciences, this is simply because of imperfections in our measurement procedures; in most cases it is because effects are usually the result of a variety of causes operating together, many of which are themselves subject to random influences. What we therefore have to do is look for general trends in our data, estimating the relationship between x and y and also the accuracy with which values of y can be derived from this estimated relationship.

The situation where there is a relationship may be contrasted with that which obtains when x and y are statistically independent. In this case we cannot predict y from x, or, rather, knowledge of x does not improve our prediction of y; the stronger the dependence the more accurate our prediction will be.

As will appear more clearly below, the graph provides the link between the scattergrams we have seen already and the mathematical equations.

If we think of the best known type of example of regression analysis in archaeology, fall-off in the quantities of a particular type of material being distributed from a source with distance from that source – let us say obsidian from Lipari in the west Mediterranean – we can imagine that for every fixed value of the independent variable, distance, there will be a distribution of quantities of the material; not all sites at a given distance will have the same amount. But each of these quantity distributions (for each of the given values of the x variable, distance) will have a mean, and we can plot the position of these means. The line traced out by these means of y's for fixed x's is known as the *regression equation* of y on x. (In actual fact it is rarely the case in practice that there will be a number of y values for a given x value; this generally only occurs in designed experiments where it can be arranged to do so. Nevertheless, the method does not depend on this; the assumptions on which it does depend will be considered below.)

The line itself can take any form but we will only consider the simplest case, when the regression equation is a linear one and the relationship is a *straight* line. This is not such a restriction as might be imagined, because many empirical relationships do take this form and because it is often possible, as we will see, to transform variables so that the relationship between them becomes linear. Such linear relations have the virtue of being easier to understand at an intuitive level. We can write an equation for this linear relationship, as follows

$$y = a + bx$$

where y is the dependent variable, x is the independent variable, and the coefficients a and b are constants, i.e. they are fixed for a given set of data.

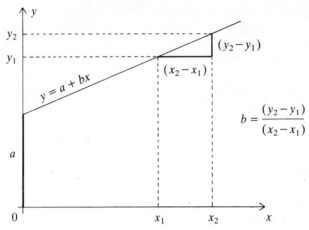

Figure 9.8. The slope and intercept (a and b coefficients) of a regression line.

If $x = 0$ then the equation reduces to $y = a$, so a represents the point where the regression line crosses the y axis (see figure 9.8); this is generally known as the intercept. The b constant defines the slope of the regression line, the amount of change in a vertical direction (along the y axis) for a given horizontal distance (along the x axis). Thus, for the pottery quantity in relation to distance from source example illustrated above, the b value represents the amount of decrease in pottery quantity for a given increase in distance from the source (it is calculated below, p. 126); for the height and rim diameter example it is the amount of increase in rim diameter associated with a given increase in height. Figure 9.8 illustrates what is involved.

As the slope becomes steeper so the amount of change in y for a given change in x becomes greater. When the line is horizontal, on the other hand, b is obviously zero and there is no change in y for any amount of change in x. It is clear that this means that there is no relationship between the two variables concerned; or, looked at from another point of view, knowing the x values of a set of observations does not help to predict their y values. But we have to qualify this. If *b* is zero it means that there is no *linear* relationship between the two variables; certain forms of nonlinear relationship could produce a *b* value of zero. Finally, it should be noted that if *y* decreases as *x* increases, in other words the relation between the two is an inverse one, then the sign of the *b* coefficient will be negative. How all this works out we will now see with out pottery example.

Having produced the scattergram of the relationship between pottery quantity and distance from the source (figure 9.1) on the basis of the information in table 9.1, we now want to describe the relationship mathematically. This means finding the appropriate intercept and slope values (*a* and *b* coefficients) for this particular set of data, to put in the equation $y = a + bx$. However, a glance at the scattergram (figure 9.1) will soon show that the relationship is not a perfect one: there is no straight line which will go exactly through all the data points. What we want to do is find the straight line which gives the *best fit* to the data points. How do we do this?

One intuitively appealing way is to plot the scattergram of the observations and then simply draw in by eye a best-fitting straight line through the dots; we could then work out the slope and intercept values for the line. Unsurprisingly perhaps, this is not entirely satisfactory. The usual method of fitting a line through the data points is by means of *least squares*. For each data point we can note the actual *y* value. It is obvious that the *y* value predicted by the regression for that point will almost certainly not correspond exactly to the real *y* value: there will be a discrepancy. What is involved for a particular data point is illustrated in figure 9.9, which looks at one particular segment of a regression line.

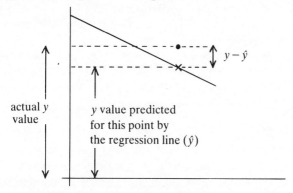

Figure 9.9. The difference between the actual *y* value of a data point and the value predicted by a regression.

The least-squares method finds the straight line which minimises

$$\sum_{i=1}^{n}(y_i - \hat{y}_i)^2$$

where n = the number of data points, y_i = the actual y value of point i, and $\hat{y}_i$ = the value of point i predicted by the regression. Let's go through what this means in words.

For each data point we can obtain the difference between its actual and predicted y values (in our example the difference between the actual quantity of New Forest pottery at a site and the quantity predicted by the regression line); this is the $(y_i - \hat{y}_i)$ term. We are then told to square this difference, to repeat the whole operation for each of our data points, then add up all the resulting quantities. This total must be minimised. In other words, we must 'juggle around' the exact position of the regression line until we find the line which produces the smallest possible sum of squared differences between actual and predicted values.

We use the squared deviations for the same reason as we use squared differences from the mean to define dispersion in calculating the variance and standard deviation of a single variable: if we simply took the differences without squaring them they would sum to zero. Inevitably, however, the result of the procedure is that the slope and position of the regression line are most influenced by the points with the largest deviations from the mean, and this is one of the sources of weakness of least-squares regression, because one or two extreme values can have a big effect on the results.

It is worth noting here that it is the sum of the squared *vertical* distances which are being minimised, since we are interested in the regression of y on x, or the effect of x on y. If we wanted to regress x on y we would use the horizontal distances. In later chapters we will see some methods which involve using the distances perpendicular to a best-fit line.

In fact, we don't actually need to do any juggling round to find the position of the best fit regression line satisfying the least squares criterion. Equations have been obtained which enable the appropriate a and b coefficients for any given set of data to be calculated:

$$b = \frac{\sum_{i=1}^{n}(x_i - \bar{x})(y_i - \bar{y})}{\sum_{i=1}^{n}(x_i - \bar{x})^2}$$

In words, starting with the top line: we take the x value of a particular data point and subtract the mean of the xs. We then take the y value of that data point and subtract the mean of the ys. Having done that we multiply the two x and y quantities together.

We carry out this operation for each of our data points and add up all the results. This quantity, known as the *covariation* between x and y, is then divided by the denominator. For the latter we take the x value of each data point in turn, subtract the mean of the x's from it, square the resulting difference, repeat the operation for all data points, and again add up all the results. This sum is used to divide the sum on the top line to give the b value, the slope of the regression line.

For the a coefficient we have

$$a = \frac{\sum\limits_{i=1}^{n} y_i - b\sum\limits_{i=1}^{n} x_i}{n} = \bar{y} - b\bar{x}$$

As you can see, this is much more straightforward.

For b there is also another version of the formula which is in general less laborious from the point of view of hand calculation, although this is a consideration fast declining in importance:

$$b = \frac{n\sum\limits_{i=1}^{n} x_i y_i - (\sum\limits_{i=1}^{n} x_i)(\sum\limits_{i=1}^{n} y_i)}{n\sum\limits_{i=1}^{n} x_i^2 - (\sum\limits_{i=1}^{n} x_i)^2}$$

where n is the number of data points; $\sum\limits_{i=1}^{n} x_i y_i$ means for each data point multiply the x value by the y value and add them all up; $(\sum\limits_{i=1}^{n} x_i)(\sum\limits_{i=1}^{n} y_i)$ means sum all the x values of the data points, then sum all the y values and multiply the two totals. There is a similar distinction in the denominator between $\sum\limits_{i=1}^{n} x_i^2$ and $(\sum\limits_{i=1}^{n} x_i)^2$.

Table 9.2. Quantities of New Forest pottery recovered from sites at varying distances from the kilns.

Site	Distance (x) in km	Quantity (y) (sherds per m^3 of earth)
1	4	98
2	20	60
3	32	41
4	34	47
5	24	62

We can now calculate the actual a and b values to describe the relationship between pottery quantity and distance from the kilns in our example. The figures are reproduced in table 9.2 for convenience. Using the computing formula above for b, the various quantities relevant to its calculation are as follows: $n = 5$; $\Sigma y_i = 308$;

$\Sigma x_i = 114$; $\Sigma x_i y_i = 5990$; and $\Sigma x_i^2 = 3172$. Then

$$b = \frac{(5 \times 5990) - (114 \times 308)}{(5 \times 3172) - 12996}$$

$$= -\frac{5162}{2864} = -1.80$$

Having obtained the b coefficient we need the intercept value:

$$a = \frac{\Sigma y_i - b\Sigma x_i}{n}$$

$$= \frac{308 - (-1.8 \times 114)}{5}$$

$$= \frac{513.2}{5} = 102.64$$

On the basis of this information we can now write the regression equation as

$$\hat{y} = 102.64 - 1.8x$$

which says that at the source there should be 102.64 sherds of the pottery type/m^3 of earth according to the regression line, and that this quantity declines by 1.8 sherds/m^3 for every kilometer of distance from the source. The resulting line is shown in figure 9.10.

(b) *The Strength of the Relationship: Correlation*
So far we have seen how to establish the two parameters of a regression equation, a and b, and thus indicate the form of the relationship between x and y. But this does not tell us anything about the accuracy of the estimates of y that are given by the regression line. To find out how good the line is we need to use the correlation coefficient, which measures the strength of the relationship between two variables. Strength of a relationship is a topic with which we are already familiar, having looked at it in relation to nominal scale variables in chapter 7. With interval scale variables the general idea of measuring the strength of a relationship is the same but the specific details of going about it are different.

The correlation coefficient has been of absolutely central importance in the applications of quantitative techniques to archaeology which have occurred in the last 25 years. As we saw in chapter 1, one of the most important themes which emerged in processsual

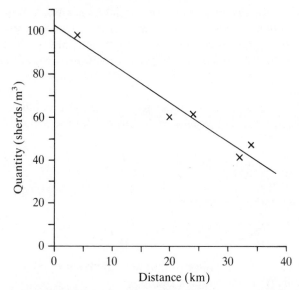

Figure 9.10. Graph of the regression equation $\hat{y} = 102.64 - 1.8x$.

archaeology was the study of the way things vary in relation to one another. The correlation coefficient has probably been the most important single mathematical tool for investigating patterns of covariation in archaeological data. It is important both for its own sake and as a basis for more complex methods such as principal components and factor analysis (see chapter 12).

Considered in graphical terms, the correlation coefficient is a measure of the extent to which data points are scattered around the regression line. When they are close to it, it means that correlation is strong and that a prediction of the value of y at a given point based on the x values will be very good. If the points are widely scattered around the line, it means that correlation is weak and prediction of y based on x will be poor. This point may be clearly demonstrated with reference to figure 9.5. The correlation coefficient would be higher for the scattergram on the left than that on the right: the data points in (a) are are obviously much more closely bunched around the regression line which would go through this point scatter. It is also obvious from these scattergrams that predictions of y based on x will be much better for (a). If we look at (b) we can see that for a given x value there is a wide range of possible y values. If the scatter of points is circular, correlation will be zero and knowledge of x will be no help in predicting y. Thus, the correlation coefficient is a measure of the extent to which two variables *covary*, although it is important to remember that it is a measure of *linear* correlation and that certain kinds of curvilinear relationship could produce a correlation value of zero even for perfect relationships (a point which demonstrates again the importance of looking at the scattergram; cf. figure 9.4).

All this discussion is very similar to that for the *b* coefficient, which is no surprise when we look at the formula for the correlation coefficient (*r*):

$$r = \frac{\Sigma(x_i - \bar{x})(y_i - \bar{y})}{\sqrt{[\Sigma(x_i - \bar{x})^2 \Sigma(y_i - \bar{y})^2]}}$$

A hand computation version is:

$$r = \frac{n\Sigma x_i y_i - (\Sigma x_i)(\Sigma y_i)}{\sqrt{\{[n\Sigma x_i^2 - (\Sigma x_i)^2][n\Sigma y_i^2 - (\Sigma y_i)^2]\}}}$$

As you can see, the numerator of the expressions for *r* and *b* is the same, the covariation between *x* and *y*.

The difference between the two lies in the denominator: for the correlation coefficient the covariation is standardised in terms of the variation in both *x* and *y*. The maximum possible value that the covariation can reach is equal to the denominator, the square root of the product of the variation in *x* and *y*. Thus, the maximum value that *r* can take is 1.0, which will be positive when the covariation term is positive and negative when it is negative. The maximum value will be reached when all points are on the straight line (figure 9.11). As we have already noted in passing, when *x* and *y* are independent of one another the correlation coefficient, like the slope (because it has the same numerator), will be zero.

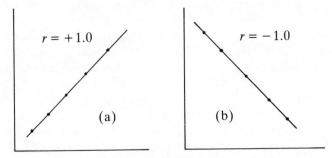

Figure 9.11. Scattergram and regression line for which there is (a) perfect positive correlation, (b) perfect negative correlation.

There are, however, two important differences between r and b which arise from the difference in their denominator. First, because the correlation coefficient is standardised in terms of the variation in both the variables it is symmetrical: it does not matter which of the variables is taken to be independent, nor indeed if neither of them is; the correlation between x and y is the same as that between y and x. The slope of the regression of y on x, however, is not the same as the slope of the regression of x on y, unless the angle of the regression line is 45°. You can see this by looking at figure 9.10, which shows the regression line for the regression of pottery quantity on distance from the source. If you turn it on its side for a moment and imagine that pottery quantity is the horizontal axis you can see that the slope with reference to this axis is much steeper than the slope in relation to the real x axis. In addition, it is obvious that a rate of change in pottery quantity per kilometre increase in distance from source, is something different from a rate of change in distance per sherd decrease in pottery quantity. Secondly, whereas a slope is measured in the units of the original variables (for example, the amount of change in pottery quantity for a given increase in distance) correlation is a unitless quantity which can thus be used as a basis for comparison in a wide variety of different circumstances.

Before we leave the correlation coefficient we need to consider its squared value (r^2). This is known as the *coefficient of determination* and has its own interesting properties, which must now be examined.

We saw above that one way of looking at a regression analysis is to see the regression as improving our estimates of the y value of particular points by using information we have about their x values. If knowledge of x does improve our predictions of y it means that the two variables are in some way related, although we have to bear in mind the *caveats* from previous chapters that association does not necessarily, or even very often, mean explanation of one in terms of the other.

If knowledge of x does not help us to predict y then our best estimate of any particular y value is the mean of y ($\bar{y}$). As we saw in chapter 4, how far this is a typical value depends on the degree of dispersion of the distribution around the mean (assuming for the moment that the distribution is symmetrical and not skewed). Thus one way of assessing how good our prediction of y based on $\bar{y}$ is likely to be is to note the dispersion around the mean, given by $\Sigma(y_i - \bar{y})^2$. This, of course, is the sum of squares, or variation, in y, the first stage of calculating the variance or standard deviation.

If we then carry out the regression of y on x to improve our prediction of y, we can assess the general quality of our predictions by looking at the dispersion of the observations not around the mean of y now but around the regression line, given by $\Sigma(y_i - \hat{y}_i)^2$. This is the quantity already referred to earlier in this chapter as that which least squares regression tries to minimise. It is known as the *residual variation* around the regression line. $\Sigma(y_i - \hat{y}_i)^2$ cannot be any greater than $\Sigma(y_i - \bar{y})^2$. To the extent that it is smaller we have achieved an improvement in prediction by using the regression line (i.e. our knowledge of the x values of the data points) as a basis for prediction rather than the mean of the y values. Thus the amount of improvement $= \Sigma(y_i - \bar{y})^2 - \Sigma(y_i - \hat{y}_i)^2$. Or alternatively, in words: variation accounted for by the regression equals the original variation minus the residual variation. This 'improvement' quantity, the amount of variation 'accounted for' by the regression is sometimes referred to as the 'explained' variation, but it is really rather misleading to use such a word in this context.

If we divide the variation accounted for by the regression by the original variation, we obtain the proportion of the original variation accounted for by the regression and it is this which is known as r^2, the coefficient of determination, the square of the correlation coefficient; in many ways it is more intuitively meaningful than the latter quantity. Its value is often multiplied by 100 to put it on a percentage scale and it is then sometimes known as the 'percentage level of explanation'.

It is now time to illustrate these two coefficients with reference to the pottery and distance example for which the regression equation was obtained above. Using the computation formula for r,

$$r = \frac{(5 \times 5990) - (114 \times 308)}{\sqrt{\{[5 \times 3172) - 12996][(5 - 20938) - 94864]\}}}$$

$$= \frac{-5162}{\sqrt{(2864 \times 9826)}} = -0.973$$

This tells us that the relationship between pottery quantity and distance from the source is a virtually perfect negative linear one, as we would indeed expect from the scattergram. If we now square this value to obtain the coefficient of determination we have

$$r^2 = -0.97^2 = 0.94 \text{ (or } 94\% \text{)}$$

This tells us that by using distance to estimate pottery quantity at our sites we reduce the original variation in the data (the variation around the mean value of quantity) by nearly 95 %, i.e. nearly 95 % of the variation in pottery quantity is related to distance; only 5 % or so is left over as variation around the regression line. Whether distance itself 'explains' the variation in pottery quantity is another matter, but any explanation must obviously take this strong relationship into account.

To be told that 95 % of the variation in quantity of this New Forest pottery at different sites relates to the distance of the site from the source kilns may seem to be attaching an unnecessary number to something which was already obvious from the scattergram with its regression line, since it is clear from this that the relationship between quantity and distance is very close. To some extent such a comment would be justified at this point! The pay-off comes in two areas. First, if we are making comparisons, for example of the relationship between quantity of a commodity and distance from source for a range of different commodities, comparing a series of definite numbers is much more satisfactory than comparing one's visual impressions of a series of scattergrams. Second, once we get on to investigating the relationships between larger numbers of variables than two we again need numbers, both to compare and to manipulate further, as we will see.

We can finish this section by noting that r^2 generally provides a more realistic assessment of the strength of a relationship than r when we come to considering what the numbers mean for interpretation purposes. Thus, an r value of 0.4 suggests at least a moderate relationship between two variables. When we square it, however, we see that it means that only 0.16 (or 16.0%) of the variation in the one variable is related to the other, not a very high proportion.

CONCLUSION

We have now seen the basics of investigating a relationship between two variables when they are measured at an interval scale or above. The most important aspect of the whole process is producing and examining the scattergram, but we can go further than this in two respects. We can obtain the equation of the regression line which best fits the scatter of points, thus specifying the way in which the dependent variable changes in relation to changes in the independent. We can also obtain a measure of the goodness-of-fit of the data to the regression line by means of the correlation coefficient and coefficient of determination.

A great many uses exist in archaeology for these techniques since archaeologists regularly want to investigate relationships between pairs of numeric variables. The methods may be used both as an end in themselves, as in the various examples referred to in this chapter, or as the basis for more complex and advanced techniques described in chapters 11 and 13.

Before we look at some of the more complicated aspects of correlation and regression on interval scale variables, in the next chapter, it is worth saying a brief word about *rank-order correlation,* so that you are aware of the possibilities.

Chapter 7 looked at ways of examining relations between nominal scale variables and this chapter has examined relations between interval scale variables, but methods also exist that are appropriate for ordinal scale, or rank-order, data. As you might expect by now, such rank-order correlation methods are more powerful than those for nominal scales but not as powerful as interval scale ones. Probably the best known of these is Spearman's coefficient of rank correlation, but Kendall's tau b and tau c are better if there are large numbers of ties, that is to say if large numbers of observations have the same rank. Details of the techniques may be found in such texts as Blalock (1972) or Norusis (1983).

An example of the use of rank correlation is given in Shennan (1985). As part of a study of field survey methods an investigation was made of the abilities of the different fieldwalkers to spot different kinds of material on the field surface. By a rather complex series of methods it was possible to rank each walker in terms of their abilities at picking up pottery and lithics. The rank order of ability at picking up pottery could then be compared with that of picking up lithic artefacts, to see if, in general, high or low ability on one was related to high or low ability on the other. In fact they weren't: someone who is good at seeing pottery on the surface won't necessarily be especially good with lithic artefacts.

In this example there were no tied ranks, i.e. no ties between several people for, say, third place in the rank order. In other cases there often are. Let us suppose, again on the basis of survey data, that we can divide the sites of a particular period in an area into the rough size categories large, medium and small; as in the example of the Mann–Whitney and runs tests this is something we might feel able to do even if we don't feel justified in estimating exact site sizes. Let us suppose also that a categorisation of the soils in the region exists in terms of whether they are excellent, average or poor for the purposes of arable agriculture, and that we know which sites are on which of these soil categories. All the sites in a particular rank category, whether for size or soil quality, may be said to be tied for that category. To what extent is site size related to soil quality?

Table 9.3. Site size category tabulated against soil quality category.

| | | Soil quality | | |
	Excellent	Average	Poor	Total
Large	15	7	2	24
Medium	6	11	4	21
Small	7	7	8	22
Total	28	25	14	67

We can construct a table of our observations (table 9.3). Kendall's tau (not to be confused with Goodman and Kruskal's tau, referred to in chapter 7) can then be calculated to find out whether there is indeed any correlation between the size category of the site and the arable agricultural potential of the soil on which it is located.

EXERCISES

9.1. As part of an investigation of palaeolithic stone tool technology and its complexity a study is being carried out of the factors affecting the number of flake scars on hand-axes. One suggestion is that it is simply a result of overall hand-axe size, which can be measured in terms of weight. Given the information below, what is the relationship between weight and number of flake scars? Is it a good one?

No. of flake scars	Weight (g)	No. of flake scars	Weight (g)
18	210	37	620
19	300	72	510
33	195	57	565
28	285	53	650
24	410	46	740
36	375	78	690
45	295	68	710
56	415	63	840
47	500	82	900

9.2. An archaeological survey has been carried out in southern England. Its approach has not been to look for sites but to collect information on artefact densities in terms of one-hectare quadrats. Below are the iron age and Romano-British pottery densities for a series of quadrats. Investigate the relationship between them.

Iron Age	Roman	Iron Age	Roman
4	5	12	55
3	20	9	61
7	20	7	62
6	33	13	79
6	46	9	81
9	45	14	98

Ten

When the Regression Doesn't Fit

In the previous chapter we saw the basics of regression and correlation analysis but were very careful to avoid any complications. It was noted, however, that we were only concerned with straight line regression and that we should always look at the scattergram to check whether the scatter of data points really does show a linear trend, rather than some kind of non-linear pattern. This point leads on to the general question of the assumptions required to carry out a valid regression analysis; obviously a very important topic which we have not yet examined.

Problems about the relationship between the data and the assumptions required by regression analysis can be seen particularly clearly in the *residuals* from the regression: where the regression doesn't fit, the difference between the actual y values and those predicted by the regression. But the residuals are also important from another point of view. In fact, they may be more interesting archaeologically than the regression itself, but it requires the regression analysis for the interest to emerge.

As an example, let us suppose again that we are dealing with the fall-off in quantity of a material with increasing distance from its source. We might note that at a particular distance the majority of sites have only a small quantity of the commodity, but a small number have much more. The question naturally arises why this should be the case. We can then find out which sites these are and see what features they share, not shared with the others, which could explain the phenomenon. They might all be close to a particular main transport route for example. Hodder and Orton (1976, 115–17), in an analysis of the distribution of Romano-British pottery from the Oxfordshire kilns were able to show that the sites which had more of this pottery than expected given their distance from the source were those where water transport could have been involved. In another study Shennan (1985) used regression methods to pick out flint scatters with exceptionally large and small

135

numbers of retouched pieces. Plotting the distribution of these on the map it was apparent that they were characteristic of certain specific types of location.

For both substantive and methodological reasons then, it is necessary to look at the residuals from a regression, even though in one or two places the topic involves an increase in the level of difficulty over earlier chapters.

RESIDUALS

In the same way as we use $\Sigma(y_i - \bar{y})^2$ in the calculation of the variance or the standard deviation of a single variable, so we can use $\Sigma(y_i - \hat{y}_i)^2$ to calculate the variance or the standard deviation around the regression line:†

$$s_{y-\hat{y}}^2 = \frac{\Sigma(y_i - \hat{y}_i)^2}{n}$$

where $s_{y-\hat{y}}^2$ is the variance of the distribution around the regression line, y_i is the actual y value at the ith point, $\hat{y}_i$ is the estimated y of the ith point according to the regression, and n is the number of observations.

Table 10.1. Information for calculating the standard error of the regression for the Romano-British pottery quantity data from table 9.1.

y_i	$\hat{y}_i{}^*$	$(y_i - \hat{y}_i)^2$
98	95.44	6.55
60	66.64	44.09
41	45.04	16.32
47	41.44	30.91
62	59.44	6.55
		104.42

* Calculated from $y = 102.64 - 1.8x$

The square root of this is the standard deviation of the distribution, known as the *standard error* of the regression. For the pottery

† The denominator in this version of the formula is n, which presupposes that we are only interested in the variation around the regression for the particular data set analysed. If we wanted to estimate the variation around the line for a population of which this was a sample, the divisor would be $n - 2$, since two degrees of freedom are lost in calculating the regression. MINITAB uses this divisor in its regression procedure.

quantity example we have the information in table 10.1. Applying the formula above we have

$$s_{y-\hat{y}}^2 = \frac{104.42}{5} = 20.88$$

$$s_{y-\hat{y}} = \sqrt{20.88} = 4.57$$

The standard error of the regression of pottery quantity against distance is 4.57.

As we will see shortly below, one of the stipulations of the regression model is that the distribution of the residuals around the line should be normal. This being so, we can note that if we put standard error bands around the regression line, then these bands will include approximately 68 % of all the observations, while bands at ± 2 standard errors will include 95 % of all observations; the point is illustrated in figure 10.1.

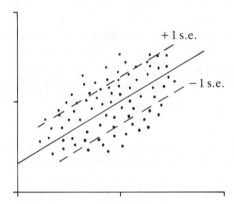

Figure 10.1. One-standard-error band around a regression line.

In fact, as well as using r or r^2 as a general indication of the fit of the regression, we can also use the standard error of the regression as an indication of the precision of the estimates, in the same way as we use the standard deviation for the dispersion of a single variable normal distribution. We can put an extra term in the regression equation to recognise this:

$$\hat{y}_i = a + bx_i \pm s_{y-\hat{y}}$$

where $\hat{y}_i$ is the estimated value of y_i, a and b are the intercept and slope, x_i is the x value of the relevant point, and $s_{y-\hat{y}}$ is the standard error of the regression. In the pottery quantity example the specific figures in the formula are:

$$\hat{y}_i = 102.64 - 1.8x_i \pm 4.57$$

When the distribution of residuals is normal then we can say that about 68% of the residuals will fall within this range. Assuming a normal distribution for the pottery example, approximately 68% of them will fall within the ± 4.57; or, alternatively, an estimate that any given quantity value is in the range ± 4.57 around the regression line will have about a 68% probability of being correct. An estimate such as this is known as an *interval estimate,* since we are specifying the interval within which some quantity should lie with some specified degree of probability; we will return to these again when we look at sampling (see chapter 14). In actual fact for these particular data $\frac{3}{5}$ of the observations (60%) fall within one standard error of the regression line and all of them within two standard errors; given the very small number of observations the correspondence with the expected values is about as close as it could be.

One other useful property follows from the normal distribution of residuals. We saw in chapter 8 that any observation in a distribution could be transformed into a Z score by expressing the observation in terms of standard deviation units away from the mean, where

$$Z = \frac{x - \bar{x}}{s}$$

For a normal distribution the score can then be looked up in the normal table to find the proportion of the distribution which lies between the mean and a point that distance away from it.

In the same way, if we take any given residual term $(y_i - \hat{y}_i)$ from the regression and divide it by the standard deviation (error) of the distribution of residuals around the regression, we produce a quantity analogous to the Z score called the standardised residual:

$$\text{standardised residual} = \frac{y_i - \hat{y}_i}{s_{y-\hat{y}}}$$

The standardised residual from the regression has the same properties as the Z score and can be linked to the standard normal distribution in the same way using the normal table (assuming, of course, that the residuals are normally distributed).

For the second observation in the pottery quantity and distance example we have

$$\text{standardised residual} = \frac{60 - 66.64}{4.57} = -1.45$$

This *y* value is 1.45 standard errors less than the value estimated by the regression.

As we will see in the following section, the standardised residual, with its link to the normal distribution, has properties which make it extremely useful for investigating whether the regression assumptions really are met or not, and indeed more generally for picking out interesting patterns in regression results.*

THE REGRESSION MODEL

Everything we have done so far in relation to regression is valid only insofar as certain assumptions concerning the residual terms in the model are satisfied. These assumptions are of a variety of types but failure to meet them, of whatever type, is always reflected in the residuals. For this reason it is very important to use graphs, not just to look at the original data but also to look at the structure of the residuals. Analyses based simply on an examination of summary statistics are insufficient. Least-squares regression is quite robust with regard to minor violations of the assumptions but gross violations can seriously distort conclusions. What I want to do is go through the assumptions, then indicate how violations of them can be detected and what can be done about them.

Assumptions
1. In the version of regression considered here it is presupposed that the independent variable as well as the dependent are measured at an interval scale or above.

2. It has been noted already that we are concerned only with simple linear regression, where the relationship between the two variables takes the form of a straight line. Obviously, if the trend is not a linear then an analysis which assumes that it is will not be very satisfactory; an example is shown in figure 10.2.

In this example *y* does increase with increasing *x* but at different rates in different parts of the *x* scale. Simply calculating the linear regression and its associated correlation coefficient would in fact suggest that there was a strong linear trend. It is examination of the graph which shows that the straight line represents an unsatisfactory

---

* Recently the trend has been towards using not the *standardised* but the *studentised* residual in this way. In this case the value of each residual is standardised not by dividing by the standard error of the regression as a whole but the standard error calculated without including the value of that particular data point; in effect the values are individually standardised.

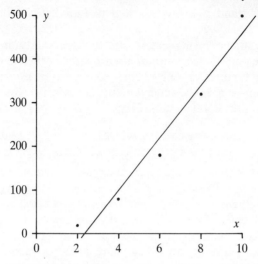

Figure 10.2. Scattergram of a non-linear relationship between *x* and *y*.

description of the relationship since it underpredicts at the beginning and end of the line and overpredicts in the middle.

3. The distribution of the residuals around the regression line must be normal. This is particularly important if we want to use the regression to obtain interval estimates for *y* in the way discussed in the previous section, or if we want to carry out significance tests; see figure 10.3 for exaggerated examples of normal and non-normal distributions of residuals.

4. The mean of the distribution of residuals must be zero for

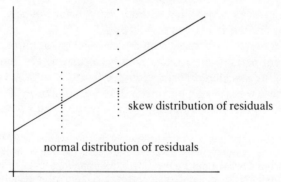

Figure 10.3. Distribution of residuals around a regression line.

every x value; in other words, the distributions of residuals must be centred on the regression line. If they are not it usually comes down either to a violation of the linearity assumption (see above), or to the presence of autocorrelation (see below).

5. One of the most important assumptions of regression analysis is that variation around the line is *homoscedastic*. In other words, the amount of variation around the line is the same at all points along it. If it is not then the variation is said to be *heteroscedastic*. There is a variety of ways in which heteroscedasticity can arise. Two of the most common ones are illustrated in figure 10.4. In figure 10.4(a) observations with small x and y values tend to be fairly close to the line while those with large x and y values are more dispersed. In (b) there is only a small number of cases with large values of x and y, the bulk of the values being small.

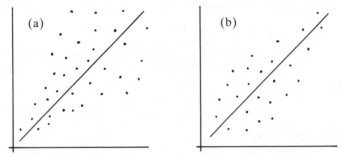

Figure 10.4. Heteroscedastic distribution of residuals.

6. Autocorrelation. One of the main assumptions of regression analysis is that the error terms associated with particular observations are uncorrelated. In other words, the residual in y for one value of x should not be related to that for other x values. An example of what this may look like is shown in figure 10.5.

Here numbers of positive residuals are grouped together and followed by numbers of negative residuals grouped together, a pattern which repeats itself along the line resulting in a nonlinear relationship. As with the other regression assumptions, failure to take autocorrelation into account is likely to produce misleading results. In the case illustrated above the value of the correlation coefficient for a linear relationship would in fact be very high, implying that for any given increase in x there is a corresponding increase in y; in fact, depending on precisely where we are on the x axis, the increase in y for a given increase in x will vary considerably.

Autocorrelation can arise for a variety of reasons, which will be

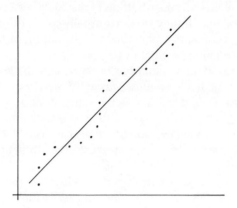

Figure 10.5. An example of autocorrelation
in the residuals from a regression.

discussed below.

The regression model is fairly robust with regard to minor violations of the assumptions. The most important ones are those of
linearity (which as we have seen subsumes several of the others),
homoscedasticity and uncorrelated errors.

Detection and Remedy of
Violations of the Regression Assumptions

As has already been suggested, one of the best and simplest ways of
detecting discrepancies between model and data is through examination of the regression residuals. We have already defined the
residual value of y as the difference between the actual and estimated values of y:

$$\text{res } y_i = y_i - \hat{y}_i$$

We have also defined the standardised residual for each y:

$$\text{st. res. } y = \frac{y_i - \hat{y}_i}{s_{y-\hat{y}}}$$

where

$$s_{y-\hat{y}} = \sqrt{\frac{\Sigma(y_i - \hat{y}_i)^2}{n}}$$

As we said earlier, the standardised residuals are like Z scores in
that they have zero mean and unit standard deviation. With a
moderately large sample these residuals should be distributed ap-

proximately normally. Graphing the residuals will reveal whether or not this is the case. If it is not, then problems of some sort exist.

The most commonly used plots are those in which the standardised residuals are plotted as the ordinate (or y axis) against either (a) the estimated value of y, i.e. $\hat{y}$, or (b) the independent variable x. Examples of both are illustrated in figure 10.6. There is really nothing to choose between them for bivariate regression although the first plot, against the independent variable, probably makes interpretation rather more straightforward. As we will see in the next chapter, however, in multiple regression there is no option but to plot the residuals against $\hat{y}$.

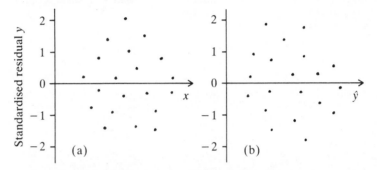

Figure 10.6. Examples of standardised residual values of data points (vertical axis) plotted against (a) their x values, (b) the $\hat{y}$ values predicted for them by the regression.

If the model is correct, the standardised residuals tend to fall between $+2$ and -2 in value and are randomly distributed (see figure 10.6); they should not show a distinct pattern of variation. When the assumptions do not hold, there is patterning; not only does this tell us that we have to take action to make the data fit the assumptions if we are going to use the technique, it also often has substantive insights to give us, in terms of revealing unsuspected structures in the data. As we have seen above, the residuals can often be more interesting than the regression itself since frequently the regression line only systematises what we thought we knew already. It is when that systematisation reveals that the patterning in the data is more complex than we thought that new knowledge may potentially be gained. In such cases the mathematically defined regression provides a secure baseline for comparison and the detection of irregularities. A good example of the patterning which can emerge has also been referred to above: Hodder and Orton's demonstration that in a regression analysis of the quantity of a certain type of Romano-British pottery against distance from source, high positive residuals were obtained in areas accessible to water transport (Hodder and Orton 1976). It is always possible in bivariate regression to obtain an idea whether problems exist simply by looking at the scattergram of the raw data, but the residual plots are much more effective – they act like a magnifying glass on the errors. When we come on to multiple regression in the next chapter, dealing with more than two variables, then residual plots are the only available option.

We can now turn to the detection and remedying of failure to meet assumptions of the linear regression model.

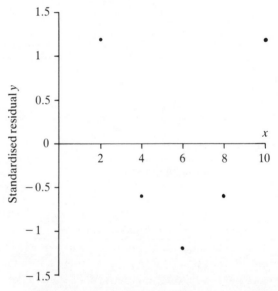

Figure 10.7. Plot of the standardised residuals from the regression line of figure 10.2 against their *x* values.

1. *Non-linearity*. It has already been noted that non-linearity in the relationship between two variables can arise in a number of different ways. An example has been shown in figure 10.2, and although the lack of linearity emerges clearly enough from the scattergram, figure 10.7 shows how the problems are magnified in the corresponding residual plot, which certainly does not show a random scatter of points.

There are several commonly met non-linear relationships between y and x which can be made linear by means of transformations. We may detect this non-linearity through looking at the data, as here, or we may have theoretical reasons for postulating a particular form of non-linear but 'linearisable' curve to which we want to see if our data will fit; such fitting is generally more straightforward if the relationship is in a linear form. In archaeological applications the most likely context in which we will have theoretical reasons for postulating a particular form of curvilinear relationship is in distance decay studies of the type already illustrated, in which we are looking at the relationship between the changing value of some variable and distance from some point. A considerable amount of work has been carried out on the forms such curves are likely to take (see Hodder and Orton 1976, Renfrew 1977).*

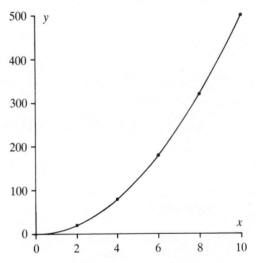

Figure 10.8. Graph of the Pareto relationship $y = 5x^2$.

One common form of curvilinear relation is the double-log or Pareto relationship, where the equation of the regression line (see figure 10.8) takes the form

$$y = ax^b$$

* In cases where we do not have the theoretical basis for postulating particular curves but do have a non-linear relationship it is possible to allow the data to determine the choice of the appropriate transformation, but the techniques involved are beyond a text such as this; for an example see McDonald and Snooks (1985).

To make this linear the appropriate transformation is

$$\log y = \log a + b \log x$$

What this means is that we have to take the logarithms of both the x and the y values of our data and use these, first as the axes of a new scattergram, and second for calculating a regression equation and correlation coefficient. In fact, the scattergram of a non-linear relationship in figure 10.2 is of this form. What happens when the x and y axes are logged is shown in figure 10.9.

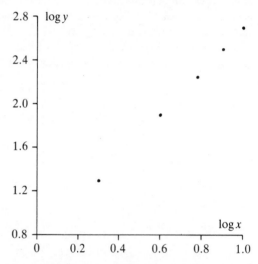

Figure 10.9. Data from figure 10.2 with the x and y values transformed to the logarithms of their original values.

The other common form of non-linear relationship is the exponential curve (figure 10.10) with the equation

$$y = ab^x$$

The linear version of this curve is given by the formula

$$\log y = \log a + \log bx$$

This involves taking logarithms of the y values of our data and using these we can produce a scattergram with a new vertical axis in units of $\log y$. It is the fact that the y axis is logged that results in the logged exponents, a and b, because both of these are expressed in terms of y: a is the point where the regression line cuts the y axis, and b is the amount of change in y for a given change in x. In this

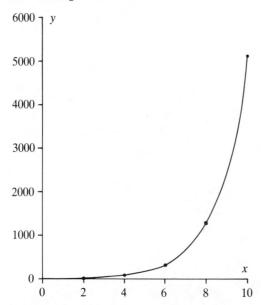

Figure 10.10. Graph of the exponential relationship $y = 5(2^x)$.

case the x axis stays the same.

The cases we have looked at are some of the most common non-linear but linearisable situations which are likely to arise in archaeological contexts because they frequently occur in spatial fall-off studies, although it is important to remember that it is the negative versions of these curves which will be relevant in fall-off studies rather than the positive versions illustrated above. If non-linearity is present it will show up in plots of the data and the standardised residuals. If the plot corresponds to one of the graphs we have just looked at then you should carry out the appropriate data transformation and try the linear regression again, remembering to check it as before by plotting the residuals.

The preceding discussion of non-linear functions and ways to turn them into linear ones has been very abstract and at this point it may help to present a worked example; once again a hypothetical distance decay study, this time of the quantity of a certain type of Mesoamerican obsidian at sites at various distances from the source, based on weight $(g)/m^3$ of excavated earth. The figures are shown in table 10.2. The first stage of the analysis will be to calculate the regression and correlation for these data:

Table 10.2. Density of a certain type of Mesoamerican obsidian for sites at varying distances from the source.

Distance (km)	Density (g/m^3)	Distance (km)	Density (g/m^3)
5	5.01	44	0.447
12	1.91	49	0.347
17	1.91	56	0.239
25	2.24	63	0.186
31	1.20	75	0.126
36	1.10		

$n = 11$ $\Sigma x_i y_i = 284.463$
$\Sigma x_i = 413$ $\Sigma y_i = 14.715$
$(\Sigma x_i)^2 = 170569$ $(\Sigma y_i)^2 = 216.531$
$\Sigma x_i^2 = 20407$ $\Sigma y_i^2 = 40.492$

$$b = \frac{(11 \times 284.463) - (413 \times 14.715)}{(11 \times 20407) - 170569}$$

$$= \frac{-2948.202}{53908} = -0.055$$

$$a = \frac{14.715 - (-0.055 \times 413)}{11} = 3.403$$

Thus the regression equation is:

$$\hat{y} = 3.403 - 0.055x$$

$$r = \frac{(11 \times 284.463) - (413 \times 14.715)}{\sqrt{\{[(11 \times 20407) - 170569][(11 \times 40.492) - 216.531]\}}}$$

$$= \frac{-2948.202}{\sqrt{(53908 \times 228.881)}} = -0.839$$

$$r^2 = -0.839^2 = 0.704$$

The correlation coefficient has the value of -0.839 and the r^2 value of 0.704 indicates that just over 70% of the variation in lithic quantity is related to distance from the source.

These values indicate a strong linear relationship between the two variables and if we simply examined the numbers calculated above we might take the investigation no further. If we look at the scattergram (figure 10.11(a)), however, we see that the distribu-

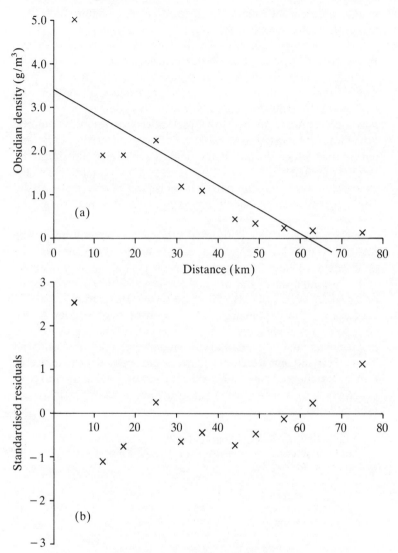

Figure 10.11. (a) Plot of obsidian densities against distance from source with the regression line $y = 3.403 - 0.055x$ superimposed. (b) Plot of the standardised residual obsidian densities against distance from source.

tion of points is not in a straight line, so that the linear regression underpredicts at the beginning and end of the line and overpredicts in the middle. The standardised residual plot (figure 10.11(b)) brings this out even more clearly.

Since the regression does not fit some action must be taken. Inspection of the raw data scattergram suggests that a linear relationship would fit all the data points except the first one quite well. This first point could therefore be regarded as an 'outlier' and excluded from consideration, and the analysis re-run without it. It may be legitimate to exclude observations in this way but the procedure obviously has considerable dangers; at the worst any data points which do not fit the analyst's model could simply be thrown out. There must therefore be a good reason for doing it; for example, reasons why this particular observation may not be a valid one, perhaps poor excavation procedure or a very small excavated sample.

In this case we will suppose that there is no reason to reject the first data point; it is therefore necessary to find a model which fits all the data, obviously in this case some sort of curvilinear relationship. Examination of the original scattergram and knowledge of other similar cases (cf. Hodder and Orton 1976, Renfrew 1977) suggests that an exponential curve might be appropriate. As we have said, it is much more straightforward to fit the regression in a linear form than in the original curvilinear one, so a transformation must be carried out. Reference to the account given above indicates that an exponential curve may be linearised by logging the y axis, in other words by working with the logarithms of the original y values (see table 10.3).

Table 10.3. Density and logged density of a certain type of Mesoamerican obsidian for sites at varying distances from the source.

Density (y)	Logged density ($\log y$)	Density (y)	Logged density ($\log y$)
5.01	0.6998	0.447	-0.3497
1.91	0.2810	0.347	-0.4597
1.91	0.2810	0.239	-0.6216
2.24	0.3502	0.186	-0.7305
1.20	0.0792	0.126	-0.8996
1.10	0.0414		

We can now calculate the regression using the transformed y values:

$$n = 11 \qquad\qquad \Sigma x_i y_i = -161.865$$
$$\Sigma x_i = 413 \qquad\qquad \Sigma y_i = -1.3285$$
$$(\Sigma x_i)^2 = 170569 \qquad (\Sigma y_i)^2 = 1.7649$$
$$\Sigma x_i^2 = 20407 \qquad\qquad \Sigma y_i^2 = 2.8412$$

$$b = \frac{[(11 \times (-161.865)] - [413 \times (-1.3285)]}{(11 \times 20407) - 170569}$$

$$= \frac{-1231.6795}{53908} = -0.0229$$

$$a = \frac{-1.3285 - (-0.0229 \times 413)}{11} = 0.739$$

Thus the regression equation is:

$$\log \hat{y} = 0.739 = 0.0229x$$

$$r = \frac{[11 \times (-161.865)] - [413 \times (-1.3285)]}{\sqrt{\{[(11 \times 20407) - 170569][(11 \times 2.8412) - 1.7649]\}}}$$

$$= \frac{-1231.6795}{\sqrt{(53908 \times 29.488)}} = -0.9769$$

$$r^2 = -0.9769^2 = 0.9543$$

It is obvious that an exponential relationship fits the data far better than a simple linear one. The r^2 value indicates that over 95 % of the variation in logged obsidian density is related to distance from the source when the fall-off is postulated to be an exponential one; in fact, no other fall-off function fits as well. Obviously though we should now look at the scattergram for the transformed relationship and the associated residual plot (see figures 10.12 and 13).

It is clear from examination of these plots that the fit of the line to the data along its length is much better. The previous under- and overprediction have been removed and the distribution of the residuals is much closer to the amorphous scatter to be expected when the regression assumptions are met. There remains, however, a slight suggestion of heteroscedasticity and autocorrelation in the residuals; they would probably deserve further investigation in a real study. It is worth noting that this slight indication was completely swamped in the first version of the regression by the nonlinearity.

The main potential problem with this or any other transformation is in interpretation. The regression equation $\log y = 0.739 - 0.0229x$

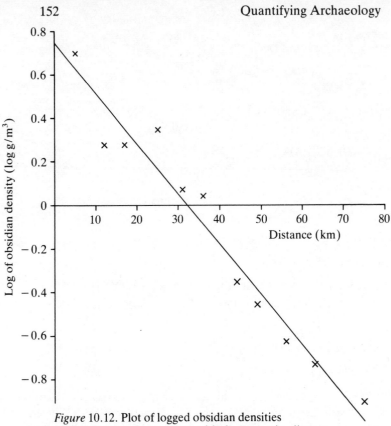

Figure 10.12. Plot of logged obsidian densities against distance from source with the regression line $\log \hat{y} = 0.739 - 0.0229x$ superimposed.

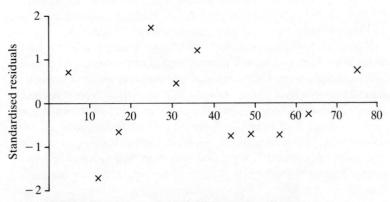

Figure 10.13. Standardised residual logged obsidian densities against distance from source.

means that there is a decrease of 0.0229 in log y for a unit increase in x. It is all too easy to forget that the transformation has been carried out and to discuss the results as if it had not. By taking antilogs it is possible to put the regression line back on the original scattergram as the appropriate exponential curve (see figure 10.14). But although this may be intuitively helpful – it puts you back in touch with the 'real' data – it tends to emphasise the point that straight-line relationships are easier to understand and it is easier to pick up deviations from them.

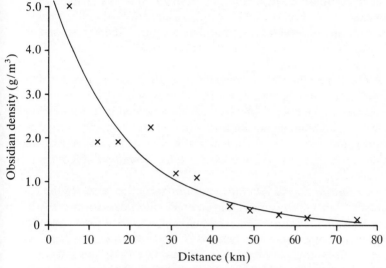

Figure 10.14. Plot of obsidian density against distance from source with the anti-logged version of the regression line log $\hat{y} = 0.739 - 0.0229x$ superimposed.

2. *Heteroscedasticity*. It is now necessary to turn to the question of heteroscedasticity and methods of stabilising the error variance to make it homoscedastic. As with other violations of the regression assumptions, heteroscedasticity will emerge clearly from examination of raw data scattergrams and residual plots. There are two rather different ways in which it often arises, those illustrated above in figure 10.4. In figure 10.4(a) dispersion of the observations around the line increases as the value of the independent variable increases. This is the type of situation which often arises in studies of the relationship between settlement size and population size; for settlements with larger populations there is much greater variation in their surface area than for those with small populations (see for

example Carothers and McDonald 1979). In 10.4(b) dispersion around the line decreases for higher valued observations, essentially because there are very few data points with high values. This might occur, for example, in studies involving the sizes of sites at the top of a settlement hierarchy, where the small number of sites at the very top may well have sizes very markedly larger than the rest.

In this second case we might again want to consider the question of whether any of the larger observations are 'outliers' which it might be appropriate to remove from the analysis. If not, then logging one or both variables will have the effect of 'pulling back' the extreme observations so that they are closer to the rest, and as a result it is very likely that the variances along the line will be equalised.

More generally, if the dispersion along the line is proportional to x we can use *weighted* least-squares regression techniques, varying the weight or influence of particular data points on the regression results. This topic is outside the scope of this text, but weighted regression techniques are now available on the MINITAB package and are described in the MINITAB *Student Handbook* (Ryan *et al* 1985).

3. *Autocorrelation.* The presence of correlation between the residuals from a regression should emerge quite clearly from study of the relevant scattergram and residual plot, but a test for it may also be carried out, using the Durbin–Watson statistic (see, for example, Chatterjee and Price 1977). Consideration of this statistic is probably only sensible if the data are collected in the sequential numerical order of the xs, for example in a time sequence.

Often the presence of correlated errors suggests that there is some other variable having an effect on the dependent, y, as well as the x variable already in the model. If this is the case it will be necessary to try adding other explanatory variables to the model which your knowledge of the situation suggests might be relevant to the apparent autocorrelation; the regression will then be a multiple one (see next chapter).

Very often autocorrelation is related to the distribution in time or across space of the observations: adjacent observations in time or space tend to have similar residuals. In these circumstances the inclusion in the analysis of a further independent variable which seems substantive to the problem and which varies in relation to time or space may well remove the autocorrelation effect.

Often, however, the autocorrelation is intrinsic to the spatial or temporal trend and it is then necessary to devise an appropriate transformation to take it into account. Let us consider an example. An intensive investigation of an area of the south western United States has produced information on the density of settlement sites per km^2 for a succession of chronological phases (table 10.4). The questions that arise are how does site density change with time and how good is the fit of the data to this proposed relationship?

Table 10.4. Number of settlement sites per square kilometre for a succession of chronological phases in an area of the south-western United States (data from Plog 1974).

Time period (years)	Sites per km^2	Time period (years)	Sites per km^2
0-50	0.25	300-350	1.05
50-100	0.25	350-400	1.00
100-150	0.55	400-450	1.15
150-200	0.60	450-500	1.30
200-250	0.95	500-550	1.65
250-300	1.00		

Before starting the analysis it should be noted that our chronology variable is in terms of intervals rather than fixed points so that we have some measurement error in this variable. For the purpose of this example I propose to assume that all the sites of a given phase were in occupation at the midpoint of that phase so that we can take the midpoint as a fixed value.

The scattergram of these data with the regression line superimposed is shown in figure 10.15. The equation for the line is

$$\hat{y} = 0.191 + 0.0025x$$

It tells us that the site density increases by 0.25 sites/km^2 every 100 years. The coefficient of determination, or r^2, value is 0.932, indicating that 93.2% of the variation in site density is associated with the time trend, and thus that the fit of the data to the regression relationship is extremely close.

But can we accept this at its face value, or is it misleading? The distribution of the points around the regression line suggests the possibility of autocorrelation in the residuals, although it is not great enough to produce a significant value for the Durbin–Watson statistic. It does, however, point towards a substantive problem with the analysis since a glance at the relation between the points and the line suggests that there is some variation in the difference between adjacent points, despite the extremely high r^2 value and its indication of a very close fit between regression and data. How does this arise?

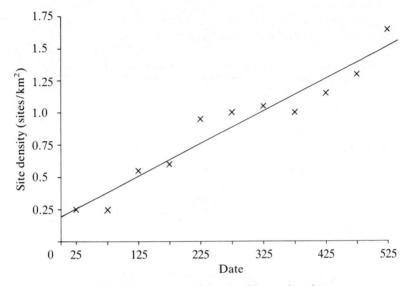

Figure 10.15. Scattergram of site densities against date.

It is highly likely that in cases such as this one many of the sites occupied in one period will also be occupied in the subsequent one, and quite probably the one after as well. Thus, the observations are not independent of one another because that for one period will be related to that for the previous one. The result of this process of accumulation is that when the regression tells us that there is a constant rate of increase of 0.25 sites/km² every 100 years, with an r^2 value of 93.2%, it may be giving a very misleading impression of the rate of change over time, how constant it is and the goodness-of-fit of the data to it.

To remove this accumulation effect, instead of regressing the original density values against the time sequence we can calculate the difference between the density of a given phase and that of the preceding one, for all phases, and plot this against the time sequence; in other words, our new definition of density change is not the original y_i values of the observations but the $y_i - y_{i-1}$ values of them (resulting in the loss of the first observation from consideration). The resulting scattergram is shown in figure 10.16. It is not,

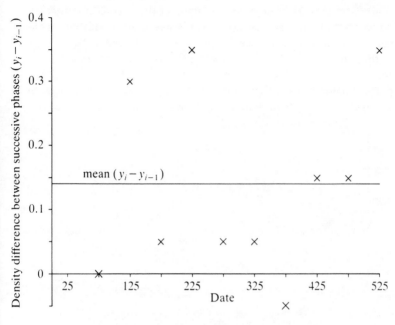

Figure 10.16. Plot of density differences between
successive phases against the chronological sequence.

of course, a regression like others we have seen since the vertical
axis is in terms of increments of change between one phase and the
next and we are expecting the line to be a horizontal one. That is to
say, if there really was a constant rate of change through time with
a close fit to the data, as the original regression and r^2 imply, then
the difference between each phase and the preceding one should be
virtually constant throughout the period: it will be represented by
the mean of the $y_i - y_{i-1}$ differences and there should be negligible
variation around this value. In fact, as the scattergram shows, there
is a great deal of variation, demonstrating how much the rate of
change in site density from phase to phase varies during the course
of the period. Thus, it appears that the original regression does
indeed give a totally misleading impression of the way in which site
density changes with time and the closeness with which the relationship defined fits the data.

Looking at the changes between adjacent points in this way
shows clearly the variation in rates of change but it does not give us
a new overall picture of the relationship between site density and
time or the extent to which it is almost constant, as the original

regression implies. One way of looking at the overall relationship between the two is to use not the original density and time measures, nor just the difference between adjacent points, but to look at the differences between all points; that is to say, we measure the time difference and the site density difference between all possible pairs of data points and plot one against the other. The scattergram is shown in figure 10.17 with the regression line superimposed.

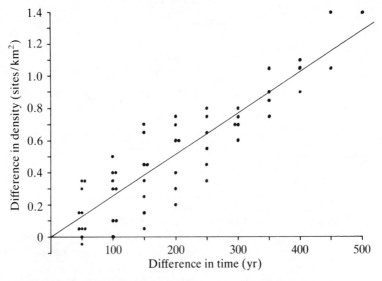

Figure 10.17. Settlement density differences between all pairs of phases plotted against the time difference between the two phases.

The slope is almost identical to that of the original regression, as indeed it should be, but we now have a much less misleading picture of the goodness-of-fit of the data to the relationship. The variation in density between adjacent phases illustrated in the previous scattergram is shown in the range of y values for $x = 50$; the range of variation in density differences for phases 150 years apart is even greater. All this is reflected in an r^2 value of 78.9% compared with the 93.2% of the original regression.

Thus it appears that the rate of change in settlement density in this area varied considerably during the period in question and was not the constant that it first appeared. This result raises a further set of archaeological questions concerning the reasons behind these varying growth rates. Even here care is necessary, however; there are signs of heteroscedasticity in the variances and there is still a tendency for adjacent density difference residuals to be correlated with one another, as witnessed in this case by the fact that the value of the Durbin–Watson autocorrelation statistic for these data is statistically significant at the 5 % level.

Finally, it should be mentioned that the procedure of taking differences in this way is illuminating in the context of this particular problem, but it should not be taken as a universally appropriate recipe for overcoming problems of this kind.

The preceding discussion of some of the problems which can arise with least-squares regression analysis and the methods which may be employed to try and overcome them has introduced some of the complexities of the method, although even so it has barely scratched the surface. The aim has been to show that the object of using the technique is not to calculate mechanically two or three coefficients which simply put a number on what we knew already, but to obtain information about patterning in our data which would not otherwise be apparent. In this modern approaches to normal-theory based regression are similar to the exploratory data analysis approach, with its emphasis on distinguishing the 'rough' from the 'smooth' in a relationship. Before turning to the EDA approach to regression, however, it is necessary to comment briefly on one aspect of least-squares regression which has not so far been mentioned.

Statistical Inference
In our account of regression and correlation we have only been concerned with analysing the data at hand and describing the form and strength of the relationship between the two variables of interest in a particular data set. It is, of course, possible to use statistical inference in a regression context, when our data are a genuine random sample of some population or can be conceived of as a random sample of some hypothetical population. It may then be meaningful to make statements to the effect, for example, that a particular value for the correlation coefficient is statistically significant at some given level, i.e. that it differs significantly from a correlation value of zero.

More often than not in archaeological cases we are not interested in such questions but simply in the data at hand, or in making comparisons with other data sets, which may or may not benefit from testing for statistical significance. Furthermore, it is arguable how often archaeological regression data meet the necessary re-

quirements for statistical inference. For these reasons regression
and correlation significance tests are not included here; they may
be found in any of the standard textbooks (e.g. Blalock 1972).

ROBUST REGRESSION:

THE EXPLORATORY DATA ANALYSIS APPROACH

The EDA approach rejects the standard forms of regression for the
same reason as it rejects the use of the mean and standard deviation
in describing the distribution of single variables: they are both
unduly affected by the values of extreme cases in the data set. The
argument is that the description of the relationship between two
variables should be *robust* and not influenced by extremes, which,
as we have noted before, are almost bound to be atypical. This is a
good argument as far as it goes but it is worth noting that the various
transformations discussed above can reduce the influence of extreme observations in least-squares regression and also make the
data conform more closely to the specifications of the regression
model. To resort to the use of EDA methods at the first sign that the
data do not meet the assumptions of standard regression analysis
may actually result in a loss of information; or rather, not all the
information present in the data may emerge. In the autocorrelation
case-study described above it would actually have been positively
misleading not to consider the substantive implications of the
suggestion of autocorrelation which emerged from the first analysis.

Nevertheless, where robust description of a relationship is required, as it often will be, then the EDA alternative to least-squares
regression known as the *Tukey line* may be used. Like the EDA
approach to single variable description it is based on the median
rather than the mean because the median is a resistant measure;
compared with least-squares regression it also has the virtue of
simplicity.

The first step is to divide the observations into three roughly
equal sized groups, based on their values on the x axis; in effect,
those with small, medium and large x values. Once this has been
done the median of the x values and the median of the y values in
the first and last groups are obtained. From this point on there are
two different ways of arriving at the Tukey line.

The first method is a direct graphical one and involves establishing the position of the median x and y values of the first and last
groups of observations on the scattergram, joining them up with a
straightedge, and then moving the straightedge up or down parallel
to this line until half the data points are above the line and half

below (Hartwig and Dearing 1979, 35).

The alternative is to use arithmetical methods to calculate the slope and intercept of the line, where the equation for the line is the same as in least-squares regression, $\hat{y} = a + bx$, but the basis of calculating the coefficients is different:

$$b = \frac{(\text{median } y_3 - \text{median } y_1)}{(\text{median } x_3 - \text{median } x_1)}$$

where median y_3 means the median y value in the third group of observations, that with the largest x values; median y_1 means the median y value in the first group of observations, that with the smallest x values; median x_3 means the median x value in the third group of observations; median x_1 means the median x value in the first group of observations.

a = the median of the values d_i, where $d_i = y_i - bx_i$

Once the coefficients have been calculated the equation can be written and the line plotted in the usual way.

It is helpful to illustrate the procedure with an example (see figure 10.18), a hypothetical study from Mesoamerica of the relation between settlement sizes and the quantity of imported obsidian found at those settlements. It is fairly characteristic of the type of situation in which a Tukey line might be employed, in that the data do not appear to meet the requirements of least-squares regression especially well; in particular, there are a couple of outlying observations, only to be expected in a study involving settlement sizes, which would be likely to have an excessive influence on the coefficients of an ordinary regression; in other words, the regression relationship defined would not really be relevant to the bulk of the observations.

The application of the graphical method of obtaining the Tukey line is illustrated on the scattergram (figure 10.18). There are five data points in each of the three groups; in the third group the same point has both the median x and median y value, in the first group this is not the case. In this particular example the line joining the two medians does itself have half the data points below it and half above it so there is no need to move the straightedge to any other position; the line joining the two medians is the Tukey line required.

For the arithmetic method we have

$$b = \frac{(73.0 - 32.0)}{(42.5 - 7.0)} = \frac{41}{35.5} = 1.15$$

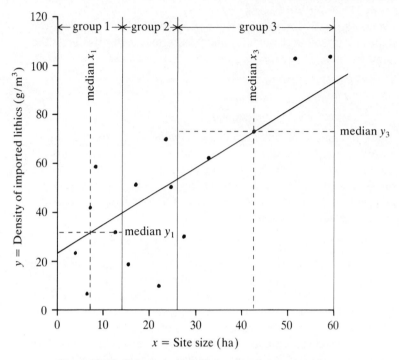

Figure 10.18. Calculation of a Tukey line for a scatterplot of densities of imported lithics at a series of sites in Mesoamerica, against the size of the sites where they occur.

Finding the intercept value is more tedious, since we must use the formula

$$d_i = y_i - 1.15x_i$$

to obtain the d values of all the points before we can find the median d value. As an example, for the point with the lowest y value

$$d = 7 - (1.15 \times 6.5) = -0.48$$

For that with the highest y value

$$d = 104 - (1.15 \times 59) = 36.15$$

The median d value is 23.9, and a glance at the scattergram confirms the correctness of this as the intercept value. Thus the equation for the Tukey line is

$$\hat{y}_i = 23.9 + 1.15x_i$$

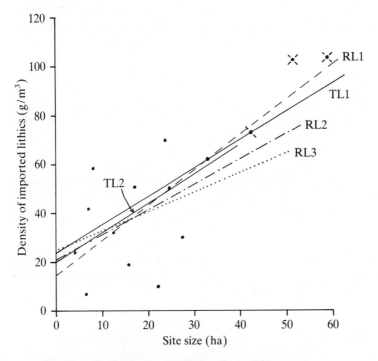

Figure 10.19. Comparison of Tukey lines and least-squares regression lines for all the data and with large observations deleted: TL1 is the Tukey line for all data; TL2 is the Tukey line for data with the 3 largest observations deleted; RL1 is the least-squares regression line for all data; RL2 is the least-squares regression line with the 2 largest observations deleted; and RL3 is the least-squares regression line with the 3 largest observations deleted.

This tells us that from a starting point of 23.9 there is an increase in lithic density of 1.15 g/m^3 of earth for each one-hectare increase in site size.

This line will be considerably more robust than the corresponding least-squares regression in that removal of the top two or three cases from consideration will have a much less drastic effect on the form of the relationship for the data set as a whole. That is to say, in the case under consideration the rate of increase in lithic density indicated by the Tukey line equation applies to the bulk of the cases and is not just a result of the difference between the biggest sites and the rest. Even if the largest sites are removed it has little effect on the rate of increase in lithic density with increasing site size indicated by the Tukey line, whereas the effect on the corresponding least-squares line is considerable (see figure 10.19).

As Hartwig and Dearing (1979, 35) point out, in many cases the basic idea of carrying out such forms of analysis as fitting a line is to define general patterns (the smooth) and distinguish them from deviations from the patterns (the rough); a resistant characterisation of the smooth is likely to keep the distinction between the smooth and the rough as clear as possible.

EXERCISES

10.1. Investigate the relationship between obsidian percentage and distance from source for the following lithic assemblages using regression techniques to specify its form and strength.

Distance	% Obsidian	Distance	% Obsidian	Distance	% Obsidian
12	98	85	21	210	8
25	92	82	44	233	16
67	77	112	56	300	10
30	67	150	33	329	5
42	39	154	15	381	8

10.2. Many recent processual studies in archaeology have considered changing population to be a crucial variable. Population is often inferred on the basis of settlement size. In this case the relationship between settlement area and population has been investigated in modern villages in the research area as a basis for making population estimates for the past. The data (from Carothers and McDonald 1979) are as follows:

Settlement size (ha)	Population	Settlement size (ha)	Population
0.6	20	3.7	300
1.0	70	4.0	250
1.1	100	4.5	500
1.2	130	5.4	270
1.6	120	5.9	190
1.9	170	6.1	630
2.3	195	6.4	650
3.0	190	8.9	310
3.1	210	10.0	730
3.3	360	12.0	850

What is the relationship between settlement size and population? How good is it? Do the data present any problems for this kind of analysis? If so, is there anything to be inferred from them?

10.3. Shaft length and the number of tooth marks are recorded on a set of ten animal bones from a palaeolithic cave:

Shaft length (cm)	4	4	5	6	7	8	9	11	13	14
No. of tooth marks	0	0	1	2	0	5	0	2	7	0

(a) Plot the data, and fit a Tukey line, superimposing it on the plot. (b) Calculate the regression line for these data. Explain your choice of dependent variable. Plot the regression line on the graph from part (a). Are the regression assumptions satisfied? (c) Briefly comment on the interpretation of the two lines drawn in parts (a) and (b).

Eleven

Facing Up to Complexity:
Multiple Correlation and Regression

By the end of chapter 10 considerable complexities had been introduced into the basic concepts of regression and correlation with which we began. Nevertheless, the treatment considered only the relationship between two variables, in general one dependent and one independent variable.

As we saw in chapter 7, it is very often necessary to deal with more variables than this if we wish to obtain any real understanding of a given situation. Thus, to take a topic from the previous chapter, we may be interested in why the quantities of some imported material vary between a number of different settlements. There most of the examples concerned themselves only with distance from the source as the reason for the variation. The last example, however, was a hypothetical investigation of the way in which imported material quantity on a settlement might relate to the settlement's size. Any real study, of course, would want to take into account the effect of both distance from source and settlement size on the density of imported material (cf. Sidrys 1977). As we will see, this cannot be done by simply carrying out two separate bivariate regression analyses; all three variables must be included in a *multiple regression analysis,* in which there will be a single dependent – material quantity – and two independents. In general in multiple regression analysis there will always be a single dependent variable but there may be any number of independents – variables which we think may have some effect on variation in the dependent, on the basis of some hypothesis we have developed.

This added complexity has an effect on the practicalities of the way we go about our analyses. Whereas virtually all the techniques which have been presented up to now can be carried out quite straightforwardly with a simple calculator, multiple regression and the majority of the other techniques to be described in the next few chapters require the use of a computer to carry them out, except in the simplest and most trivial cases, because of the complexity of the

166

calculations involved. This complexity is associated with a significantly higher order of mathematical difficulty, in particular involving the use of matrix algebra.

It seemed inappropriate in a text such as this to present an introduction to matrix algebra and then to go through the mathematics of the techniques in detail. It would have taken up a large amount of space and moved the text up to a level of mathematical sophistication unsuitable for most of the intended audience. Nevertheless, there is a price to be paid for this. Whereas, up to now, we have seen the detailed workings of virtually all the methods described, in much of what follows the detailed workings will remain a 'black box'. This obviously has its dangers and pitfalls, into which many archaeologists have fallen in the past (cf. Thomas 1978); for those who intend to be serious practitioners of these techniques there is no alternative to acquiring the detailed knowledge and (rather than 'or') seeking advice from professional statisticians. However, the view taken here is that it is possible to obtain an understanding of the theoretical structure of the techniques without a detailed knowledge of the mathematics involved, and thus to gain a valid intuitive insight into them and their role.

The chapter begins with a brief introduction to the basics of the multiple regression model. A more detailed examination of various aspects of multiple regression and correlation then follows; this is done with reference to an archaeological example, so that the discussion does not become too theoretical and the implications of the techniques for archaeological data analysis become apparent.

THE MULTIPLE REGRESSION MODEL

The principles of multiple regression are the same as for simple regression. In general, we want to estimate a regression equation by fitting it to some empirical data. It will be assumed that the relationship is linear and we will be using the least-squares criterion to obtain the best fit of the regression to the data. Whereas in the simple regression case the equation was $y = a + bx$, now it is

$$y = a + b_1x_1 + b_2x_2 + \ldots + b_kx_k$$

In the simple regression case we were fitting a line to our two-dimensional scatter of points (figure 11.1). If, for the sake of visualisation, we take the simplest multiple regression case, when we have two independent variables, we can see that what we are trying to fit is a plane rather than a line (figure 11.2). Once we move beyond three variables the situation becomes very difficult to visualise but the principle remains the same: we will be trying to fit a plane not of two dimensions, as in the case illustrated, but of as many dimensions are there are independent variables.

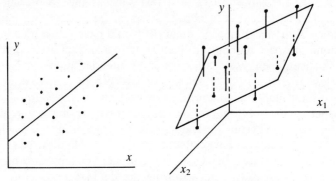

Figure 11.1 (*left*) Scattergram of the relationship between a dependent variable (y) and an independent (x) with the regression line drawn in.
Figure 11.2 (*right*) Scattergram of the relationship between a dependent variable (y) and two independents (x_1 and x_2): the regression *line* has become a regression *plane*, which is drawn in. (After Blalock 1972.)
(After Blalock 1972.)

To return to our three-variable case. Where $x_1 = x_2 = 0$ we have $y = a$, which is the height at which the regression plane crosses the y axis. The b coefficients work as follows. Imagine a vertical plane perpendicular to the x_2 axis, projected so that it intersects the regression plane (figure 11.3). At the point of intersection with the

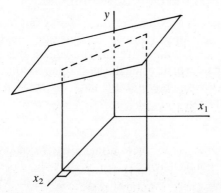

Figure 11.3. A vertical plane at right angles to x_2 projected upwards until it intersects the regression plane: the line of intersection represents the regression of y on x_1.

regression plane this vertical plane is simply a straight line on the regression surface. Because the vertical plane, and therefore the line of intersection, is perpendicular to the x_2 axis, all the points on it have the same value for the x_2 variable. The slope of this line is b_1 in the multiple regression equation; that is to say, it is the slope of the regression of y on x_1, since for this particular line all the x_2 values are constant. In the same way, if we construct a vertical plane perpendicular to the x_1 axis, then the line along which it intersects the regression plane will have slope b_2 and will represent the regression of y on x_2 with x_1 held constant. In multiple regression the aim is to find the a, b_1 and b_2 coefficients which produce the regression plane giving the best fit to our data on the least-squares criterion. We will see below the way in which the overall goodness-of-fit of this plane to the data may be measured using the multiple correlation coefficient.

But multiple regression and correlation are not just about finding the overall effect of a set of variables on a dependent variable. As has been implied already, we are also interested in the effect of our independent variables one at a time, with the others held constant. The laboratory experimenter can achieve this situation in reality by manipulating the conditions of his experiment. Archaeologists obviously cannot do this; we have to control our experiments, insofar as this is possible, during the analysis phase. To control in this way we have to use partial coefficients, as we did in the case of dichotomous variables, but here we are using partial correlation and partial regression coefficients.

PARTIAL CORRELATION

We will start with partial correlation, which is the more important of the two, and illustrate what is involved with an example. We will suppose that a programme of survey and excavation has given us information on the sizes (in terms of area) of a number of settlements in a region of Mexico. We are interested in the reasons for the variation and suspect that they may have something to do with the available agricultural resources in the vicinity (cf. Brumfiel 1976). Information is therefore collected on the area of available agricultural land around each of the sites, and on the productivity of the land (see table 11.1).

In terms of a regression analysis:
Dependent (y) variable = site size
First independent (x_1) variable = area of available
  agricultural land

Table 11.1. Information about site size, area
of available agricultural land and land productivity (in arbitrary units) for 28 hypothetical Formative Period sites in Mexico.

	Site size (ha)	Available agricultural land (km^2)	Relative productivity index
1	30.0	17.9	0.75
2	33.0	12.7	0.87
3	37.0	17.6	0.71
4	42.0	6.0	0.85
5	42.0	21.6	0.83
6	44.9	29.4	0.73
7	47.0	19.6	0.89
8	53.2	29.0	0.87
9	55.0	21.4	0.72
10	55.0	50.8	0.89
11	55.2	31.8	0.90
12	60.0	24.8	0.81
13	62.0	26.4	0.92
14	63.1	34.0	0.94
15	64.5	39.1	0.99
16	65.0	35.4	0.82
17	67.7	34.8	0.96
18	69.7	53.0	0.91
19	74.0	54.2	0.94
20	75.0	73.3	1.01
21	76.0	95.9	1.09
22	77.0	66.8	1.05
23	80.5	51.0	1.23
24	86.0	61.2	1.06
25	88.0	72.5	1.29
26	90.0	54.7	1.22
27	95.3	89.9	1.00
28	99.0	89.9	1.26

Second independent (x_2) variable = relative productivity
   of land

We can start by carrying out a simple regression of site size on
available agricultural land, and obtain the following results

$\hat{y} = 35.4 + 0.656x_1$

$r_{yx_1} = 0.864$

$r^2_{yx_1} = 0.746$

The corresponding scattergram is shown in figure 11.4. In words

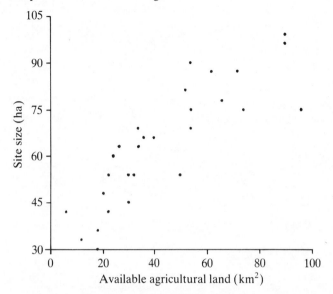

Figure 11.4. Scattergram of site size against area of available land, from the data in table 11.1.

this result states that where there is no available land, site size is estimated to be 35.4 ha; and that for every increase in available land of 1 km^2, site size increases by 0.656 ha. The correlation between the two variables is 0.864. Given that available land is the independent variable and site size the dependent, we can say that variation in the area of available agricultural land accounts for 74.6% of the variation in site size.

Similarly, if we carry out a regression of site size on land productivity we have:

$$\hat{y} = -28.9 + 97.9x_2$$
$$r_{yx_2} = 0.832$$
$$r^2_{yx_2} = 0.693$$

The scattergram is shown in figure 11.5, and the result suggests that for every increase in the productivity index of 1.0 there is an increase of 97.9 ha in site size. Correlation is 0.832 and variation in productivity accounts for 69.3% of the variation in site size.

Together the two r^2 figures we have just seen appear to suggest that our two independents – area of available land and land productivity – account for $74.6 + 69.3 = 143.9\%$ of the variation in site size. Clearly this gives us grounds for suspicion! But what is actually

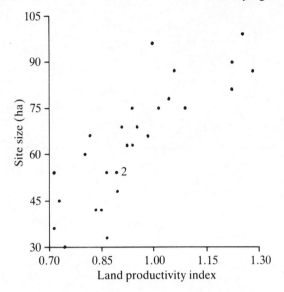

Figure 11.5. Scattergram of site size against productivity index of available land, from the data in table 11.1.

wrong with the procedure?

Suppose we ask whether land productivity and available land area are related to each other. They might be, if, for example, the geomorphological conditions in which larger areas of soil were produced were different from those in which smaller areas originated; the contrast between large alluvial plains and small colluvium-filled basins might be an instance of this. The point may be investigated by regressing x_2 (productivity) on x_1 (available land area):

$$\hat{x}_2 = 0.74 + 0.0048x_1$$

$$r_{x_2x_1} = 0.738$$

$$r^2_{x_2x_1} = 0.545$$

A scattergram (with productivity as the vertical axis) is shown in figure 11.6, and it appears from this result that 54.5% of the variation in productivity is in fact accounted for by variation in the area of the land concerned.

This poses problems for the initial two regressions we carried out since it means that they were not independent of each other. The second regression, y on x_2, was partly also a regression of y on x_1, because x_2 and x_1 are both related to each other. This situation

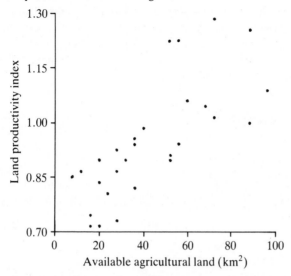

Figure 11.6. Scattergram of area of available land against productivity index of land, from the data in table 11.1.

raises two difficulties. First, we cannot tell how much of the variation in site size is related to available land area, how much to land productivity, and how much to the two of them together. Secondly, it means that, as we suspected, the conclusion that the two independents together account for about 144% of the variation in site size was indeed incorrect: because it included an element of double counting. We cannot simply add the two separate r^2 values together because the two overlap with one another as a result of the relationship between x_1 (available land area) and x_2 (land productivity). It is in the solution of these problems that partial and multiple correlation have their role.

It is convenient here to make a slight change in notation and to designate our dependent variable, y, as x_0. Our partial correlation coefficient can then be expressed as e.g. $r_{01.23}$ which reads as the correlation between variables 0 and 1 with the effects of variables 2 and 3 being controlled. This is much neater than having to include xs and ys in the subscript. Of the two variables before the point, the first is usually the dependent and the second the independent variable currently of interest. Any number of independent variables can be controlled; the number being controlled is known as the order of correlation, so that with two controls it is a second-order correlation coefficient, with no controls it is a zero-order coefficient.

It is important to note that with the partial correlation coefficient e.g. $r_{01.2}$ we remove the effect not just of the relation between x_0 and x_2, but also of the relationship between x_1 and x_2.

The first-order partial correlation coefficients, i.e. those holding only one other variable under control, can be obtained by means of the following formula:

$$r_{ij.k} = \frac{r_{ij} - (r_{ik})(r_{jk})}{\sqrt{(1 - r_{ik}^2)}\sqrt{(1 - r_{jk}^2)}}$$

$$\text{e.g. } r_{01.2} = \frac{r_{01} - (r_{02})(r_{12})}{\sqrt{(1 - r_{02}^2)}\sqrt{(1 - r_{12}^2)}}$$

If we want to obtain second-order partials the procedure is essentially the same:

$$r_{ij.kl} = \frac{r_{ij.k} - (r_{il.k})(r_{jl.k})}{\sqrt{(1 - r_{il.k}^2)}\sqrt{(1 - r_{jl.k}^2)}}$$

It is easily possible to see that computation of these becomes very tedious if you have to do it by hand because of the large numbers of coefficients which have to be calculated. In fact, they are easily available from computer packages such as s p s s-x (see appendix 2).

At this point, now that we have seen in the abstract what a partial correlation coefficient is and how it may be calculated, it is important to return to the example with which we started, to see how the partial coefficients may be obtained in practice and how they differ from the zero-order coefficients seen above.

We need to investigate the relationship between site size and area of available agricultural land, holding land productivity constant; and between site size and land productivity holding area of available agricultural land constant. To do this we simply put the relevant numbers in the expression for the first-order partial:

$$r_{01.2} = \frac{r_{01} - (r_{02})(r_{12})}{\sqrt{(1 - r_{02}^2)}\sqrt{(1 - r_{12}^2)}}$$

$$= \frac{0.864 - (0.832)(0.738)}{\sqrt{(1 - 0.832^2)}\sqrt{(1 - 0.738^2)}}$$

$$= 0.6678$$

$$r_{01.2}^2 = 0.6678^2 = 0.446$$

This figure of just over 44% of the remaining variation in site size accounted for by variation in the area of available land, once variation in productivity has been taken into account, compares with the figure of nearly 75 % accounted for by area of available land when productivity was not controlled, in the zero-order correlation analysis.

The corresponding procedure is now carried out for the relationship between site size and productivity with available land area held constant. From the usual expression for first-order partials we have

$$r_{02.1} = \frac{r_{02} - (r_{01})(r_{21})}{\sqrt{(1 - r_{01}^2)}\sqrt{(1 - r_{21}^2)}}$$

$$= \frac{0.832 - (0.864)(0.738)}{\sqrt{(1 - 0.864^2)}\sqrt{(1 - 0.738^2)}}$$

$$= 0.572$$

$$r_{02.1}^2 = 0.572^2 = 0.327$$

Thus, it can be seen that just over 32 % of the remaining variation in site size is accounted for by variation in land productivity when area of available land is held constant, i.e. when the effect of area of available land on the other two variables is taken into account. This compares with over 69 % accounted for by productivity when area of available land was not controlled.

It should be obvious from this example that any serious investigation of the relationships between variables cannot simply be left at the level of zero-order coefficients. Nevertheless, the analysis and understanding of the relations between large numbers of zero-order and partial correlation coefficients is a complex business; the procedures involved are the same as those shown in the examination of the Q coefficient. It is necessary to examine the differences in sign and magnitude between partials and zero-orders, to see whether the control variable(s) is suppressing, explaining or having no effect on the relations between the variables of interest. As before, it is clearly helpful to have definite hypotheses about relationships to investigate.

MULTIPLE CORRELATION

The previous section of this chapter concentrated on how to isolate the effect of individual variables in the context of a regression analysis with a number of independent variables. What we have not yet considered, however, is how we assess the overall effect of all the independents taken together on variation in the dependent. The multiple correlation coefficient (R) measures the goodness of fit of the least-squares regression surface as a whole to the dependent variable values. The square of the multiple correlation coefficient (R^2) indicates the percentage of the variation in the dependent variable accounted for by the least-squares surface.

This is all very well as a matter of definition, but how is the quantity, or its square, actually found, in the light of the problems we saw in the preceding section about adding together zero-order coefficients and the need to calculate partials. Clearly, as our example showed, the percentage of variation in the dependent accounted for by the regression overall cannot be simply the sum of the zero-order r^2 values, for the same reason – that of double counting.

At this point the obvious answer would seem to be that we sum the partials we have obtained to find the overall effect. But this too is incorrect. Whereas summing the zero-order values involves double counting, summing the partials has the converse problem that it is not sufficient. This is because each partial only gives us the effect of an individual variable by itself, with no influence from the other independent variables; so summing them only gives the total effect of all the individual variables taken alone on that part of the variation in the dependent which doesn't relate to any of the other independent variables. What is missing is that when independents are correlated with one another they will not only each have an individual effect on the dependent; there will also be an effect of the joint action of the relevant variables.

If we take the case of two independent variables, $r_{01.2}$ is concerned with the variation in x_0 not associated with x_2, and $r_{02.1}$ is concerned with the variation in x_0 not associated with x_1; however, because the two independents are intercorrelated, some of the variation in x_0 is accounted for by the joint variation of x_1 and x_2, and therefore is not included in the partials (cf. Johnston 1978, chapter 3). Accordingly, we need something different from any of the coefficients we have seen so far.

The formula for multiple R^2 for the three-variable case is:

$$R_{0.12}^2 = r_{01}^2 + r_{02.1}^2 (1 - r_{01}^2)$$

where $R_{0.12}^2$ is the multiple coefficient of determination between x_0 and both x_1 and x_2. It is the proportion of the variation in x_0 accounted for by the two independents both separately and together.

To obtain it we first let one of the independents do all the 'explaining' it can. This is the meaning of the r_{01}^2 term: it is the proportion of the variation in the dependent accounted for by the first independent. If the total variation in the dependent is defined as 1.0 then after the first independent has accounted for its share of the variation, the proportion remaining to be accounted for is $(1 - r_{01}^2)$. Now we see how much of the remaining variation in the dependent can be accounted for by the second independent and add this to the variation accounted for by the first, to obtain the overall effect of the two together. Why then is the second part of the formula $r_{02.1}^2(1 - r_{01}^2)$ and not simply $r_{02}^2(1 - r_{01}^2)$?

It is because by including the term r_{01}^2 we already have in the equation all the effect of the first variable. If x_1 and x_2, our independents, are correlated then there will be some effect of x_1 expressed in r_{02}^2, so if we used this in the equation we would again be making the mistake of double counting. We must remove any effect of x_1 on r_{02}^2 and we do this, of course, by controlling for it, and taking the partial $r_{02.1}^2$.

To make the argument more concrete it will be helpful at this point to return to our example and obtain the multiple R^2 value, i.e. establish the proportion of the variation in site size accounted for by the overall effect of area of available land and land productivity, acting both separately and together. In the course of this chapter we have already calculated the relevant quantities:

$$r_{01}^2 = 0.746$$
$$1 - r_{01}^2 = 0.254$$
$$r_{02.1}^2 = 0.327$$
$$R_{01.2}^2 = 0.746 + (0.327)(0.254)$$
$$= 0.746 + 0.083 = 0.829$$

That is to say, area of available land and land productivity altogether account for 82.9% of the variation in site size for this set of data, made up by letting area of available land account for all the variation it can – 74.6% – and letting land productivity 'explain' what it can of the remainder – 8.3%.

But we can break this down further, since as it stands we do not yet know how much of the 74.6% is the effect of area of available land alone and how much is the joint effect of this and land productivity together. The partial $r_{01.2}^2 = 0.446$ tells us that 44.6% of the variation in site size (x_0) not accounted for by land productivity (x_2) is accounted for by variation in available land area alone, i.e. 44.6% of the $(1 - r_{02}^2)$ value of 30.7%. To find out what proportion of the total variation in site size is accounted for by variation in available land alone we therefore calculate:

$$r_{01.2}^2(1 - r_{02}^2) = (0.446)(1 - 0.693) = 0.137$$

That is to say, 13.7% of the variation in site size is accounted for by variation in available land alone.

The corresponding quantity for land productivity has already been calculated in the course of obtaining the multiple R^2 value.

$$r_{02.1}^2(1 - r_{01}^2) = (0.327)(1 - 0.746) = 0.083$$

Thus 8.3% of the variation in site size is accounted for by productivity alone.

Given that overall multiple R^2 was 82.9%, and only $8.3 + 13.7 = 22\%$ is attributable to the separate effects of area of available land and land productivity, it appears that 60.9% of the variation in site size is accounted for by the joint effect of the two independent variables, in that larger areas of available land tend to have greater fertility.

In this case then, as in many empirical situations, there is a not inconsiderable degree of overlap in the effects of the two variables, so that the multiple R^2 is not very much larger than the largest single r^2 value. The opposite extreme, of course, is when the independent variables are actually uncorrelated with one another and then the R^2 formula reduces to

$$R_{01.2}^2 = r_{01}^2 + r_{02}^2$$

i.e. the variance accounted for is simply the sum of the two zero-order r^2 values. R^2 is obviously at its maximum in this situation, which is clearly preferable since it means that the two independents are each accounting for *different parts* of the variation in the dependent. When they are correlated, on the other hand, they are explaining the same variation and thus introduce ambiguity into our interpretations. This problem, which can have complex technical ramifications in regression analysis (see e.g. Chatterjee and Price 1977), is known as *collinearity* or *multicollinearity*.

One obvious way of recognising collinearity is by means of comparing the simple and multiple correlation coefficients. Suppose we have two independent variables, x_1 and x_2, and one dependent, x_0. If we work out first the zero-order r_{01}^2 and then the multiple $R_{0.12}^2$, the difference is the improvement in statistical explanation achieved by adding in the second independent variable. If this is very small it suggests that the second variable is strongly correlated with the first, or that it is simply having no effect on the dependent. Which of these two possibilities is the case may be established by looking at the value of r_{12}^2, the coefficient of determination between the two independents themselves; if this is large it confirms that collinearity exists.

One way of getting round this problem is simply to drop one of the independent variables from the analysis; another way is to make the independent variables uncorrelated, for example, by means of principal components analysis, and then to regress the dependent variable against the principal components; principal components will be examined below in chapter 13. On the other hand, we do not necessarily want to neglect or re-define the various relationships out of existence since they may themselves be quite informative, as in our site-size example.

THE MULTIPLE REGRESSION COEFFICIENT

It remains to look in a bit more detail at the multiple regression equation itself, a task postponed until now because of the greater importance of multiple and partial correlation.

It was stated at the beginning of the chapter, when the multiple regression model was introduced, that the slope coefficients (the bs) referred to the amount of change in the dependent for a given change in a specific independent, with the other independents held constant. In the light of our discussion of partial correlation it is clear that these slope coefficients represent something very similar. In fact, they are known as *partial regression coefficients*. The notation in the equation is also very similar, so that we have

$$\hat{x}_{0.1\ldots k} = a_{0.1\ldots k} + b_{01.2\ldots k}x_1 + b_{02.1,3\ldots k}x_2 + \ldots + b_{0k.1\ldots k-1}x_k$$

or in the two-variable case

$$\hat{x}_{0.12} = a_{0.12} + b_{01.2}x_1 + b_{02.1}x_2$$

a represents the intercept value, when the values of all the independent variables are zero.

The formulae for the a and b coefficients are:

$$a_{0.12} = \bar{x}_0 - b_{01.2}\bar{x}_1 - b_{02.1}\bar{x}_2$$

$$b_{01.2} = \frac{b_{01} - (b_{02})(b_{21})}{1 - b_{12}b_{21}}$$

It is easy to see that the formula for b is really very similar to that for partial r.

We now have a partial regression coefficient which indicates the absolute increase in our dependent variable associated with a unit increase in our first independent variable, the other independents being held constant, and, of course, we can do the same for all our independents.

In general, we will not actually have to do the calculation to obtain the quantities required above since multiple regression is usually a computer-based procedure. The multiple regression equation produced by the MINITAB program package (see below) for our example of site size regressed on area of available land and land productivity is

$$\hat{x}_0 = -1.87 + 0.416x_1 + 50.3x_2$$

If, for illustrative purposes, we calculate the coefficient for x_1 using the formula given above and the results of the bivariate regressions calculated earlier in this chapter for these variables, we have

$$b_{01.2} = \frac{0.656 - (97.9)(0.0048)}{1 - (114.0)(0.0048)}$$

$$= \frac{0.1861}{0.4528} = 0.411$$

Rounding error is responsible for the slight difference between this and the coefficient of 0.416 above.

The equation tells us that the value of site size is best predicted by assuming that when available land and land productivity are zero, site size is -1.87 ha, and that it increases thereafter by 0.416 ha for each 1 km^2 increase in available land and by another 50.3 ha for each unit increase in the productivity index.

Suppose, however, that we want to compare our slope coefficients so that we have a measure of the amount of increase/decrease in the dependent associated with a unit increase in each independent variable, in terms which are comparable from one variable to the next. This is likely to cause problems because the independent variables will almost certainly be measured on different scales; in the example given above, for instance, of the relationship between site size and land, available land was measured in square kilometres and productivity on an arbitrary scale with a much smaller range. In these circumstances it is meaningless to compare a unit change in one variable with a unit change in another.

If we are interested in such relative rates of change what we have to do is transform our b coefficients into what are known as *beta coefficients,* or *beta weights,* standardised partial regression coefficients. To do this we standardise each variable by dividing it by its standard deviation, in other words we obtain its Z score, and on the basis of these scores we obtain adjusted slopes which are comparable from one variable to the next. In mathematical symbols we obtain

$$Z_{x_i} = \frac{(x_i - \bar{x}_i)}{s_{x_i}}$$

This, of course, gives us a variable with mean $x_i = 0$ and $s_{x_i} = 1.0$. We then have a transformed regression equation, which for the two variable case is

$$\hat{Z}_{x_{0.12}} = \beta_{01.2}Z_{x_1} + \beta_{02.1}Z_{x_2}$$

As we are dealing with Z scores, the mean of every variable is zero, so that the a coefficient is also zero and therefore drops out of the equation.

Our standardised partial regression coefficients, or beta weights, thus indicate relative changes in variables on a standard scale. They are actually obtained through standardising the b coefficient by the ratio of the standard deviation of the two variables:

$$\beta_{01.2} = b_{01.2}\frac{s_{x_1}}{s_{x_0}}$$

or, more generally,

$$\beta_{ij.k} = b_{ij.k}\ \frac{s_j}{s_i}$$

This formula tells us the amount of change in the dependent produced by in this case a *standardised* change in one of the independents, when the others are controlled. Clearly, whether you use the ordinary b coefficient or the beta weight depends on whether you are interested in relative or absolute changes.

We can complete this section by calculating the multiple regression equation for our example using beta weights (not output by MINITAB but given by many other programs).

$$\beta_{01.2} = \frac{0.864 - (0.832)(0.738)}{1 - 0.545}$$

$$= 0.549$$

$$\beta_{02.1} = \frac{0.832 - (0.864)(0.738)}{1 - 0.545}$$

$$= 0.427$$

Thus we have

$$\hat{Z}_{x_{0.12}} = 0.549Z_{x_1} + 0.427Z_{x_2}$$

That is to say, according to the equation, for each increase of one standard deviation in area of available land there is a corresponding increase of 0.549 standard deviations in site size; and for each one standard deviation increase in productivity there is an increase of 0.427 standard deviations in site size. The sum of these two effects gives our best prediction of site size, measured in terms of standard deviations from its mean, on the basis of the least-squares criterion. Comparison of the coefficients of each of the two independent variables indicates that a given increase in area of available agricultural land has a greater effect on site size than a given increase in land productivity, a comparison which may now be made in a valid fashion because the scales of the two variables have both been converted into the same units – units of standard deviation from the mean of their distribution.

An interesting recent example of an analysis using such multiple regression techniques models the income of English manors given in Domesday Book in terms of the various resources of the manors for which data are also given (McDonald and Snooks 1985).

INTERPRETING MULTIPLE REGRESSION COMPUTER OUTPUT

In the preceding sections of this chapter much reference has been made to the fact that multiple regression is normally carried out by means of a computer, and virtually all the results for the example followed through in the course of the chapter were obtained by this means, which is why few calculations were presented. An enormous number of multiple regression programs is now available, all differing slightly from each other with regard to what is included in their output. The aim of the present section is to go through as an example the output from the multiple regression analysis of our example produced by the MINITAB multiple regression program, to briefly elucidate its various sections, relating them to the points which have been covered in the chapter. The output is shown in table 11.2. Much of it relates to questions of statistical inference, which, as we saw in the previous chapter, are not relevant to most archaeological uses of regression analysis.

The regression equation (1) we have already seen and it requires no further comment. The next section (2) repeats the values of the regression coefficients but gives further information about them.

Table 11.2. MINITAB computer print-out for regression of site size against area of available land and productivity, from the data in table 11.1. Numbers in parentheses refer to references in the text.

```
THE REGRESSION EQUATION IS                                          (1)
Y = -  1.87 + 0.416 X1 +   50.3 X2
```

	COLUMN	COEFFICIENT	ST. DEV. OF COEF.	T-RATIO = COEF/S.D.	
	--	-1.87	11.10	-0.17	(2)
X1	C2	0.41596	0.09286	4.48	
X2	C3	50.33	14.39	3.50	

```
THE ST. DEV. OF Y ABOUT REGRESSION LINE IS                         (3)
S = 8.107
WITH (  28- 3) =  25 DEGREES OF FREEDOM                             (4)

R-SQUARED = 83.0 PERCENT                                            (5)
R-SQUARED = 81.6 PERCENT, ADJUSTED FOR D.F.                         (6)
```

ANALYSIS OF VARIANCE

DUE TO	DF	SS	MS=SS/DF	
REGRESSION	2	7998.80	3999.40	
RESIDUAL	25	1643.21	65.73	(7)
TOTAL	27	9642.01		

FURTHER ANALYSIS OF VARIANCE
SS EXPLAINED BY EACH VARIABLE WHEN ENTERED IN THE ORDER GIVEN

DUE TO	DF	SS	
REGRESSION	2	7998.80	(8)
C2	1	7194.53	
C3	1	804.27	

	X1	Y	PRED. Y	ST.DEV.		(9)
ROW	C2	C1	VALUE	PRED. Y	RESIDUAL	ST.RES.
21	95.9	76.00	92.87	3.94	-16.87	-2.38RX
23	51.0	80.50	81.24	3.90	-0.74	-0.10 X
25	72.5	88.00	93.21	3.79	-5.21	-0.73 X
27	89.9	95.30	85.85	4.09	9.45	1.35 X

R DENOTES AN OBS. WITH A LARGE ST. RES.
X DENOTES AN OBS. WHOSE X VALUE GIVES IT LARGE INFLUENCE.

First of all the standard deviations of the coefficients; these would enable us to construct a confidence interval for an estimate of their value in the population from which the sample used in this particular analysis was drawn, if it were appropriate for us to do this (for the procedure involved see e.g. Blalock 1972, chapter 18; Ryan *et al.* 1985, 161–2).

Similarly, the next column, T-RATIO = COEF./S.D., taken together with the figure for the number of degrees of freedom two lines below, gives us the information to find out whether the various coefficients are significantly different from zero (see again Blalock 1972, chapter 18; Ryan *et al.* 161–2).

The next line, (3), the standard deviation of y (or x_0) about the regression line, refers to the variation of the actual y values round the regression line, (see chapter 9). The standard deviation of this distribution of points around the line is 8.107 in this case. Assuming a normal distribution of residuals around the regression (see chapter 10) this tells us that about 68% of them lie within 8.107 ha either side of their predicted value.

Any estimate of a population quantity in regression must be based not on the size of the sample, but on the number of degrees of freedom associated with it (4), or the estimate will be biased. One degree of freedom is lost in estimating the mean y value, and one each for every independent variable used as a predictor of the y value. In our site size example there were 28 observations and three degrees of freedom are lost: one each for the two independent variables and one for the estimate of the mean.

The R^2 value (5) has already been discussed at length; the adjusted version (6) takes into account the fact that the value is obtained from a sample of a given size, and that degrees of freedom are lost in the process of analysis, as described in the previous paragraph.

The next section (7), headed analysis of variance, provides the information to carry out an F test of the significance of the regression (Blalock 1972, chapter 18). Degrees of freedom have already been discussed. The meaning of the quantities in the sum of squares column has been outlined in the previous chapter, but is worth repetition in relation to this example. The *total* sum of squares is the sum of the squared deviations around the mean value of the dependent variable: $\Sigma(y_i - \bar{y})^2$. In this case it has a value of 9642.01 around the mean value of site size. The *regression* sum of squares is the amount of this total accounted for by the regression overall, using both independent variables – in this case 7998.8. The R^2 value, of course, is obtained by dividing this quantity by the total sum of squares. The *residual* sum of squares is the sum of the squared residuals around the regression line (or plane in this case): $\Sigma(y_i - \hat{y}_i)^2$. This is the variation not accounted for by the regression.

The final column, MS = SS/DF, is self-explanatory and provides the two quantities whose ratio is the F statistic.

The next section (8), further analysis of variance, gives a breakdown of the variation actually accounted for by the regression, in terms of the amount accounted for by each of the independents. The top line repeats the total regression sum of squares from the previous section. The next line tells us that C2 is associated with a sum of 7194.53. Higher up in the print-out it tells us that C2 is the column in MINITAB's working memory which contains the variable x_1, in this case area of available land. As we saw earlier in the chapter, the first variable in the regression accounts for as much of the variation as it can, and which will include not only its own direct effect, but any joint effect it may have with others; again in terms which we have seen above, this is the sum of squares used in the calculation of r_{01}^2.

The sum of squares associated with C3 is that accounted for by the x_2 variable, land productivity, alone, after all joint effects of x_2 and x_1 have been removed; in other words, the value of 804.27 is the sum of squares from which $r_{02.1}^2$ is obtained.

The last main section of the print-out (9) provides information about those data items which are in some way unusual, either because they have large residual values from the regression or because their x values are such that they have a major influence on the slope of the regression line. We saw in the discussion of robust regression at the end of the previous chapter that it is possible for a small number of data points with large values to have a major impact on the slope of a regression line, so that if they are deleted the slope of the line changes considerably (see figure 10.19). As we also saw then, it is inevitable that points with y values a long way from the mean of y will have this effect since regression is based on minimising *squared* differences. Accordingly, in interpreting a regression it is important to appreciate how much reliance may be placed on the validity of disproportionately few observations, and to note which those are. It is in fact possible to obtain the information given here for all data items rather than just the extreme ones if that is required; it simply needs the appropriate MINITAB command.

The information given is the x_1 value of each case listed, its actual y value, the y value it is predicted to have according to the regression (PRED. Y VALUE), the difference between the observed and predicted value (residual), and the value of the residual expressed as a number of standard deviations of the residual distribution (ST. RES.).

Standard deviation of predicted Y value (ST. DEV. PRED. Y) requires a little more comment since we have not previously seen it, and it is once again associated with statistical inference from the regression. The predicted y value for a particular x is the mean value of the ys at that particular point for that particular sample, given that the regression assumptions outlined in the previous chapter have been met. It is also the best single estimate (or point estimate) of the mean y value for that x value in the population as a whole. If, on the other hand, we want to specify an interval within which the population mean y should lie with some given probability (an interval estimate) then we need to know the standard deviation, or standard error, of the prediction, so that we can calculate the interval, on the basis of an assumption that the sampling distribution of predicted y values for the population is normal (see Blalock 1972, 404–5).

ASSUMPTIONS

The previous section has referred in passing to the question of the regression assumptions and it may be appropriate to complete this chapter with a comment on these in relation to multiple regression.

The first point to emphasise is that all the assumptions outlined in the previous chapter for simple regression also hold for multiple regression, with the extra ramification that in the latter they must hold for the relationship between the dependent and each of the independents. Furthermore, as we have seen already, the independent variables themselves should not be intercorrelated.

It will be obvious from this that the process of investigating whether the assumptions do indeed hold for a particular multiple regression analysis can be a complex one if there are many independent variables. Moreover, it is quite likely that for at least one or two of the relationships the assumptions will not be perfectly met, and the question then arises of the extent to which they may be ignored before the analysis becomes a meaningless one, a question to which there is not a straightforward answer.

The previous chapter provided guidance on the detection of problems and the solution of them and what was said there applies equally to multiple regression. It is worth reiterating, however, that it is never satisfactory simply to store data on a computer and then carry out multiple regression analyses related to some problem of interest. The first step should always be to study the distributions of the individual variables to see that they are approximately normal; then to investigate the scattergrams of the various bivariate relationships to see that they are linear. Finally, the residuals from the multiple regression itself should be examined for patterning in their distribution.

Again to reiterate what was stated in the previous chapter, if the assumptions are not met it does not mean that a regression analysis cannot be carried out, but that appropriate action must be taken first. Very often this will raise complexities which require the involvement of a professional statistician.

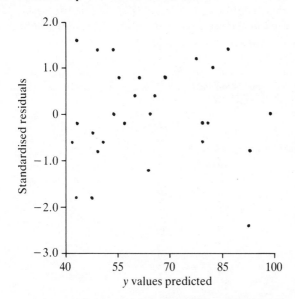

Figure 11.7. Scattergram of standardised residuals from multiple regression of site size on area of available land and land productivity, plotted against the site size values predicted by the multiple regression, from the data in table 11.1.

As far as the example followed through in this chapter is concerned, it was noted above that some collinearity is present, leading to ambiguity in assessing the separate effects of area of available land and land productivity, but the extent of it is not so great as to cause the drastic problems illustrated by Johnston (1978, 74–7). The variables for our example were constructed so as to have reasonably normal distributions, while the scattergrams shown earlier in this chapter (figures 11.4–11.6) indicate that the various bivariate relationships are approximately linear. Finally, the scatterplot of the standardised residuals from the multiple regression against the y values predicted by it (figure 11.7) shows no very obvious patterning to indicate that the assumptions are violated.

EXERCISES

11.1. In an archaeological study of factors affecting the density of obsidian at a series of large early classic sites in Mesoamerica it is hypothesised that distance from the source and site size, reflecting functional importance, are the important variables. Given the information below (data from Sidrys 1977), is this the case? Use multiple regression and multiple and partial correlation methods to assist you in drawing your conclusion.

Obsidian density (g/m^3 earth)	Distance from source (km)	Site size (ha)
38	70	32
32	105	16
35	110	24
23	110	14
18	145	33
23	160	30
27	150	29
30	165	40
14	195	65
22	205	44
16	240	37
21	260	48
7	280	59

11.2. In a study of the faunal remains from a number of Pleistocene cave sites it is decided to investigate the relationship between the number of wolf bone fragments and the number of bovid fragments (data from Boyle 1983). Is there any relation between the two, bearing in mind that the overall size of the assemblage must be taken into account?

Assemblage	Bovid fragments	Wolf fragments	Total no. of fragments in assemblage
1	31	1	1211
2	0	111	618
3	1622	278	4260
4	150	63	820
5	13	48	137
6	12	161	2916
7	0	24	249
8	33	0	128
9	58	0	505
10	107	18	998

11.3. In a study of the relationship between the economies of Roman villas and adjacent towns, the proportions of cattle in the faunal assemblages at a number of villas are noted, together with the distances of the villas from the nearest town and the dates at which they were occupied. The correlations are as follows:

Distance from town–proportion of cattle $r = 0.72$

Date–proportion of cattle $r = 0.55$

Date–distance from town $r = 0.60$

Discuss the relationship between these variables.

Twelve

Numerical Classification in Archaeology

HISTORICAL INTRODUCTION

Since the discipline's inception classification has had a central role in archaeology. In Europe, for example, much of the most important work of the nineteenth century, from Thomsen's Three Age system to Montelius, was concerned with grouping and ordering archaeological material in such a way that the ordering would have chronological significance. With the development of the concept of the archaeological culture at the beginning of the twentieth century the spatial dimension too became of importance, and a key aspect of archaeological work became the definition of coherent temporal and spatial units, a task which continues to be of significance.

The basis of defining these units was an assessment of similarities and differences in archaeological material. This assessment had two aspects. On the one hand there was the search for groupings and discontinuities within particular classes of material, such as pottery. On the other, once groupings within individual classes of material had been obtained, there was the question of the association between groupings of material of different kinds; for example, were particular types of pottery usually found together with particular types of stone tool in the context of similar houses or forms of burial?

The basis of the decisions to group the archaeological material in certain ways and not in others was the expertise of the archaeologists involved in making them. Their training steeped them in the handling of archaeological material that was accessible to them and in the examination of *corpora* of material from elsewhere. Travel was important because it made possible a first-hand acquaintance with material in foreign museums and thus provided a wider knowledge base for individuals in their handling and assessment of differences and similarities. Among his many other achievements Childe was the classic exponent in the field of European prehistory

190

of this kind of approach, which remains of great importance in everyday archaeological practice today.

It was in the 1950s that approaches began to change, with the first application of quantitative techniques to the problems of defining and ordering the similarities and differences in archaeological material. One of these approaches was that of Spaulding (1953), who proposed that artefact types could be defined in terms of patterns of association between the different variables or attributes describing the artefacts in question, and that these associations could be assessed for significance by means of the chi-squared test (see chapter 6).

The other problem that led to the use of quantitative methods was not the definition of types but the ordering of assemblages in a chronological sequence. In fact, a problem of this type had already been tackled in a quantitative fashion in a famous study by the Egyptologist Sir Flinders Petrie (1901), in an examination of burials of the predynastic period in Egypt. What Petrie had was information on grave goods found in a large number of graves and what he was interested in finding out was the chronological order in which the burials were deposited, given the assumption that one of the most important factors affecting the goods deposited in a particular grave would have been variation in the types which were in fashion at any given time. As Kemp (1982) describes, Petrie's conclusion was that the ordering of the graves which would best approximate their chronological sequence would be one in which the life-spans of the individual types would be the shortest possible; the idea being that a type comes into fashion, has a period of increasing popularity, is widely used for a time, then declines in popularity and disappears from use. Petrie's practical solution to the problem involved writing out the contents of each grave on a strip of cardboard, laying all the strips in a line and then shuffling them around to try and get all occurrences of a given type bunched together. This is by no means a straightforward procedure since the life-spans of different types overlap, so that grouping together the occurrences of one type may have the effect of dispersing those of another, but eventually Petrie achieved an ordering with which he was satisfied. Kemp (1982) describes an analysis of Egyptian predynastic cemetery material using modern techniques which broadly confirms Petrie's result.

At the beginning of the 1950s Brainerd and Robinson (Brainerd 1951, Robinson 1951) wished to order pottery assemblages. They made the same assumption as Petrie about the way in which types come into fashion and go out again, but rather than working with strips of cardboard they took their assemblages and on the basis of a comparison of the relative proportions of different pottery types in each pair of assemblages, they calculated a measure of similarity between each assemblage and every other (see below p. 208). They produced a table, or matrix, of these similarities and then shuffled around the order of the assemblages in the table with the aim of grouping all the highest similarities together to produce a sequence (see Doran and Hodson 1975, 272–4, for a more detailed account).

The process of seriation itself will be examined below (pp. 208–12, but for the moment we may note, from a historical point of view, that there was a period from the 1950s up to the mid-1960s when seriation studies were at the forefront of quantitative archaeological research. It was in the early to mid-1960s that an impetus came from a different source to develop quantitative approaches to the assessment of similarity and relationships in archaeology. This source was biology, and specifically biological taxonomy.

Traditional classifications of plants and animals in biology were not based on large numbers of characteristics of the items being studied. As in archaeology, the taxonomist, with his experienced eye, selected a small number of key attributes which seemed to vary significantly between the items and based his classification on these. It came to be felt by some of those involved in the discipline that more satisfactory classifications, specifically classifications which would have greater phylogenetic significance, would be produced if large numbers of the attributes of the plants or animals under study could be used, and it was felt that the classification would also be more satisfactory if no *a priori* differential weighting was attached to the significance of particular characteristics of the items being classified. The result of such an approach, it was argued, would be 'natural' groups.

Since it is impossible for any human taxonomist to consider simultaneously a large number of characteristics of a large number of items and to weight them all equally, some form of automated procedure becomes essential, hence the rise of *numerical taxonomy* (Sokal and Sneath 1963, Sneath and Sokal 1973).

Numerical taxonomy was really introduced to archaeology by David Clarke (1962, 1970) in his so-called 'matrix analysis' of British Bell Beakers. What Clarke wanted to do was to produce a 'natural' classification of his Beaker pots, using all their attributes and not weighting them differentially, in the belief that such 'natural' groups would relate to human group social traditions

(Clarke 1966), although in fact the actual methods he used were an adaptation of the Robinson–Brainerd approach to seriation.

Since that time the dubious theoretical baggage concerned with 'natural' groups has been jettisoned for the much more tenable approach which lays emphasis on classification for a purpose, but the methods of numerical taxonomy have come to play an increasing role in archaeological classification, despite the undeniable problems inherent in them (see, for example, Doran and Hodson 1975, Whallon and Brown 1982).

The technical details of the various procedures involved will be described in the following sections of this chapter and in the next, but here it is appropriate to comment briefly on certain aspects of their use in archaeology in the last two decades, a period in which there has actually been relatively little change in the essentials of the way in which the methods are employed, although some technical improvement has taken place.

On the whole, the methods of numerical taxonomy have been used to group together items in terms of the values of the variables, or states of the attributes, which characterise them, rather than to group variables or attributes in terms of their patterns of association. This is because it is the former process which has been regarded as corresponding to the traditional intuitive approach to defining artefact types in archaeology – the grouping together of some actual physical items, or descriptions of them. One result of this has been that to an extent numerical classification has simply been traditional archaeology with a computer, and the classifications produced have themselves been evaluated in terms of the success with which they approximate traditional classifications made by 'experts'. This hardly seems a justification for the elaborate methodology employed and has been one of the reasons why this area of archaeology tends to be regarded by students (and others) as extremely boring and even pointless.

Spaulding (e.g. 1977) has in fact taken the view that this approach to the definition of types is misconceived, arguing, as we have seen above, that types are defined in terms of statistically significant associations of *attributes,* while the proponents of grouping together *items* in their turn have questioned the validity of Spaulding's approach (e.g. Doran and Hodson 1975). The latest expression of this disagreement may be seen in the book *Essays in Archaeological Typology* (Whallon and Brown 1982, chapters 1, 2, 3 and 6), but some recent methodological developments (see chapter 13) mean that the dispute is no longer as relevant as it was.

It remains to consider why numerical taxonomy has become so popular, even among traditional archaeologists who have generally been sceptical about many of the innovations in archaeological method and theory of the last two decades. There are a number of answers to this question, some hinted at above, but I believe the most important has been that the methods are regarded as in some sense 'objective'. This is a highly dangerous notion which we must briefly subject to examination.

As we will see in subsequent sections of this chapter, the use of numerical taxonomy involves the definition of a measure of similarity between the items or variables we wish to group together, and then definition of a procedure for carrying out the grouping on the basis of the similarities. These measures and procedures have different properties which produce different results. They are 'objective' in the sense that once the choices are made they can be carried through consistently and mechanically by means of a computer. Nevertheless, the choices must be made in the light of the particular data and problem in question: they should not be arbitrary, nor can they be regarded as 'objective', but they should be reasoned, on both archaeological and methodological grounds.

Even prior to the definition of similarity, however, the very possibility of defining any such measure presupposes the existence of a description of the objects of interest from which the measure may be derived. As we have said already, the idea that we can and should describe every aspect we can think of concerning our objects of interest, as a basis for numerical taxonomy, has long been abandoned. Since then Gardin (1980) has been at pains to emphasise the problematical nature of archaeological description. We describe with a purpose in mind, implicit or explicit, and it is far better that it should be explicit so that we give active thought to the descriptive variables we select, and the way in which we construct them, in relation to the purpose which we have, whether that be the definition of spatial and chronological variation or any other (see e.g. Gardin 1980, Whallon 1982, Vierra 1982). Decisions taken at this point largely determine the results of subsequent analysis.

This discussion does not mean that in our description of our data and our use of analytical methods upon them we are simply *imposing* order on the world. The view taken here is that structure and order in our data may or may not exist, but their existence and form, if any, are waiting to be *discovered*. Any structure will be with respect to our description, and our methods of analysis may hide it, distort it or reveal it, but the very possibility of these alternatives indicates the contingent reality of its existence.

We have digressed slightly from the question of 'objectivity' as a basis for using numerical classification, albeit to make what is an important point. But if objectivity is a chimera, and numerical classification studies are often justified in terms of their approximation to traditional typologies, what do constitute valid reasons for using such methods? First, their use helps us to make the bases of our classification decisions more explicit. Second, given the frequent need to seek order in large numbers of items described in terms of large numbers of variables (or in large numbers of variables in relation to their occurrence on large numbers of items), they make the grouping process consistent (not 'objective'), and more importantly, they can reveal patterning present in the material which would otherwise fail to emerge from the complexities of the raw data. In this last respect the various methods described in this and the following chapter have a role which is indispensable.

NUMERICAL CLASSIFICATION:
SOME PRELIMINARY DEFINITIONS

From this point on the chapter will be concerned with describing the technical details of various aspects of numerical classification, and the archaeological issues raised by their use on the whole will be considered only in passing; you are referred to Doran and Hodson (1975) and Whallon and Brown (1982), and the references therein, for more detailed discussion of these questions. Before going any further, however, it is necessary to clarify some terms.

Classification is essentially concerned with the identification of groups of similar objects within the set of objects under study (the 'objects' may be items or variables). It can be seen as a process of simplification, so that generalisations may be made and used on the basis of within and between group similarities and differences. Such generalisations can be purely descriptive or they can form the basis of hypotheses which can be tested by other means; in these respects it can be seen as an extension of the exploratory data analysis approach discussed in earlier chapters.

It is helpful to distinguish now between what is meant here by *classification proper* and certain rather similar procedures. Broadly speaking, classification is concerned with the definition of groupings in a set of data, based on some idea that the members of a group should be more similar to one another than they are to non-members; within-group similarity should be in some sense greater than between-group similarity; alternatively expressed, groups (or

clusters as they are usually known) should exhibit internal cohesion
and external isolation (Cormack 1971). The aim in classification
studies is generally to *discover* the pattern of groupings in a set of
data, with as few assumptions as possible about the nature of the
groupings (cf. Gordon 1981, 5). The process is usually referred to
as *cluster analysis*.

This may be contrasted with the procedure of *discrimination,*
which presupposes the existence of a given number of known
groups and is concerned with the allocation of individual items to
those groups to which they belong most appropriately. It might be
used, for example, to allocate a new find to the most appropriate of
the categories in an existing classification. Alternatively, it can be
employed to investigate the way in which a categorisation relates to
another set of variables. For example, we may have a number of
ceramic vessels from different sites and the vessels may be characterised in terms of a number of measurements describing their
shape; do the vessel shapes differ from site to site? The problem
becomes: given the division of vessels between sites, is that division
reproduced when we attempt to divide up the vessels on the basis of
the variables defining their shape (cf. Shennan 1977, Read 1982)?
Answering such a question involves discrimination and not classification.

Another procedure again is *dissection.* In some cases we may
know that our data are not divisible into groups which exhibit
internal cohesion and external isolation: there is simply a continuous scatter of points in which no natural division can be made.
Nevertheless, it may be that for some purpose we wish to divide
them up; such a more or less arbitrary division would be a dissection
(cf. Gordon 1981, 5). Dissection is not really very important, but a
class of procedures which will concern us a great deal, and which
are mainly discussed in the next chapter, goes under the heading of
ordination.

We saw in chapter 9 on regression analysis that if we have information about a number of items in terms of their values on two
variables we can represent the relations between the items by
means of a scattergram, the axes of which are defined by the two
variables in question. In the chapter on multiple regression we saw
that such a representation is problematical with three variables and
impossible with any more. Clearly then, looking visually for groups
of similar items when they are described in terms of a large number
of variables is impossible: there are too many dimensions. The aim
of ordination methods is to represent and display the relationships

between items in a low-dimensional space – generally of two or at most three dimensions – while still retaining as much as possible of the information contained in all the descriptive variables. Points, representing objects, are close together if their mutual similarity is high and far apart if it is low. A visual check of the scattergram will indicate whether groups – defined as areas of relatively high point density – are present. As a further stage in the operation grouping (classification proper) methods can be applied to the distribution of points in the scattergram.

We have now distinguished classification proper from discrimination, dissection and ordination. Within classification proper we can usefully make some further distinctions, in terms of the different ways in which it is possible to go about group formation, or clustering.

One category is known as *partitioning* methods (Gordon 1981, 9–10). The use of these involves making a decision about the number of groups in which we are interested (this point will be qualified below), but unlike discrimination does not require any specification of the sizes of the different groups. Individuals are grouped together with those with which they are in some defined sense most similar, so that the specified number of groups is formed.

The other main category is that of *hierarchical* methods, which can themselves be subdivided into *agglomerative* and *divisive* groups. Hierarchical agglomerative methods start with all the items under consideration separate and then build up groups from these, starting by grouping the most similar items together, then grouping the groups at increasingly low levels of similarity until finally all the items are linked together in one large group, usually at a very low level of similarity. Divisive methods start with all the items in a single group and then proceed to divide the groups up successively according to some criterion. In both types of hierarchical method the relationships between the items and groups may be represented in the form of a tree diagram or *dendrogram*.

All these cluster analysis methods, but perhaps particularly the divisive ones, to some extent impose their own patterning on the data, as we will see. A divisive method, for example, will impose a series of divisions on a set of data, regardless of whether the resulting groups represent genuine distinctions or an arbitrary dissection. For this reason the process of validation of the results is important and has been unjustifiably neglected in archaeology (see Aldenderfer 1982). The topic is considered later in this chapter (pp. 228–32) but it may be noted here that the results of a single cluster analysis method should never be taken at face value. Results of different methods should be compared with one another and other validation methods also employed.

It has already been said that prior to the use of any cluster analysis method it is necessary to have some measure which expresses the relationships between the individuals in the analysis. We have generally talked about assessing the similarity between items but we can also talk about distances rather than similarities and in general terms one can be regarded as the converse of the other (cf. Späth 1980, 15–16).

Table 12.1. Matrix of similarities between four hypothetical ceramic assemblages, using the Robinson coefficient of agreement.

	1	2	3	4
1	200	14	11	9
2	14	200	147	163
3	11	147	200	157
4	9	163	157	200

Methods of numerical classification then are based on an $n \times n$ matrix of similarities or distances between the n objects being studied, so the first step in an analysis will be to compute this matrix. An example of such a matrix of the similarities between four items, in this case hypothetical ceramic assemblages, is shown in table 12.1. Down the *principal diagonal* of the matrix run the similarities of each object with itself, obviously the maximum possible value, in this case 200. In fact, of course, we don't need all of this matrix because the two halves, above and below the principal diagonal, are mirror images of one another. Thus s_{12}, the similarity between items 1 and 2, is the same as s_{21}, in this case 14. A matrix such as this is said to be a *symmetric* matrix and only one or other half is needed for analysis. Most distance or similarity matrices are symmetric in this way although we will have occasion later on to note an example which is not.

The similarity or distance coefficients which it is possible to enter into such a matrix are many and varied (see e.g. Sneath and Sokal 1973, Wishart 1978). They have different properties and some are appropriate for quantitative numeric data while others are based on qualitative presence/absence data; choices should not be made without thought. Here it will only be possible to examine a few of the most important ones.

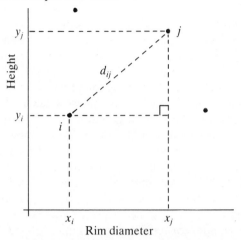

Figure 12.1. Scattergram of height against rim diameter for four ceramic vessels, showing the definition of Euclidean distance between vessels *i* and *j*.

The measure most commonly used with interval or ratio scale data is the *Euclidean distance coefficient*. Given two individuals *i* and *j*, measured in terms of a number of variables *p*, the Euclidean distance coefficient d_{ij} is defined as

$$d_{ij} = \left(\sum_{k=1}^{p} (x_{ij} - x_{jk})^2 \right)^{\frac{1}{2}}$$

This is simply the straight-line distance between two points and what its calculation involves, of course, is Pythagoras' theorem. It is best illustrated with a two-dimensional example. Suppose we want to measure the straight-line distance between a number of vessels described in terms of their height and rim diameter (figure 12.1). We take the distance between each pair of objects, *i* and *j*, on the *x* axis $(x_i - x_j)$, that between them on the *y* axis $(y_i - y_j)$, square these two distances, add them together and take the square root. Thus, in this case

$$d_{ij} = \left((x_i - x_j)^2 + (y_i - y_j)^2 \right)^{\frac{1}{2}}$$

(Remember that raising a number to the power ½ is another way of symbolising taking the square root). Carrying out this operation for every pair of points gives us the matrix of distances between them.

If there are more than two variables then we have to add in extra $(x_{ik} - x_{jk})^2$ terms so that there is one for every descriptive variable, before taking the square root, and that is what the general formula tells us to do.

When two points are in the same place – the items are identical, in other words – d_{ij} is zero; the opposite possible extreme value of d_{ij} is infinity – the two points are infinitely far apart and there is total dissimilarity.

A problem arises with this measure concerning the scale of the axes. This is particularly the case when the measurements of the items under study are all to the same scale but range within quite different limits. Such a problem would arise if, for example, we were interested in classifying bronze swords in terms of measurements of their length, breadth and thickness. Clearly length is likely to vary over a much greater range than thickness and accordingly will have a much greater effect on the classification. If we want to counteract effects of this kind it is necessary to standardise the measurement scales and the convention most commonly used is to give each variable equal weight by transforming the observed values into standard scores.

There is, however, another problem in the use of the Euclidean distance measure since it presupposes that the axes of the space defined by the variables in the analysis are at right angles to one another, so that we have a rectangular coordinate system. This point will become clearer to you when you have read the next chapter, but we can say now that the axes will only be at right angles to one another (or *orthogonal* to use the jargon term) when the variables are completely independent of one another, which in practice will never be the case. If the variables are intercorrelated and therefore the axes are not at right angles, then the d_{ij}s will be over- or under-estimated by an amount depending on the size of the correlation and whether it is positive or negative.

The most common solution to this problem is to make sure the axes are at right angles by defining the distance measure not on the original variables but on the axes defined by the principal components derived from the variables, which are at right angles to one another by definition, as we will see in the following chapter; but alternative methods are also available (see, e.g., Johnston 1978, 217–19; Mather 1976, 313–14; Everitt 1980, 57).

Although a variety of other similarity/distance measures in addition to Euclidean distance are available for use with interval and ratio scale data (see Sneath and Sokal 1973), only one more will be mentioned here, a measure based on summing the absolute differences rather than the squared differences between the points, for each variable, thus:

$$d_{ij} = \sum_{k=1}^{p} |x_{ik} - x_{jk}|$$

This tells us to take the difference between points i and j in terms of their values on each variable in turn, for as many variables as there are in the analysis, and to add the differences together, without squaring them and without regard to whether they are positive or negative (the modulus symbol | tells us to ignore the sign of the differences). This distance measure is known as a *city-block metric*; why this is so may be shown by a two-dimensional example, illustrated in figure 12.2. The formula in this case requires one to take the difference between i and j on the first variable $|x_i - x_j|$ and the difference between them on the second variable $|y_i - y_j|$ and add the two together. This gives us a distance measure made up of two straight lines turning a corner.

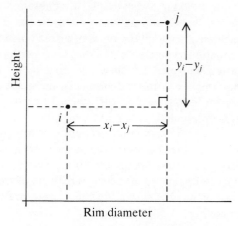

Figure 12.2. Scattergram of height against rim diameter for two ceramic vessels (i and j), showing the definition of city-block distance between the two.

If we now turn to appropriate measures of similarity between items for use with presence/absence (or dichotomous) data we find an enormous variety of coefficients, all of which do slightly different things. The major difference among them is on the question of whether or not they take *negative matches* into account, a negative match being the situation when neither of the units or individuals under consideration possess the attribute in question. The point may be illustrated by means of an example. Suppose we have two graves scored in terms of whether or not they possess certain grave goods types, as in table 12.2.

Table 12.2. Two graves scored in terms of the presence/ absence of ten different grave-goods types.

				Goods types						
	1	2	3	4	5	6	7	8	9	10
Grave 1	1	0	1	1	0	0	0	1	1	0
Grave 2	1	0	0	1	1	0	0	1	0	0

In this example we have assumed that there are ten different grave good types present in our data set as a whole, but that types 2, 6, 7 and 10 are not actually present in either of these two hypothetical graves. It is arguable that in a case such as this absence of a particular type does not have the same status as its presence, and that in particular one would not wish to give joint absence of a type from a pair of graves the same weight as joint presence. This would be especially the case if some of the types occurred only very infrequently. Such a situation, where zero and one have a different status may be contrasted with that which would arise if, for example, we were coding the sex of the individuals in the graves as zero for male and one for female, where the two values have the same status and are simply labelled arbitrarily.

An enormous range of coefficients appropriate for binary (presence/absence) data is available, but only two of the most important ones are described here. These take contrasting positions with regard to their treatment of negative matches. What sort of treatment is appropriate in a given case should be considered carefully at the beginning of an analysis.

The Simple Matching Coefficient

For each pair of items their scores for each attribute are compared and it is noted whether they match (i.e. are the same) or not. The number of matches is then expressed as a proportion of the total number of attributes. What this involves can usefully be illustrated by looking at the comparison between any two individuals in the form of a 2×2 table (table 12.3). For each pair of individuals we count the number of attributes present in both (a), the number present in j but not i (b), the number present in i but not j (c), and the number absent from both (d). Putting in the data for our

Table 12.3. General table for the comparison of two items in terms of the presence/absence of a series of attributes.

		Individual i	
		Attribute +	Attribute −
Individual j	Attribute +	a	b
	Attribute −	c	d

Table 12.4. Comparison of graves coded in table 12.2 with regard to presence/absence of the ten coded attributes.

		Grave 1	
		+	−
Grave 2	+	3	1
	−	2	4

example of the two graves from table 12.2 gives us table 12.4.

For the simple matching coefficient then

$$S = \frac{a+d}{a+b+c+d}$$

In words: positive matches plus negative matches, divided by the total number of attributes. In the case of our two graves

$$S = \frac{3+4}{3+1+2+4} = \frac{7}{10} = 0.7$$

The Jaccard Coefficient

This takes the opposing principle with regard to negative matches: they are disregarded altogether. If two items are the same in the sense of not possessing some attribute this is not counted either as a match or in the total number of attributes which forms the divisor for the coefficient; for any given pair of items the divisor is the number of attributes actually present in one or other of the items in the pair. In terms of our general 2×2 table (table 12.3)

$$S = \frac{a}{a+b+c}$$

With regard to our example we have

$$S = \frac{3}{3+1+2} = \frac{3}{6} = 0.5$$

As we have noted above, it would obviously be preferable to use the Jaccard coefficient if you had a data set in which there was a large number of variables which only occurred rarely, so that a given individual or case possessed only a small proportion of the total range. In this situation, if the simple matching coefficient was used all the cases would be defined as more or less identical to one another.

So long as they are chosen appropriately, these coefficients and the many others available will provide a satisfactory definition of the similarity between the two items, but suppose we want a measure of association between presence/absence *variables* in the same way as the correlation coefficient provides such a measure for continuous variables. This presents some problems. Measures based on the 2×2 contingency table are likely to be unsatisfactory because they are bound to depend on the value in the *d* cell of the table, the sum of those cases where neither of the two attributes under consideration occurs; in other words, they will be strongly affected by the negative matches; and for the strength of association between two attributes to be in effect determined by the number of cases in which neither of the attributes occurs seems unsatisfactory, especially if the numbers of occurrences of some attributes are low relative to the total number of cases (cf. Speth and Johnson 1976). One solution would appear to be to use the Jaccard coefficient again. Let us take an example.

We can suppose that in a study of a cemetery we may be interested not simply in the similarities between the graves but in the patterns of association between the different types of grave goods occurring in them; details of the occurrence of two hypothetical grave goods types are shown in table 12.5. For this example, using the Jaccard coefficient, $S = 3/6 = 0.5$.

But there are two ways of looking at this question, of which the Jaccard coefficient represents only one. It tells us that half the occurrences of type 1 are associated with type 2. However, if we look at this from the point of view of the less common attribute 2, we can think of it in a different way: we could say that it has a perfect association with attribute 1 since every time it occurs attribute 1 is present as well.

Table 12.5. Two grave-good types scored in terms of whether or not they are present in a series of graves.

	Grave numbers								
	1	2	3	4	5	6	7	8	9
Grave goods type 1	1	1	0	1	0	0	1	1	1
Grave goods type 2	1	0	0	0	0	0	1	0	1

Doran and Hodson (1975) see this asymmetry as a reason for more or less rejecting altogether the study of this type of association, but such a view seems excessively drastic because the association of presence/absence variables can certainly provide us with useful information. Their scepticism fits in with their general preference for studying similarity between individuals or cases rather than association between variables, and their rejection of a contingency table type approach to typology and classification. Their recommendation to those who do want to study association between presence/absence variables is, in effect, to use the Jaccard coefficient and accept its limitations; this is what Hodson does in his analysis of the Hallstatt cemetery (Hodson 1977). An alternative solution, however, especially if the attributes occur with widely differing frequencies is to use the following coefficient:

$$S = \frac{1}{2}\left(\frac{a}{a+c} + \frac{a}{a+b} \right)$$

where the letters refer to the general 2×2 table presented in table 12.3.

This coefficient takes the positive matches as a proportion of the total occurrences of the first attribute (here grave goods type) under consideration, then as a proportion of the second attribute, and finally averages the two. It is clear that with this coefficient the less frequent attribute receives much more weight than with the Jaccard coefficient, although it might still be argued that the average is rather spurious.

The matrix of association coefficients produced by this technique, like all the coefficient matrices we have seen so far, is symmetric: the half below the principal diagonal is a mirror image of that above the diagonal. Another approach to the problem posed by such cases as that just outlined is to produce an asymmetric matrix in which the two halves are different from one another; thus, one half of the matrix will be made up of terms of the form $a/(a+c)$ and the other half of terms $a/(a+b)$. Methods of analysing such matrices have

been proposed (Gower 1977, Constantine and Gower 1978) but
they seem to have found very little, if any, use in archaeology.

Up to now the contrast has been drawn between numeric variables on the one hand and binary variables on the other, but
archaeological data are sometimes characterised by neither of
these; *multistate* attributes occur very frequently. An example from
the field of pottery studies might be *rim type*. This is the attribute or
variable and it will have a series of attribute states; for example,
simple rim, notched rim, rolled rim, everted rim, etc., which are
mutually exclusive – only one state can occur on any one vessel –
and exhaustive – they cover all the different varieties of rim form
which occur in the data set under consideration.

Such variables can in fact be recorded as a series of binary
variables. To take our rim form example, we can have four variables, one for each rim type; the one occurring in any given case is
coded as present and the other three as absent. Nevertheless, it is
important to be careful over the choice of similarity coefficient in
these circumstances: ones which exclude negative matches from
consideration are satisfactory but those which include them are not,
because the variables are logically interconnected so that a certain
number of negative matches will occur simply because of the way
they are defined.

Often a given archaeological data set may be described in terms
of both quantitative, presence/absence and multistate variables.
The desire to use all of these in a single analysis of a given data set
has been a strong one among archaeologists, which they have been
able to realise thanks to the development of Gower's *general coefficient of similarity* (Gower 1971). The formula is

$$S = \sum_{k=1}^{p} s_{ijk} \Big/ \sum_{k=1}^{p} w_{ijk}$$

Here two individuals, i and j, are being compared over a series of
variables in turn, the similarity s_{ijk} being evaluated for each variable
in turn and all the s_{ijk}s being summed at the end. The sum of all
these values, however, is standardised by division by the sum of the
'weights' w_{ijk} associated with each variable in the comparison of any
particular pair of individuals i and j.

The idea of weights is one we have referred to above only in
passing, but the notion is the intuitive one of using some means of
varying the importance attached to particular variables in a given
analysis. In the context of Gower's general coefficient the weights
are generally used in a very simple manner. Thus, the weight is set
at 1 when comparison between objects i and j for the kth variable is

possible, and 0 when the value of variable k is unknown for either or both objects i and j.

When presence/absence variables are involved s_{ijk} is set to 1 for a positive match and 0 for a mismatch. Since in these circumstances the weight attached to the variable in question will be 1, the result of this comparison will be fully taken into account in the evaluation of the final similarity coefficient. If the match is negative, i.e. both i and j do not possess the particular attribute in question, then we have to again make the choice whether we want to count it in or not. If we do not, the weight for that particular variable is set at zero, so that the treatment corresponds to the Jaccard coefficient; otherwise the weight is set at 1.

For qualitative or multistate variables $s_{ijk} = 1$ if the attribute states for the two units i and j are the same, and 0 if they differ; w_{ijk} is generally set at 1 unless the attribute is non-applicable, although again there is no reason in principle why it should not be varied to reflect any ideas the analyst may have about the relative importance of the different states.

For quantitative variables

$$s_{ijk} = 1 - \frac{|x_{ik} - x_{jk}|}{R_k}$$

where R_k is the range for variable k. In words, we take the value of variable k for object j and subtract it from the value of object i, ignoring the sign of the result. We then divide the result by the range of the variable, i.e. the difference between its lowest and highest values, before subtracting the result from 1. Obviously, in the specific case where objects i and j are those with the highest and lowest values, then the result of evaluating this $|x_{il} - x_{jk}|/R_k$ term will be 1, which when subtracted from 1 will produce a similarity of 0 for the comparison on this particular variable.

Gower's coefficient is discussed by Doran and Hodson (1975, 142–3) and in recent years has found fairly extensive archaeological use, as we noted above. This is, I think, at least partly due to a tendency on the part of archaeologists to want to throw all the information on a particular set of items into some form of cluster analysis or ordination procedure and see what comes out. This can be dangerous to the extent that it serves as an excuse for not giving serious thought to the variables in the analysis and what they are supposed to represent – the underlying dimensions, as Whallon (1982) calls them. For many purposes it may not be either relevant or appropriate to include in an analysis all the variables which have been recorded for a particular set of data. In other cases more may be gained by analysing subsets of the variables separately, selected on carefully thought-out grounds, and then comparing the results for the different subsets with one another.

To complete this discussion of measuring similarity, a final coefficient worth examining, despite its undoubted drawbacks (Doran and Hodson 1975), is the Robinson coefficient of agreement (Robinson 1951), specifically devised for the archaeological purpose of measuring similarity between pottery assemblages described in terms of percentages of different types. This coefficient is one kind of city-block metric. It totals the percentage differences between defined categories for pairs of archaeological assemblages. The maximal difference between any two units is 200%. By subtracting any calculated difference from 200 an equivalent measure of similarity or agreement is obtained. The formula is:

$$S = 200 - \sum_{k=1}^{n} |P_{ik} - P_{jk}|$$

where P is the percentage representation of attribute or type k in assemblages i and j.

It may be useful to demonstrate the two extreme possibilities with simple examples:

a)

	Type 1	Type 2
Assemblage 1	50%	50%
Assemblage 2	50%	50%

$\Sigma |P_{ik} - P_{jk}| = |50 - 50| + |50 - 50| = 0$

$S = 200 - 0 = 200$

b)

	Type 1	Type 2
Assemblage 1	100%	0%
Assemblage 2	0%	100%

$\Sigma |P_{ik} - P_{jk}| = |100 - 0| + |0 - 100| = 200$

$S = 200 - 200 = 0$

SEARCHING FOR PATTERNING
IN SIMILARITY (AND DISTANCE) MATRICES

Once the matrix of similarity coefficients has been obtained, what do you do with it? In general you want to look for patterning in it which will be interpretable in an archaeologically meaningful way.

How you go about looking for that patterning depends both on what you are trying to do and on what patterning you actually expect to exist.

As we have seen already, the patterning which initially interested archaeologists experimenting with quantitative methods was chronological patterning, particularly the establishing of sequences of archaeological units solely on the basis of comparison between them, in a situation in which external dating evidence is either unavailable or put to one side. There is now an extensive archaeological literature on this subject of seriation (e.g. Cowgill 1972, Doran and Hodson 1975, Marquardt 1978, Ester 1981) and no attempt is made here to deal with the topic since it is already so well covered.

Nevertheless, one particular seriation technique will be presented here because it provides a useful introductory insight of a practical nature into the process of investigating the patterning in matrices of similarity coefficients. The method is known as *close-proximity analysis* (Renfrew and Sterud 1969), a rapid pencil and paper method of seriation which does not, however, force the data into a linear ordering.

The basic idea is that you select any of the units to be seriated, find the unit most similar to it and place this beside the first, thus beginning a chain. You then find the unused unit most similar to either end of the chain and add it on, until in the ideal case all the units are linked in a continuous sequence. The detailed procedure is given below (Renfrew and Sterud 1969, 266–8) and an example follows:

1. Mark the two highest similarity coefficients in each column of the complete matrix (excluding the values along the diagonal).

2. Take any unit as a starting point and note the two closest neighbours to it, i.e. select a column of the matrix and note the two marked coefficients in it. Link the starting unit and its neighbours with lines marked with arrows showing the direction of the similarity; indicate the value of the coefficients on the lines.

3. Take one of the units with only one neighbour (at one or other end of the line), note its two closest neighbours and repeat the procedure of step 2. If it is already linked to one of these as a result of being a mutual nearest neighbour with one of the units already in the diagram then the mutual nature of the link should be shown by arrows in both directions.

4. Carry on this procedure for each unit in turn until it can go no further. If not all the units in the matrix have been linked together

at this point then a separate set of links should be started with one of the items not yet linked with the others. Repeat this procedure until all units are included.

5. Where there are loops in the resulting diagram the link with the lowest coefficient should be cut, subject to the stipulation that chains may not be broken into separate blocks. Usually it is one-way links which are cut in this way and single bonds should be broken in preference to double ones if both have the same value. When this has been done the final order has been achieved.

It should be noted that while the method forces the breaking of loops it does not prevent branching: side chains are not forced into a linear order where this is inappropriate.

6. If at the end of stage 4 entirely separate clusters have emerged with no links between them, then at this point they are linked together in the most appropriate fashion, i.e. by finding the two highest similarity coefficients which will link members of the given cluster with the others. Each separate cluster should be treated in this way. The links between the separate groups of already linked units may be marked by dotted rather than solid lines to indicate their relative weakness.

It was noted above that this method does not force the units into a linear chain but allows the possibility of branching if in fact the patterning in the data is not linear. Renfrew and Sterud (1969, 267) also suggested a means of assessing the degree of clusteredness as opposed to one-dimensional linear ordering in the data. This depends on the fact that if a perfect seriation can be achieved there will be two marked coefficients in each row of the matrix, except for two rows, corresponding to the ends of the linear ordering, which will have three. The formula is:

$$\text{clustering coefficient} = \frac{\sum_{i=1}^{n} N_{i>2} - 2}{2n - 3} \times 100$$

where $N_{i>2}$ is the number of ringed coefficients in row i beyond 2. The clustering coefficient has a value of zero for perfect seriation and of 100 for maximal clustering.

The whole procedure may be illustrated by means of an example (figure 12.3) using the Robinson coefficient of agreement to represent the similarities between four ceramic assemblages. For this case the clustering coefficient is $(0 + 1 + 1 + 0 - 2)/(8 - 3) = 0$. In other words we have a perfectly 'seriatable' matrix.

The method of close-proximity analysis is very good when a linear chain type of ordering exists in the data, but when the

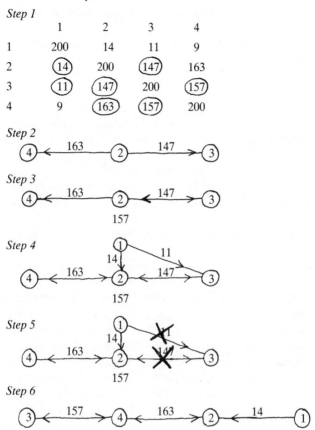

Figure 12.3. Close-proximity analysis.

relations between the units are more complex or the number of units is large then it is not very satisfactory. Furthermore, its use presupposes that a matrix of similarity coefficients already exists. To obtain such a matrix is really only practicable with a computer and once the data are held in a computer file it is just as easy to use computer-based techniques to search for patterning in the matrix as it is to use close-proximity analysis. The latter technique then is more a helpful way of illustrating how similarity matrices are analysed than of real practical use. Nowadays seriation studies are usually carried out by means of the sort of ordination method discussed in the next chapter (e.g. Kemp 1982). In this chapter, however, we are concerned with examining patterning in the matrix from the point of view of classification proper, defined above as concerned with the definition of groupings in a set of data, based on some idea that the members of the group should be more similar to one another than they are to non-members. This involves the use of cluster analysis.

It was noted above that these can be divided into two categories, partitioning methods and hierarchical methods, and that within the latter agglomerative and divisive techniques may be distinguished.

1. *Hierarchical Methods*

We have already seen that behind this group of techniques lies the idea that objects can be similar to one another at different levels, so that the results can be represented in the form of a dendrogram: a tree diagram representing the relationships between individuals and groups.

These techniques, like those of numerical taxonomy generally, came to archaeology, as we have seen, from biological classification studies. Within this field the hierarchy of relations between individual organisms and groups of them representing their similarities to one another was seen as relating to their phylogenetic connections – their evolutionary tree. In archaeological data there is no such obvious hierarchy of interrelationships between items and groups to which a hierarchical representation of similarities corresponds and this has occasionally been seen as a reason for rejecting the use of such hierarchical techniques in archaeology. Clarke (1968) argued that in fact it was possible to define a hierarchy of archaeological entities, in terms of which relationships could be described and which had a substantive significance for the history and nature of individual examples of the entities involved – assemblages, cultures, culture groups and techno-complexes. The view taken here is that the notion of similarity in some respects and not in others, and of greater and lesser similarity, is an entirely familiar one in archaeology which it is often both helpful and legitimate to conceptualise and represent in a hierarchical fashion.

i) *Agglomerative Techniques*

As we have seen, these start with a series of individuals and then build up groups from these. First the most similar items are grouped together, then individuals are added to these groups and the groups themselves are linked together, at decreasing levels of similarity, until finally they are all joined in a single group.

The task which the agglomerative methods perform is to carry out the operation in the best possible way, according to some defined criterion. A variety of such methods exist because a variety of criteria exist in terms of which the similarity between a given individual and a group, or between two groups, may be evaluated.

a) *Nearest Neighbour or Single Link Cluster Analysis.* This is probably the simplest clustering method and for that reason is very useful for illustrating what procedures are actually involved in cluster analysis. The criterion of linkage in this case is that to join a group a given individual must have a specified level of similarity with any member of the group; for two groups to join any member of the one group must have a specified level of similarity with any member of the other. In other words, similarities or distances between individuals and groups, or between groups and other groups, are defined as those between their nearest neighbours.

Table 12.6. Matrix of similarities between five ceramic vessels, on the basis of their decorative motifs (after Everitt 1980).

	1	2	3	4	5
1	1.0	0.8	0.4	0.0	0.1
2	0.8	1.0	0.5	0.1	0.2
3	0.4	0.5	1.0	0.6	0.5
4	0.0	0.1	0.6	1.0	0.7
5	0.1	0.2	0.5	0.7	1.0

The procedure is best illustrated by actually carrying out analysis of a small similarity matrix of the relationships between five ceramic vessels on the basis of their decorative motifs (see table 12.6; cf. Everitt 1980, 9–10). The highest similarity is that between vessels 1 and 2 so the first step in the procedure is to join these two together. These no longer have separate identities in the matrix; they are a group and the similarities between this group and the other individuals in the matrix must be evaluated according to the nearest neighbour criterion, as the basis for producing a revised similarity matrix.

As an example, to find the similarity between the group and vessel 3, you look at the similarity between vessels 1 and 3, and between 2 and 3, and whichever is the larger counts as the similarity between the group, of vessels 1 and 2, and vessel 3. Here the similarity between 1 and 3 is 0.4 and between 2 and 3 it is 0.5, so the latter is chosen. The same procedure is carried out for the group and vessels 4 and 5, and the matrix produced is shown in table 12.7.

Table 12.7. Reduced matrix of similarities between five
ceramic vessels, after first stage of nearest-neighbour
cluster analysis which has grouped vessels 1 and 2
together (after Everitt 1980).

	(12)	3	4	5
(12)	1.0	0.5	0.1	0.2
3	0.5	1.0	0.6	0.5
4	0.1	0.6	1.0	0.7
5	0.2	0.5	0.7	1.0

This matrix in turn is examined for its largest value, the similarity
between vessels 4 and 5 of 0.7, so these two now become another
group, whose similarity with the first group and the remaining
individual vessel must be established so that a third matrix may be
produced. The procedure is as before. The similarity between the
first group (vessels 1 and 2) and vessel 3 is unchanged at 0.5. To find
the similarity between the first group and the second group on our
nearest neighbour criterion we look for the larger of the two similarities between group 1 and vessel 4 and group 1 and vessel 5, and
see that it is 0.2 for the latter. The remaining entry for the matrix is
found in similar fashion to give table 12.8.

Table 12.8. Reduced matrix of similarities between five
ceramic vessels, after second stage of nearest-neighbour
cluster analysis which has grouped together vessels 4 and
5, in addition to 1 and 2 (after Everitt 1980).

	(12)	3	(45)
(12)	1.0	0.5	0.2
3	0.5	1.0	0.6
(45)	0.2	0.6	1.0

The next stage is for vessel 3 to join the second group at a
similarity level of 0.6, while the final step is to join the two groups
together, on the same criterion, at a similarity level of 0.5. The
sequence of links may now be represented as a dendrogram, with a
similarity scale down the side (figure 12.4).

b) *Furthest Neighbour or Complete Linkage Cluster Analysis.*
The criterion specified by this method is that to join a group a given
individual must have a specified degree of similarity with the member of the group from which it is most dissimilar; for two groups to

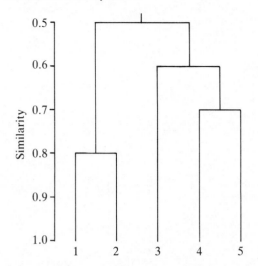

Figure 12.4. Dendrogram of results of single-link cluster analysis of the matrix of similarities between 5 ceramic vessels shown in table 12.6 (after Everitt 1980).

join, the two individuals, one from each group, which are most dissimilar from one another must have a specified degree of similarity. Once again then we are looking for the highest similarity values in the succession of matrices, but defined on the basis of furthest rather than nearest neighbours.

The dendrogram resulting from furthest neighbour cluster analysis of the matrix used in the nearest neighbour example is shown in figure 12.5. In this case the relative similarities have changed but the actual configuration of the dendrogram is identical to that for single linkage. This is unusual; more often than not the configurations are very different.

c) *Group Average or Average-Link Cluster Analysis.* This is also sometimes known as the unweighted pair group method. Here the similarity or dissimilarity between groups is defined as the arithmetic average of the similarities between pairs of members, i.e. as

$$\frac{\sum_{i=1}^{n_i}\sum_{j=1}^{n_j} S_{ij}}{n_i n_j}$$

where S_{ij} is the similarity between a member of group i and a member of group j, n_i is the number of individuals in group i, and n_j is the number of individuals in group j. The formula tells us to take the first individual of group i, obtain the similarity between it and

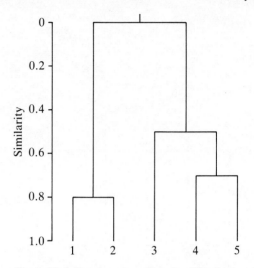

Figure 12.5. Dendrogram of results of furthest-neighbour
cluster analysis of the matrix of similarities between
5 ceramic vessels shown in table 12.6 (after Everitt 1980).

all members of group j, sum these similarities, then go on to the
second member of group i and repeat the process, and so on until
all members of group i have been accounted for. The resulting
overall sum of similarities is then divided by the product of the
number of individuals in each of the two groups. What this involves
may be illustrated diagrammatically (figure 12.6).

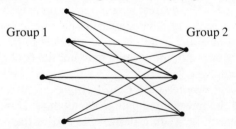

Figure 12.6. Diagram illustrating the calculation of
average similarity between two groups.

Here there are two existing groups, 1 and 2. The lines linking the
members of the two groups are the S_{ij}s (or d_{ij}s in this case), of
which there are 12. These are summed and then divided by $n_1 \times n_2$,
the number of items in each of the two groups; here $4 \times 3 = 12$. At
each stage of the average-link cluster analysis the similarities/dis-

tances between the groups and/or individuals are calculated, following the group average criterion where groups are involved, and the pair of groups and/or individuals with the greatest similarity or smallest distance at each step are linked together.

d) *Ward's Method.* There is a variety of other hierarchical agglomerative techniques (see e.g. Sneath and Sokal 1973, Everitt 1980), although a number of them can be shown to be variations of a more general procedure (Everitt 1980, 16–17; Gordon 1981, 46–9). Only one more will be described here, Ward's method, which has had a considerable amount of use within archaeology for the analysis of continuous numeric data such as the results of trace element analyses, and recently by Whallon (1984) in the context of an interesting approach to intra-site spatial analysis.

The idea behind this is that satisfactory clusters should be as homogeneous as possible. One way to define homogeneity is in terms of the distance of the members of a cluster from the mean of that cluster. In Ward's method the distance is the *error sum of squares* (ESS): the total sum of squared deviations or distances of all points from the means of the clusters to which they belong. The aim of the method is to join individuals and groups successively in such a way that at each step in the fusion process the error sum of squares is the minimum possible; in other words, the clusters remain as homogeneous as possible. The method is best understood by means of an example (cf. Everitt 1980, 16–17).

Table 12.9. Matrix of squared Euclidean distances between five projectile points, based on measurements describing their shape.

	1	2	3	4	5
1	0.0	1.0	36.0	64.0	121.0
2	1.0	0.0	25.0	49.0	100.0
3	36.0	25.0	0.0	4.0	25.0
4	64.0	49.0	4.0	0.0	9.0
5	121.0	100.0	25.0	9.0	0.0

A matrix of squared distances between five projectile points based on quantitative measurements of variables describing their shape is shown in table 12.9. At the beginning, when all the individuals are separate from one another, the total ESS has a value of zero. Then those two individuals with the smallest distance between them, i.e. those whose fusion will produce the minimum increase in ESS, are linked, here individuals 1 and 2, separated by a squared distance of 1.0. In the case when we are dealing with only two individuals the increase in ESS is given (Gordon 1981, 42) by

$$I = \tfrac{1}{2}d_{ij}$$

Here

$$I_{(12)} = \tfrac{1}{2}(1.0) = 0.5$$

As with our single-link cluster analysis example we now need to calculate a new reduced matrix, giving the distances between the group mean and the other items in the analysis. A general formula for obtaining the new distances is given by Gordon (1981, 42):

$$d_{k(ij)} = \frac{n_k + n_i}{n_k + n_i + n_j} d_{ki} + \frac{n_k + n_j}{n_k + n_i + n_j} d_{kj} - \frac{n_l}{n_k + n_i + n_j} d_{ij}$$

where $d_{k(ij)}$ is the distance between group or items k and the new group made up of groups or items i and j, n_i is the number of items in group i, n_j is the number of items in group j, n_k is the number of items in group k, d_{ki} is the distance between group/item k and group/item i, d_{kj} is the distance between group/item k and group/item j, and d_{ij} is the distance between group/item i and group/item j. In the present example the calculations are as follows (in practice, of course, such calculations are always carried out by computer):

$$d_{3(12)} = \frac{1+1}{1+1+1}\,36 + \frac{1+1}{1+1+1}\,25 - \frac{1}{1+1+1}\,1$$

$$= 24.0 + 16.666 - 0.333$$

$$= 40.333$$

$$d_{4(12)} = \frac{2}{3}\,64 + \frac{2}{3}\,49 - \frac{1}{3}\,1$$

$$= 42.666 + 32.666 - 0.333$$

$$= 75.0$$

$$d_{5(12)} = \frac{2}{3}\,121 + \frac{2}{3}\,100 - \frac{1}{3}\,1$$

$$= 80.666 + 66.666 - 0.333$$

$$= 147.0$$

The other distances in the new matrix are as before, so the result is table 12.10.

The smallest distance is now that between individuals 3 and 4, a distance of 4.0. Again we need to find the increase in ESS resulting

Table 12.10. Reduced distance matrix between five projectile points after the first stage of a Ward's method cluster analysis which has linked together items 1 and 2.

	(12)	3	4	5
(12)	0.0	40.333	75.0	147.0
3	40.333	0.0	4.0	25.0
4	75.0	4.0	0.0	9.0
5	147.0	25.0	9.0	0.0

from the formation of the new group, in the same way as above:

$$I_{(34)} = \frac{1}{2}(4) = 2.0$$

and once more we need to produce a new matrix (table 12.11):

$$d_{(12)(34)} = \frac{2+1}{2+1+1}40.333 + \frac{2+1}{2+1+1}75.0 - \frac{2}{2+1+1}4$$

$$= 30.25 + 56.25 - 2 = 84.5$$

$$d_{5(34)} = 16.666 + 6 - 1.333 = 21.333$$

Table 12.11. Reduced distance matrix between five projectile points after the second stage of a Ward's method cluster analysis which has linked items 3 and 4, in addition to 1 and 2.

	(12)	(34)	5
(12)	0.0	84.5	147.0
(34)	84.5	0.0	21.333
5	147.0	21.333	0.0

Looking at the new matrix we can see that the smallest distance is that between the group of 3 and 4 and individual 5 of 21.333. As before, the increase in ESS resulting from including a new individual in a group is equal to half the distance between them. In this case 21.333/2 = 10.666.

It remains to evaluate the single entry in the final matrix (table 12.12), the distance between group (12) and group (345):

$$d_{(12)(345)} = \frac{2+2}{2+2+1}84.5 + \frac{2+1}{2+2+1}147.0 - \frac{2}{2+2+1}21.333$$

$$= 67.6 + 88.2 - 8.532 = 147.268$$

Table 12.12. Reduced distance matrix between five
projectile points at the final stage of a Ward's
method cluster analysis.

	(12)	(345)
(12)	0.0	147.268
(345)	147.268	0.0

Again, the increase in ESS is half the distance, giving a value of
73.65. The results may be summarised in the form of a table (12.13)
and the links represented in the form of a dendrogram (figure 12.7).

Table 12.13. Increase in error sum of squares (ESS)
associated with successive linkages in the Ward's method
cluster analysis of the matrix in table 12.9.

Fusion	ESS increase	Cumulative ESS
1 2	0.5	0.5
3 4	2.0	2.5
(34)5	10.7	13.2
(12)(345)	73.7	86.9

ii) *Divisive Techniques*

Divisive methods of cluster analysis start off with all the individuals
or units together in a single group which is then successively subdivided. There are two main groups of divisive methods, polythetic
and monothetic; the former are based on the consideration of the
values of all the variables in the analysis at any given division step,
the latter on the values of a single variable (cf. Everitt 1980, 18).
Only the monothetic approach is considered here since it is the
only one which has had any impact on archaeology (Tainter 1975,
Peebles 1972).

  Its use in practice has largely been restricted to cases where the
data are of presence/absence type, so that division is in terms of the
presence or absence, or 1/0 value, of a particular attribute: all
items with a 1 value go in one group, all those with a zero value in
the other. When there is a series of successive division steps, producing smaller and smaller subdivisions, the result once again is a
hierarchy.

  Divisive methods have been particularly used by ecologists, for
classifying areas of land by the species present, or species in terms

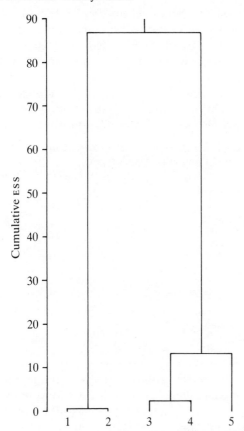

Figure 12.7. Dendrogram resulting from analysis by
Ward's method of the distance matrix in table 12.9.

of their presence in particular areas, and the main method is generally known as *association analysis*; this corresponds to the DIVIDE
program in the well-known CLUSTAN cluster analysis computer
package (see appendix 2).

Having said that the series of divisions is made in terms of the
presence or absence, or 1/0 value, of a single attribute at any given
time, the question arises as to the means of selecting the best
attribute for making such a division: what is meant by 'best'? The
basic idea is that the two groups produced at any given division step
should be as dissimilar as possible from each other, not just in terms
of their value on the variable used to make the division, but overall,
in terms of all the variables in the analysis. In other words,

presence/absence of the attribute used for division should be related to the presence/absence values of the other attributes; the attribute whose presence/absence is most closely related to the values of the other variables in the data set being split will be the one to choose. Even so, there is still a variety of ways in which this general criterion may be defined. The one chosen to illustrate the method is widely used although not particularly satisfactory, as we will see below. Nevertheless, it provides a straightforward example.

Table 12.14. Data matrix for ten graves scored in terms of the presence/absence of four grave-goods types.

Grave	Grave goods types			
	1	2	3	4
1	0	0	1	1
2	0	0	1	1
3	1	1	1	0
4	1	1	1	0
5	0	1	1	1
6	1	1	0	0
7	1	1	1	1
8	1	0	0	0
9	0	0	0	1
10	0	0	0	1

Suppose we have ten graves scored in terms of the presence/absence of four grave-goods types (table 12.14). One way of seeing whether the values on one variable are related to the values on another is to calculate the chi-squared statistic for the association between those two variables. The idea behind the approach is that the chi-squared values actually measure strength of association in this context, because sample size is a constant for all the comparisons. If a particular variable is strongly related to other variables, it means that for a given case its value on the first variable will be a good predictor of its value on the others. The result is that a group defined on the basis of presence or absence of the one variable will be relatively homogeneous since the state of that variable will specify the particular states taken by the other attributes, for the members of that group. The variable most closely related to the others, and therefore most appropriate for making a division, will be the one with the highest chi-squared values for its relations with the others. Thus we have to calculate the chi-squared value for each attribute's association with every other and then sum the results for each variable to see which is the highest, as shown in table 12.15.

Table 12.15. Contingency tables showing associations between each pair of grave-goods types for the data presented in table 12.14.

(a)

Type 1		+	−		
Type 2	+	4	1	5	$\chi^2_{12} = 3.6$
	−	1	4	5	
		5	5	10	

(b)

Type 1		+	−		
Type 3	+	3	3	6	$\chi^2_{13} = 0$
	−	2	2	4	
		5	5	10	

(c)

Type 1		+	−		
Type 4	+	1	5	6	$\chi^2_{14} = 6.666$
	−	4	0	4	
		5	5	10	

(d)

Type 2		+	−		
Type 3	+	4	2	6	$\chi^2_{23} = 1.666$
	−	1	3	4	
		5	5	10	

(e)

Type 2		+	−		
Type 4	+	2	4	6	$\chi^2_{24} = 1.666$
	−	3	1	4	
		5	5	10	

(f)

Type 3		+	−		
Type 4	+	4	2	6	$\chi^2_{34} = 0.278$
	−	2	2	4	
		6	4	10	

We now sum the chi-squared values for each variable:

$$\text{Goods type 1} = \chi^2_{12} + \chi^2_{13} + \chi^2_{14}$$
$$= 3.6 + 0.0 + 6.666 = 10.266$$
$$\text{Goods type 2} = \chi^2_{21} + \chi^2_{23} + \chi^2_{24}$$
$$= 3.6 + 1.666 + 1.666 = 6.932$$

$$\text{Goods type 3} = \chi_{31}^2 + \chi_{32}^2 + \chi_{34}^2$$
$$= 0.0 + 1.666 + 0.278 = 1.944$$

$$\text{Goods type 4} = \chi_{41}^2 + \chi_{42}^2 + \chi_{43}^2$$
$$= 6.666 + 1.666 + 0.278 = 8.61$$

It appears from this that variable 1 is overall more closely associated with the other variables; that is to say, presence or absence of the other grave-goods types is most closely related to the presence or absence of grave goods type 1. The result of this is that the best division of the graves is into those where type 1 is present and those where it is absent. It is not possible to obtain two more dissimilar groups on the criterion we have used. In table 12.16 the graves are arranged in their two groups. It can be seen that types 2 and 4 are markedly differently distributed in the two subdivisions, although type 3 is identically distributed in both and its presence/absence is obviously not related to that of type 1, as the relevant chi-squared statistic indicated.

Table 12.16. Graves listed in table 12.14 sorted so that all those in which goods type 1 is present and all those in which it is absent are grouped together.

| | Grave | Grave goods types | | |
		2	3	4
Type 1 present	3	1	1	0
	4	1	1	0
	6	1	0	0
	7	1	1	1
	8	1	0	0
Type 1 absent	1	0	1	1
	2	0	1	1
	5	1	1	1
	9	0	0	1
	10	0	0	1

Only one division step has been illustrated in this example but in association analysis a succession of subdivisions of this type is carried out.

There are undeniable problems in using chi-squared in this way (see Cormack 1971); one obvious one is the question already discussed above of how seriously one takes the *d* cell of the contingency table, the joint absences or negative matches. The chi-squared method has been presented here for illustrative purposes rather than as a recommendation of its suitability. Other division criteria are available, in particular one known as the *information statistic*. The use of the information statistic in classification arises from the concept of entropy, or disorder. It gives a measure of the disorder in a group. Thus, it has a value of zero when all members of a cluster are identical, and increases as the group becomes more diverse (see Sneath and Sokal 1973, 141–4, 241–4). This statistic, which is available on CLUSTAN, is favoured by Peebles (1972) and by Tainter (1975), while Doran and Hodson (1975, 180) also appear to find it satisfactory.

2. *Partitioning Methods*

All the cluster analysis methods we have seen so far have been hierarchical, but it is now time to turn to the partitioning methods, to which reference has already been made. Instead of there being multiple levels of grouping at different levels of similarity a decision is made as to an appropriate number of clusters and then individuals are assigned to the one to which they are closest. This process of assignment is not a trivial one because as new individuals are added to a cluster the definition of the cluster changes. The methods which have been devised to carry out this task are not analytical techniques which can produce a single correct answer, since the number of possible variations in the assignment of items to groups quickly becomes enormously large as the number of items in the analysis increases; they are techniques which use the great speed of the computer in carrying out large numbers of calculations to search through the data, assigning individuals to groups according to a set of rules based on some criterion. The assignment that results should be as close as possible to an optimum but this cannot be guaranteed.

The first decision that has to be made then concerns the number of clusters to be started, although, as we shall note, in practice it is possible to operate in a more or less hierarchical manner, successively reducing the number of clusters of interest. Once the initial number has been decided then it is necessary to provide a basis for starting the clusters. Procedures suggested for defining the starting points include random selection of a specified number of individual cases, corresponding to the number of clusters required, and the use of the results of some other clustering method for the relevant number of groups. When the starting cluster centres have been chosen individuals are allocated to the cluster to whose centre they are nearest.

This idea of allocating individuals to the groups to whose centre they are nearest is clearly the same as that in Ward's method, and very often an error sum of squares based on squared Euclidean distance is used in partitioning methods as well. In Ward's method the best fusion of individuals into groups is achieved by the hierarchical pattern of linkage, but as with all hierarchical methods of cluster analysis a cluster, once formed, can never be broken and its members redistributed to another group or group. This can lead to anomalous situations, in that an individual's membership of a group may be appropriate when it joins, but as other items join the group and its definition changes the initial item may become peripheral to it, to such an extent that it should really now join a different group with which initially it did not have much in common. The idea of reassessing a classification at any stage, and if appropriate, re-allocating individuals to other groups, is intuitively attractive (Doran and Hodson 1975, 180).

This is precisely what the partitioning methods known as *iterative relocation* (or sometimes *k-means*) techniques do. As individuals are added to the clusters the centre of each cluster is recalculated, either every time a new individual is added to it or at the end of the process of allocating items to clusters. At this point the question arises of whether all items are in the most appropriate cluster, so each item is considered in turn to see if it should be re-assigned to another cluster. A variety of criteria have been proposed for making these decisions but the basic idea of them all is that the dispersion of the different clusters should be reduced and the distinctions between them maximised, again a concept similar to the idea of minimising ESS in Ward's method.

Of course, once one item is moved then the centre of the cluster it comes from and the one it has moved to both need recalculating so the process of relocation is a laborious one for which efficient computer algorithms are required. It continues until any further moves fail to cause an improvement in the criterion being used. A very much simplified version of the procedure is illustrated in figure 12.8, in which only two clusters are considered.

The solution achieved at the end of the relocation process may or may not represent the best possible overall allocation (or *global optimum* as it is sometimes known in the jargon). One way of checking on this is to repeat the process using a different set of starting points for the clusters, again perhaps either randomly chosen or arising from the results of another clustering technique.

As noted already, although the procedure is carried out for a specific number of clusters, it can also be carried out in a quasi-

1. Two individuals are selected as starting points for
the two clusters; a third individual is introduced and
allocated to its nearest cluster:

2. The position of the centre of cluster 2 is recalculated; another case is introduced and allocated:

3. Position of centre of cluster 1 is recalculated;
another case is introduced and allocated:

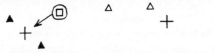

4. Position of centre of cluster 2 is recalculated;
another case is introduced and allocated:

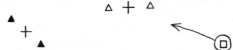

5. Position of centre of cluster 1 is recalculated;
another case is introduced and allocated:

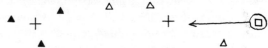

6. Position of centre of cluster 2 is recalculated;
another case is introduced and allocated:

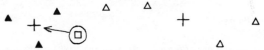

7. Position of centre of cluster 1 is recalculated;
left-most individual of cluster 2 is now closer to the
centre of cluster 1, so is allocated to it:

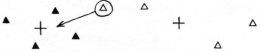

8. Centres of both clusters finally recalculated;

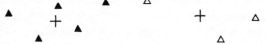

Figure 12.8. Successive stages of an iterative relocation
partitioning procedure for two clusters.

hierarchical fashion. Thus, once the best-fit solution for a given number of clusters is found the two nearest ones can be joined and the relocation procedure repeated. When this has been done the number of clusters may be reduced again and the whole process repeated for as many clusters as are required. It is important to note that this process is not hierarchical in the sense of the hierarchical methods we've seen above. They produced clusters whose members were unchanging except that new members were added as the number of clusters decreased. With the iterative relocation methods described in this section clusters can also change their membership as well as gain new members as their number is reduced.

As for all the procedures we have described, a program for iterative relocation is available in the CLUSTAN suite of programs for cluster analysis.

CLUSTER ANALYSIS EVALUATION

It was pointed out earlier in this chapter that cluster analysis methods impose their own patterning on the data to a greater or lesser extent. It will also have become clear in the course of the presentation of the various techniques which have been described that they embody very different ideas of the way in which clusters should be defined. Inevitably this means that they will very often produce different results when used to analyse the same set of data. Two important questions therefore arise. How do we know then whether our clusters represent some kind of genuine distinctions in our data rather than being merely a product of the method used? And what basis have we for preferring the results of one clustering method to another? A subsidiary question related in some ways to the first is how do we decide on the number of clusters we should be taking seriously?

The answers to these questions are by no means unequivocal, because it is not simply a matter of distinguishing between right and wrong methods but of considering the criteria in terms of which a particular technique defines good clustering and whether these are appropriate to the structure of the data at hand. However, cluster analysis is generally used in precisely those situations where we know very little about the structure of our data, while the theoretical foundation of many of the methods is itself uncertain. A great deal of literature has been generated by these problems which it is impossible to go into here; they are discussed among others by Doran and Hodson (1975), Everitt (1980) and Gordon (1981), who give references to further studies.

In early work on these techniques in archaeology much emphasis was placed on the extent to which the results of numerical classification studies matched those produced by traditional typological methods. This was important at the stage when a case was being made for the respectability of the new methods. Furthermore, such comparisons can provide useful information, as can the comparison of results with external information not actually used in the cluster analysis. Nevertheless, they cannot be regarded as validating or otherwise the results of cluster analyses. Moreover, as we have noted already, if the touchstone of numerical classification methods is the extent to which the results match traditional typologies there is in any case no point in using them.

Recently a paper by Aldenderfer (1982) has reviewed some of the most important ways in which the results of cluster analyses can be evaluated, suggesting that it is unsatisfactory to use any of them in isolation; they are listed below.

1. The use of a stopping rule – a means of testing for a significant number of clusters in a hierarchical sequence (Mojena 1977); available through CLUSTAN.

2. The use of Wilk's lambda statistic, a measure based on the ratio of within-group variation to overall variation in the data, tested by means of a randomisation procedure (see below for what this involves).

3. The use of scatterplots of the data, pairs of variables at a time, to see whether there are any indications of clustering and the form any clusters may take.

4. By means of discriminant analysis, which attempts to maximise the separation between existing groups and provides an indication of the extent to which this is possible (see chapter 13 and cf. Everitt and Dunn 1983, 106–9).

5. By means of plotting the distribution of the data not in terms of their values on the original variables but on their scores on a series of transformed axes produced by some form of data reduction technique such as principal components analysis. These are the ordination methods referred to earlier in this chapter; they are described in chapter 13.

Another way of trying to ensure the validity of clustering results on a particular data set is to analyse it by a variety of different methods. If they all give very similar answers in terms of strongly overlapping cluster membership then it suggests that the patterning is genuine; ways of systematising this idea are discussed by Gordon (1981, 132–6). On the other hand, if different methods do not give the same result it does not necessarily mean that there is not real patterning to be found, or that one of them is not representing it correctly. It may be that the cluster structure is successfully identified by one method based on one set of assumptions but not on another based on a different set.

A number of variations on the theme of randomisation may also be used in the evaluation process. For example, a data set may be randomly divided into two subsets and analyses carried out on each of these to see if they match each other. A more radical approach is randomly to permute the values of the variables across the different cases, thus destroying any structure of association or similarity which may exist, and to compare the results with those of the real data, either visually and intuitively, for example in terms of dendrogram structure, or perhaps using the measures for measuring overlapping membership of clusters discussed by Gordon (1981, 132–6). Aldenderfer (1982, 66) uses a randomisation procedure to generate a distribution of Wilk's lambda with which to compare the observed one since the standard significance test is inappropriate. He randomly assigned his data items to clusters and calculated the resulting lambda value. The procedure was repeated ten times and a mean value obtained with which to compare the observed result.

Finally, another approach to validation considers the extent to which the grouping of the individual items into clusters distorts the patterning of similarities or distances between the individual items; it can also be used to compare the amount of distortion between different clustering methods. The CLUSTAN suite of programs has two such measures: Jardine and Sibson's Δ (Jardine and Sibson 1968) and the so-called cophenetic correlation coefficient. The second of these will be illustrated with an example to show what is involved; the similarity matrix used in the single-link cluster analysis example presented above will be compared with the grouping of similarities resulting from that analysis.

The original similarity matrix (table 12.6) is reproduced below for ease of reference (table 12.17); these similarities will be designated s_{ij}. The next stage is to derive the patterning of similarities produced by the cluster analysis; these similarities will be designated s_{ij}^*. The s_{ij}^* values between each pair of units may be read from the single-link dendrogram (reproduced as figure 12.9) by noting the coefficient value at which the units become linked. Thus, units 1 and 2 become linked at 0.8, 4 and 5 at 0.7, 3 to 4 and 5 at 0.6, 1 and 2 to 3, 4 and 5 at 0.5. From these figures we can produce the new matrix s_{ij}^* (table 12.18), and we can plot corresponding ele-

Table 12.17. Matrix of similarities (s_{ij}) between five
ceramic vessels, on the basis of their decorative motifs.

	1	2	3	4	5
1	1.0	0.8	0.4	0.0	0.1
2	0.8	1.0	0.5	0.1	0.2
3	0.4	0.5	1.0	0.6	0.5
4	0.0	0.1	0.6	1.0	0.7
5	0.1	0.2	0.5	0.7	1.0

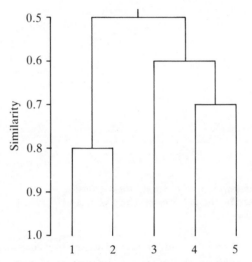

Figure 12.9. Dendrogram of results of single-link cluster
analysis of the matrix of similarities between 5 ceramic
vessels shown in table 12.17.

ments of these two matrices against one another on a scattergram
(figure 12.10).

We can also obtain the correlation coefficient between the matrices on the basis of their corresponding elements; it is calculated in exactly the same way as a normal correlation coefficient and is known in this context as the cophenetic correlation coefficient. In this case its value is 0.44. As noted already, the technique can also be used to compare the s_{ij}^* matrices resulting from different clustering methods.

This example completes our treatment of the evaluation of the results of cluster analysis but it is important to be aware that decisions made before the choice of clustering technique, concern-

Table 12.18. Matrix of similarities (s_{ij}^*) between five
ceramic vessels derived from the dendrogram linkages in
figure 12.9.

	1	2	3	4	5
1	1.0	0.8	0.5	0.5	0.5
2	0.8	1.0	0.5	0.5	0.5
3	0.5	0.5	1.0	0.6	0.6
4	0.5	0.5	0.6	1.0	0.7
5	0.5	0.5	0.6	0.7	1.0

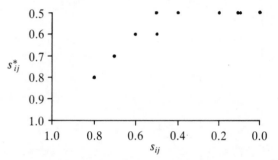

Figure 12.10. Scattergram of s_{ij}^* similarities against s_{ij}
similarities, based on the matrices in tables 12.18 and
12.17 respectively.

ing the variables used and the similarity or distance measure selected, will also have an effect on the results. In numerical classification, perhaps even more than in other areas of the application of
quantitative methods in archaeology, clear thought about aims, the
nature of the data, the properties of the numerical description and
its analysis, and the appropriate means of evaluating the results are
essential.

12.1. Carry out a close-proximity analysis in an attempt to seriate the following matrix of similarity scores between ten Upper Palaeolithic artefact assemblages.

	1	2	3	4	5	6	7	8	9	10
1	200	142	124	135	90	78	69	73	70	52
2	142	200	122	131	92	89	79	82	81	63
3	124	122	200	117	95	87	83	85	86	69
4	135	131	117	200	98	110	92	98	75	58
5	90	92	95	98	200	94	95	95	102	77
6	78	89	87	110	94	200	134	132	122	95
7	69	79	83	92	95	134	200	119	129	125
8	73	82	85	98	95	132	119	200	125	103
9	70	81	86	75	102	122	129	125	200	146
10	52	63	69	58	77	95	125	103	146	200

12.2. Because of a lack of vertical stratigraphy an attempt is being made to understand the chronology of a site by seriating the pits present on the basis of their ceramic contents. Below is a matrix of similarities between 10 pits, based on the pottery in the pits. Attempt to seriate the pits using close-proximity analysis. Does the seriation seem to you a good one or is the seriation too complex to be arranged in a good linear sequence?

Pits	1	2	3	4	5	6	7	8	9	10
1	100	36	6	69	48	50	58	83	87	38
2	36	100	74	38	48	93	42	52	62	30
3	6	74	100	38	99	22	28	15	7	75
4	69	38	38	100	36	15	19	90	73	27
5	48	48	99	36	100	57	17	86	57	62
6	50	93	22	15	57	100	93	71	61	68
7	58	42	28	19	17	93	100	32	88	65
8	83	52	15	90	86	71	32	100	92	5
9	87	62	7	73	57	61	88	92	100	95
10	38	30	75	27	62	68	65	5	95	100

12.3. Carry out a close-proximity analysis of the following matrix of Robinson–Brainerd coefficients, representing the degree of similarity between the ceramic assemblages from fifteen sites.

	1	2	3	4	5	6	7	8	9	10	11	12	13	14	15
1	—	181	179	182	162	164	154	144	148	146	143	147	150	147	132
2	181	—	181	186	156	157	147	141	146	145	149	146	148	146	127
3	179	181	—	184	153	157	155	146	151	147	150	151	153	145	130
4	182	186	184	—	153	157	150	144	149	145	148	147	152	148	130
5	162	156	153	153	—	173	151	145	143	137	133	142	134	160	135
6	164	157	157	157	173	—	159	165	160	155	147	159	152	155	132
7	154	147	155	150	151	159	—	148	149	141	137	155	140	148	144
8	144	141	146	144	145	165	148	—	181	175	167	172	168	137	121
9	148	146	151	149	143	160	149	181	—	178	173	177	177	139	121
10	146	145	147	145	137	155	141	175	178	—	185	175	176	127	123
11	143	149	150	148	133	147	137	167	173	185	—	173	179	122	118
12	147	146	151	147	142	159	155	172	177	175	173	—	177	135	132
13	150	148	153	152	134	152	140	168	177	176	179	177	—	128	120
14	147	146	145	148	160	155	148	137	139	127	122	135	128	—	128
15	132	127	130	130	135	132	144	121	121	123	118	132	120	128	—

12.4. On p. 236 is a series of measurements describing the shape of a number of Bevel Rim Bowls of the Uruk period in Mesopotamia. The diagram below shows what the different measurements refer to (information from Johnson 1973). Carry out a cluster analysis of these data to try and establish groupings within it. Remember that simply carrying out a single analysis and interpreting the results is insufficient. You should compare different methods and use validation techniques. Can you see any problems with this analysis?

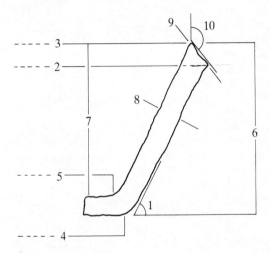

Key: 1 Base angle; 2 Rim diameter (estimated to 0.5 cm); 3 Interior rim diameter (to 0.5 cm); 4 Base diameter (to 0.5 cm); 5 Interior base diameter (to 0.5 cm); 6 Side height (measured to 0.1 cm); 7 Interior side height (to 0.1 cm); 8 Side thickness; 9 Rim thickness; 10 Rim angle.

Exercise 12.4

	1	2	3	4	5	6	7	8	9	10
1	58	160	150	80	70	73	65	108	145	128
2	57	140	130	70	65	67	62	94	111	137
3	55	175	155	70	70	71	61	107	110	137
4	58	180	170	70	65	84	80	106	121	154
5	62	195	180	80	70	86	72	108	135	150
6	60	165	160	70	65	85	78	111	130	159
7	53	180	170	80	65	85	75	120	123	148
8	68	130	120	60	50	71	65	108	104	150
9	48	150	140	70	60	70	55	133	129	165
10	58	200	190	80	75	96	84	159	141	147
11	47	210	200	85	75	79	74	114	135	163
12	60	160	150	80	70	87	80	110	121	136
13	55	180	170	80	80	88	83	109	118	160
14	65	190	165	80	75	91	79	132	169	150
15	63	190	170	75	70	89	85	137	129	155
16	67	220	210	80	75	118	105	145	138	170
17	44	170	150	80	70	58	44	103	123	154
18	63	185	170	75	80	80	74	117	139	148
19	52	160	150	60	55	75	69	109	126	148
20	62	215	200	90	85	97	81	138	128	133
21	41	175	160	65	60	70	62	110	137	151
22	47	190	170	75	80	69	58	120	129	148
23	50	185	160	70	65	94	80	126	143	152
24	55	195	180	70	65	85	80	130	129	151
25	49	195	180	70	65	77	69	124	102	148
26	58	140	120	65	60	66	54	113	143	130
27	62	170	160	65	60	90	70	94	131	137
28	55	135	120	70	65	73	64	109	102	136
29	53	170	160	70	65	78	64	123	124	135
30	60	175	160	70	60	83	70	112	142	155
31	52	140	120	70	65	73	62	116	126	145
32	59	150	140	75	70	88	76	101	126	135
33	61	140	130	70	60	92	85	116	103	152
34	56	145	130	65	60	72	65	125	134	136
35	60	175	160	75	65	93	78	111	160	130
36	53	165	160	70	60	74	65	111	62	160
37	49	165	150	80	75	75	62	129	147	154
38	60	160	140	70	65	78	66	114	146	143
39	59	170	160	70	60	91	77	138	119	146
40	57	165	160	80	63	77	60	91	124	170
41	55	170	160	80	65	70	66	140	121	149

12.5 Below is information about a number of hoards from period II of the Danish Bronze Age (information from Levy 1982). Carry out a cluster analysis of the hoards to find out whether there are any clear groupings of hoards of particular types. Use only the information on the content of the hoards at this stage and give careful thought to the problem of coding the data for the cluster analysis.

Again remember to use more than one clustering method, together with validation techniques, involving the use of stopping rules where appropriate.

Look at the relationship between the clustering results and (i) the region where the hoards were found (Zealand, Funen, Jutland), (ii) the find circumstances, and (iii) Levy's categorisation of the hoards as ritual or non-ritual.

Zealand

1. Two beltplates, two neckcollars, four spiral fingerrings, 33 tutuli [a type of small bronze ornament], 113 tubes for cord skirt. Found in a meadow in damp, peaty soil, during deep ploughing. Weight = 1986 g. Ritual hoard.

2. Two neckcollars, two armrings, three spiral armrings, 13 tutuli, one belt hook. Found in a bog. Estimated weight = 735 g.

3. One weapon palstave, one spearpoint. Found in a bog. Estimated weight = 750 g. Ritual hoard.

4. Two beltplates, two neckcollars, several armrings, one sickle. Found in a bog. Weight = 868 g. Ritual hoard.

5. Two plain palstaves, one knife, one beltplate, one unique bronze plate (pre-deposition fragmentation). Found on a field. Weight = 1211 g. Non-ritual hoard.

6. One neckcollar, one spiral armring, two armrings, pin to a fibula. Found in a bog. Weight = 160 g. Ritual hoard.

7. Three spearheads, one plain palstave, one sickle. Found in a field. Estimated weight = 955 g. Non-ritual hoard.

8. Three beltplates, four large tutuli, 27 small tutuli, four spiral armrings, one neckcollar. Bone fragments and a stone maul are now missing. Found in a bog, circa .5 metre deep. Weight = 1530 g (partially estimated due to fragmentation). Ritual hoard.

9. Ninety-four palstaves (many unfinished), celts, sword hilt, knife blade, sixty spearheads, lump of raw metal (most objects now missing). Found in a blue clay layer in peat. Weight not estimated. Non-ritual hoard.

10. Two neckcollars, spiral armring fragments. Found together in a field. Weight = 400 g (partially estimated due to post-deposition fragmentation). Ritual hoard.

11. Three spearheads, fragments of sword blade, chisel, unidentifiable tool with flat pointed blade and socket. Found in an irrigation ditch. Weight = 853 g. Non-ritual hoard (?).

12. Two matching armrings. Found together. Weight = 51 g. Ritual hoard.

13. One celt, two plain palstaves. Found in a field. Estimated weight = 900 g. Non-ritual hoard.

14. Fragment of a sword hilt, fragment of an armring (probably N. German), six plain palstaves, fragments of palstaves, belthook, raw metal (pre-deposition fragmentation). Found in a field. Weight = 4530 g. Non-ritual hoard.

15. Two spearheads. Found in a bog. Weight = 227 g. Ritual hoard.

16. Two swords with metal hilts. Found together in a field. Weight = 2446 g. Ritual hoard.

17. Two neckcollars, one beltplate, one armring, spiral armring fragments, one rounded tutulus, two sickles, one plain palstave, three awls. Found on a heath with the neckcollars encircling the smaller objects and the beltplate covering all of them. Weight = 1150 g (partially estimated due to post-deposition fragmentation). Ritual hoard.

18. One beltplate, two spiral armrings, one knife. Found in a bog. Weight = 1189 g. Ritual hoard.

19. One sword with metal hilt, one sword blade and related hilt button. Found in a bog (slight possibility not a closed find). Weight = 1169 g. Ritual hoard.

20. Two plain palstaves. Found in a peat bog, 1.26 metres deep. Weight = 760 g. Ritual hoard.

21. One spearpoint and one beltplate. Found in a bog at bottom of thin peat layer (slight doubt about association). Weight = 310 g. Ritual hoard.

22. Three neckcollars, three beltplates, 21 tutuli, 7–8 spiral finger-rings, 3–4 spiral armbands, one sawblade, one sickle. Found in a field lying above a gravel layer. Weight = 1760 g (partially estimated due to post-deposition fragmentation). Ritual hoard.

22a. A hollow-cast, model horse attached to a disc covered with gold on one side; both are set on a model cart resting on six wheels. Found in a bog, apparently dismantled before deposition. Weight = 4190 g (from literature; an estimated 15 g of weight is of gold). Ritual hoard.

23. One sword with metal hilt, two sword blades, one hilt button. Found next to an ancient watercourse, lying horizontal with points to southwest. Weight = 1457 g. Ritual hoard.

24. Four spearpoints and six sickles (or sawblades). Found in a bog, 1.25 metres deep, far from dry land. Weight = 365 g. Ritual hoard.

25. Two beltplates, one fishhook. Found together in a bog, 2 metres deep. Weight = 229 g. Ritual hoard.

26. One sword with metal hilt, two plain palstaves, one spearpoint, one arm- or anklering. Found together in a bog. Weight = 1888 g. Ritual hoard.

27. Three swords with metal hilts, three sword blades, two hilt buttons. Found together, horizontal, hilts to east, at bottom of an ochre layer just above a chalk layer; this is evidence of the former presence of a spring. Weight = 4157 g. Ritual hoard.

28. Two neckcollars. Found in a bog. Weight = 322 g. Ritual hoard.

29. Two beltplates, one neckcollar, two tutuli, two saw or sickle blades, one knife blade. Found in limey, water-bearing soil, two metres deep. Weight = 694 g. Ritual hoard.

30. One weapon palstave, one large celt. Found in a wet field, during draining work, 1.25 metres deep. Ritual hoard. Weight = 1122 g.

31. Three belt plates, 17 tutuli, one celt, one sickle, at least four saw or sickle blades. Found at bottom of peat layer, on clay. Weight = 838 g. Ritual hoard.

32. Five plain palstaves. Found in a garden, edges to north. Weight = 2233 g. Non-ritual hoard.

Funen

33. Sixteen spearpoints, 15 sickles, two plain palstaves, two fragments of sword blade, two knives, one metal rod. Found by machine digging in sandy subsoil of a field. Weight not estimated. Non-ritual hoard.

34. Five spearpoints, eight saws or sickles, one weapon palstave, one knife, one chisel. Found in a bog. Estimated weight = 1600 g. Ritual hoard (?).

35. Two massive swords with metal hilts, one dagger blade. Found in a bog. Weight = 2398 g. Ritual hoard.

36. Three beltplates, one armring, one spearpoint, two plain palstaves, one chisel, four saw or sickle blades. Found in a boggy meadow. Weight = 1575 g. Ritual hoard.

37. Three beltplates, seven tutuli, one neckcollar. Found in a bog. Estimated weight = 759 g. Ritual hoard.

38. Two twisted neckrings. Found in a ditch. Weight = 77 g. Ritual hoard.

39. Three massive swords with metal hilts. Found in a depression by edge of a watercourse. Weight = 2818 g (weight of one sword estimated). Ritual hoard.

40. Three spearpoints, two saws or sickles. Found in a bog. Estimated weight = 450 g. Ritual hoard.

41. Seven spearpoints. Found at edge of bog. Weight = 1200 g (partially estimated due to post-deposition fragmentation). Ritual hoard.

Jutland

42. One plain palstave, two sickles. Found on a field. Weight = 513 g (partially estimated, palstave missing). Non-ritual hoard.

43. One neckcollar, four varying armrings. Found in a bog. Weight = 96 g. Ritual hoard.

44. Two dagger blades, one beltplate, one celt (some fragmentation, apparently modern). Found in a field. Weight = 327 g. Ritual hoard (?).

45. Seventeen tutuli, one pin, one awl, amber beads. Found in a bog. Weight = 148 g. Ritual hoard.

46. Two plain palstaves, one socketed hammer. Found among stones. Weight not estimated. Non-ritual hoard.

47. Marstrup. Two plain palstaves, never used. Found in a field. Weight = 425 g. Non-ritual hoard.

48. One neckcollar, one beltplate, six tutuli, tubes for cord skirt. Found in a bog. Estimated weight = 416 g. Ritual hoard.

49. One beltplate, four tutuli. Found by a cliff. Weight = 200 g (partially estimated due to post-deposition fragmentation). Ritual hoard.

50. Two spiral armrings. Found in a ditch. Weight = 129 g. Ritual hoard.

51. One massive sword with metal hilt, massive shaft-hole axe. Found in a bog, one metre deep. Weight = 2735 g. Ritual hoard.

52. One celt, seven sickles, fragment of sword blade (broken in antiquity). Found beside a big stone. Weight = 804 g. Non-ritual hoard.

53. Two fragmented neckcollars and approximately two kilograms of unworked amber in numerous chunks. Found in a small natural mound. Metal weight = 88 g. Non-ritual hoard.

54. Four unused plain palstaves. Found on a hill under a stone. Weight = 1403 g. Non-ritual hoard (?).

55. Seven plain palstaves, one weapon palstave. Found in a bog. Weight = 2970 g. Ritual hoard.

56. Five tutuli, five varied armrings, one twisted neckring, one awl. Found in a field. Estimated weight = 342 g. Ritual hoard.

57. Two plain palstaves, one celt, one socketed chisel, hilt button to a sword. Found near the surface of a field near the remains of a firepit ; no clear evidence that the bronzes and firepit were associated. Weight = 1596 g. Non-ritual hoard (?).

58. Massive celt, weapon palstave. Found under a big stone in marly soil. Estimated weight = 1000 g. Ritual hoard.

59. Four plain palstaves, one celt, chisel, sickles, dagger blade, two neckcollars, two beltplates, 18 tutuli, spiral armrings, three spearpoints. Found at edge of a bog. Weight = 3331 g. Ritual hoard.

60. Nineteen plain palstaves, two spearpoints, fragments of other spearpoints. Found close to the surface on a field. Weight = 7911 g (partially estimated). Non-ritual hoard.

61. One beltplate, two spearpoints. Found in a bog. Estimated weight = 475 g (some objects now missing). Ritual hoard.

62. One sword, one shafthole axe, six spearpoints, celt, palstave. Found at the side of a grave mound, the spearpoints thrust vertically into the ground. Weight = 3280 g. Ritual hoard.

63. Four plain palstaves, two sickles. Found in a field. Weight = 1677 g. Non-ritual hoard.

12.6. Turn the hoard analysis around and instead of clustering the hoards themselves carry out a cluster analysis of the artefacts, coded in terms of the hoards they occur in. Are there any particularly marked groupings of associated artefacts?

Thirteen

Simplifying Complex Spaces:
The Role of Multivariate Analysis

The previous chapter introduced us to the idea of describing objects of interest to us in terms of a number of variables and then seeking patterning in the similarities or distances between the objects with respect to their values on the variables used to describe them. The approach taken was to use methods of cluster analysis to place similar objects together in the same group and we saw that different methods represented different ideas of how a group should be defined. At the same time it was noted that to some extent these methods tended to impose their own structure on the data and that this was a problem which could not be neglected.

The methods to be described in this chapter follow a different line of approach, already referred to in passing in the previous chapter, known as *ordination*. They involve many of the concepts we have seen in our discussion of cluster analysis and also ideas from regression analysis.

In the context of simple bivariate regression we used scattergrams to see if any trends were present in the distribution of the observations, but we could also have used them to see which points were similar to one another and which were not by looking at the distances between them; at the same time we could, if we had wished, have noted whether or not there was any indication that the observations fell into distinct groups. The axes of the scattergrams were formed by the variables. Our examination of multiple regression showed, among other things, that with any more than three variables, at most, representing our data by means of scattergrams in this way is simply impossible. If we want to do this we have to plot them two or at most three at a time. This is certainly worth doing for its own sake but obviously does not give us an overall picture: we cannot look visually for overall trends for multiple regression purposes, or at inter-point distances for classification or grouping purposes.

The aim of ordination methods is to compress the information

contained in a large number of variables into a much smaller number of new variables, ideally only two or three. We can then produce
scattergrams of our data expressed in terms of these new variables
which will allow visual appreciation of a large amount of information. By examining these scattergrams we can see whether or not
there are any groups or clusters in the data; the objects are not
forced into a particular grouping pattern simply as a result of the
adoption of a particular clustering technique. Furthermore, as we
shall see, the process of obtaining the new variables to create the
scattergrams itself produces interesting information, and in some
cases forms the main object of the exercise.

An archaeological example of the general ideas involved may be
helpful at this juncture. Let us suppose that we are analysing the
graves from a cemetery and in the course of this we have decided
to calculate a matrix of similarities between the graves by some
method such as those described in the last chapter, on the basis of
some set of descriptive variables which we believe to be relevant to
the question we are investigating. We now want to investigate the
patterning in the matrix. Cluster analysis is likely to be relevant, but
if the number of graves is large then any dendrogram resulting from
it is likely to be rather confusing; furthermore, we still have the
problem that the method may be imposing its own structure on that
of the data. An ordination approach would be as follows.

We can imagine trying to represent the graves under study as
points in a space, such that the similarities between the graves are
represented by the distances between the points. In order to represent the relationships accurately we would need a space of many
dimensions. We can further imagine that within this space the
points will not necessarily be equally scattered in all directions;
they may be distributed over a relatively short distance in some
directions and a considerably longer one in others. It is possible to
define the orientation of these different directions or axes and also
the lengths over which the points are distributed along them. Once
we have established the orientation of the longest axis and its length
we can then define the axis which goes through the next longest part
of the point scatter, subject to the proviso that it must be at right
angles to the first, and we can obtain its length too. It is possible to
go on doing this for as many independent dimensions of our space
as exist. These axes often have a substantive interpretation in terms
of the data from which they were derived. In the case of our graves,
for example, it may be that the axis along which our graves are most
widely scattered, i.e. in terms of which the variation in distances

between the graves in our space is greatest, is one relating to chronological differences between the graves, so that early graves (as suggested by independent evidence) are very much different from late ones (also independently attested). We can establish a set of coordinates for the points (here graves) in relation to these axes and use these new coordinates to produce scattergrams, which may be interpreted in terms of both the clustering of graves, which are closest to which, and also in terms of the nature of the axes, referred to above. Rather than relying on a visual assessment of the scattergrams a cluster analysis could if necessary be carried out using the coordinates of the objects on the new axes as input, rather than the original raw data.

The application of procedures such as this to the analysis of cemeteries (e.g. Shennan 1983) and many other types of archaeological data has proved helpful in a large number of cases because it is a way of disentangling complex patterns of variation which are not otherwise easily assimilated.

This example brings out the twin aspects of ordination. The concern with similarities or distances and patterning within them is common to cluster analysis. The idea of looking for trends in the variation is something we have already seen in regression. Nevertheless, there are some major differences between ordination and regression and it is worth drawing attention here to one in particular. In regression analysis the aim is to model and account for the variation in a dependent variable in terms of the effect of one or more independents. In the example of the graves above the original variables did not come into the analysis once the similarities had been calculated. However, as we shall see, in the case of those ordination methods which do analyse the original variables directly, we do not make any assumptions about which variables are dependent or independent. We simply obtain a measure of correlation or covariation between each variable and every other and analyse the matrix which results.

There has been a pronounced tendency within archaeology for the ordination methods to be preferred to multiple regression, for two reasons at least. First, many archaeological data are highly complex and it is by no means obvious in many cases which variables should be regarded as dependent and which as independent. This is the case, for example, when we are dealing with quantitative descriptions of ceramic vessel or projectile-point shape. There may well be correlations between the different measurements and an understanding of them will be extremely helpful to grouping the objects in question and vital to accounting for why they vary in the way they do. On the other hand, to treat one of the variables as the dependent does not correspond to the realities of the situation; they are interrelated with one another.

A second, and perhaps less creditable, reason why archaeologists have preferred ordination methods is precisely that it is possible to analyse the data and see what patterns emerge without much prior thought as to relevant models and hypotheses. Such an approach corresponds to the exploratory data analysis philosophy which has been emphasised throughout this book but it undoubtedly has its dangers (cf. Speth and Johnson 1976); it seems to reflect a deeply ingrained tendency among archaeologists to prefer to interpret patterns rather than develop and test hypotheses.

MULTIVARIATE ANALYSIS

So far we have only talked in very general terms about ordination and the process of simplifying complex spaces, without any attempt to make distinctions between different methods. It is now necessary to be a bit more specific and to give an indication of the different techniques involved and the way in which they will be covered in this chapter. For the most part they come within an area of statistics known as *multivariate analysis.* They differ from the techniques used in cluster analysis in that whereas the latter is in many respects a group of *ad hoc* heuristic techniques without a secure theoretical foundation, multivariate analysis has a secure basis in mathematics and statistical theory. As we have had occasion to remark already (chapter 11), the mathematics behind these methods is often complex and for this reason they have been regarded as very deep and mysterious. While care, knowledge and expert advice are essential for their use, the aim of this chapter is to show that in essence they are readily comprehensible, certainly to the extent that it should be possible for anybody to understand and evaluate (properly) published analyses. To achieve an understanding of them is important because they have been so widely used and because some major recent debates have revolved around particular examples of such analyses.

In what follows there will be a detailed account of the method of *principal components analysis,* and to a lesser extent of the related method of *factor analysis.* Once these have been described and explained we will be in a position to present briefer and much more generalised accounts of *principal coordinates analysis, non-metric multidimensional scaling* and *correspondence analysis.*

Principal Components and Factor Analysis

Factor analysis was developed in the field of psychology in the 1930s and its original aim was to extract fundamental measures of intellect from scores on intelligence tests. The belief was that any single test does not really provide an adequate measure of intelligence. The scores of individuals are related to their mental ability but are also affected by differences between them in terms of education, cultural background and the circumstances of the test. Psychologists believed that factor analysis was capable of extracting the common intelligence factor from the score of individuals on several tests even though no single test was capable of measuring intelligence directly. Nowadays principal components and factor analysis are used in a great variety of different disciplines involved in data analysis.

The general idea is to pull out something in common from a number of different variables. If we can isolate such a common underlying dimension behind our initial variables we may be able to suggest that it means something in terms of our problem, as the psychologists did with the factor behind their intelligence test scores. Further, if there is a common factor underlying the variation in a whole set of variables, we can forget about the variation between the original variables and just look at what they have in common. If we then look at the scores of our cases on the small number of common factors underlying the original data values we can use these as the basis for our ordination in a small number of dimensions. In fact, all the methods not only allow us to pull out separate dimensions of variation, they also tell us how important they are.

The above discussion mainly refers to factor analysis. The distinction between this and principal components analysis is explained below. The emphasis in what follows is on principal components analysis, as the more straightforward technique.

An Introduction to Principal Components Analysis

It has already been stated that the mathematics involved are too complex for this to be an appropriate place to present a mathematically rigorous account of principal components analysis (see, for example, Morrison 1967). In these circumstances the best way of presenting an intuitively comprehensible account is by means of pictures and geometry. That which follows relies heavily on the very lucid presentation of Johnston (1978), designed for a fairly

similar level of readership; a very good alternative is presented by
Davis (1973).

In the case of principal components (and factor) analysis the
starting point is the covariation between the variables. If a set of
variables possesses some underlying common factor the implication
is that their values are correlated with one another – they are closely
related to one another. The common factor can be seen as in some
sense the average of the group of variables; the more closely related
they are the stronger the common factor will be and the more
meaningful on its own as a substitute for the original variables.

To see how principal components arise we need to look again at
how the covariation between variables is measured. We saw in
chapter 9 that covariation in its technical sense was given by
$\Sigma(x - \bar{x})(y - \bar{y})$; this can be divided by the sample size to give an
average covariation or covariance. If the variables we are dealing
with have been standardised, i.e. transformed to Z scores in which
the values are expressed in numbers of standard deviation units
from the mean (see chapter 8), then the value of the covariance
between any two variables will also be automatically standardised
and will correspond to the correlation coefficient between the two
variables; it follows from this transformation that the variances of
the individual variables are also standardised, to a value of 1.0. In
what follows we will assume that the relationships between variables are expressed as correlation coefficients (rather than covariances), although such a standardisation is not necessarily something which we would wish to adopt in a real analysis (this point is
discussed further below, p. 262; see also Davis 1973, Everitt and
Dunn 1983, 42 and 47).

To develop a geometrical presentation of principal components
then we first need a geometrical method of representing correlations. If we imagine our variables as vectors of equal length emanat-
ing from a common origin then one way of representing their
relations with one another is in terms of the angular distance between them. This is best illustrated visually (figure 13.1). Here we
have four variables each represented as a line with a direction
starting from a common origin. In terms of our pictorial representation and our convention for its interpretation x_1 and x_2 are closely
interrelated, neither is very closely related to x_3 although x_2 is closer
to it than x_1; finally, x_4 is more or less diametrically opposed to x_1
and x_2 and very little related to x_3.

The reason that this is a very useful representation is that the
sizes of the angles can be directly related to the values of the

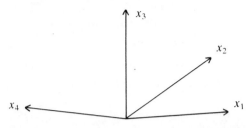

Figure 13.1. Geometric representation of the correlations between four variables.

Figure 13.2. Geometric representation of two perfectly correlated variables.

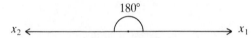

Figure 13.3. Geometric representation of two variables showing perfect inverse correlation between them.

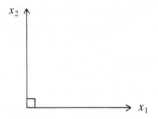

Figure 13.4. Geometric representation of two uncorrelated variables.

correlation coefficients, since these correspond to the cosines of the angles concerned. Thus, in our pictorial convention, when two variables are perfectly correlated the angle between them is zero: they are superimposed (figure 13.2). Obviously in such a case the value of the correlation coefficient is 1.0; similarly, the cosine of an angle of zero degrees is 1.0.

Again, when two variables are diametrically opposed we represent the angle between them as 180° (figure 13.3). The value of the correlation coefficient here would be −1.0; the cosine of an angle of 180° is −1.

Unsurprisingly, an angle of 90° has a cosine of 0.0 (figure 13.4).

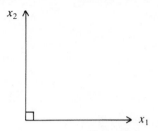

Figure 13.5. Two uncorrelated variables.

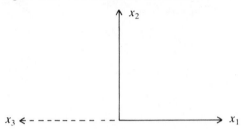

Figure 13.6. A failed attempt to represent a third
uncorrelated variable on a two-dimensional surface.

In these circumstances the correlation between x_1 and x_2 is also
zero, so we can represent two variables which are completely unrelated to one another by two vectors at right angles; in statistical
jargon the two variables are *orthogonal*.

When dealing with two variables we can always represent the
correlation between them in terms of angular distance correctly on
a flat piece of paper, i.e. in two dimensions. Above, we also saw a
diagram which represented the correlations between four variables
in two dimensions but this is by no means always possible. Imagine
a case in which the four variables were uncorrelated with one
another; in other words, each has a correlation of zero with every
other. We can draw the first two correctly (figure 13.5), but try
putting in the third (figure 13.6): This is obviously incorrect; although x_3 has a correlation of zero and angle of 90° with x_2, it is at
180° to x_1, with a perfect negative correlation of -1.0. The only way
to put in the third vector correctly is to have it coming up out of the
paper, although a distorted representation can be given (figure
13.7): If we add in the fourth orthogonal variable even this becomes
impossible; the relations between all the variables can only be
represented correctly in a four-dimensional space.

In general, the maximum number of dimensions required to
represent the correlations between a specified number of variables

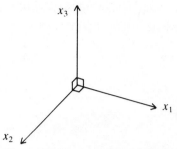

Figure 13.7. Geometric representation of three uncorrelated variables.

is given by the number of variables, but it may be less. In the extreme case that all of them were perfectly correlated with each other than only one dimension would be required.

In principal components analysis we start with the matrix of correlation coefficients (or covariances) between our variables and the aim is to produce from these a new set of variables which are uncorrelated with one another. Precisely how this relates to our aim of defining underlying dimensions of variation in our data, and thus being able to present scattergrams of two dimensions which summarise the information from ten variables, will probably only be fully clear when we examine an archaeological example in detail. Nevertheless, we can note here that if it is possible to represent the relations between ten variables correctly in two dimensions then we can replace the ten by two new ones at right angles *which contain all the original information.*

The idea is not dissimilar from the kinds of statistical summary which we have already seen. We may have a large number of values of some variable, which together make up a normal distribution. Given its shape, once we know its mean and its standard deviation there is an enormous amount we can say about it just on the basis of the two summary numbers, without needing to worry about the original data values.

In the present case, rather than obtaining a mean number we want to start by obtaining a mean variable. This will be a new, synthetic variable, in the same way that a mean rarely coincides exactly with any of the numbers in a distribution. It will also be the variable which is overall closest to all the original variables in the analysis, again a similar concept to that behind the mean of a distribution. In the present context we can define closeness in terms of angular distance. The variable which is overall closest to all the original ones will be in such a position that the sum of the angles between it and each of them will be the smallest possible.

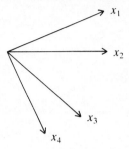

Figure 13.8. Geometric representation of the correlations between four variables.

Let's look at this by means of a simple example (figure 13.8). Here we have a diagram representing the relations between four variables whose correlations are represented by the angle between them. Obviously, the average variable summarising these four will be somewhere between x_2 and x_3. How good such averages are at representing the original variables is a relevant question which may strike you here. We'll see how this may be assessed later but for the moment the immediate question is how do we find out precisely where the average is.

Table 13.1. Angles between variables shown in figure 13.8.

	x_1	x_2	x_3	x_4
x_1	0	22	61	84
x_2	22	0	40	62
x_3	61	40	0	24
x_4	84	62	24	0

The first thing to do is note the exact values of all the angles and then the corresponding correlations/cosines (tables 13.1–2). Having done this we can obtain the total sum of correlations for each variable (table 13.2), remembering that the largest sum of correlations corresponds to the smallest sum of angles. We can see that as expected x_2 and x_3 have the largest sum of correlations and are therefore closest to the average, but we still haven't obtained the position of the average itself. This requires several more steps.

The total number of entries in this matrix is 16, the square of the number of variables. If each correlation value were 1.0 then the total sum of correlations in the table would be 16.0. In the present case, of course, it isn't: the total sum of correlations is found by adding the separate sums for each variable: $2.517 + 3.162 + 3.165 + 2.488 = 11.332$.

Table 13.2. Correlations between variables shown in figure 13.8.

	x_1	x_2	x_3	x_4
x_1	1.000	0.927	0.485	0.105
x_2	0.927	1.000	0.766	0.469
x_3	0.485	0.766	1.000	0.914
x_4	0.105	0.469	0.914	1.000
Sum	2.517	3.162	3.165	2.488

Going back to our hypothetical example for a moment, if the total sum of correlations in the table was 16.0 then the maximum possible for any single variable would be 4.0, the square root of 16.0. Similarly here, the total sum of correlations is 11.332; the total sum possible for any single variable is $\sqrt{11.332}$, which is 3.366. This is the variable with the largest possible overall correlation with all the other variables, or the one which is overall closest to the other variables in terms of angular distance. In other words, it is the average variable we are looking for, otherwise known as the first *principal component*. What we still do not know though is where this component lies in relation to the other variables.

Let us suppose that one of the original variables in this case coincided with the average variable or first principal component, i.e. the angle between them was zero degrees. It too would have a sum of correlations of 3.366 and its correlation/cosine with the component would be 1.0; that is to say it would be the ratio of the sum of correlations for the original variable to the sum of correlations for the principal component; here $3.366/3.366 = 1.0$, corresponding to zero degrees.

The same rationale applies, of course, whether or not any of the original variables coincides with the component: if we divide the sum of correlations for a variable by the sum of correlations for the component, the result is the correlation between the two, which can then be turned into an angle via the cosine. Let us carry out this operation for our example (table 13.3), and put the component on our original diagram of the relations between the variables (figure

Table 13.3. Correlations and angles between the four
original variables and the first principal component.
Total sum of correlations (TS) = 11.332, $\sqrt{TS}$ = 3.366.

	x_1	x_2	x_3	x_4
Sum	2.517	3.162	3.165	2.488
Sum/$\sqrt{TS}$	0.748	0.939	0.940	0.739
Angle	42°	20°	20°	42°

13.9). By finding this component we have obtained a single variable
averaging the four original ones, whether or not for the moment we
think it's a good summary or average and would be prepared to use
it in some analysis instead of the original variables.

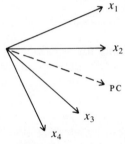

Figure 13.9. Geometric representation of the
correlations between four variables, with
the first principal component added.

The method works in exactly the same way in the case where
there are strong negative correlations, as we may briefly illustrate
with the following example, in which x_1 and x_2 are highly correlated
with each other and both strongly negatively correlated with x_3
(figure 13.10).

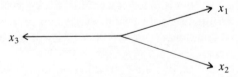

Figure 13.10. Geometric representation of the
correlations between three variables.

The actual angles are shown in table 13.4, and the correlations/
cosines in table 13.5. Putting in the component results in figure
13.11. In this instance, then, x_1 and x_2 have strong positive correla-

Table 13.4. Angles between variables shown in figure 13.10.

	x_1	x_2	x_3
x_1	0	34	164
x_2	34	0	162
x_3	164	162	0

Table 13.5. Correlations between variables shown in figure 13.10. $\text{TS} = 0.884$, $\sqrt{\text{TS}} = 0.913$.

	x_1	x_2	x_3
x_1	1.000	0.829	-0.961
x_2	0.829	1.000	-0.951
x_3	-0.961	-0.951	1.000
Sum	0.868	0.878	-0.912
Sum/$\sqrt{\text{TS}}$	0.950	0.962	-0.999
Angle	18°	16°	177°

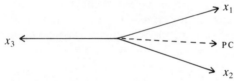

Figure 13.11. Geometric representation of the correlations between three variables, with the first principal component added.

tions with the principal component and x_3 a strong negative one.

These examples should have given you a feel for what a principal component is since they show one way in which they may be derived. It may be worth adding that this is not how they are actually calculated by the computer programs which carry out principal components analyses; nevertheless, these arrive at the same end by a different means.

At this point I want to look again at the results of the first example to see what more may be said now that the first component has been located. As we saw, the angle between the component and the original variables was obtained by dividing the sum of correlations for a given variable by the square root of the total sum of correlations, to give a value for the correlation of the variable with the component, corresponding to the cosine of the angle between them.

It is these correlations with the variables which actually define the component; they are known as the *component loadings* and they have exactly the same interpretation as ordinary correlation coefficients. In particular, we can use them now to get an answer to the question of how representative our new average variable is of those already present, for the squared values of the correlations between the variables and the component (of the component loadings in other words) correspond precisely to the r^2 coefficient of determination values which we have seen in our discussion of regression. That is to say, by squaring the component loading of a variable we can find out the percentage of the variation in that variable that is accounted for by the new component (but see the footnote for eigenvalue below). The figures for our example are presented in table 13.6. In this case it appears that the new component accounts for 56% of the variation in variable x_1, 88.2% of the variation in x_2, and so on. If we sum all these values we have the sum total of all the variation accounted for by the component. For reasons arising from the matrix algebra derivation of the quantity this sum total is usually known as the *eigenvalue* (or *latent root*) of the matrix, the matrix in question being the original matrix of correlations/cosines describing the relations between our four variables.* The formula for the eigenvalue is

$$\lambda_i = \sum_{j=1}^{n} L_{ij}^2$$

where λ_i is the eigenvalue for component i, L_{ij} is the loading of variable j on component i, and the summation is over all variables from 1 to n. In this case we have

$$\lambda_1 = 0.56 + 0.882 + 0.884 + 0.546 = 2.872$$

As it stands it is difficult to attribute much meaning to this quantity of the sum of the squared loadings. It is more helpful from the point of view of interpretation of a component to relate its eigenvalue to the total variation in the variables. Because we are

---

* Some computer programs normalise the component loadings so that their squared values sum to 1.0 rather than to the eigenvalue; in these circumstances the squared loadings do not correspond to r^2 values or the loadings themselves to correlation coefficients. To produce this correspondence the normalised loadings should be squared and then multiplied by the eigenvalue for the component. This gives the corrected squared loading corresponding to an r^2 value; the square root of this in turn gives a loading corresponding to a correlation coefficient.

Table 13.6. Correlations and squared correlations
of four variables with the first principal component,
from the data in table 13.3 and figure 13.9.

Variable	Component loading	Squared loading (r^2)
x_1	0.748	0.560
x_2	0.939	0.882
x_3	0.940	0.884
x_4	0.739	0.546

dealing with a matrix of correlation coefficients in which the variance in each variable has been standardised to 1.0, the sum total of the variation in the data is given by the number of variables in the analysis. To find the percentage of the variation in all the variables taken together accounted for by the component, we divide the eigenvalue for the component by the number of variables and multiply by 100:

$$\text{percentage accounted for} = \frac{\lambda_1}{n} \times 100$$

Here

$$\text{percentage accounted for} = \frac{2.872}{4} \times 100 = 71.8\%$$

We can see that our new variable or principal component accounts for 71.8% of the variation in the original four variables. To reiterate the point, the idea here is exactly analogous to that we have already seen in regression analysis. In multiple regression we were using a number of independent variables to account for variation in a dependent; here we are using a new variable we have defined to account for variation in the set of variables with which we started. In terms of our aim of trying to reduce the complexity in our data by reducing the number of variables with which we have to deal, we are already doing quite well in this case; we have replaced just over 70% of the variation in four variables by a single new one. In the case of two of our original variables the component accounts for 88% of the variation, for the other two, x_1 and x_4, it is not so high, at around 55%.

The next question is whether we cannot account for at least some of the balance, both in the individual variables and overall, by obtaining a second component. To relate what is involved to the topic of regression again, we can say that the variation unaccounted for by the first component is the residual variation from it – the variation which has zero correlation with it. Accordingly, the best way of accounting for this variation will be in terms of a component which is uncorrelated with the first, that is to say at right angles, or orthogonal, to it.

Table 13.7. Correlations and angles between the four variables represented in figure 13.8 and tables 13.1-2, with the second principal component derived from them.

Variable	Loading on second component	Angle between variables and second component
x_1	−0.661	131°
x_2	−0.336	110°
x_3	0.335	70°
x_4	0.676	47°

The loadings of the four variables on the second component, together with their conversion into angles, are shown in table 13.7. If we now draw in the second component on our original diagram of the relations among our four variables and between them and the first component, we can see that the second one is indeed at right angles to the first (figure 13.12).

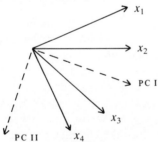

Figure 13.12. Geometric representation of the correlations between four variables, with the first two principal components added.

We can also go on, as with the first component, to calculate the amount of variation in each of the individual variables, and the sum overall, accounted for by the second component, by simply squaring the component loadings. Likewise, these squared loadings can be summed to give the eigenvalue for the second component. The results of this operation are presented in table 13.8, together with the results for component 1 already given, for reasons which will become clear in a moment.

Table 13.8. Squared correlations of four variables with principal components 1 and 2, from figure 13.12.

Variable	Squared loading on component 2	Squared loading on component 1
x_1	0.437	0.560
x_2	0.113	0.882
x_3	0.112	0.884
x_4	0.457	0.546
Sum	1.118	2.872

From this we can see that component 2 accounts for 43.7% of the variation in variable x_1, 11.3% in x_2, and so on. Overall the eigenvalue of the component is 1.118; to find the percentage of the variation in all the variables taken together accounted for by the second component we carry out the same calculation as for the first:

$$\text{percentage accounted for} = \frac{\lambda_2}{n} \times 100$$

Here

$$\text{percentage accounted for} = \frac{1.118}{4} \times 100 = 28.0\%$$

At this point we can start looking at the results for the two components together. The first component accounted for 71.8% of the variation; the two together account for 99.8%, or 100% within the limits of rounding error. Similarly, if we look directly at the eigenvalues we see that they sum to 3.99, while the sum total of variation in the correlation matrix from which the components were derived was 4.0, the number of variables. Likewise, if we look at the results for the individual variables and sum the squared loadings for each, they all come to more or less 1.0, or 100%, again within the limits of rounding error.

In other words, our two new components have accounted for 100% of the variation in the original four variables. This tells us that we can describe the variation in four variables in terms of two new ones without losing any of the information originally present. This is satisfactory in itself since it means that our data are immediately simplified and we are therefore more likely to be successful in detecting and understanding patterning within them. In visual

terms, instead of looking at a series of scattergrams of the relationships between our four variables two at a time, we can simply look
at one scattergram in two dimensions. In fact, we can note in this
case that if we had not been able to account for all the variation with
two components then it would have been impossible to represent
the relationships between the original four variables correctly on a
flat piece of paper. Conversely, if we could draw a diagram of the
correct relations between 100 variables on a sheet of paper, we
would know in advance that they could be reduced to two components.

Nevertheless, as we've noted already, our new variables may not
only give us a simplification, useful in itself, they may also define
underlying dimensions of variation, substantively interesting to us,
affecting the values of the variables we have measured. In order to
see how this might work we first need to switch our perspective.

So far we have only looked at components in connection with a
series of abstract variables arbitrarily defined to have certain relationships. When dealing with real data we start off with cases
which have values on a set of variables and it is in terms of these
values and their relationships that we arrive at the correlations
between the variables. Presumably then, if we can replace a set of
correlated variables with new uncorrelated ones then we can replace the values of our cases on the original variables with their
values on the new ones and it is these new values with which we
construct our now simplified scattergrams; these new values are
known as *component scores*. As usual, how they are obtained is best
illustrated graphically with a two-variable example.

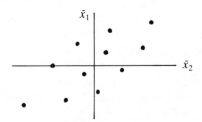

Figure 13.13. Scattergram of data points
with values on two variables, x_1 and x_2.

When the observations on two variables are correlated, the scattergram will appear as in figure 13.13, with the centre of gravity of
the distribution at the intersection of the two means. Where are the
axes of the space defining this scatter of points? They are the axes

of the ellipse enclosing the scatter of points and the angle between them is given by the correlation between the two variables concerned; the origin is at the intersection of the two means. What is involved is shown in figure 13.14.

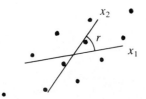

Figure 13.14. Axes of the ellipse defining the scatter of data points in figure 13.13. The angle between the axes corresponds to the correlation between the variables.

When we find the principal components we are defining different axes for this scatter. The first principal component corresponds to the long axis of the ellipse and the second component to the short axis, at right angles to the first. The lengths of the new axes or components correspond to their eigenvalues. The result is shown in figure 13.15.

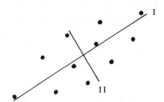

Figure 13.15. The principal components of the scatter of data points on figure 13.13.

When we are simply moving from one pair of dimensions to another pair, as in this example, we are not perhaps doing a great deal, but as we've seen already it is the possibilities of space reduction which are particularly attractive.

You may wonder what all this has to do with the topic of component scores, for we seem to have done little more than repeat our derivation of principal components from a slightly different point of view. The component scores come in when we focus on what happens to a particular point when the axes are transformed in the way we have seen: How do we get from its values on the two original variables to its values on the new components? Again the

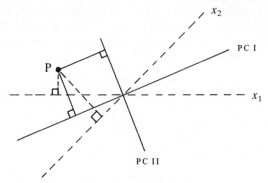

Figure 13.16. The relationship between the value of a
data point on the original variables x_1 and x_2, and its
score on the components PC I and PC II.

matter is best illustrated by a diagram (figure 13.16).

The position of point P is initially defined by its value on variables
x_1 and x_2; the dashed lines projected down from the point to meet
these two axes at right angles show the values of point P on these
two variables. When we find the principal components we don't
actually do anything to point P – it stays where it is – but we now
have a new coordinate system in terms of which to describe its
position. Its position in terms of the new axes is given by the solid
lines projected from point P to meet the component axes at right
angles. The point's position on each of these new axes is known as
its component score for that axis, and just as we plotted scattergrams of our data points in terms of their values on the original
variables so we can plot scattergrams of our data points in terms of
their component scores; we will see below ways in which this can be
helpful to us.

Component scores are obtained from the formula

$$S_{ik} = \sum_{j=1}^{n} x_{ij} L_{jk}$$

where S_{ik} is the score of observation i on component k, x_{ij} is the
standardised value for observation i on variable j, L_{jk} is the loading
of variable j on component k, and n is the number of variables. In
words, we start by taking the standard score for observation i on
variable j; we noted at the beginning of our account of principal
components that we would be describing it in terms of a matrix of
correlation coefficients, which therefore implied that we were dealing with standardised values for our variables. We then multiply
this standardised value by the loading of that variable on the compo-

nent of interest, i.e. by the correlation of the variable with the component, which in turn gives us the angle between the variable and the component. It is obviously necessary to know this angle if we are to change from one set of coordinates to another. In fact, of course, we need to know the relationship between every variable used in the analysis and the component currently of interest to make the transformation of coordinates successfully. We have to note each loading and the value of our data point on each variable, multiply them together and then sum all the results, for as many variables as we have.

At the end of the process of calculating component scores – which does not have to be done by hand but is available in standard principal components analysis computer programs – we have a table of the scores of our individual cases on each of the components, in the same way as initially we had a table of their scores on the variables we'd measured.

Summary of Principal Components Analysis. In summary, PCA is extremely versatile and does a number of very useful things all at the same time (Doran and Hodson 1975, 196):

1. It gives a helpful indication of the relationships between variables.

2. It also provides information about the relationships between units.

3. It suggests whether there are any major trends behind the raw data, and which variables are mainly involved in the trends.

4. It provides a transformation of the data in which in general a very large percentage of the variation in a large number of variables is compressed into a smaller number of variables.

5. The transformation effected is such that the new variables are uncorrelated with one another.

It is this last property which, as we have seen, makes principal components so suitable as a method for overcoming the problem of collinearity in multiple regression. It is possible to use as input data for the regression not the scores of the individuals on the original variables but their component scores. Use of the components as independent variables removes the possibility of bias or ambiguity in the regression coefficients. The only problem about this is that the components are not always easy to interpret so that it may not be altogether clear what is going on in the regression.

Finally, it is appropriate to say something about the assumptions involved in PCA. PCA itself is simply a mathematical method for extracting the principal axes from matrices and may be applied to any symmetric matrix of coefficients defining relations between variables. It is usually applied to matrices of correlation coefficients and it is therefore important to be satisfied that the linear correlation coefficient, r, does provide a satisfactory picture of the relations between the variables. This point may be investigated by examining the bivariate scattergrams of relations between pairs of variables. Alternatively, if the individual variable distributions are normal it is likely that use of the correlation coefficient will be satisfactory.

If the matrix analysed is not a correlation matrix it is generally a matrix of variances and covariances. The correlation coefficient, of course, as we saw above, is the covariance between two variables which have been transformed into standardised (Z score) form. Consequently, the comments relevant to correlation coefficients also apply to covariances.

In fact, probably the majority of statisticians are extremely cautious about using the correlation matrix rather than the covariance matrix for principal components analysis, on the grounds that it tends to destroy the validity of available statistical distributional theory; it can make the results difficult to interpret; and it allows the dubious possibility of combining different types of measurements (Fieller, pers. comm.).

As noted already then, the decision to analyse the covariance or the correlation matrix should not be made without thought in the case of principal components analysis. In addition to what has just been said, you should note that analysis of the two different matrices may give very different results – unsurprising if you think what is involved in variable standardisation.

A further point to be borne in mind is that since principal components analysis is designed to extract axes from matrices, it will do this regardless of any substantive meaning they may or may not have. In any matrix of correlations between even a moderate number of variables there will be a large number of values. Some of these will be quite large and statistically significant purely by chance, even if the raw data are simply a set of computer-generated random numbers. On the basis of these chance large values apparently significant components may result from a PCA, which may even be apparently interpretable in substantive terms to the archaeologist eagerly searching for patterns. This problem is discussed in an archaeological context by Vierra and Carlson (1981), who suggest testing the correlation matrix prior to PCA to see if there is a significantly large number of significant correlations. By this means illusory results may be avoided.

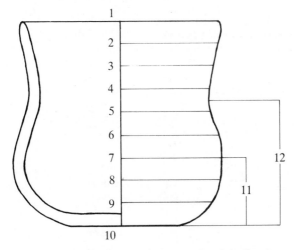

Figure 13.17. The measurements used to describe the
shape of a number of late neolithic ceramic vessels from
Central Europe.

An Archaeological Example. At this point we are badly in need of
an archaeological example to bring together all the strands of our
methodological account in a concrete substantively comprehensible
fashion. The analysis to be described is concerned with the problem
of understanding variation in the shape of 65 ceramic vessels dating
to the end of the neolithic period in Central Europe. The shapes of
the vessels are described in terms of twelve measurements, shown
in figure 13.17.* Ten measurements were taken at intervals from
the top to the bottom of the vessel (cf. Shennan and Wilcock 1975) ;
the measurements were taken from, and at right angles to, the
centre line of the vessel drawing to the nearest point on the exterior
surface of the vessel. Two further measurements were also taken :
the height of the belly of the pot and the height of the bottom of the
neck. In order that vessel size, as measured by overall vessel height,
should not be a major factor behind the variation, all the measurements were standardised by division by overall vessel height. The
correlations between the resulting ratios were then obtained and a
principal components analysis was carried out on the matrix of
correlation coefficients of each variable with every other variable.
The eigenvalues and the variance accounted for by the components

* More sophisticated methods of vessel shape description are now
available ; see, for example, the use of contour codes by Kampffmeyer
and Teegen (1986).

Table 13.9. Eigenvalues and variance accounted for
by 12 principal components resulting from the analysis
of a group of vessels described in terms of shape.

Component	Eigenvalue	Percentage variance	Cumulative variance
1	7.30	60.87	60.87
2	2.05	17.07	77.93
3	1.41	11.77	89.69
4	0.58	4.85	94.54
5	0.45	3.74	98.27
6	0.08	0.64	98.91
7	0.06	0.48	99.38
8	0.04	0.30	99.68
9	0.02	0.16	99.82
10	0.01	0.09	99.90
11	0.01	0.06	99.96
12	0.00	0.05	100.00

are shown in table 13.9.

As you can see, we started with twelve variables and there are twelve components, but the majority of them only account for minute proportions of the variance. The question obviously arises here, as in many other cases, how many of the components should be taken seriously. There is no fixed rule for this but the guideline most often adopted is to take seriously only those components with an eigenvalue of 1.0 or more. The reasoning behind this is that 1.0 represents the variance of a single variable in the correlation matrix so that if a component has an eigenvalue of less than this it actually accounts for less of the variation in the data than any one of the original variables (Johnston 1978, 146). An alternative is to plot the eigenvalues as the vertical axis against the components as the horizontal axis and to look for a kink in the curve of declining eigenvalues.

If we adopt the first approach in this case we see that we only have to deal with three components, all together accounting for 90% of the variation in the data. Thus, in terms of one of the main aims of principal components analysis, data reduction and simplification, we have achieved a reduction from twelve variables to three new ones while still retaining the vast majority of the original information. Of these three, of course, the first is by far the most important.

It appears then that there are some major trends behind the initially confusing variation in the raw data, and the next step is to see which variables are involved in these trends. To do this we need to look at the loadings of the variables on the components, and also at their squared values, to see the percentage of the variation in the variables accounted for by the components. These are shown in table 13.10.

Table 13.10. Loadings and squared loadings of 12 variables defining vessel shape on the first three principal components arising from a principal components analysis of the matrix of correlations between the 12 shape-defining variables.

Variable	Component I loading	Squared loading	Component II loading	Squared loading	Component III loading	Squared loading
1	0.730	0.532	−0.460	0.211	−0.437	0.191
2	0.811	0.657	−0.395	0.156	−0.393	0.154
3	0.897	0.805	−0.235	0.055	−0.331	0.110
4	0.924	0.854	0.229	0.052	−0.216	0.048
5	0.911	0.829	0.384	0.147	−0.014	0.0002
6	0.919	0.844	0.322	0.104	0.076	0.006
7	0.929	0.864	0.132	0.017	0.223	0.050
8	0.894	0.800	−0.064	0.004	0.384	0.147
9	0.794	0.631	−0.241	0.058	0.521	0.272
10	0.576	0.331	−0.435	0.189	0.215	0.046
11	0.349	0.121	0.727	0.529	−0.454	0.206
12	0.184	0.034	0.726	0.527	0.297	0.085

If we look first at component I we can see that the vast majority of the variables have high positive correlations with it; it accounts for more than 50% of the variance for variables 1 to 9. Component I defines a pattern of variation common to all these. On the basis of the series of high correlations we can say that when a case has high values on one of these it will have high values on the others, and when it has low values on one it will have low values on the others. This pattern is condensed to a single trend defined by component I and, as we have seen, accounting for 60% of the variance in the data. Precisely what that trend is will become clearer when we examine the score of our individual cases on component I, because that is where the abstractions of the analysis can be directly related to the raw archaeological data. For the moment, however, we will continue with our examination of the component loadings.

A glance at these for component II shows immediately that in general this is much less important than the first – it accounts for only very small proportions of the variation in most of the variables. The exceptions are variables 11 and 12 and it is clear that it is with these that component II is associated, accounting for more than 50 % of the variance in each case. It appears that these two have a common pattern of variation defined by this component: when height of belly is high then so is height of neck; when one is low the other is low.

Component III, of course, is even less significant, in no case accounting for more than just over 25 % of the variation in a variable. If we look at the loadings we see that variables 1 and 2 have moderate negative correlations with the component, as does variable 11; variable 9, on the other hand, has a moderate positive correlation. This would seem to suggest that in terms of this component high values on 9 tend to be associated with low values on 1, 2 and 11, but what this actually means in terms of vessel shape is not clear. In order to make more progress we need to look at the component scores.

Table 13.11. Scores of 22 vessels on the first three principal components derived from a matrix of correlations between 12 variables describing vessel shape.

Case no.	Component scores			Case no.	Component scores		
	I	II	III		I	II	III
1	2.426	−1.403	−1.550	34	−1.801	3.318	−0.501
4	−2.546	0.586	−0.460	37	4.555	2.965	−1.075
4	−0.362	0.184	0.926	40	−2.593	1.214	−0.974
10	0.871	−0.282	2.436	43	−1.657	0.500	1.281
13	3.296	−0.573	0.676	46	1.505	1.878	2.178
16	−1.517	−0.051	−1.001	49	0.819	0.338	0.468
19	−4.392	−0.061	−0.351	52	−1.759	−2.298	−0.696
22	−2.891	0.496	−0.257	55	−0.544	−0.786	−0.426
25	−3.672	−1.238	−3.329	58	−3.352	0.131	0.445
28	−3.886	−0.627	0.401	61	3.771	0.292	0.557
31	−1.544	4.143	−0.350	64	4.185	−2.577	−2.139

In table 13.11 the scores of the cases on the first three principal components are listed; only every third case out of the 65 is included as the information is merely required for illustrative purposes. These scores provide us with a means of obtaining a direct insight into the archaeological meaning of the components. If we note which cases have the highest negative values on the component and which have the highest positive values we can refer to our measurements or drawings of the individual vessels and see what it is that the vessels at each end have in common and what differentiates those at one end from those at the other. The component will then represent a trend from one to the other of these extreme types.

If we look at component I we see that cases 19, 25, 28 and 58 have large negative values and 13, 37, 61 and 64 have large positive values. For component II cases 1, 25, 52 and 64 have large negative values, 31, 34 and 37 have high positive ones. Finally, for component III cases 1, 25 and 64 are at the negative end and 10, 43 and 46 at the opposite end.

The raw data values for all the cases whose component scores are given – measurements expressed as percentages of vessel height – are presented in table 13.12. If we look at the cases which have high negative values on component I we see that they all have generally low values on the first nine variables, while those cases at the opposite end have high values for these variables. Remembering that all these values are width measurements in relation to height we can see that all those with low values are slim vessels, all those with high values fat or squat ones. In other words, component I represents a trend from slim to squat in vessel shape, a trend summarising the majority of the covariation between these width measurements; obviously, in general if one of them tends to be either large or small then the others will tend to follow suit, hence the values of the loadings which we have already seen. Referring back to the loadings, the only width measurement which does not fit this pattern so strongly is the base.

We can now turn to component II. As we'd expect from the loadings, the distinctions here concern the height of the belly and neck (variables 11 and 12). For those vessels at one end the belly and neck are relatively low in relation to the overall height, for those at the other end they are relatively high. Component II represents a trend from one to the other. By definition this trend in variation is independent of that defined by the first component.

For component III the pattern is more complex and difficult to discern, unsurprising in view of the generally weak loadings and the relatively complex pattern they indicate, with variables 1, 2 and 11 showing weak to moderate negative correlations with the component and variable 9 a moderate positive one.

Examination of the values of these variables for the cases at either end of component III shows that those at the negative end have relatively wide rim and next-to-rim measurements while those at the positive end have relatively narrow ones; it also reveals a contrast between the two ends in the relation between variables 9

Table 13.12. Raw data values for the 22 vessels whose component scores are given in table 13.11.

Case no.	1	2	3	4	5	Variables 6	7	8	9	10	11	12
1	60.36	55.86	51.35	48.65	50.45	53.15	54.05	50.45	42.34	27.93	37.84	65.77
4	41.28	37.61	35.78	36.70	39.45	43.12	42.20	38.53	33.03	25.69	38.53	77.06
7	40.96	38.55	37.35	37.35	48.19	53.01	54.22	50.60	43.37	21.69	33.73	68.67
10	34.88	34.88	38.37	40.75	50.00	56.98	59.30	55.81	47.67	33.72	34.88	62.79
13	54.84	50.54	47.31	48.39	53.76	59.14	62.37	58.06	46.24	31.18	34.41	75.27
16	47.62	41.90	39.05	40.00	41.90	44.76	45.71	42.86	36.19	20.00	36.19	70.48
19	38.40	34.40	32.00	32.00	33.60	36.80	39.20	38.40	32.00	16.80	30.40	71.20
22	40.00	36.47	34.12	35.29	36.47	41.18	44.71	42.35	36.47	17.65	36.47	72.94
25	48.24	44.71	38.82	35.29	31.76	38.82	40.00	35.29	25.88	15.29	37.65	51.76
28	37.50	31.94	30.56	31.25	34.72	38.89	42.36	40.28	34.03	24.31	31.25	64.58
31	32.18	27.59	28.74	49.43	52.87	50.57	47.13	41.38	33.33	22.99	55.17	81.61
34	32.86	34.29	37.14	42.86	48.57	51.43	50.00	44.29	34.29	8.57	41.43	84.29
37	50.75	47.76	47.76	64.18	70.15	70.15	64.18	56.72	41.79	20.90	49.25	79.10
40	35.71	34.52	35.71	39.29	44.05	46.43	45.24	39.29	30.95	20.24	41.67	66.67
43	35.29	34.31	33.33	36.27	44.12	49.02	50.98	49.02	41.18	20.59	32.35	70.59
46	37.33	36.00	36.00	45.33	54.67	61.33	62.67	60.00	48.00	21.33	37.33	78.67
49	44.00	42.67	41.33	41.33	50.67	56.00	57.33	54.67	42.67	21.33	36.00	69.33
52	51.39	45.83	38.89	37.50	37.50	40.28	44.44	45.83	37.50	22.22	26.39	59.72
55	46.74	43.48	40.22	41.30	44.57	48.91	52.17	46.74	38.04	22.83	32.61	63.04
58	32.17	32.17	31.30	33.04	39.13	43.48	44.35	42.61	35.65	21.74	34.78	62.61
61	50.53	48.42	48.42	54.74	60.00	62.11	62.11	58.95	48.42	27.37	36.84	73.68
64	66.15	64.62	56.92	52.31	52.31	55.38	55.38	53.85	46.15	33.85	41.54	56.92

and 11. At the negative end next-to-base width (9) and height of belly (11) are relatively similar, but at the positive end next-to-base width tends to be large and height of belly to be small.

Examination of the component scores then is important for understanding precisely what the principal components analysis is telling us about our data. It is, as we have seen, where the abstract analysis and the archaeological evidence confront each other directly. Component scores are much more immediate in this respect than component loadings. But the identification of the individual cases in relation to the components is important in another respect. In this example we have simply defined the archaeological meaning of the components in terms of variation in vessel shape. It might easily be, however, that these trends in shape relate for example to change through time, so that the vessels at one end of a component are early and those at the other end are late. By being able to consider the individual vessels, or whatever our cases might be, we have access to information which may exist about other aspects of their archaeological context: are they associated, for example, with other items for whose dating we have independent evidence. If we simply look at the overall correlations or loadings this information is not available to us.

So far, however, we have only looked at the scores of the cases on each individual component taken separately. This is obviously essential if we're trying to define what the components mean in archaeological terms. Nevertheless, the possibility clearly arises of producing scattergrams of the scores of the cases on two components together. In the example of our vessels a scattergram just using the first two components includes 78 % of the variation in the data, while if we use different symbols for the cases according to their scores on component III a further 12 % is included, bringing the total to 90 %. The possibilities of visual assessment of patterns in these circumstances, as compared with dealing with the original twelve variables are certainly far greater.

But what patterns are we likely to be looking for? First, it may be that such patterns as chronological trends in the variation in our data will not be apparent in terms of a single dimension but will become clear when we are dealing with two. Second, as was noted already in the previous chapter, such scattergrams can provide a supplement or alternative to cluster analysis. They provide an ordination of the data in very few dimensions containing a large amount of information. We can tell, for example, whether genuine clusters of data items exist, or whether clusters would represent a relatively arbitrary division of a continuum; or which points are outliers and do not really belong with any others. Again, as with the results of the cluster analysis of data items, we can see, for example, whether all the cases in a particular part of the scattergram come from a particular site.

A scattergram of the cases whose component scores were listed above is shown in figure 13.18. It is based on the first two compo-

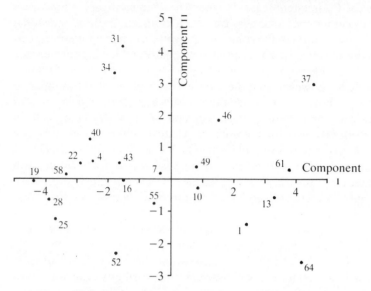

Figure 13.18. Scattergram of ceramic vessel scores on the
first two principal components. Data from table 13.11.

nents. It is clear from this that while there are marked trends in the
data and some of the vessels are distinctly unusual, lying well to the
fringes of the main distribution, there is little evidence for any
discrete clustering. This is not to say that we might not want to
break up the continuum for some purpose, but if we are going to do
that we should be aware that we are breaking up a continuum and
not picking out clearly defined discrete clusters.

This consideration of component scores completes our illustration
of principal components analysis. It should be clear that so long as
it is used on data for which it is appropriate it can provide a great
deal of archaeologically relevant information about a given data set
which would not necessarily be accessible or apparent to an intuitive
approach to the same data, especially if the number of cases was
large. The eye and the brain are excellent for providing an overall
feel for what is going on in a particular set of aretfacts (if it is
artefacts that are being studied), in terms of morphological variation between them. Separating out that overall variation into
different aspects, analysing it, is better done by appropriate
methods and can provide new insights; after the analysis process
visual assessment can again play an important role.

Factor Analysis

Now that we have outlined principal components analysis it is necessary to consider factor analysis, since it has been very widely used in archaeology and understanding a not inconsiderable number of papers depends on a knowledge of it. It is a topic which has generated a considerable amount of discussion both among professional statisticians and among users of the technique in various disciplines, and it would probably be true to say that opinions are still divided on the subject of its usefulness. The fact that this is so should certainly be taken as a warning to the innocent archaeologist. What follows again makes much use of Johnston's (1978) approach; a rather more technical account is Dunn and Everitt (1983, chapter 1).

The essential difference between factor analysis and principal components analysis may seem fairly minor but it does have quite important consequences. Principal components analysis extracts components from all the variance in the data. Factor analysis works on a different principle. It assumes that the variance in a variable can be divided into two segments, one segment which it has in common with other variables and reflects its relations with them, and another part which is unique to itself and does not relate to anything else; these two parts are referred to as the *common variance* and the *unique variance*. The argument is that as factor analysis is concerned with defining underlying patterns of variation common to several variables then it should only operate on the common variance and leave the unique variance out of account: to include all the variance in the analysis is to confuse the issue. The first question which arises then is how to estimate the unique variance of the variables in the analysis so that it may be removed from consideration; the remaining common variance of a variable is often referred to as its *communality* in the jargon of factor analysis.

What is involved in technical terms in the factor analysis case is best illustrated by a comparison with principal components. We saw above that when components were extracted from a correlation matrix the entries down the principal diagonal of the matrix were all 1.0, the standardised variance of each variable. In factor analysis the value along the diagonal are not 1.0, but are the communality estimates for the different variables. These are usually the multiple R^2 values of the individual variables and will, of course, vary from one variable to another. You will remember from chapter 11 on multiple regression that the multiple R^2 value gives the proportion of the variation in a dependent variable accounted for by the effect of all the independents acting together and separately. Thus, to obtain the communalities each variable in turn is treated as dependent on all the others. The argument is that the amount of variance accounted for by the other variables is a measure of what a given variable has in common with them; whatever the source of the rest of the variance it is not relevant to the point at issue. The sum of the communalities is the total amount of variation in the analysis. If a given variable has only a small communality – in other words, the way in which it varies has little in common with the others – then it will play only a small role in the analysis.

In terms of our graphical illustration of the extraction of principal components, there the lines or vectors representing the individual variables were of equal length and each variable played an equal role in defining the position of the first component; in factor analysis the vectors corresponding to the variables would be of different lengths, the lengths corresponding to the communality value, and the position of the first average variable, or factor in this case, would be more strongly affected by those with the larger communalities; a variable with twice the communality of another would have twice the influence on the position of the factor.

As with principal components analysis, but using this different matrix, we obtain the loadings of each of the variables on the factor. Correspondingly, the squared factor loadings give us the proportion of the variance in the variables accounted for by the factor. At this point, however, we come to another major difference between the two. In a principal components analysis of a given matrix the components are obtained successively according to a fixed mathematical procedure and that is the end of the matter. Factor analysis, on the other hand, with its emphasis on finding the underlying pattern of variation behind groups of variables takes things a step further.

The point is best illustrated with reference to figure 13.19, in which all the vectors are drawn of equal length to simplify presentation. Here we have four variables, together with the two factors accounting for all the variation within them. As with principal components analysis, the first represents the average pattern of the four variables, based now on their communalities, and the second the average of the remainder, by definition at right angles to the first. But do these really represent the underlying dimensions of variation behind what are clearly two pairs of variables? We tend to feel intuitively that if the factors could somehow be moved round, so that one corresponded to one pair of variables and the other to the other then we would have a better representation of the relations between the variables in the simplified space defined by these new underlying dimensions.

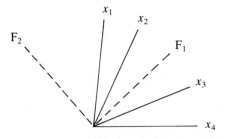

Figure 13.19. Geometric representation of the correlations between four variables, and the two factors accounting for all the variation between them (after Johnston 1978).

This is precisely the step which factor analysis takes: the axes are rotated in order to achieve this kind of correspondence. The rules which have been devised and implemented for carrying out this procedure are many and varied. Some of them even drop the stipulation that the new axes should be at right angles to one another, but these are not considered here and the most commonly used ones keep this constraint; they are therefore known as *orthogonal rotations*. The idea is to rotate the axes to a position which is as close as possible to an ideal referred to as *simple structure*. This ideal is that each variable should be completely identified with one single factor and no other: all its variance should be accounted for by a single factor, not split between several as we saw with principal components analysis. In numerical terms the aim is that each variable should have a loading of 1.0 on one factor and 0.0 on all the others. Obviously it is impossible to achieve this ideal with any real data set in practice, but computer methods are available which approximate it as closely as possible for any given case. As far as our example in figure 13.19 is concerned we can simply do the rotation visually (figure 13.20) but this again will be impossible in real examples.

As you can see, once rotation has taken place we have not only reduced the variation in the data to a smaller number of dimensions, we have identified the new dimensions as far as possible with specific sets of variables, which can potentially be very helpful in

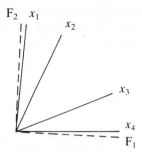

Figure 13.20. The two factors from figure 13.19 after
orthogonal rotation as near as possible to simple structure
(after Johnston 1978).

understanding what is behind the variation in our data.

But rotation brings its own set of problems, since the decision
about the number of factors to be rotated in effect determines the
number of underlying dimensions supposedly behind the variation
in the variables and also the way in which the dimensions are
defined: rotating two will give two groups of variables, rotating
three will give three. Furthermore, the introduction of the third will
not simply add a dimension associated with a group of variables to
the first two groups; it will change the definition of the first two.
This is intuitively obvious if you think about what is involved in
rotating a fixed set of axes at right angles to one another through a
cloud of data points: the best position for three axes in terms of the
criterion specified above is most unlikely to be the same as that for
two. When not only the number but the nature of what are in some
sense supposed to be 'objectively existing' underlying dimensions
of the data can be affected, or even determined, by relatively
arbitrary choices about the number of axes to be rotated, then one
quite rightly feels that caution is required unless there are very good
reasons for the number of axes chosen. If the data are multivariate
normally distributed then maximum likelihood factor analysis provides a statistically rigorous method for deciding on an appropriate
number of factors for rotation (see e.g. Everitt and Dunn 1983,
200).

Factor Scores. When we come to look at the scores of the individual observations on the new axes then factor analysis presents
further problems. We saw that with principal components analysis
individual scores on the principal components could be obtained,
and that they could provide us with much useful information. Unfortunately, precise factor scores for individual observations cannot

be obtained in the same way, because, as we have seen, factor analysis does not use all the variation in the data, only the common variance, 'whereas the observed values on the original variables combine common and unique elements in unknown proportions' (Johnston 1978, 173). Because of this discrepancy between the basis of the analysis and the nature of the individual observations factor scores can only be estimated, by a form of regression procedure. Consequently, although most factor analysis programs have options for the production of factor scores, and in essence they are the same kind of thing as component scores, whose derivation we have outlined at length above, it is important when interpreting them to bear in mind that they are only estimates, which may be better for some observations than others, and not fixed scores.

An Archaeological Example. As an archaeological example of factor analysis we will take that described by Bettinger (1979). Bettinger was concerned with understanding the subsistence-settlement system of Owens Valley, in California. He had carried out a surface survey of the area and had information on over 100 sites in terms of the frequency of occurrence of nine different categories of features and artefacts. On the basis of this information he was interested in making inferences about the functions of the different sites.

Bettinger specifically addressed the factor analysis versus principal components analysis issue and the question of whether or not it was meaningful in his particular case to make a distinction between common and unique variance. He argued that as far as the regional distribution of features and tools was concerned idiosyncratic variation in variables from site to site would result from such factors as differential curation or differential access to raw materials. Common variance, on the other hand, patterns of variation which the different variables had in common with each other in a systematic kind of way, 'would most likely result from their use in complementary activities synchronised by the aboriginal economic schedule' (Bettinger 1979, 457). Since it was the economic schedule which interested Bettinger, his argument ran, an analytical method which considered only common variance would be the most appropriate one, hence factor rather than principal components analysis.

His starting point was a correlation matrix obtained from the frequencies of the different types of artefact and feature of interest to him at the individual sites; it is reproduced as table 13.13. As Bettinger himself remarks, the distributions of these frequencies are extremely skew, a common occurrence with distributions of

Table 13.13. Correlation matrix for settlement variables
(after Bettinger 1979).

	Fl	Ms	Cer	Pp	Bi	R	Uni	Core	Deb
Floor	—								
Milling stone	0.80	—							
Ceramic	0.02	0.39	—						
Projectile point	0.51	0.61	0.50	—					
Biface	0.40	0.62	0.51	0.83	—				
Roughout	0.06	0.21	0.44	0.59	0.58	—			
Uniface	0.13	0.21	0.17	0.40	0.33	0.60	—		
Core	0.16	0.29	0.16	0.24	0.26	0.36	0.82	—	
Debitage	0.08	0.19	0.29	0.35	0.31	0.48	0.84	0.82	—

frequencies of this type, and in these circumstances the product moment correlation coefficient, *r,* is unlikely to provide a very good description of the covariation between the variables. Nevertheless, he uses it, on the argument that in general such data will tend to produce correlation values lower than they really are, consequently his analysis will err on the conservative side. Although this may be true to a degree it is also likely that the description of the relationships by this means will be misleading to some extent since at many points along the implied linear regression line the relationships will be misspecified by the line – there will be marked patterning in the residuals. A more appropriate technique than factor analysis would probably have been correspondence analysis (see below p. 283), which does not require the same assumptions, although this would almost certainly have been unknown and unavailable to the author at the time he carried out his study. Despite these doubts about the appropriateness of the use of the correlation coefficient, the analysis remains an interesting one, and particularly useful from the point of view of illustrating a substantive interpretation of factor analysis results.

Examination of the correlation matrix suggests that occurrences of milling stones and floors are strongly related to one another, that this is also true of bifaces and projectile points, and that frequencies of occurrence of cores, debitage and unifaces are also highly inter-correlated.

The procedure adopted by Bettinger to analyse this matrix was first to carry out a principal components analysis to find the number of components with eigenvalues greater than 1.0, and then to obtain and rotate this number of factors using a matrix containing communality estimates along the principal diagonal. Three components had eigenvalues greater than 1.0 so three factors were obtained from the matrix based on communalities and then rotated. The loadings of the variables on the rotated factors are shown in table 13.14, together with the variable communalities. We can note from the latter that the occurrence of ceramics does not appear to be closely related to the other variables, and the same is true to a lesser extent of the occurrence of roughouts.

Table 13.14. Varimax rotation of factor matrix
(after Bettinger 1979). Factor definers are
indicated by parentheses.

Variable	Factor I	Factor II	Factor III	Communalities
Floor	0.05	0.07	(0.95)	0.91
Milling stone	0.11	0.37	(0.81)	0.80
Ceramic	0.10	(0.61)	0.06	0.38
Projectile point	0.17	(0.79)	0.43	0.84
Biface	0.14	(0.80)	0.37	0.80
Roughout	0.40	(0.67)	−0.05	0.61
Uniface	(0.91)	0.25	0.05	0.89
Core	(0.89)	0.07	0.15	0.82
Debitage	(0.88)	0.24	0.02	0.83
% variance	59.6	26.5	14.0	

If we now look at the loadings we see that three variables are very closely associated with factor I: unifaces, cores and debitage. Bettinger states that unifaces represent woodworking and the cores stone-working, while debitage results from stone tool manufacture and repair. His conclusion therefore is that factor I 'reflects the heavy-duty manufacturing of wood and stone tools' (1979, 466).

Factor II is identified with projectile points, bifaces, roughouts and ceramics. This obviously represents a range of different activities and Bettinger concludes that it indicates 'the basic assemblage needed to engage in and sustain procurement at camps occupied for more than a few days at a time, i.e. base camps' (1979, 466).

The final factor is obviously defined by the co-occurrence of floors and millingstones. 'Denoting dwellings, storage features and food preparation equipment, these categories leave little doubt that factor III is a complex of domestic facilities that would be employed year-round at occupation sites and seasonally, fall and winter, at pinyon camps' (1979, 466).

At this point it is necessary to note that Bettinger's factor analysis was part of a larger study and that he had already defined a set of three different site functional categories: occupation sites, temporary camps and pinyon camps, the latter being small camps occupied in late autumn and winter primarily serving as bases for obtaining pine nuts.

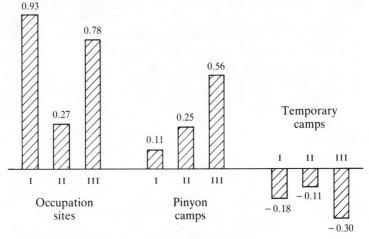

Figure 13.21. Mean factor scores for each settlement category: I, factor 1; II, factor 2; III, factor 3 (after Bettinger 1979).

To investigate the relationship between these already defined site categories and the results of the factor analysis Bettinger made use of the factor scores of his sites, computing mean factor scores for each site category on each of the three factors (figure 13.21) and drawing a number of conclusions from the results:

i) 'Heavy-duty manufacturing tools and by-products, camp maintenance and resource procurement tools, and domestic facilities are all prominently represented at occupation sites but virtually non-existent at temporary camps' (1979, 467).

ii) 'Pinyon camps are characterised by camp maintenance and resource procurement tools and domestic facilities, which is consistent with their function as fall and winter base camps' (1979, 467).

iii) 'Both are somewhat less strongly represented at pinyon camps than at occupation sites, probably because use of pinyon camps is more seasonally restricted.'

iv) 'Heavy-duty manufacturing tools and by-products are relatively insignificant at pinyon camps. Unlike occupation sites, both pinyon camps and temporary camps were primarily places for resource procurement, so much so that manufacturing activities . . . were systematically excluded' (1979, 468).

Bettinger's analysis provides a good example of the way factor analysis can be used in the context of a larger study to provide substantively useful and interpretable results. Sets of interrelated variables are defined and connected to the archaeological problem in terms of a clearly formulated model. However, to show the care with which all results of complex multivariate methods should be treated when it comes to substantive interpretation, the loadings of the variables on a set of unrotated principal components derived by this author from Bettinger's correlation matrix are presented, together with the relevant eigenvalues, in table 13.15.

Table 13.15. Summary of results of principal components analysis: eigenvalues of components, and loadings of variables on first three principal components, derived from the matrix of correlations between artefact types presented in table 13.13. N.B. These loadings are normalised so that their squared values sum to 1.0. See footnote on p.254 for the method of converting them so that they correspond to correlation coefficients.

Component	1	2	3	4	5	6	7	8	9
Eigenvalue	4.319	1.980	1.228	0.627	0.305	0.233	0.134	0.101	0.074

Variable	Component I	Component II	Component III
Floor	−0.230	0.413	0.539
Milling stone	−0.323	0.402	0.299
Ceramic	−0.267	0.123	−0.519
Projectile point	−0.394	0.262	−0.149
Biface	−0.381	0.261	−0.211
Roughout	−0.346	−0.122	−0.389
Uniface	−0.358	−0.409	0.147
Core	−0.322	−0.397	0.314
Debitage	−0.345	−0.419	0.112

Both sets of results are perfectly correct but they are not the same, and which set one uses depends on one's interest. Bettinger was interested in defining groups of related variables rather than in just summarising the main dimensions of variation in the data, hence the choice he makes. Another archaeologically based discussion of this issue may be found in Forsberg's (1985) analysis of hunter-gatherer subsistence settlement patterns in Sweden.

These relatively detailed descriptions and examples of principal components and factor analysis should have given you a feel for what is involved in multivariate analysis and the kinds of useful task it can be used to carry out. The remaining multivariate methods referred to at the beginning of this chapter will be treated much more briefly, for several reasons. In the light of the account of principal components and factor analysis much less space is required to give an idea of what they involve; space is simply not available to provide detailed examples of all of them; and archaeologically oriented accounts already exist (Doran and Hodson 1975; Bølviken *et al.* 1982).

i) *Principal Coordinates Analysis*

In many cases when we are dealing with qualitative and multistate variables we will have a matrix of similarities between a large number of items, of the type discussed in the previous chapter. The similarities may in fact be based on variables of a variety of different types put together using Gower's general coefficient of similarity. This is the type of example referred to at the beginning of this chapter to give you an indication of what ordination procedures involved. The process described in an intuitive fashion in that example concerning burials, to which you are referred again (p. 242), is in fact the process of principal coordinates analysis. In other words, in order to create a low-dimensional space for the purpose of understanding patterning in data we don't need to define the space in terms of *variables*; we can do so in terms of the space defined by the *similarities between the units*. In the same way as we could define principal components and their associated eigenvalues for the space created by the variables, we can define principal axes and eigenvalues for the space created by the similarities, that is to say, for the similarity matrix. The size of the eigenvalue gives the importance of a given dimension in accounting for variation in inter-point distances and can be converted in the same way as before into a figure for the percentage of the inter-point distance in the data accounted for by that particular dimension. Again, the first two or three dimensions often account for the major part of it. The principal axes of the space enable us to obtain the equivalent of a component score for each of our cases on each of the orthogonal axes of the space. Thus, we move from a relative representation of the cases or data points in relation to one another, to their representation in terms of their positions on the new axes. Again we can use these axes to produce scattergrams of our data points which we can examine for trends and clusters as we did with our scattergram of component scores.

However, the consequence of the fact that principal coordinates analysis works on similarities between cases rather than correlations between variables is that there are no loadings of variables on components to be considered and to be used as a basis for the interpretation of the results. It is *only* the equivalent of the component scores which principal coordinates analysis produces and it is these which must be interpreted to arrive at the substantive meaning of the new axes. Nevertheless, as we saw with the component scores this is not a problem. One has to note which cases are at one end of a given axis, which at the other, and then go back to the raw data on which the coordinates were based to see what it is that differentiates these from one another. Thus, if we were dealing with the results of a principal coordinates analysis of a matrix of similarities between graves then we could refer back to our initial listing of the values of the variables which were used to characterise the graves, different grave goods types for example. By this means we would obtain a substantive archaeological knowledge of the main factors behind the variation in the burials.

ii) *Non-Metric Multidimensional Scaling*
This technique approaches essentially the same problem as principal coordinates analysis from a rather different angle; for a given set of data it should produce very similar results, in terms of the relationships between points in the low-dimensional space which the method tries to achieve.

The conceptual basis of the technique is straightforward. The starting point is the same as for principal coordinates analysis: a measure of similarity or dissimilarity between our n cases, and a representation of the relationships between the cases in a multidimensional space, the number of dimensions being one less than the number of cases. From this starting point the method successively reduces the number of dimensions in which the points are represented, at the same time trying to keep to a minimum the distortion in the relations between the points which begins to arise as the number of dimensions is reduced. The specific feature of the method is that in contrast to principal coordinates analysis it is 'non-metric': it works not on the actual numerical values of the similarities/distances between the cases, but on their rank-ordering. That is to say, it is the rank-ordering of the distances/similarities between the points which the method tries to preserve as the dimensions are reduced. Thus, if the distance between point (case) x_i and point (case) x_j is the tenth smallest distance in the original distance matrix, it should remain the tenth smallest as the number of dimensions of the multidimensional representation is reduced.

Of course, the method has to do this not just for one pair of distances but for all of them at the same time: the rank-ordering of all the distances in the reduced space should correspond to the original ordering of all of them. It goes without saying that the relevant juggling is difficult – in fact, for large numbers of cases it is quite time-consuming even for a computer – and that it is almost impossible for the original arrangement of the points in terms of the rank-order of their distances to be perfectly preserved in a space of few dimensions. A key part of the method of non-metric multidimensional scaling is that it provides a measure of the success with which the ordering is maintained as the number of dimensions is reduced. The measure is known as 'stress' (perhaps a reflection of the psychological circles in which the method has much of its use?), an indicator of the extent to which the ordering in the reduced number of dimensions departs from the original ordering.

In the same way as the eigenvalues associated with axes in principal components or coordinates analysis indicate the importance of those axes in accounting for variation in the data, so stress gives a measure of the number of dimensions important in representing the data in non-metric multidimensional scaling. Stress is calculated for each successively decreasing number of dimensions and the idea is to look for the number of dimensions at which a large increase in stress suddenly occurs: this indicates a sudden increase in the amount of distortion in the data, which would arise when a dimension important in accounting for the variation in the data is removed; some multidimensional scaling computer programs have an option to carry out a significance test for the correct number of dimensions.

The idea, as with principal components and coordinates analysis, is that if the variation in a set of data is reducible to a small number of major trends or patterns (as in the case of our vessel shape measurements above) then the stress at the appropriate small number of dimensions will be lower than for comparable data where the variation is not reducible in this way. A low stress value would correspond to the case in principal coordinates analysis where the same number of dimensions accounts for a high percentage of the variance. Furthermore, the substantive archaeological meaning of the dimensions can be established in the same way as for principal coordinates analysis, by looking at which cases lie where on the various axes or dimensions.

Non-metric multidimensional scaling has been used extensively in archaeology. Kemp's (1982) analysis of Egyptian predynastic cemeteries is one example while Cherry and others have used it to construct maps of Aegean Bronze Age states (e.g. Cherry 1977, Kendall 1977). A number of other examples are cited by Doran and Hodson (1975), who also discuss the technique at some length. A full account of it, still essentially at an introductory level, is given by Kruskal and Wish (1978). Much discussion of the technique centres on its various advantages and disadvantages relative to other techniques such as those with which we have been comparing it. It is not possible to go in to these here but Doran and Hodson (1975, 214–17) provide a good account of the issues, as does Gordon (1981, 91–101).

iii) *Correspondence Analysis*
This technique is a relatively recent introduction to archaeology, a fact reflected by the lack of discussion by Doran and Hodson. In fact, it was only really developed in the late 1960s and much of the development took place in France (although see Hill 1973). To a degree the relative slowness of its adoption by Anglo-American quantitative archaeologists must be ascribed to a certain lack of communication between them and the rather different French archaeological world; the contrasting speed with which the potential of the technique was appreciated in French archaeology is indicated by Djindjian (1980).

The method has now been very well described for English-speaking archaeological audiences by Bølviken *et al.* (1982) and thus does not require detailed treatment here, for which in any event space is not available. The main purpose of including it at all is to draw attention to it as an important technique and to note the special features which make it particularly useful.

Of the techniques which we have examined so far correspondence analysis is most like principal components analysis, with which it shares the same general principles. But as we have seen already, the latter generally involves the analysis of a matrix of correlations, or the covariances or sums of squares and products from which correlations are derived, and these are only satisfactory measures of association when data are numeric and the distributions of the individual variables are not too far from normality.

Correspondence analysis does not have this constraint in that it is designed to analyse data which consist of frequencies, such as the frequency of occurrence of the various artefact types analysed by Bettinger in the example described above. In fact, as we have seen, principal coordinates analysis can be used to get round some of the problems which arise when the variables in an analysis are not normally distributed numeric ones. However, principal coordinates analysis, like non-metric multidimensional scaling, involves the prior calculation of similarity coefficients rather than working on the raw data directly as principal components analysis does, and the calculation of similarity coefficients involves a loss of information. We may have a certain value for, say, the Jaccard coefficient of similarity between two particular cases but we do not know precisely what it is the two have in common and what distinguishes them. Correspondence analysis does not require this intervening step; like principal components analysis it starts from the values of the variables for the particular cases.

It does, however, have a further property which principal components analysis does not possess (although a related technique, known as the *biplot,* does (see Gabriel 1981)). As we saw, with principal components analysis it is possible to study the distribution of the component scores on a scattergram and see which cases are similar to which. Likewise, we saw that the relationships between variables, and between variables and components, can also be represented graphically. With correspondence analysis the relationships between cases, those between variables, and those between variables and cases, may all be analysed together and represented in the same scattergram or series of scattergrams produced by the plotting of pairs of orthogonal axes. The ability to link relations between particular variables directly with similarities between particular cases is very significant from the point of view of interpretation, and to some extent undercuts the arguments which have raged in the archaeological literature on this subject, particularly as it relates to the definition of archaeological types and whether they should be treated in terms of correlations between variables or similarities between cases (see the papers in Whallon and Brown 1982).

It may be helpful to indicate what is involved in correspondence analysis by briefly summarising one of the examples presented by Bølviken *et al.* (1982). Information was available from the excavation of a late stone age site on the frequencies of 37 lithic types from 14 house sites. After a preliminary analysis it was decided to group the 37 types into only 9 categories on the basis of assumptions as to their function. The aim of the study was to see which houses were similar to one another, which functional categories were related in terms of associational patterning on deposition, and the way in which the similarities between the houses related to the functional categories. Accordingly, a correspondence analysis was carried out with the 14 houses as the cases and the frequencies of the 9 functional tool categories as the variables.

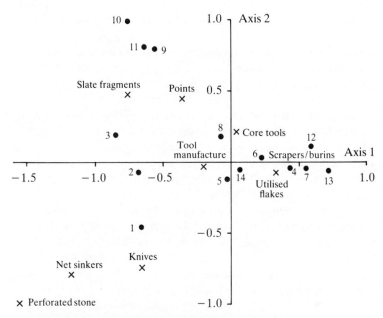

Figure 13.22. Correspondence analysis plot of the functional categories and house site units from the Iversfjord locality (after Bølviken *et al.* 1979).

The scattergram based on the first two axes, together accounting for 73% of the variation, is shown in figure 13.22. It will be seen that both the houses and the variables are represented on it. The first axis, accounting for 53% of the variation, opposes scrapers, burins and utilised flakes on the one hand to net sinkers and perforated stones on the other, and is interpreted by the authors as a contrast between maintenance activities and fishing. The second axis, accounting for 20% of the variation, has projectile points and slate fragments at one end and slate knives, net sinkers and perforated stones at the other. The authors regard this as representing a contrast between hunting and fishing.

The investigators were particularly interested in the question of whether groups of houses such as that excavated were winter fishing villages. They argued that if this was indeed the case then all the houses ought to fall in a single cluster based on artefacts indicative

of winter fishing activities. As they point out, there is no indication
from the scattergram that this is the case: on the contrary, there
appear to be three clusters of houses. Moreover, since we are
dealing with the results of a correspondence analysis, we can look
at the scattergram further to see which cases are associated with
which variables. Houses 4, 5, 6, 7, 8, 12, 13 and 14 are in the same
area of the scattergram as scrapers, burins and utilised flakes, and
were thus associated with maintenance activities. Houses 9, 10 and
11 lie near slate fragments and points, interpreted by the authors as
hunting related tool categories, while houses 1, 2 and 3 were more
associated with fishing. They conclude that, 'The present analysis
indicates a greater diversity in economic orientation (hunting, fishing and maintenance) as well as different degrees of settlement
permanence (long-term diversified activity patterning vs. short-
term specific activities) than previously believed possible for Stone
Age coastal sites' (Bølviken *et al.* 1982, 47).

It may be possible to argue with the author's interpretation of the
results in terms of their model of the relationship between activity
patterns and archaeological deposition (cf. Binford 1981, 1983),
but the usefulness of the technique in making explicit the relationships among the cases and the variables, and between the two,
seems undeniable.

Discriminant Analysis

Before finally leaving multivariate analysis there is one more technique that must be mentioned, albeit only briefly, even though it is
rather different in nature from any we have looked at so far. All
these have been concerned with looking for patterning in a set of
data, with very little in the way of prior assumptions as to what that
patterning will be like, except to a degree for the case of factor
analysis. The technique of *discriminant analysis* presupposes that
we can divide our observations into groups on the basis of some
criterion and then attempts to find a way of distinguishing those
same groups on the basis of some independent criterion derived
from the data.

In fact, the procedure has already been refered to early in chapter
12, where we distinguished *classification* from *discrimination* and
gave an example of the latter. We may have a number of undecorated ceramic vessels of a particular type which were found at different sites. Do the vessel shapes, described in terms of a series of ratio
measurements, differ from site to site? In discriminant analysis we
tell the program which vessels come from which sites and the

analysis then attempts to reproduce correctly the assignment of the vessels to the sites, but based solely on the measurements describing the vessel shape. If it is successful at doing this it means that the vessels from the different site do differ from one another; if it isn't, it means they do not. This can be a very useful thing to do. One area of archaeological research in which it has found a lot of use is artefact characterisation studies, where quantities of trace elements in lithic artefacts or pottery are used to try to discriminate materials from different sources.

Discriminant analysis comes into this chapter rather than the previous one because the methods used are those of multivariate analysis. It involves constructing a set of variables from the original variables, rather like principal components, but with the criterion that these variables must maximise the differences between the different groups, the different sites in the example outlined above.

What is involved is, as usual, best indicated by a diagram of the two-variable case (figure 13.23). Suppose we have groups of flint flakes from two distinct phases at the same site and have described the size and shape of the flakes in terms of measurements of length and breadth. Do the sizes or shapes of the flakes in the two phases differ?

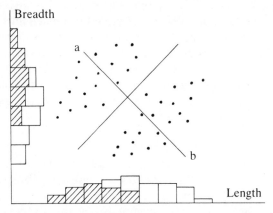

Figure 13.23. Discriminating between two groups of lithic debitage on the basis of the length and breadth of the individual pieces.

Clearly we can see in this particular two-dimensional case that they do (of course, in a real multivariate case we would not be able to see this). On the other hand, neither of our original variables, length and breadth, distinguishes the two groups. There is an overlap between them, as the histograms of the two groups projected onto each of these axes show. However, a single axis does exist that would distinguish the two groups perfectly – the line a-b in the diagram, which is a composite of both length and breadth. This is the *discriminant function* in this case; a line bisecting it at right angles between the two groups divides them with complete success.

Discriminant analysis programs carry out this operation for the multivariate case and in the same way as for principal components we are told the eigenvalue of each function and the contribution of each of the original variables to it.

The above account is intended to do no more than give you an idea of what is involved in the technique, which is too important to omit altogether. It is described more fully in a number of texts (e.g. Davis 1971, Norusis 1985) and is widely available in the computer statistical packages listed in appendix 2. As already indicated, it is not an exploratory technique in the same way as cluster analysis or principal components analysis, but it can be extremely useful when it comes to testing archaeological hypotheses.

This account of discriminant analysis completes our introduction to multivariate analysis in archaeology. It should be obvious that it is a complex topic of which we have only just begun to scratch the surface. Doran and Hodson (1975) take the subject much further, as does Johnston (1978) from a geographical point of view. On the basis of this chapter you shouldn't attempt to embark on your own multivariate data analysis projects unless you have expert advice and assistance, but you should now have some idea of why people have made use of the techniques and a basis for understanding published archaeological examples.

EXERCISES

13.1. Carry out a principal components analysis of the data on Uruk bevel rim bowls provided for exercise 12.4. Comment on all aspects of the results which you consider to be relevant, giving special attention to the archaeological interpretation of the components and their significance.

13.2. Carry out a factor analysis on the same data, distinguishing between common and unique variance. Rotate an appropriate number of factors and again interpret the results.

13.3. In a study of spatial and temporal variation in prehistoric rock art 83 art sites in Australia were examined (Morwood 1980). For each site the colour of the design elements of the art was recorded. Each site was then coded for the number of occurrences of design elements of a particular colour, and for the relative percentage occurrence of the different colour categories.

The colours are as follows:

1. Red   5. White
2. Purple   6. Black
3. Orange   7. Brown
4. Yellow   8. Pink

A principal components analysis was carried out on the two sets of data. Figure 13.24 shows the scattergrams of the variables in relation to the principal components, and relevant data pertaining to these scattergrams. Discuss the results given from a statistical and an archaeological point of view.

13.4. Tables 13.16 and 13.17 are the results of a principal components analysis of 15 stone tool assemblages from southern Africa described in terms of the percentage composition of different tool types (Cable 1984). Discuss these results from a statistical and an archaeological point of view, giving particular attention to (a) indicating what you regard as the main patterns of variation in the assemblage, and (b) describing and explaining the relationship between the data in the correlation matrix and that in the factor matrix.

13.5. The data involved are again the 15 stone tool assemblages from southern Africa. Figure 13.25 shows a tripolar graph of the relations between the 15 assemblages, based on the data concerning three tool types in the attached key.

Figure 13.26 shows the results of a cluster analysis of these assemblages based on the complete list of tool types given above for exercise 13.4, using Ward's Method. Figure 13.27 shows the same assemblages as figure 13.26, again based on the full list of tool types, plotted against the first two principal components as given in the data for exercise 13.4.

Note that assemblages B and D are not present in figures 13.26 and 13.27, only the amalgamated version, assemblage X, is present. Assemblages L and M are also deleted from these latter two analyses.

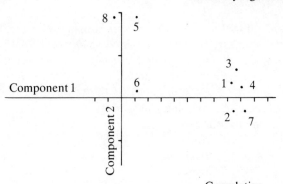

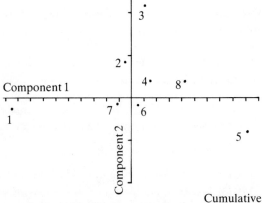

(a)

Component	Eigenvalue	Variance %	Cumulative variance %
1	4.04	50.6	50.6
2	1.51	18.9	69.4
3	1.02	12.8	82.2

Variable communalities:

1 0.81   2 0.81   3 0.73   4 0.83   5 0.79   6 0.79   7 0.88   8 0.80

(b)

Component	Eigenvalue	Variance %	Cumulative variance %
1	1.92	23.9	23.9
2	1.37	17.2	41.1
3	1.08	13.6	54.7

Variable communalities:

1 0.97   2 0.24   3 0.81   4 0.60   5 0.95   6 0.93   7 0.63   8 0.29

Figure 13.24. (a) Principal components analysis of raw colour frequencies. (b) Principal components analysis of percentage colour frequencies (after Morwood 1980).

Discuss the relationship between the results presented in these three figures, referring where necessary to your answer to exercise 13.4. What archaeological conclusions, in particular concerning the reasons behind the assemblage variation, is it possible to draw?

13.6. Excavation of a settlement midden in northern Norway produced large numbers of animal bones from the fourteen layers (layer 1 being the most recent and layer 14 the oldest). The bone frequencies are presented in table 13.18. In order to investigate patterning in the composition of the bone assemblage through time a correspondence analysis was carried out. The scattergram of the layers and species against the first two axes is given in figure 13.28. The first axis accounts for 68.8% of the variation, the second for 29.54%. Discuss the results for the layers and for the species and the relation between them. (Data from Mathiesen *et al.* 1981).

Table 13.16. Tool counts from 15 Natal sites, and their correlation coefficients (after Cable 1984).

Variable	Label	Mean %	s.d.
P2	Convex scrapers	63.9720	15.0613
P3	Backed blades	6.5337	7.2994
P4	Segments	3.1457	4.7784
P5	Tanged/pressure-flaked points	0.6480	0.7627
P6	Backed pieces	1.3701	2.0794
P7	Notched scrapers	22.6633	18.0055
P8	Reamers	0.0698	0.1853
P9	Borers	0.8013	0.9494
P10	Backed adzes	0.7960	1.4124

Correlation Coefficients

	P2	P3	P4	P5	P6	P7	P8	P9
P2	1.00000	-0.21502	-0.26859	-0.03987	-0.24972	-0.66241	0.13254	0.16628
P3	-0.21502	1.00000	0.95950	0.35566	0.81085	-0.57833	-0.20933	0.01052
P4	-0.26859	0.95950	1.00000	0.31807	0.81109	-0.51279	-0.24782	0.00711
P5	-0.03987	0.35566	0.31807	1.00000	0.38298	-0.27684	0.21841	-0.35674
P6	-0.24972	0.81085	0.81109	0.38928	1.00000	-0.46210	-0.24550	0.11475
P7	-0.66241	-0.57833	-0.51279	-0.27684	-0.46210	1.00000	0.01090	-0.19299
P8	0.13254	-0.20933	-0.24782	0.21841	-0.24550	0.01090	1.00000	0.24369
P9	0.16628	0.01052	0.00711	-0.35674	0.11475	-0.19299	0.24369	1.00000
P10	0.08089	-0.11428	-0.27892	0.14748	-0.10471	-0.00265	0.31651	-0.07173

Table 13.17. Tool counts from 15 Natal sites: the factor matrix (after Cable 1984).

Factor	Eigenvalue	% of variance	Cumulative variance
1	3.38154	37.6	37.6
2	1.79047	19.9	57.5
3	1.46956	16.3	73.8
4	1.10192	12.2	86.0
5	0.72836	8.1	94.1
6	0.35722	4.0	98.1
7	0.14690	1.6	99.7
8	0.02400	0.3	100.0
9	-0.00000	-0.0	100.0

Factor matrix using principal factor, no iterations

	Factor 1	Factor 2	Factor 3	Factor 4	Factor 5	Factor 6	Factor 7	Factor 8
P2	-0.14224	0.85984	-0.20478	-0.44221	-0.21555	0.02352	-0.04362	0.00811
P3	0.95873	-0.02408	0.02118	0.09423	0.08752	-0.20689	0.09981	-0.10247
P4	0.95713	-0.11986	-0.06601	0.08458	-0.03734	-0.20109	0.05742	0.11365
P5	0.45268	0.12302	0.73469	-0.13820	-0.32945	0.30397	0.14199	0.00353
P6	0.89934	-0.06437	0.00905	0.18148	0.11008	0.25582	-0.27644	-0.00641
P7	-0.62763	-0.72569	0.12421	0.23780	-0.05558	0.06618	-0.00204	0.00340
P8	-0.27343	0.47956	0.43771	0.53560	-0.38088	-0.23932	-0.12023	-0.00435
P9	0.00186	0.41236	-0.54669	0.67641	0.01094	0.23200	0.14002	0.00420
P10	-0.20894	0.30053	0.61410	0.19336	0.67076	-0.01033	0.03315	0.02048

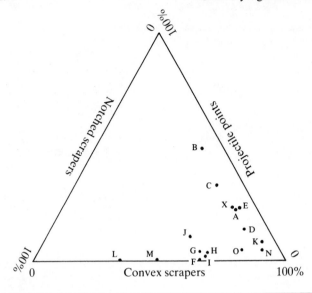

	Assemblage	Zone*	n	Tools		
				% CS*	% NS*	% PP*
A	Umbeli Belli	C.B.	98	69.4	8.2	22.4
B	Borchers Shelter Layers 1+2	C.B.	123	42.3	8.9	48.8
C	Borchers Shelter Layer 3	C.B.	173	56.6	11.0	32.4
D	Borchers Shelter Annexe	C.B.	325	77.2	9.2	13.5
E	The Falls	C.B.	44	70.5	6.8	22.7
F	Good Hope Layer 1	H.S.	41	65.9	34.1	0
G	Good Hope Layer 2	H.S.	497	64.2	31.6	4.2
H	Bottoms Up Shelter	H.S.	140	67.1	29.3	3.6
I	Giant's Castle	H.S.	246	67.1	30.9	2.0
J	Belleview, Spits 1–4	H.S./A.G.	92	56.5	32.6	10.9
K	Belleview, Spits 5–8	H.S./A.G.	192	87.0	5.2	7.8
L	Grindstone Shelter	H.S.	49	34.7	65.3	0
M	Karkloof	M.B.	149	49.0	50.3	0.3
N	Moshebi's Shelter	A.G.	309	88.7	6.8	4.5
O	Sehonghong	A.G.	206	80.6	15.0	4.4
X	Borchers Site Complex (Borchers 1+2 & Annexe)	C.B.	446	67.9	9.2	23.3

* C.B. = Coastal Belt   CS = Convex scrapers
  H.S. = Highland Sourveld   NS = Notched scrapers
  A.G. = Alpine Grassland   PP = Projectile points
  M.B. = Mist Belt Forest

Figure 13.25. Natal and eastern Lesotho: tripolar graph
of assemblage variability, and key (after Cable 1984).

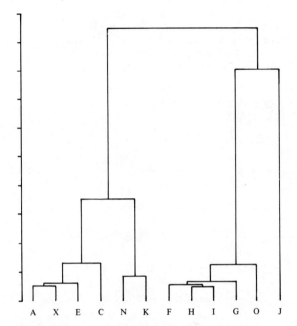

Figure 13.26. Cluster analysis of the stone tool
assemblages by Ward's method (after Cable 1984).

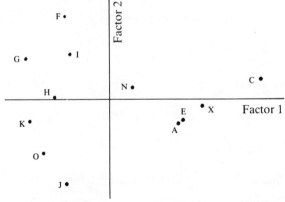

Figure 13.27. The stone tool assemblages plotted against
the first two principal components (after Cable 1984).

Table 13.18. Osteological material from layers 1-14
of trench 1 of the farm mound of the island of Helgøy
(see key to figure 13.28 for details of assemblage).
(After Mathiesen *et al.* 1981.)

	A	B	C	D	E	F	G	H	I	J	K	L	M	N	P	Q	Sum
1	27	42	33	1	3	0	272	5	40	31	3	0	0	0	17	0	474
2	54	122	35	0	4	0	1080	36	115	73	11	1	0	0	47	0	1578
3	44	83	54	3	4	0	842	24	71	81	35	12	0	0	32	0	1284
4	101	151	90	2	6	0	3247	14	128	81	20	23	3	0	34	1	3901
5	101	202	58	4	0	4	3204	95	99	216	24	92	33	0	22	4	4158
6	43	61	33	6	13	1	1082	37	170	138	17	1	5	0	4	4	1615
7	24	40	17	0	23	4	545	23	3	88	3	0	1	3	2	1	777
8	17	24	14	1	30	3	597	22	4	46	4	1	0	0	2	0	765
9	27	42	10	2	14	2	294	8	7	33	2	11	0	0	9	0	461
10	24	53	20	0	6	0	100	6	3	22	0	28	0	0	14	1	277
11	45	78	35	0	30	1	128	4	9	20	0	17	1	0	2	9	379
12	109	367	167	1	142	8	348	1	13	38	1	80	1	0	13	6	1294
13	15	18	17	0	7	8	25	0	0	4	0	14	0	0	0	1	109
14	42	41	34	0	15	3	93	0	0	0	0	14	0	0	6	0	248
Sum	673	1324	617	20	297	34	11857	275	662	871	118	294	44	3	204	27	17320

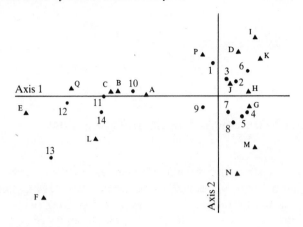

Layers 1-14

A	Cattle	*Bos taurus*
B	Sheep/goat	*Ovis aries / Carpa hircus*
C	Pig	*Sus scrofa dom.*
D	Reindeer	*Rangifer tarandus*
E	Seal	Phocidae
F	Grouse	*Lagopus*
G	Cod	*Gadus morrhua*
H	Haddock	*Melanogrammus aeglefinus*
I	Coalfish	*Pollachius virens*
J	Ling	*Molva molva*
K		*Brosme brosme*
L	Halibut	*Hippoglossus hippoglossus*
M		*Sebastes marinus*
N		*Anarchichas lupus*
P	Auk	Alcidae
Q	Hen	*Gallus gallus f. dom.*

Figure 13.28. Correspondence analysis of the data from table 13.18 (after Mathiesen *et al.* 1981).

Fourteen

Probabilistic Sampling in Archaeology

'Sampling' has been an important part of new approaches to archaeology for more than two decades (Vescelius 1960). It has been singled out in the literature by both advocates and opponents of modern approaches as a key part of a new methodology of archaeology (Binford 1964, Hole 1980). When a method becomes part of the ideology of an approach the results are likely to be unsatisfactory and sampling in archaeology has been no exception to this (cf. Wobst 1983), often accepted or rejected on principle rather than on the basis of reasoned argument or appropriateness. What is involved in 'sampling' and why has it had this importance?

In its most general sense it embodies the idea of using information from a part of something to make inferences about the whole. Since archaeologists have always been acutely aware of the partial nature of the evidence they recover – they only ever recover a 'sample' – the idea of a methodology which could help to solve the problems posed by this situation has an almost mystical attraction. Some decidedly sophisticated mathematically based models are now being developed to tackle this question (e.g. Orton 1982), but 'sampling' is certainly not the answer. Unfortunately, misconceptions resulting from the belief that it is have been rife, leading to overoptimism on the one hand and the rejection of what are believed to be unrealistic claims for the potential of 'sampling' in archaeology on the other.

It is important to be clear from the start that 'sampling' is concerned with the making of inferences about some defined piece of the extant archaeological record on the basis of a study of some part of that piece of the record. It is *not* concerned with making inferences from the extant record (or physical finds populations as Cowgill (1970) has called them) to the material results of human behaviour in the past (Cowgill's physical consequences populations), still less to the nature of the behaviour which produced them.

298

Of course, in this sense archaeologists have always practised sampling. They have selected sites to excavate in regions, and places to put trenches within sites, and they have not restricted their conclusions to those specific trenches or sites. The change which occurred 25 years ago was the introduction and advocacy of *probabilistic* sampling: the selection of the part of the archaeological record to be investigated in such a way that probability theory can be used to evaluate the inferences made from that part to the whole from which it was selected, in terms of the probability that the inferences are correct. The idea then is to ensure that the sample selected is representative of the whole. Probability theory provides the rules for both making the selection and making the inferences from it.

But what inferences can be made in this way and are they ones in which we are really interested? This brings us onto the question of the aims we have in carrying out any particular project and the research design appropriate for their realisation. Unfortunately, this part of the research process has not always been given the attention it deserves. More often than not the extent of an investigation is determined by financial constraints in one form or another and there has been a tendency to move directly from the realisation, for example, that the excavation of a threatened site can only be partial, to a consideration of statistically based sampling schemes, with a consequent lack of clarity over objectives. The investigator has no idea of what statements may be made on the basis of the sample but simply feels that if the sample selected is statistically based it must in some sense be better. Such an approach may not be harmful and the distribution of excavation or survey units which stems from it may produce interesting results, but they will not have much to do with statistical inference.

Statistical sampling theory becomes relevant when the aim of the study is to use the sample selected to make estimates of characteristics of the population from which it was drawn. The aim in these circumstances is to draw a sample which is an 'honest representation' of the population and which leads to estimates of population characteristics with as great a precision as we can reasonably expect for the cost or effort expended (cf. Barnett 1974).

It is now well established that the 'pragmatic' approaches to sampling which have been followed in archaeology are not very satisfactory in this regard, although in fairness to early investigators it should be pointed out that they rarely had the goal of achieving an honest representation of a population in mind. Two types of 'pragmatic' sampling which have been important in archaeology are worth distinguishing:

1. Accessibility sampling: In this approach the key factor is the ease of access of the observations; the most easily obtainable ones are chosen. An archaeological example might be surveys looking for settlements in the Near East which consist of driving along roads and looking out for mounds visible from them. A converse version of this might be called inaccessibility sampling, as practised by some archaeologists in the Mediterranean area, who look for all the prominent hills in an area and then climb them to see if there are early settlements on top! There is nothing necessarily wrong with such an approach so long as it is not thought that it provides representative information about the density or relative proportions of different types of site in an area.

2. Judgemental or purposive sampling: This involves investigators making their own choice about which part of a site to excavate or of a region to survey. The aim may or may not be to obtain a representative sample. If it is, and the investigator possesses a great deal of relevant subject matter knowledge, then the sample may indeed be an excellent representation of the population. The main problem with this approach to sampling, if the aim is to achieve representativeness, is not that the estimates resulting from it may be distorted, but that we have no means of evaluating the representativeness of the sample selected other than through an evaluation of the selector and our own knowledge of the substantive situation.

If we use a probabilistic sampling scheme, on the other hand, it means that we consider, notionally at least, all possible samples of a given size from the population, we assign a probability to each sample on the basis of the sampling scheme chosen, and then go on to select one particular sample in accordance with the scheme. The result will be an estimate whose reliability and precision may be quantified; in other words, one for which we can supply a *confidence interval*. In specifying a confidence interval we are saying that in a given percentage of the samples generated by this means the population characteristic (or parameter) concerned will fall within some specified interval estimated from the sample. In fact, as we shall see, we can use our theoretical knowledge either after the event, when our data have been collected, to obtain a confidence interval for the estimate in which we are interested; or to obtain an estimate, before starting the investigation, of the sample size required to obtain a confidence interval of a desired width. It is obviously better, of course, to follow the latter procedure rather than finding out late in the day that from the data collected we can only specify an unhelpfully wide interval within which our population characteristic should lie. It may be worth emphasising again here that all such estimates are based on the archaeological record as recovered and refer to the record as potentially recoverable: we are making inferences about a 'physical finds population' from a sample of it.

To summarise. It should be clear from this that the point of using probability sampling methods is to obtain estimates of some aggregate quantity whose reliability and precision we can assess. At the regional level, for example, it may be of interest to estimate the mean density of neolithic sites in an area, or their total; at the site level we may wish to estimate the proportion of flakes which are retouched, or of rim sherds of a certain type. Whether such aggregate measures are of interest to us in any given study depends on our *aims*. For example, if we are comparing them from site to site or area to area in some macro-scale analysis they will be highly relevant.

In the following section the technicalities of obtaining such measures by means of simple random sampling will be described, then some more complex procedures will be outlined in general terms. Finally, some of the problems posed will be discussed and it will be argued that there are many archaeological questions to which the standard techniques of probability sampling are not relevant, even in those cases, the vast majority, where our archaeological information is only partial.

CALCULATING CONFIDENCE INTERVALS AND SAMPLE SIZES

Here we need to recall some points made in earlier chapters. First of all, a reminder of the distinction made in chapter 5 between characteristics of populations and characteristics of samples: *parameters* and *statistics*. For a given population any parameter value will be fixed but unknown. In probability sampling the aim is to use statistics calculated from a sample to estimate the population parameters. Since we do not know the population parameters, and would not need to take a sample if we did, we can never know how close our estimates are to the parameter value. Our rationale for having some confidence in the estimates therefore has to be based on a method of sample selection which has secure theoretical foundations to justify the claims we make.

In this chapter we will look at the estimation of three population characteristics: the population mean (e.g. the mean density of sites in an area); the population total (e.g. the total number of sites in an area); the proportion of values in a population which satisfy some condition of interest (e.g. the proportion of sites in an area which are fortified). In fact, all these three different measures are closely related and in the following preliminary discussion of the concepts which it is necessary to understand before the description of the estimation methods, it will be assumed that we are interested in the population mean.

If we want an estimate of a population mean for a simple random sample (to be defined below), the sample mean will be perfectly satisfactory since it is unbiased. Unfortunately, but unsurprisingly, this does not mean that any simple random sample mean will always correspond to the mean of the population from which it is drawn. Rather, if we take a series of simple random samples from a population and obtain the mean of each of those samples then each of those means will be slightly different – there will be a distribution of means. It is the mean of the distribution of sample means which will correspond to the population parameter.

The upshot of all this is that while obtaining a specific sample mean is fine as far as it goes, we have no basis for knowing whether the particular one we have obtained from a given sample is a good estimate or not. If we are dealing with the mean of a continuous variable – for example, the mean length in millimetres of a sample of projectile points, calculated to three places of decimals – then the probability that this corresponds exactly to the population mean is almost infinitely small.

If we want to have some given degree of confidence in our estimate of the population mean we must take into account the dispersion of the distribution of sample means to which we have referred above. But how do we do this when in at least 9 cases out of 10 all we will have is a single sample?

The answer is that we start from the dispersion of the sample itself – its standard deviation. We are not interested in this estimate of the dispersion of the population for its own sake, however, but in the dispersion of the distribution of sample means. Nevertheless, the more variable the population is, the more variable are likely to be the means of a series of samples drawn from it. Statistical theory which it is not possible to go into here enables us to go from the sample-based estimate of the population standard deviation to an estimate of the standard deviation of the notional distribution of sample means – known as the *standard error of the mean*. The formula is

$$s_{\bar{x}} = \frac{s}{\sqrt{n}}$$

In words, we can obtain an estimate of the standard error of the mean by dividing an estimate of the population standard deviation by the square root of the number of observations in the sample. It makes sense intuitively that the dispersion of a distribution of means will not be as great as the dispersion of the individual population values, and that as the sample gets larger and therefore increasingly representative of the range of population variability, the standard error should decrease.

But there is another aspect of sample size which also makes a difference to our estimates of the standard error of the mean. If our sample was so large that it included the entire population of interest we would know the population mean and our estimate would have no error at all. By extension of this, as our sample becomes an increasingly large fraction of our population, our estimate of the standard error can be narrowed down. This is done by adding to the formula which we have just seen something called the *finite population correlation factor*. Now we have

$$s_{\bar{x}} = \left(\frac{s}{\sqrt{n}} \right) \bigg/ \sqrt{\left(1 - \frac{n}{N} \right)}$$

where *n* is sample size and *N* is population size.

But having seen how to calculate an estimate for the standard error of the mean, how does this help us to arrive at an estimate of the population mean in which we can have some specified degree of confidence? The answer to this is that it depends on some properties of the normal distribution, which we have seen in an earlier chapter.

Recapitulating the ground just covered we can say that the distribution of interest to us if we are to obtain the estimate we want is the notional distribution of sample means, whose standard deviation, the standard error of the mean, we have just seen how to calculate. It can be shown, again by means of statistical theory which we cannot go into, that so long as the sample size is reasonably large, greater than, say, 30 or so, the shape of this distribution of means will be normal, even when the shape of the *population* is not normal but is quite skew. As we saw earlier (chapter 8), it is characteristic of the normal distribution that there will be a constant proportion of the observations within a given number of standard deviations either side of the mean. Thus, if we have a normal distribution of sample means we can say, for example, that 68.2% of the means will fall within one standard error either side of the overall mean; or that 95% of the means will fall within 1.96 standard deviations either side.

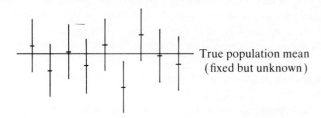

Figure 14.1. Relationship between population mean and a series of sample means; each bar shows a sample mean and the range covered by a fixed number of standard errors.

Since this overall mean is the population mean in which we are interested, we can say, for example, that the means of 95% of the simple random samples which we select from this population will fall within 1.96 standard errors of the population mean. However, since we don't know the population mean we have to work this the other way round: for 95% of the samples drawn from the population a distance of 1.96 standard errors either side of the sample mean will include the true population mean; for 5% of the samples it will not. Of course we can change the percentages by changing the number of standard errors. What is involved may be usefully illustrated by a diagram (figure 14.1). The procedure enables us to produce a confidence interval: a range within which our parameter should lie, with a specified level of probability, the range being expressed in terms of the number of standard errors associated with the level of probability in which we are interested.

It's now about time that this theoretical discussion was illustrated by means of a simple example. Let us suppose that we have selected a simple random sample (we'll see how this is done later) of 50 arrowheads from a collection of 2000, for the purpose of obtaining an estimate of the mean length for the collection as a whole, and that we want our estimate to have a 95% probability of being correct. We will suppose that our measurements have produced a mean length for our sample of 22.6 mm, with a standard deviation of 4.2 mm. The first step is to obtain the standard error of the mean. Using the formula

$$s_{\bar{x}} = \left(\frac{s}{\sqrt{n}} \right) \Big/ \sqrt{\left(1 - \frac{n}{N} \right)}$$

we have

$$s_{\bar{x}} = \left(\frac{4.2}{\sqrt{50}} \right) \Big/ \sqrt{\left(1 - \frac{50}{2000} \right)}$$

$$= (0.594)(0.987) = 0.586$$

The sample mean, as we have seen, is 22.6 mm. In order to obtain an interval which will have a 95% probability of including the population mean and assuming that the notional distribution of sample means is normal, we know that we have to take an interval of 1.96 standard errors either side of the sample mean. Thus, our interval is defined by the sample mean ± 1.96 standard errors. Here

$$22.6 \pm (1.96)(0.586) = 22.6 \pm 1.15$$

and we can say that there is a 95% probability that the mean length of the collection of arrowheads as a whole lies in the interval 21.45–23.75 mm. We may, of course, have been unlucky and the simple random sample we have selected may be one of the 5% which does not include the true population mean. If we are worried about this we can decide to increase our probability of being correct, but only at the expense of widening the interval within which the population mean is estimated to lie. Thus, if we want a probability of 99% of being correct, then to include 99% of a distribution we have to go out 2.58 standard errors either side of our sample mean. In this case

$$22.6 \pm (2.58)(0.586) = 22.6 \pm 1.51$$

so there is a 99% probability that the mean length of the population of arrowheads lies between 21.09 and 24.11 mm.

For constructing a confidence interval in general we can write

$$\bar{x} \pm Z_{\alpha} \left(\frac{s}{\sqrt{n}} \right) \Big/ \sqrt{\left(1 - \frac{n}{N} \right)}$$

where Z_{α} is the Z score, or number of standard deviations, associated with a particular probability level.

Here we must interject a brief footnote. Using the Z score, as we have done throughout our example, is perfectly satisfactory if our sample size is larger than say 40 or so, but if it is smaller then we have to take account of the fact that s, our estimate of the population standard deviation, is itself of course based on a sample and that different samples will produce different values for it. Small samples will in general be more variable from one to the next and we have to take account of this by using in our estimates not the normal distribution but Student's t distribution (see e.g. Blalock 1972, 188–93), which varies in the proportion of observations within a given number of standard deviations of the mean according to the size of the sample, converging on the normal distribution as the sample size gets larger. Thus, instead of the formula above we have

$$\bar{x} \pm t_{\alpha,\text{d.f.}} \left(\frac{s}{\sqrt{n}} \right) \Big/ \sqrt{\left(1 - \frac{n}{N} \right)}$$

where $t_{\alpha,\text{d.f.}}$ is the t value for a given number of degrees of freedom ($= n - 1$), associated with a particular probability level (see appendix 1, table c; note that for the boundaries of the confidence interval you need to use t for the 2-sided test, i.e. the 2α row at the top of the table).

Let us return to the main thread of our argument. In our arrowhead example we supposed that we already had a sample of a given size and on the basis of that we were able to construct a confidence interval. This is all very well, but in the situation in which we find ourselves at the beginning of the archaeological investigation for which we only have limited resources, one of the key questions is precisely how large a sample we should select. If it is too small the confidence intervals for our estimates of the quantities in which we are interested will be too wide to be of any use; if it is larger than we need then resources are being wasted which could be used for something else. How then can we calculate a required sample size?

Let us look again at the formula for constructing a confidence interval, assuming that we are dealing with the normal distribution and ignoring for a moment the finite population correction. The formula for the interval around the mean is

$$\pm Z_\alpha \left(\frac{s}{\sqrt{n}} \right)$$

Let us designate this tolerance (or $\pm$) factor as d. We then have

$$d = Z_\alpha \left(\frac{s}{\sqrt{n}} \right)$$

This can be rearranged to give

$$\sqrt{n} = \frac{Z_\alpha s}{d}$$

or

$$n = \left(\frac{Z_\alpha s}{d} \right)^2$$

We have then a formula for estimating what the sample size should be in a given case, provided that we can specify the three quantities on the right-hand side of the equation.

Fixing a value for Z_α is straightforward enough: it is simply a matter of deciding on the probability we wish to have that our interval will include the parameter in which we are interested. Specifying the tolerance, the $\pm$ factor, which we are prepared to accept, is also straightforward enough in principle, although less so in practice. Why should we decide on any particular tolerance value? Ideally, it should stem from the specific question which we are investigating, but in practice the decision may be rather arbitrary. The point is that if we are prepared to settle for an estimate with an error factor rather than insisting on obtaining the exact value of the population parameter, we can save a great deal of effort in terms of the number of units or items we have to examine.

The third quantity, s, has been written in lower case here and throughout because although it is the population standard deviation, S, which interests us, we have been using s, the sample-based estimate of S, since the latter is, of course, unknown. When we wish to calculate a sample size, however, even obtaining s is problematical. In the case of constructing a confidence interval we could obtain it from our sample. Before taking the sample, trying to decide on the sample size, we are not in this position! What can we do?

In general terms there are two possible answers, neither of which is ideal. One is to carry out some sort of pilot study on the population of interest, before the main investigation, and thus obtain a preliminary sample-based estimate of the population standard deviation with which to work. Another is to use the results of previous work on similar populations which has already produced variability estimates. In both cases we might want to increase the resulting estimate of the population standard deviation slightly in case it turns out to be an underestimate and our confidence intervals end up being wider than we would wish.

Having used the formula presented above to obtain an initial estimate of the required sample size we should then consider whether or not this represents a sufficiently large fraction of the total population for the finite population correction to be required. To obtain the required size taking the sampling fraction into account we have

$$n' = \frac{n}{1 + n/N}$$

where N is the population size and n is the sample size as initially calculated.

At this point it is worth going through a numerical example of calculating the correct sample size to estimate a mean, to see how the procedure is carried out (cf. Van der Veen and Fieller 1982). Let us look again at our 2000 hypothetical arrowheads and ask how many we should measure in order to estimate their mean length, on the assumption of selection by means of simple random sampling. Prior knowledge tells us that such a distribution of lengths will probably have a tendency to be positively skewed, i.e. have a long positive tail, but this skewness is unlikely to be so great as to have a major effect on the normality of the notional distribution of sample means, which is what matters. Applying the formula

$$n = \left(\frac{Z_\alpha s}{d} \right)^2$$

we need to fill in some numbers:

Z_α: we will assume that we are interested in the 95 % probability level so this may be set at 1.96.

s: we will assume that we have selected a small number of arrowheads for measurement as a pilot sample and that this has given us a value of 4.00 mm as an estimate of the population standard deviation. To be on the safe side we have decided to increase this by 1.0 mm and to use an estimate of 5.0 mm for the population standard deviation.

d: we will assume that we want to estimate the mean within a tolerance of ± 1.0 mm, an effectively arbitrary decision.

$$n = \left(\frac{1.96 \times 5.0}{1.0} \right)^2 = 96$$

Applying the finite population correction

$$n' = \frac{n}{1 + n/N}$$

$$n' = \frac{96}{1 + {}^{96}\!/\!_{2000}} = 91.6$$

In this case, because n is such a small fraction of N, applying the finite population correction does not make a great deal of difference.

To show the difference that varying the tolerance makes, let us recalculate the sample size figure supposing that we will be satisfied with a tolerance of ± 2.0 mm, instead of 1.0 mm.

$$n = \left(\frac{1.96 \times 5.0}{2.0} \right)^2 = 24$$

Alternatively, if we wanted it to within ± 0.5 mm:

$$n = \left(\frac{1.96 \times 5.0}{0.5} \right)^2 = 384$$

It is obviously worth giving the matter of the tolerance level some thought, as it has an enormous efect on the required sample size.

It may be, of course, that our sample size is going to be determined simply by the amount of time and money available. On the basis of knowledge of the cost of collecting information on one item, or of experiments or prior knowledge of the time taken to collect it, we may know our maximum number in advance. If, given an estimate of the likely population standard deviation, it turns out that a sample of this size will only produce a confidence interval which is too wide to be at all informative about the parameter in question, then we really need to rethink our whole project.

ESTIMATING TOTALS

Now that we have seen the procedure for estimating the confidence interval for a population mean with a given probability level, and how to rearrange the information to estimate required sample sizes, we can look at the question of estimating population totals; this can be done much more briefly since it is closely related to what we have just seen.

You may be puzzled by the whole idea of estimating a total. After all, do we not in effect need to have a total list of our population in order to select a sample? The answer is that the list of items which we are sampling may not be the same as the list of items in which we are interested. An archaeological example arises in regional survey. A normal procedure would be to divide the region up into a number of squares and to sample the squares: the squares then form the list of items we are sampling, a list we can completely enumerate if required. What we are interested in, however, will never be the total number of squares, but it may be the total number of sites within the area, perhaps of a particular type or period. To find this we will need to have a sample-based estimate of the mean number of sites per square which can then be multiplied up by the total number of squares. We can write this as

$$x_T = Nx$$

where x_T is the total number of items of interest, x is the mean number of items of interest per sample unit, and N is the total number of sample units in the population.

This is straightforward enough, but, as with estimating the mean, we are generally not just interested in a point estimate but in being able to specify an interval within which the total should lie with a given degree of probability. Fortunately, this too is very easy. As you might expect, it is simply a matter of including N in the formulae for obtaining confidence intervals and sample sizes which we have already seen for the mean. Thus, for the confidence interval we have

$$\bar{x}_T \pm Z_\alpha N \left(\frac{s}{\sqrt{n}} \right) \Bigg/ \sqrt{\left(1 - \frac{n}{N}\right)}$$

with $t_{\alpha, d.f.}$ substituted for Z_α with small sample sizes. And for the sample size calculation we have

$$n = \left(\frac{Z_\alpha s N}{d} \right)^2$$

and, as before

$$n' = \frac{n}{1 + n/N}$$

ESTIMATING A POPULATION PROPORTION

This is something rather different from the two cases we have looked at so far but it is a situation which arises frequently in archaeology. We may, for example, want to estimate the proportion of sherds in an assemblage with some specified characteristic on the basis of a simple random sample from the assemblage; perhaps the proportion of a lithic assemblage characterised by a certain type of retouch. The difference between this and the previous examples lies not in what we are trying to do but in the simple structure of the values in the population and the sample, which can only take one of two states: a particular sherd, for example, either has the characteristic in question or it does not.

As with the mean, the best estimate of a population proportion will be the corresponding sample proportion, but again we want a confidence interval, and for this we need to know the standard error of the proportion.

The standard deviation of a population of ones and zeros is $[P(1-P)]^{1/2}$, where P is the proportion of interest. This can be estimated using p, the sample proportion. To obtain the standard error of the proportion we must divide this by $\sqrt{n}$, the square root of the sample size, as with the mean. Thus, the standard error of the proportion is $[p(1-p)/n]^{1/2}$.

Obviously the shape of such a distribution is not going to be normal. Nevertheless, the shape of the notional distribution of sample means will be, so long as the sample is reasonably large, say greater than 50. In these circumstances we can once again construct the confidence interval by multiplying the standard error of the proportion by Z_α, the number of standard deviations corresponding to the probability level in which we are interested, since the distribution is a normal one. Finally, the finite population correction factor has the same role as before. Thus a confidence interval for P, the population proportion, will be given by

$$p \pm Z_\alpha \sqrt{\left(\frac{p(1-p)}{n}\right)\left(1 - \frac{n}{N}\right)}$$

where p is the sample proportion.

This is straightforward enough when we have the information from a sample and want to construct a confidence interval for P on the basis of it, but how do we estimate sample size? We saw above, when looking at confidence intervals for the mean, that if we designate the interval either side of the mean which we are prepared to accept as d, we have (forgetting about the finite population correction for the moment)

$$d = Z_\alpha \left(\frac{s}{\sqrt{n}}\right)$$

And we could rearrange this to give

$$n = \left(\frac{Z_\alpha s}{d}\right)^2$$

If we now do this for the case of proportions we have

$$d = Z_\alpha \sqrt{\left(\frac{p(1-p)}{n} \right)}$$

Rearranging this gives us

$$n = \frac{Z_\alpha^2 [p(1-p)]}{d^2}$$

This tells us that in order to calculate an appropriate sample size to obtain an estimate of a proportion with a certain level of probability we first need to make an estimate of what the proportion is! This seems pretty Alice-in-Wonderland stuff even by the standards of statistics. Fortunately it is not quite as bad as it looks.

For a given tolerance and a given probability level, the maximum sample size n we will need will be when $p(1-p)$ takes the maximum value it can possibly take. Quite simply, this will be when $p = (1-p) = \frac{1}{2}$. The product of the two in this case will be $\frac{1}{4}$ and the product of no other pair of values will be so great. In other words, in the case of proportions, unlike other means and totals, we can always find the maximum size of the sample we will need to attain a certain tolerance with a certain probability simply by assuming that the population proportions P and $(1-P)$ are $\frac{1}{2}$ – we don't need to bother estimating them with sample proportions at all.

For actual values of P between about 0.3 and 0.7 this maximum value will not be too extravagant an estimate of the required sample size for a given confidence interval. On the other hand, as P gets larger or smaller than this, the required n begins to decrease fairly considerably so assuming $P = \frac{1}{2}$ will create a fairly large amount of unnecessary work. In many cases, however, it will be possible to have a reasoned guess as to whether the proportional occurrence we are investigating is very rare or very common (one is obviously the converse of the other), or only reasonably frequent.

As with the other sample size estimates we have seen we can correct for the sampling fraction

$$n' = \frac{n}{1 + n/N}$$

It remains to consider an example of estimating the required sample size for a proportion. A researcher working in the Shetland Islands (Winham 1978) wanted to know how many of the known sites to visit to obtain information on their locational characteristics, for example the proportion on particular soil types. He decided he wanted his estimates of the proportions of sites having particular characteristics to have a tolerance of $\pm 7\%$, with a 95 % probability. He did not have any prior information and furthermore he wanted to estimate the proportions for a number of different characteristics at the same time and there was every reason to believe that these would occur with widely differing frequencies. He therefore adopted the most conservative hypothesis of assuming $P = \frac{1}{2}$, giving the largest possible sample size. The population total was 198 sites. To find the necessary sample size

$$n = \frac{Z_\alpha^2[P(1-P)]}{d^2}$$

In this case

$$= \frac{Z_\alpha^2(\frac{1}{4})}{d^2} = \frac{Z_\alpha^2}{4d^2}$$

Substituting numbers:

$$n = \frac{1.96^2}{4(0.07)^2} = 196$$

This is nearly the whole population so we obviously need to take the finite population correction into account

$$n' = \frac{n}{1 + n/N} = \frac{196}{1 + 196/198}$$

$$= \frac{196}{1.989} = 98$$

So the necessary sample size for the required degree of precision and probability level is 98 sites selected by simple random sampling.

SELECTING A SAMPLE

At this point we have seen a great deal about constructing confidence intervals and estimating required sample sizes on the basis of simple random samples but we have not yet specified what a simple random sample is or how to go about selecting one.

To select any sample at all it is obvious that we need a set of *sampling units*: discrete, definable entities amongst which samples may be chosen. The list of sampling units from which samples may be drawn is known as the *sampling frame*. Without a sampling frame containing the list of all the items in the population which we wish to sample we cannot go any further.

It is important to emphasise again here that the sample units making up the list do not have to be the real items of interest: they may merely contain them. Thus, in an archaeological context, the fact that before we excavate a site we do not usually know how many features there will be, and that if we did know this, for some purposes at least we would not need to bother taking a sample, is completely irrelevant to the process of taking a sample. In all such cases we can sample from known populations which contain the one in which we are interested. At the regional level we can sample units of land and at the site level grid squares. It is then possible to discuss the attributes of these arbitrary units and talk about, for example, the number of sites per km^2, or the number of sherds per grid square. Or we can talk about aspects of the sites or artefacts themselves, in which case any statistical inference procedures have to take into account the fact that they are dealing with cluster samples (see below).

A *simple random sample* is a sample which has the characteristic that any individual, and any combination of individuals, has an equal chance of occurring in the sample. Such a sample can be obtained by drawing members from the population one at a time *without replacement*; this means that once an item has been selected it is withdrawn from the selection pool and does not have a second chance of being chosen.

The mechanism of choice is generally a *random numbers table* (see appendix 1, table D). The sampling units in the population are numbered in sequence. As many random numbers are selected from the table as are required to give a sample of the size decided, subject to the stipulation that if a number comes up which has already occurred it is ignored. How is the table to be read?

Suppose the case we saw above where we wanted to select 50 arrowheads from 2000, and each arrowhead has been given a number from 1 to 2000. Because 2000 is a four-digit number we need four-digit random numbers; these are obtained by reading four adjacent digits together from the random numbers table; a small extract from one is presented here to illustrate the procedure:

```
10  09  73  25
37  54  20  48
08  42  26  84
99  01  90  25
```

We don't need to start at the top of the table and we can make our blocks of four digits by amalgamating any adjacent four. We might, for example, begin with the second row and the fourth digit across. Reading across and then down we would have 4204, 2268, 1902.

Since only one of these falls within the range 1–2000 only this one is selected, the other two are ignored. You continue reading the table until the required number of numbers has been selected, without duplication.

If the population contained only 100 elements (0–99, or 1–100 with 00 counting as 100) then only two-digit numbers would be required.

If the sampling units are spatial ones defined in terms of a grid over an area, individual units can be selected by means of two random numbers specifying the coordinates of a corner of the unit.

If the required sample size is large the process of selecting a series of numbers by hand from a table can be a laborious one and it will be quicker to use one of the random number generators available in many suites of statistical computer programs. You should be careful when using these, however, because many of them produce a fixed set of numbers that you will obtain every time unless you take explicit action to randomise the starting point.

ALTERNATIVES TO SIMPLE RANDOM SAMPLING

Simple random sampling is a widely used procedure and it is easy to operate from a statistical point of view. Nevertheless, there will very often be circumstances in which we want to use one of the more complex procedures, because (a) they are often more efficient than simple random sampling in the sense that a more precise estimate will be obtained from the same number of sample units; (b) they are often much easier to carry out in practice than simple random sampling; (c) our aims may require us to use an alternative method; (d) sometimes, for archaeological reasons, we have no choice (e.g. we may have to use cluster samples (see below)).

Stratified Random Sampling

In a stratified random sample the sampled population is divided into a number of *strata* (nothing to do with archaeological layers) or subdivisions and an independent random sample is taken from each stratum. The subdivisions are decided by the investigator and are often chosen so that there is some difference between them. For example, if an archaeological survey of a region is being carried out it may be decided to divide the region into environmental zones on the basis of some criterion and to sample independently within each zone; or if a site is being excavated and it appears from preliminary work that it is functionally differentiated, then each of the functionally different sections may be sampled. The subdivisions may, however, be more or less arbitrary.

The reasons for stratifying are usually the advantages it has over simple random sampling in two respects. First of all, an appropriate stratification can ensure that all parts of our population are sampled. Simple random sampling does not guarantee this since some parts of the list of units may be heavily sampled and others hardly at all, purely on the basis of chance. This will not matter to the obtaining of some overall estimate for the population as a whole, but more often than not we are interested in internal comparisons within our sample, as in the examples just given; or, for example, if we are selecting a sample of sherds from a multi-period site for scientific analysis, we will probably want to ensure that all the periods, or only certain specific ones, are represented. In regional sampling we may simply want to ensure that all parts of the region are examined, without regard to any question of environmental or other variation between them.

The second reason for stratifying is that if the population characteristic of interest is more homogeneously distributed within the strata than between them (i.e. there is variation between strata but not within them), then the precision of the overall estimate obtained will be greater for a given number of sample units than with simple random sampling.

The formula for the standard error of the mean based on a stratified sample is as follows (Dixon and Leach 1978):

$$s_{\bar{x}_{\text{strat}}} = \sqrt{\frac{\sum_{i=1}^{k}(n_i s_i)^2(1 - n/N)}{n^2}}$$

where n_i is the number of units in the sample from stratum i, s_i is the standard deviation in stratum i, n is the total number of units in the sample, and k is the total number of strata. If different fractions of each stratum were sampled, however, the formula would need to be altered to take this into account (see, for example, Dixon and Leach 1978, 19–21).

Systematic Sampling

With this technique (which is in fact a special case of cluster sampling) the interval between the sample points is fixed by the relation between the size of the proposed sample and the size of the population. Thus, if we wanted to select a sample of 30 from a population of 300 we would select every 300/30th item – every 10th in other words. Whether the 1st, 11th, 21st, etc., are chosen, or the 5th,

15th, 25th, etc., or whatever, is determined by selecting a random number between 1 and 10 for the starting point.

The reasons for selecting a systematic sample generally tend to be those of practical convenience; it is often more straightforward to sample in this way. The other reason, especially if we are talking about sampling in archaeological survey or excavation, is that we will normally want our sample to serve a number of different purposes, of which estimating population characteristics will only be one. In these circumstances a systematic sample might be taken as a compromise in the face of conflicting demands.

From the strict statistical and estimation point of view systematic samples present undoubted problems, in particular for the calculation of an estimate of the standard error of the statistic of interest. These arise because of the lack of independence of the elements of the sample and because of the possibility that there may be periodicities in the values of the population elements being sampled. This is particularly likely to be the case in the sampling of spatial distributions. On a settlement excavation, for example, a regular grid of sampling units at a given interval might find all the houses or miss them, if, as is likely, they were systematically distributed in some way. Whichever turned out to be the case any estimate of the total number of houses on the site based on the number in the sample would prove erroneous (cf. Winter 1976).

A variety of reactions is possible in the face of these well-known difficulties presented by systematic samples for the calculation of standard errors. One is never to use them at all (cf. Doran and Hodson 1975), which is probably the best solution but may be excluded in a given situation for practical and non-statistical reasons. Another is to use one of the formulae presented by Cochran (1977, 224–7) for obtaining the standard error, each of which is only applicable in certain situations. The problem here is that their use involves prior knowledge of the structure of the population which we are sampling in order to use an appropriate method; such knowledge may not be available. In the particular case where the order of the items in the sampling frame has been randomised, or can be assumed to be random, then the systematic sample can be effectively treated as a simple random sample (Cochran 1977, 214–16) and the same formula for the standard error used. Nevertheless, this option should be used with caution since periodicities and trends within the population may not be at all obvious.

A further approach has been adopted by Bellhouse in an archaeological context (Bellhouse 1980, Bellhouse and Finlayson 1979).

It is in effect an extension of the idea of using prior knowledge and involves the use of a computer program which calculates the outcome of different sampling schemes, including systematic sampling, in terms of the standard error of the estimate, for estimates of means, totals and ratios. The problem is that in order to provide an appropriate sampling scheme for a particular case, whether region or site, the method presupposes that complete information is available for a similar region or site, in order to provide the information on which the performance of the sampling schemes may be assessed.

The question of spatial or area sampling to which this discussion (and systematic sampling in general) is particularly relevant is considered again below.

Cluster Sampling
It is most straightforward to describe what is involved in cluster sampling with relation to the other methods which have been described already.

We saw that in stratified sampling the population is subdivided into groups called strata and each stratum is sampled. In cluster sampling the population is again subdivided into groups but some groups are selected for examination and not others. As you might expect, and as we will see below, the principles on which the subdivision is based are different in the two cases.

An archaeological example of the differences between these two approaches, contrasted with simple random sampling as well, will help to make the differences clearer. Let us suppose that a large number of pits has been excavated at a site. We are interested in studying the pottery from them but we do not have the resources to study all of it so a sample must be taken.

If we were taking a simple random sample of the pottery we would treat all the pottery from all the pits as the population and select randomly from that population without regard to the pits from which the pottery came. It is likely that such a procedure would be extremely difficult to put into practice because of the way material is stored and organised after an excavation, and also that some pits would not be represented in the sample while others would only have very few sherds selected.

If we were using stratified random sampling we could take the individual pits as our strata and select a random sample of pottery from within each pit. Although this would be very good from the point of view of estimating various properties of the population, it would still almost certainly be very laborious to put into operation because we would have to organise the procedure of selecting a random sample from the finds bags for each pit.

The cluster sampling approach would be to take a random sample of pits and study the pottery from the pits selected. This would have the disadvantage that not all of the pits would be examined, and that cluster samples almost always give greater sampling errors than simple random samples of the same size. On the other hand, it would almost certainly be the easiest procedure to put into practice, probably by a considerable margin, which would mean that we could, if we chose, actually look at more pottery.

In cluster sampling then we do not sample among our units of interest directly but among clusters or groups of sample units. The example just described is very characteristic of the kind of situation which occurs in archaeology; often there is not a great deal of choice about dealing with cluster samples.

The main problem with clusters, for example the contents of our pits discussed above, is that they tend to be relatively homogeneous and any single cluster is likely to represent only a fraction of the full range of variation in the population as a whole. This means that in selecting only certain clusters we may be failing to consider some of the variation in the population, which will simply not be repre-sented in the sample; alternatively our sample may include some unusual clusters. In neither case will we get a very good estimate of the standard error of the characteristic in which we are interested. Ideally what we want of clusters, therefore, is that they should be heterogeneous, incorporating a wide range of the population varia-tion so that omitting some clusters from consideration isn't going to make a lot of difference. In stratified sampling, on the other hand, every stratum is represented by a sample of units; accordingly, our sampling errors arise from variability *within* the strata so that we want the individual strata to be as homogeneous as possible.

To sum up then. Strata are preferable on the whole, in the sense that their use can decrease the standard error of the estimate when compared with simple random sampling. Cluster samples are very often unavoidable for practical reasons but will usually give larger standard errors than using simple random sampling. Sometimes, however, strata can be less efficient and clusters more efficient than simple random sampling. Dixon and Leach (1978, 22) suggest that rather than using the simple random sampling formula for calculat-ing the standard error of an estimate for cluster samples we should apply a correlation factor. They suggest that a quick way of doing this is to use a factor of 1.5 as a reasonable 'rule of thumb' figure based on experience. Thus, for a confidence interval, instead of

$$\bar{x} \pm Z_\alpha \left(\frac{s}{\sqrt{n}} \right) \sqrt{\left(1 - \frac{n}{N} \right)}$$

we would have

$$\bar{x} \pm Z_\alpha \left(\frac{1.5s}{\sqrt{n}} \right) \sqrt{\left(1 - \frac{n}{N} \right)}$$

and for calculating sample size

$$n = \left(\frac{Z_\alpha 1.5s}{d} \right)^2$$

PROBABILISTIC SAMPLING
OF POPULATIONS WITH A SPATIAL DIMENSION

Now that the main techniques of probabilistic sampling and the concepts behind them have been outlined, it is necessary to go on to a discussion of their use in an archaeological context. The problems which this raises arise mostly in the context of the survey and excavation of regions and sites and they are of two kinds: technical difficulties in the use of probabilistic sampling, and wider questions of the relevance of probabilistic sampling at all in the light of the aims of survey and excavation projects. This section is concerned with the first of these two topics.

As we have noted already, both regional and site sampling involve sampling units of space for unknown distributions. The problems for probabilistic sampling arise from the *spatial* distribution of observations within and between the sampling units.

In the first place, the distribution of the number of items per spatial unit is very often highly skewed – a standard model for such distributions is the Poisson distribution (see, for example, Hodder and Orton 1976, 33–8). Although Ihm (1978, 293–4) has presented, in an archaeological context, a formula for obtaining a confidence interval for the mean of a Poisson distribution, this author at least has never seen such a formula used in a case-study. Archaeologists seem always to have used the standard estimation procedure described in this chapter which presupposes that the sampling distribution of sample means is normal. We saw above that for this to hold the sample size must be sufficiently large and Thomas (1975) showed that 'sufficiently large' can mean very large indeed if the skewness is as great as it often is with spatial distributions.

More intractable than this, however, is the problem that items are rarely scattered randomly over space but deviate from this pattern, usually in the direction of clumping or aggregation. It is this problem of aggregation which has meant that most archaeological investigations of spatial sampling techniques, whether at the site or regional scale, have been essentially *ad hoc* empirical investigations (see, e.g., Plog 1976), with all that is implied by that statement concerning limitations in their significance. They have not been soundly based in theory because the consequences of aggregation have not been explored in a theoretically based fashion.

Some of the most interesting work on this and a number of other problems associated with spatial sampling has been carried out by Nance (1981, 1983), largely using perfectly standard results from statistical theory but working at a level of statistical sophistication considerably in advance of that used in most earlier applications and much more relevant to archaeological problems. In particular, he has used the negative binomial distribution (see e.g. Hodder and Orton 1976, 86–97) for describing spatial distributions and shown how increasing aggregation drastically increases the standard error of any estimates.

Nance has also examined a rather different but important sampling question to which relatively little attention has been given compared with that devoted to obtaining assessments of the precision of estimates: the question of discovery probabilities, i.e. the number of sampling units required on average to discover the presence of some phenomenon among the sampling units; or conversely, for a given sample size, the probability that at least one sampling unit will contain an example of the phenomenon, for items of varying degrees of rarity. Here too aggregation is important since as it increases – as the number of items concentrates into an increasingly small number of the sampling units – discovery probabilities decrease.

Finally, Nance has also applied these ideas to another problem of considerable importance in regional sampling. Surface survey and sampling techniques were first developed in their modern form in the arid regions of the western and south-western United States, where surface visibility of finds is generally extremely good. Since then attention has been drawn frequently to the problems of such techniques where surface visibility is poor (e.g. Wobst 1983). In the United States, in the context of the very large funds available for contract archaeology, attempts have been made to overcome

the difficulties by excavating small test pits within the larger sampling units. Naturally, the question has arisen of the statistical properties of such observations and the inferences which may validly be
drawn from them (Lovis 1976, Nance 1983, Nance and Ball 1986,
Wobst 1983). Nance's work on discovery probabilities and estimation in such situations again provides a basis for planning future
designs and assessing the limitations of current ones. McManamon
(1981) has used these techniques in estimating site densities in
different environmental strata on Cape Cod. In principle then it is
possible to use distributions of shovel test pits in a rigorous fashion,
in a similar way to the use of surface collection. Whether the
practical problems posed by digging such pits can always be overcome is another matter. In particular, the small sample sizes which
are practically feasible, relative to the rarity in the landscape of the
items being sought, are a major obstacle to achieving worthwhile
estimates (see Wobst 1983).

Bellhouse's approach (Bellhouse 1980, Bellhouse and Finlayson
1979) to improving spatial sampling methods has been referred to
already during the discussion of systematic sampling, as have the
problems associated with it. Despite these it may prove very useful
in particular situations, and if it is widely used some generalisations
may begin to emerge.

The concentration here on aspects of spatial sampling is a reflection both of the importance of fieldwork in the archaeological
research process and of the considerable problems from a sampling
point of view inherent in it. The manipulation of the data collected
is no less important but their characteristics are, of course, ulti-
mately dependent on the fieldwork; furthermore, the intrinsic
problems associated with assemblage sampling are not as great, for
several reasons. First, the spatial dimension has been removed
from consideration, except as a basis for stratifying the sample.
Second, the external non-statistical constraints, while they exist,
are less complex and less powerful. Finally, there is usually a
considerable amount of redundancy present in the populations, in
contrast to the situation at site and regional level, so that sampling
really can make a difference as far as saving time and money are
concerned. The redundancy stems from two main sources: the
inherently greater complexity and variability present at the site and
regional levels, and the sheer number of items available for study at
the assemblage level. It tends to be forgotten in many archaeological discussions of sampling that the most important feature of
samples as far as estimation is concerned is their size and not the

sampling fraction; the fraction required of very large populations can often be minute. It might be necessary to examine 100 artefacts to obtain some estimate of interest and this could easily be a tiny percentage of the available artefact population. In contrast, if some problem required information from 100 sites this could well represent a large proportion of the sites in an area. It goes without saying that carrying out an investigation on 100 artefacts is something on a rather smaller scale than investigating 100 sites!

On the other hand, however, Nance (1981) has demonstrated that for some purposes at least it is not the total number of items in the collection which is important but the number of clusters (excavation or surface collection units) from which they come, so the issues are not always straightforward.

SAMPLING AND ARCHAEOLOGICAL AIMS: ALTERNATIVES TO PARAMETER ESTIMATION

We have seen that probability sampling is concerned with giving us estimates whose reliability and precision we can assess of aggregate population characteristics. We also noted at the beginning of the chapter that whether such measures will be of interest to us depends on what our aims are. More often than not, in fact, we are interested in variation within our site or region so that some overall blanket measure of some characteristic is not particularly helpful.

The answer to this in sampling terms is the process of stratification described above. If we are interested in whether there are any differences between certain parts of our site or area then we can divide it up into strata and sample each part separately. Nevertheless, although in principle stratification can be a good idea, its use can also raise major problems, both at site and regional level. For example, the question of whether we have enough information to produce a stratification cannot be lightly dismissed, nor can the possibility that in devising and applying a stratification scheme we will simply perpetuate existing biases in our information.

In the regional case problems arise because it is rarely feasible to carry out a regional survey devoted to a particular period or problem: covering the ground is generally so expensive that we only want to do it once and to collect information on all periods when doing it. There is usually no reason to believe that the factors affecting site or find density will be constant for all periods, indeed this is highly unlikely. The consequence of this is that a stratification relevant for one period will not be relevant for another, and the application of a number of different cross-cutting stratification schemes is likely to be impossibly unwieldy in practice.

The same problem also arises with multi-period sites, of course, which present very intractable problems if they are deeply strati-fied. However, there is also another problem at the site level, which arises both from the destructive nature of excavation and again the expense associated with it. When excavating we are invariably interested in the characteristics of a number of different populations – pottery of different types, animal bones, seeds, structures, lithics, etc. – and it is unlikely that these will be spatially distributed across the site in the same kind of way: a stratification relevant to obtain-ing good estimates of population characteristics for one will not necessarily be good for the others. Integration of different aims remains a major excavation problem.

Even when stratified sampling can be carried out, however, it will not be satisfactory for obtaining certain kinds of spatial informa-tion. It has long been pointed out (e.g. Redman 1974) that in a given case investigations of both regions and sites are likely to involve both a probabilistic and non-probabilistic element, and that to obtain full information on spatial patterning in an area may well involve total coverage of that area, whether by survey or excava-tion, in order to produce a complete map or plan. Nevertheless, even with so-called total coverage we cannot escape sampling con-siderations, because the question arises of how intensive our cover-age should be if we are to recover rare elements in the population from a surface survey, or how intensive soil processing should be to recover, for example, plant remains or lithic debitage (cf. the discussion of Nance's work above).

On the positive side, however, total continuous coverage is not always necessary to make statements about spatial patterning. De-spite what was said above about the limited use of aggregate de-scriptive statistics for telling us about internal variation, there are certain overall statistics which can be calculated on the basis of sample data and which tell us in a general way about spatial pattern-ing, in particular concerning the extent to which the distribution is clustered, random or dispersed. Morisita's index of dispersion, for example (see e.g. Rogge and Fuller 1977, Shennan 1985), unlike nearest neighbour analysis or the usual forms of quadrat analysis (see Hodder and Orton 1976) only requires data on the frequencies of sites per sample unit and these units need not be contiguous. Given the problems posed by clustering or aggregation for para-meter estimation discussed above, assessing its extent seems an important prerequisite for the evaluation of other estimates. Plog

(1974) has discussed other useful aspects of spatial pattern which can be assessed by means of such general indices.

But even when we want detailed information on spatial patterning total coverage may not always be required and is certainly not always feasible. For some mapping purposes the use of sample-based data is satisfactory, but we are not using the sample for parameter estimation purposes so the criteria for what is a good sample will be different. The most important criterion is spatial regularity: there has to be a systematic element in the sampling scheme, so that observations are recorded in all areas of interest. The paradigm here is the site contour survey, in which a regular grid for observations is laid out, a measurement is taken at each and the contours are then interpolated. In a contour survey, however, it is possible to see where the slope is going between the data points, so we know whether or not they are representative and can, if necessary, take extra readings if a particular point on the grid is obviously unrepresentative, or if there are local variations in slope which the grid observations do not characterise sufficiently. When we are interpolating patterns of spatial variation in archaeological distributions, on the other hand, we are in the dark, just as with parameter estimation, and cannot see when problems arise.

From this point of view, although an essentially even distribution of data points is essential, systematic samples present problems just as great as they do for parameter estimation: regularities in the distributions, such as that of houses on settlements referred to above, are potentially equally disastrous from both points of view. The answer which has been proposed by geographers faced with similar kinds of problem is the use of *stratified systematic unaligned sampling* (see e.g. Haggett *et al.* 1977, 272–4). This is illustrated in figure 14.2.

First of all the area is divided into grid squares. We then start with the bottom left or top left square and use two random numbers to define the coordinates of a point within this square (figure 14.2a). All grid squares along the top or bottom row of the area are then given the same x coordinate as the first square but the y coordinate for each square is selected by random numbers (14.2b). Similarly, all squares along the left-hand margin of the area have the same y coordinate as the first square but their x's are chosen randomly (14.2c). For all other squares the sample point is obtained by taking the x coordinate of its row and the y coordinate of its column (14.2d).

In effect this is a minutely stratified sample with the grid squares

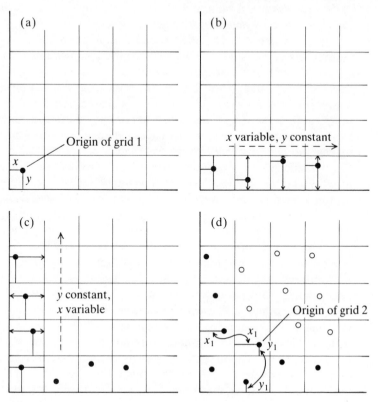

Figure 14.2. Stages in the generation of a stratified
systematic unaligned sample (after Haggett *et al.* 1977).

as the strata. The method does seem to have the potential to avoid
the periodicity problem and at the same time to provide regularly
distributed spatial information; on the other hand it rarely seems to
be used in practice in archaeology as a basis for estimating population characteristics with associated confidence intervals, the other
purpose for which such samples are normally required (with the
exception of Bellhouse 1980).

Even using such a method as stratified systematic unaligned
sampling, however, we still have no very satisfactory criterion for
telling us how good or bad our interpolations are when we make
them. One way round this is to use trend surface analysis to see if
there are any spatial trends in the values of the variables of interest.
This is a form of multiple regression in which there are two independent variables, the two spatial coordinates of the data points, and

one dependent, the values of the variable of interest at the data points (see e.g. Davis 1973, Orton 1980). A more sophisticated method of spatial interpolation is *kriging*, which involves the use of spatial autocorrelation assumptions (see Hodder and Orton 1976, 174–83, for an archaeological discussion of the latter) in estimating the value of a spatially distributed variable at a location from its values at adjacent locations; so far only Zubrow and Harbaugh (1978) seem to have used this technique in an archaeological context. As they show, its use is not restricted to spatial mapping; it can be used in a predictive fashion, as in geology, to maximise the probability of site discovery for a given amount of effort.

It is important to note that such a prospecting exercise, trying to maximise returns, is very different in its aim from obtaining representative information on, for example, site density in a region. Perhaps some authors have not always been clear about which of these aims they have been, or should have been, pursuing. If a survey of a threatened area is taking place, it could be argued that maximising site discovery is actually more appropriate than estimating regional site densities.

All the methods just described are different approaches to obtaining different kinds of spatial data. As usual, it will be the aims of the investigator which will determine which of them is the most appropriate. In making such a decision it is important to be aware of the options which are available and not to automatically assume that some fairly straightforward probability sampling scheme will be the best.

Indeed, a radical conclusion from this discussion of spatial patterning in distributions would be that estimation of means and standard errors is almost entirely irrelevant: what matters most of all is distributional shape, to which relatively little attention has been given apart from that noted in the discussion above. This point is not dissimilar to the criticisms made by the exploratory data analysts with regard to statistical distributions in general: if a distribution has peculiarities of shape these are the most important thing about it and we need to know about them. In the face of significant clustering, it could be argued, averages become irrelevant.

But we can go on from this and argue further that what matters most of all, in contrast to estimation, is to account for the variation we observe. To take an example at the regional scale, we may be less interested in estimating site densities than in understanding factors behind site location, or, more generally, behind variations in artefact density on the ground surface (e.g. Shennan 1985). In these circumstances, rather than automatically adopting a probabilistic area sampling technique we could set up a traditional experimental design, selecting combinations of factors which we believe to be relevant to the variations in density and then going out into the field and carrying out surface collections in those places where the selected combinations of factors exist. The resulting data could then be analysed using classic analysis of variance techniques (similar to regression but involving nominal scale independent variables – see, for example, Blalock 1972, chapter 16) and a measure obtained of the percentage variation in artefact density accounted for by the different factors. Of course, having identified all the various combinations of factors in which we were interested, we could if necessary sample probabilistically within them in a very straightforward fashion.

Even if we have not collected the data in such a rigorous way, and have not even collected it according to a probabilistic sampling scheme, we can still use such an approach to analyse variation in the data we have collected in a perfectly valid manner, although we will not be able to infer statistically to a larger population. The main problem in such a case is likely to stem from the fact that the resulting design may be so unbalanced that the effects of different variables are confounded with one another and cannot be distinguished.

An argument similar to this has been developed by Wobst (1983), who expresses considerable scepticism about the results of many projects based on probabilistic sampling, not least because in the many regions where surface visibility is poor actually collecting sufficient observations to produce estimates which have any worthwhile degree of precision is a virtually impossible task. Wobst's answer is that we should turn away from general purpose estimation to hypothesis testing, since the observations required for the testing of a hypothesis can almost certainly be specified much more narrowly and as a result there will be a more realistic chance of obtaining them.

It is obvious from all this that the issues involved in probability sampling are both complex and unresolved and whether Wobst is right or not its use should never be a substitute for thought.

EXERCISES

14.1. In a study of settlements in an area it is decided to begin by studying the locations of known sites in order to try and develop some predictive principles to guide subsequent survey in search of new sites. At each site various locational features are noted and the aim is to obtain an estimate of the percentage of the sites which possess specific characteristics, to an accuracy of $\pm 5\%$ with a confidence of 95%. The number of sites is 291. How many must be visited, assuming that they are selected by simple random sampling?

14.2. In the course of a study of the material from the excavation of a neolithic settlement in Hungary, it is decided that it is important to investigate pottery fragmentation as a basis for understanding the nature of the different deposits. To save time and money it is decided to select a sample of each pottery fabric from each deposit, rather than weighing all the sherds. The sample will be selected by simple random sampling.

For one particular fabric type the selection of a preliminary sample provides a standard deviation of 25 g. It is decided that a tolerance on the estimated weight of 5 g is acceptable, with a 95% probability.

Calculate a basic sample size to achieve this aim, which can then be corrected for the varying population sizes of different deposits.

14.3. An archaeological survey has been carried out of an area of 100 km^2. The survey was based on a simple random sample of one-hectare quadrats, totalling 5 km^2 in all. Densities of material in each quadrat were recorded and for lithic artefacts of the neolithic and earlier bronze age the mean density was 16.95/ha, with a standard deviation of 7.03, and a distribution not too far from normality, albeit positively skewed.

Calculate a confidence interval for the total number of lithic artefacts in the survey area as a whole, with a probability of 99%.

14.4. A hunter-gatherer occupation site was excavated on a grid of 2×2 metre squares. Below is a list of the number of lithic pieces found in each of the 50 squares excavated.

```
 2   5  15  17  11  26  25  28  23  22
38  37  35  30  39  48  47  45  48  42
47  45  41  55  50  59  51  59  56  57
53  61  67  64  63  60  79  75  77  72
71  85  82  89  96  93  95 108 103 117
```

i) Work out the mean and standard deviation for the site as a whole.

ii) (a) use random numbers to select 10 simple random samples of 30 squares; (b) obtain the mean and standard deviation for each sample, together with the mean of the means; (c) obtain the standard error of the mean for each sample, and 95% and 99% confidence intervals for the mean; (d) how do the confidence intervals relate to each other and to the overall population mean.

iii) Repeat (ii) for samples of 10 squares and 20 squares.

(N.B. The t distribution should be used for the confidence intervals.)

Fifteen

Conclusion

If you have managed to get this far you should find that you have reached a level of competence which will enable you to carry out some basic data analysis and to talk to statisticians without mutual incomprehension; you should also be able to follow many of the statistical arguments in the literature and obtain the general idea of most of the rest; and you have a firm basis for further reading and finding out about other techniques. Some appropriate further reading has already been mentioned. Blalock (1972) is very good on most of the material in the first part, although becoming rather dated in certain respects. Hartwig and Dearing (1979) and Tukey (1977) provide a firm grounding in exploratory data analysis, while at a more advanced level of the same general philosophy there is a great deal to be learnt from Mosteller and Tukey (1977). Johnston (1978) is very appropriate for extending your knowledge of the more advanced techniques.

A barrier does come, however, in that without a knowledge of calculus and matrix algebra you can only go so far on your own and you will find that you are unable to read more mathematical books on statistics and data analysis. Davis (1973) provides an accessible introduction to matrix algebra, as do Wilson and Kirkby (1980), who also cover calculus. The book by Everitt and Dunn (1983) is a good intermediate level text which requires some knowledge of matrix algebra to get the most out of it but is not impossibly difficult.

Whether you follow up quantitative data analysis, the extent to which you do so, and the direction you take are likely to be determined by the particular problems with which you are faced: of those which require it, some are susceptible to analysis by the methods described in this text and others related to them, while other problems require the development of novel techniques.

331

RECENT DIRECTIONS AND FUTURE TRENDS

Recent work provides examples of both these solutions to problems. Log-linear modelling has been finding increasing use (e.g. Hietala 1984, Leese and Needham 1986), while cluster analysis has been applied in novel ways as an important tool in intra-site spatial analysis (e.g. Whallon 1984, Kintigh and Ammerman 1982). Detailed work on problems of the application of particular techniques, such as probabilistic sampling, also continues (e.g. Shott 1985, van der Veen 1985).

In the longer term, however, it is probable that novel, or at least non-standard techniques will be required to solve many archaeological problems, and this is where co-operation between archaeologists and statisticians and mathematicians is especially important. In particular, the use of so-called 'bootstrap' techniques is likely to become far more important, in which the statistical or mathematical analysis is tailored to the complexities of the specific problem at hand, usually involving the computer simulation of distributions which take into account the constraints of the real data, and with which patterning in that data can be compared (e.g. Bradley and Small 1985, Simek 1984, Berry *et al.* 1984). Rather similar in approach is some important work on modelling the relationship between the archaeological evidence as recovered and as originally deposited, for pottery by Orton (1982) and for animal bones by Fieller and Turner (1982; Turner and Fieller 1985). These studies go considerably beyond probabilistic sampling in some important respects and again indicate further possibilities for the future in the development of rigorous models in which the mathematics closely match the archaeological problem.

Many of the developments are likely to be outside the field of quantitative data analysis in archaeology as traditionally perceived. Cluster analysis, for example, can now be seen as one part of the rapidly developing field of computerised mathematical pattern recognition (e.g. Bow, 1984), which in the future could well have an important contribution to make, for example to the analysis of shape, whether of artefacts or of spatial distributions, in archaeology; indeed, some of these techniques have long been used in archaeology for improving plots of geophysical survey readings (e.g. Scollar 1969), and have recently been applied to shapes (Gero and Mazzullo 1984).

The general trend in these recent and hypothesised future developments is clear: it is the increasing integration of archaeological knowledge and information into quantitative analyses. Standard 'off-the-peg' analyses will continue to be appropriate for many purposes, but for many others they will not. Another line of current research in archaeology points in a similar direction: it is the development of intelligent knowledge-based 'expert' systems for computers (see e.g. Huggett 1985). These involve the setting up of bodies of knowledge and rules for inference, which will enable the drawing of appropriate conclusions when new problems are presented to the system; medical diagnosis is probably their best-known field of application at present. Although their use in archaeology faces undoubted problems, as Huggett indicates, the idea behind them is undeniably attractive, not least in the context of the developments in data analysis which I have outlined above.

Some may say that developments of this kind may be interesting but they are unlikely to impinge on more than a small area of the archaeological profession. Whether or not this proves to be the case depends on two things. The first is the availability of facilities, and all the experience of the last few years suggests that increasingly high-powered facilities in terms of both hardware and software will be increasingly available in the future, even to archaeologists! The second is the level of education of the archaeological profession in data analysis and computing. With respect to the latter it is undoubtedly coming on apace. If this book makes a contribution to the former it will have been worthwhile, because it will have helped to create a climate for the realisation of the potential in the vast quantities of archaeological data whose possibilities remain almost untouched.

Appendix 1

Statistical Tables

A. Percentage points of the χ^2 distribution

B. Areas of the standardised normal distribution

C. Percentage points of the t-distribution

D. Random numbers

Tables A and C are reproduced by permission
of the Biometrika Trustees, and tables B and D
are reproduced from White, Yeats & Skipworth
(1979) by permission of Stanley Thornes
(Publishers) Ltd.

335

Table A. Percentage Points of the Chi-Squared Distribution.

The values tabulated are $\chi_\nu^2(\alpha)$, where
$Pr(\chi_\nu^2 > \chi_\nu^2(\alpha)) = \alpha$, for ν degrees of freedom.

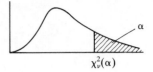

ν	$\alpha=0.995$	0.990	0.975	0.950	0.900	0.750	0.500
1	392704.10^{-10}	157088.10^{-9}	982069.10^{-9}	393214.10^{-8}	0.0157908	0.1015308	0.454936
2	0.0100251	0.0201007	0.0506356	0.102587	0.210721	0.575364	1.38629
3	0.0717218	0.114832	0.215795	0.351846	0.584374	1.212534	2.36597
4	0.206989	0.297109	0.484419	0.710723	.063623	1.92256	3.35669
5	0.411742	0.554298	0.831212	1.145476	1.61031	2.67460	4.35146
6	0.675727	0.872090	1.23734	1.63538	2.20413	3.45460	5.34812
7	0.989256	1.239043	1.68987	2.16735	2.83311	4.25485	6.34581
8	1.34441	1.64650	2.17973	2.73264	3.48954	5.07064	7.34412
9	1.73493	2.08790	2.70039	3.32511	4.16816	5.89883	8.34283
10	2.15586	2.55821	3.24697	3.94030	4.86518	6.73720	9.34182
11	2.60322	3.05348	3.81575	4.57481	5.57778	7.58414	10.3410
12	3.07382	3.57057	4.40379	5.22603	6.30380	8.43842	11.3403
13	3.56503	4.10692	5.00875	5.89186	7.04150	9.29907	12.3398
14	4.07467	4.66043	5.62873	6.57063	7.78953	10.1653	13.3393
15	4.60092	5.22935	6.26214	7.26094	8.54676	11.0365	14.3389
16	5.14221	5.81221	6.90766	7.96165	9.31224	11.9122	15.3385
17	5.69722	6.40776	7.56419	8.67176	10.0852	12.7919	16.3382
18	6.26480	7.01491	8.23075	9.39046	10.8649	13.6753	17.3379
19	6.84397	7.63273	8.90652	10.1170	11.6509	14.5620	18.3377
20	7.43384	8.26040	9.59078	10.8508	12.4426	15.4518	19.3374
21	8.03365	8.89720	10.28293	11.5913	13.2396	16.3444	20.3372
22	8.64272	9.54249	10.9823	12.3380	14.0415	17.2396	21.3370
23	9.26043	10.19567	11.6886	13.0905	14.8480	18.1373	22.3369
24	9.88623	10.8564	12.4012	13.8484	15.6587	19.0373	23.3367
25	10.5197	11.5240	13.1197	14.6114	16.4734	19.9393	24.3366
26	11.1602	12.981	13.8439	15.3792	17.2919	20.8434	25.3365
27	11.8076	12.8785	14.5734	16.1514	18.1139	21.7494	26.3363
28	12.4613	13.5647	15.3079	16.9279	18.9392	22.6572	27.3362
29	13.1211	14.2565	16.0471	17.7084	19.7677	23.5666	28.3361
30	13.7867	14.9535	16.7908	18.4927	20.6992	24.4776	29.3360
40	20.7065	22.1643	24.4330	26.5093	29.0505	33.6603	39.3353
50	27.9907	29.7067	32.3574	34.7643	37.6886	42.9421	49.3349
60	35.5345	37.4849	40.4817	43.1880	46.4589	52.2938	59.3347
70	43.2752	45.4417	48.7576	51.7393	55.3289	61.6983	69.3345
80	51.1719	53.5401	57.1532	60.3915	64.2778	71.1445	79.3343
90	59.1963	61.7541	65.6466	69.1260	73.2911	80.6247	89.3342
100	67.3276	70.0649	74.2219	77.9295	82.3581	90.1332	99.3341

ν	$\alpha=0.250$	0.100	0.050	0.025	0.010	0.005	0.001
1	1.32330	2.70554	3.84146	5.02389	6.63490	7.87944	10.828
2	2.77529	4.60517	5.99146	7.37776	9.21034	10.5966	13.816
3	4.10834	6.25139	7.81473	9.34840	11.3449	12.8382	16.266
4	5.38527	7.77944	9.48773	11.1433	13.2767	14.8603	18.467
5	6.62568	9.23636	11.0705	12.8325	15.0863	16.7496	20.515
6	7.84080	10.6446	12.5916	14.4494	16.8119	18.5476	22.458
7	9.03715	12.0170	14.0671	16.0128	18.4753	20.2777	24.322
8	10.2189	13.3616	15.5073	17.5345	20.0902	21.9550	26.125
9	11.3888	14.6837	16.9190	19.0228	21.6660	23.5894	27.877
10	12.5489	15.9872	18.3070	20.4832	23.2093	25.1882	29.588
11	13.7007	17.2750	19.6751	21.9200	24.7250	26.7568	31.264
12	14.8454	18.5493	21.0261	23.3367	26.2170	28.2995	32.909
13	15.9839	19.8119	22.3620	24.7356	27.6882	29.8195	34.528
14	17.1169	21.0641	23.6848	26.1189	29.1412	31.3194	36.123
15	18.2451	22.3071	24.9958	27.4884	30.5779	32.8013	37.697
16	19.3689	23.5418	26.2962	28.8454	31.9999	34.2672	39.252
17	20.4887	24.7690	27.5871	30.1910	33.4087	35.7185	40.790
18	21.6049	25.9894	28.8693	31.5264	34.8053	37.1565	42.312
19	22.7178	27.2036	30.1435	32.8523	36.1909	38.5823	43.820
20	23.8277	28.4120	31.4104	34.1696	37.5662	39.9968	45.315
21	24.9348	29.6151	32.6706	35.4789	38.9322	41.4011	46.797
22	26.0393	30.8133	33.9244	36.7807	40.2894	42.7957	48.268
23	27.1413	32.0069	35.1725	38.0756	41.6384	44.1813	49.728
24	28.2412	33.1962	36.4150	39.3641	42.9798	45.5585	51.179
25	29.3389	34.3816	37.6525	40.6465	44.3141	46.9279	52.618
26	30.4346	35.5632	38.8851	41.9232	45.6417	48.2899	54.052
27	31.5284	36.7412	40.1133	43.1945	46.9629	49.6449	55.476
28	32.6205	37.9159	41.3371	44.4608	48.2782	50.9934	56.892
29	33.7109	39.0875	42.5570	45.7223	49.5879	52.3356	58.301
30	34.7997	40.2560	43.7730	46.9792	50.8922	53.6720	59.703
40	45.6160	51.8051	55.7585	59.3417	63.6907	66.7660	73.402
50	56.3336	63.1671	67.5048	71.4202	76.1539	79.4900	86.661
60	66.9815	74.3970	79.0819	83.2977	88.3794	91.9517	99.607
70	77.5767	85.5270	90.5312	95.0232	100.425	104.215	112.317
80	88.1303	96.5782	101.879	106.629	112.329	116.321	124.839
90	98.6499	107.565	113.145	118.136	124.116	128.299	137.208
100	109.141	118.498	124.342	129.561	135.807	140.169	149.449

Table B. Areas of the Standardised Normal Distribution.

Z	−0.09	−0.08	−0.07	−0.06	−0.05	−0.04	−0.03	−0.02	−0.01	−0.00
−3.9	0.99997	0.99997	0.99996	0.99996	0.99996	0.99996	0.99996	0.99996	0.99995	0.99995
−3.8	0.99995	0.99995	0.99995	0.99994	0.99994	0.99994	0.99994	0.99993	0.99993	0.99993
−3.7	0.99992	0.99992	0.99992	0.99992	0.99991	0.99991	0.99990	0.99990	0.99990	0.99989
−3.6	0.99989	0.99988	0.99988	0.99987	0.99987	0.99986	0.99986	0.99985	0.99985	0.99984
−3.5	0.99983	0.99983	0.99982	0.99981	0.99981	0.99980	0.99979	0.99978	0.99978	0.99977
−3.4	0.99976	0.99975	0.99974	0.99973	0.99972	0.99971	0.99970	0.99969	0.99968	0.99966
−3.3	0.99965	0.99964	0.99962	0.99961	0.99960	0.99958	0.99957	0.99955	0.99953	0.99952
−3.2	0.99950	0.99948	0.99946	0.99944	0.99942	0.99940	0.99938	0.99936	0.99934	0.99931
−3.1	0.99929	0.99926	0.99924	0.99921	0.99918	0.99916	0.99913	0.99910	0.99906	0.99903
−3.0	0.99900	0.99896	0.99893	0.99889	0.99886	0.99882	0.99878	0.99874	0.99869	0.99865
−2.9	0.99861	0.99856	0.99851	0.99846	0.99841	0.99836	0.99831	0.99825	0.99819	0.99813
−2.8	0.99807	0.99801	0.99795	0.99788	0.99781	0.99774	0.99767	0.99760	0.99752	0.99744
−2.7	0.99736	0.99728	0.99720	0.99711	0.99702	0.99693	0.99683	0.99674	0.99664	0.99653
−2.6	0.99643	0.99632	0.99621	0.99609	0.99598	0.99585	0.99573	0.99560	0.99547	0.99534
−2.5	0.99520	0.99506	0.99492	0.99477	0.99461	0.99446	0.99430	0.99413	0.99396	0.99379
−2.4	0.99361	0.99343	0.99324	0.99305	0.99286	0.99266	0.99245	0.99224	0.99202	0.99180
−2.3	0.99158	0.99134	0.99111	0.99086	0.99061	0.99036	0.99010	0.98983	0.98956	0.98928
−2.2	0.98899	0.98870	0.98840	0.98809	0.98778	0.98745	0.98713	0.98679	0.98645	0.98610
−2.1	0.98574	0.98537	0.98500	0.98461	0.98422	0.98382	0.98341	0.98300	0.98257	0.98214
−2.0	0.98169	0.98124	0.98077	0.98030	0.97982	0.97932	0.97882	0.97831	0.97778	0.97725
−1.9	0.97670	0.97615	0.97558	0.97500	0.97441	0.97381	0.97320	0.97257	0.97193	0.97128
−1.8	0.97062	0.96995	0.96926	0.96856	0.97846	0.96712	0.96638	0.96562	0.96485	0.96407
−1.7	0.96327	0.96246	0.96164	0.96080	0.95994	0.95907	0.95818	0.95728	0.95637	0.95543
−1.6	0.95449	0.95352	0.95254	0.95154	0.95053	0.94950	0.94845	0.94738	0.94630	0.94520
−1.5	0.94408	0.94295	0.94179	0.94062	0.93943	0.93822	0.93699	0.93574	0.93448	0.93319
−1.4	0.93189	0.93056	0.92922	0.92785	0.92647	0.92507	0.92364	0.92220	0.92073	0.91924
−1.3	0.91774	0.91621	0.91466	0.91308	0.91149	0.90988	0.90824	0.90658	0.90490	0.90320
−1.2	0.90147	0.89973	0.89796	0.89617	0.89435	0.89251	0.89065	0.88877	0.88686	0.88493
−1.1	0.88298	0.88100	0.87900	0.87698	0.87493	0.87286	0.87076	0.86864	0.86650	0.86433
−1.0	0.86214	0.85993	0.85769	0.85543	0.85314	0.85083	0.84850	0.84614	0.84375	0.84134
−0.9	0.83891	0.83646	0.83398	0.83147	0.82894	0.82639	0.82381	0.82121	0.81859	0.81594
−0.8	0.81327	0.81057	0.80785	0.80511	0.80234	0.79955	0.79673	0.79389	0.79103	0.78814
−0.7	0.78524	0.78230	0.77935	0.77637	0.77337	0.77035	0.76731	0.76424	0.76115	0.75804
−0.6	0.75490	0.75175	0.74857	0.74537	0.74215	0.73891	0.73565	0.73237	0.72907	0.72575
−0.5	0.72240	0.71904	0.71566	0.71226	0.70884	0.70540	0.70194	0.69847	0.69497	0.69146
−0.4	0.68793	0.68439	0.68082	0.67724	0.67364	0.67003	0.66640	0.66276	0.65910	0.65542
−0.3	0.65173	0.64803	0.64431	0.64058	0.63683	0.63307	0.62930	0.62552	0.62172	0.61791
−0.2	0.61409	0.61026	0.60642	0.60257	0.59871	0.59483	0.59095	0.58706	0.58317	0.57926
−0.1	0.57535	0.57142	0.56750	0.56356	0.55962	0.55567	0.55172	0.54776	0.54380	0.53983
−0.0	0.53586	0.53188	0.52790	0.52392	0.51994	0.51595	0.51197	0.50798	0.50399	0.50000

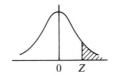

Z	0.00	0.01	0.02	0.03	0.04	0.05	0.06	0.07	0.08	0.09
0.0	0.50000	0.49601	0.49202	0.48803	0.48405	0.48006	0.47608	0.47210	0.46812	0.46414
0.1	0.46017	0.45620	0.45224	0.44828	0.44433	0.44038	0.43644	0.43250	0.42858	0.42465
0.2	0.42074	0.41683	0.41294	0.40905	0.40517	0.40129	0.39743	0.39358	0.38974	0.38591
0.3	0.38209	0.37828	0.37448	0.37070	0.36693	0.36317	0.35942	0.35569	0.35197	0.34827
0.4	0.34458	0.34090	0.33724	0.33360	0.32997	0.32636	0.32276	0.31918	0.31561	0.31207
0.5	0.30854	0.30503	0.30153	0.29806	0.29460	0.29116	0.28774	0.28434	0.28096	0.27760
0.6	0.27425	0.27093	0.26763	0.26435	0.26109	0.25785	0.25463	0.25143	0.24825	0.24510
0.7	0.24196	0.23885	0.23576	0.23269	0.22965	0.22663	0.22363	0.22065	0.21770	0.21476
0.8	0.21186	0.20897	0.20611	0.20327	0.20045	0.19766	0.19489	0.19215	0.18943	0.18673
0.9	0.18406	0.18141	0.17879	0.17619	0.17361	0.17106	0.16853	0.16602	0.16354	0.16109
1.0	0.15866	0.15625	0.15386	0.15150	0.14917	0.14686	0.14457	0.14231	0.14007	0.13786
1.1	0.13567	0.13350	0.13136	0.12924	0.12714	0.12507	0.12302	0.12100	0.11900	0.11702
1.2	0.11507	0.11314	0.11123	0.10935	0.10749	0.10565	0.10383	0.10204	0.10027	0.09853
1.3	0.09680	0.09510	0.09342	0.09176	0.09012	0.08851	0.08692	0.08534	0.08379	0.08226
1.4	0.08076	0.07927	0.07780	0.07636	0.07493	0.07353	0.07215	0.07078	0.06944	0.06811
1.5	0.06681	0.06552	0.06426	0.06301	0.06178	0.06057	0.05938	0.05821	0.05705	0.05592
1.6	0.05480	0.05370	0.05262	0.05155	0.05050	0.04947	0.04846	0.04746	0.04648	0.04551
1.7	0.04457	0.04363	0.04272	0.04182	0.04093	0.04006	0.03920	0.03836	0.03754	0.03673
1.8	0.03593	0.03515	0.03438	0.03362	0.03288	0.03216	0.03144	0.03074	0.03005	0.02938
1.9	0.02872	0.02807	0.02743	0.02680	0.02619	0.02559	0.02500	0.02442	0.02385	0.02330
2.0	0.02275	0.02222	0.02169	0.02118	0.02068	0.02018	0.01970	0.01923	0.01876	0.01831
2.1	0.01786	0.01743	0.01700	0.01659	0.01618	0.01578	0.01539	0.01500	0.01463	0.01426
2.2	0.01390	0.01355	0.01321	0.01287	0.01255	0.01222	0.01191	0.01160	0.01130	0.01101
2.3	0.01072	0.01044	0.01017	0.00990	0.00964	0.00939	0.00914	0.00889	0.00866	0.00842
2.4	0.00820	0.00798	0.00776	0.00755	0.00734	0.00714	0.00695	0.00676	0.00657	0.00639
2.5	0.00621	0.00604	0.00587	0.00570	0.00554	0.00539	0.00523	0.00508	0.00494	0.00480
2.6	0.00466	0.00453	0.00440	0.00427	0.00415	0.00402	0.00391	0.00379	0.00368	0.00357
2.7	0.00347	0.00336	0.00326	0.00317	0.00307	0.00298	0.00289	0.00280	0.00272	0.00264
2.8	0.00256	0.00248	0.00240	0.00233	0.00226	0.00219	0.00212	0.00205	0.00199	0.00193
2.9	0.00187	0.00181	0.00175	0.00169	0.00164	0.00159	0.00154	0.00149	0.00144	0.00139
3.0	0.00136	0.00131	0.00126	0.00122	0.00118	0.00114	0.00111	0.00107	0.00104	0.00100
3.1	0.00097	0.00094	0.00090	0.00087	0.00084	0.00082	0.00079	0.00076	0.00074	0.00071
3.2	0.00069	0.00066	0.00064	0.00062	0.00060	0.00058	0.00056	0.00054	0.00052	0.00050
3.3	0.00048	0.00047	0.00045	0.00043	0.00042	0.00040	0.00039	0.00038	0.00036	0.00035
3.4	0.00034	0.00032	0.00031	0.00030	0.00029	0.00028	0.00027	0.00026	0.00025	0.00024
3.5	0.00023	0.00022	0.00022	0.00021	0.00020	0.00019	0.00019	0.00018	0.00017	0.00017
3.6	0.00016	0.00015	0.00015	0.00014	0.00014	0.00013	0.00013	0.00012	0.00012	0.00011
3.7	0.00011	0.00010	0.00010	0.00010	0.00009	0.00009	0.00008	0.00008	0.00008	0.00008
3.8	0.00007	0.00007	0.00007	0.00006	0.00006	0.00006	0.00006	0.00005	0.00005	0.00005
3.9	0.00005	0.00005	0.00004	0.00004	0.00004	0.00004	0.00004	0.00004	0.00003	0.00003

Table C. Percentage Points of the *t*-Distribution.

One-Sided Test

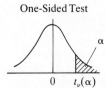

$$\Pr(T_\nu > t_\nu(\alpha)) = \alpha,$$
for ν degrees of freedom

Two-Sided Test

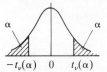

$$\Pr(T_\nu > t_\nu(\alpha) \text{ or } T_\nu < -t_\nu(\alpha)) = 2\alpha,$$
for ν degrees of freedom

ν	$\alpha = 0.4$ $2\alpha = 0.8$	0.25 0.5	0.1 0.2	0.05 0.1	0.025 0.05	0.01 0.02	0.005 0.01	0.0025 0.005	0.001 0.002	0.0005 0.001
1	0.325	1.000	3.078	6.314	12.706	31.821	63.657	127.321	318.309	636.619
2	0.289	0.816	1.886	2.920	4.303	6.965	9.925	14.089	22.327	31.599
3	0.277	0.765	1.638	2.353	3.182	4.541	5.841	7.453	10.215	12.924
4	0.271	0.741	1.533	2.132	2.776	3.747	4.604	5.598	7.173	8.610
5	0.267	0.727	1.476	2.015	2.571	3.365	4.032	4.773	5.893	6.869
6	0.265	0.718	1.440	1.943	2.447	3.143	3.707	4.317	5.208	5.959
7	0.263	0.711	1.415	1.895	2.365	2.998	3.499	4.029	4.785	5.408
8	0.262	0.706	1.397	1.860	2.306	2.896	3.355	3.833	4.501	5.041
9	0.261	0.703	1.383	1.833	2.262	2.821	3.250	3.690	4.297	4.781
10	0.260	0.700	1.372	1.812	2.228	2.764	3.169	3.581	4.144	4.587
11	0.260	0.697	1.363	1.796	2.201	2.718	3.106	3.497	4.025	4.437
12	0.259	0.695	1.356	1.782	2.179	2.681	3.055	3.428	3.930	4.318
13	0.259	0.694	1.350	1.771	2.160	2.650	3.012	3.372	3.852	4.221
14	0.258	0.692	1.345	1.761	2.145	2.624	2.977	3.326	3.787	4.140
15	0.258	0.691	1.341	1.753	2.131	2.602	2.947	3.286	3.733	4.073
16	0.258	0.690	1.337	1.746	2.120	2.583	2.921	3.252	3.686	4.015
17	0.257	0.689	1.333	1.740	2.110	2.567	2.898	3.222	3.646	3.965
18	0.257	0.688	1.330	1.734	2.101	2.552	2.878	3.197	3.610	3.922
19	0.257	0.688	1.328	1.729	2.093	2.539	2.861	3.174	3.579	3.883
20	0.257	0.687	1.325	1.725	2.086	2.528	2.845	3.153	3.552	3.850
21	0.257	0.686	1.323	1.721	2.080	2.518	2.831	3.135	3.527	3.819
22	0.256	0.686	1.321	1.717	2.074	2.508	2.819	3.119	3.505	3.792
23	0.256	0.685	1.319	1.714	2.069	2.500	2.807	3.104	3.485	3.768
24	0.256	0.685	1.318	1.711	2.064	2.492	2.797	3.091	3.467	3.745
25	0.256	0.684	1.316	1.708	2.060	2.485	2.787	3.078	3.450	3.725
26	0.256	0.684	1.315	1.706	2.056	2.479	2.779	3.067	3.435	3.707
27	0.256	0.684	1.314	1.703	2.052	2.473	2.771	3.057	3.421	3.690
28	0.256	0.683	1.313	1.701	2.048	2.467	2.763	3.047	3.408	3.674
29	0.256	0.683	1.311	1.699	2.045	2.462	2.756	3.038	3.396	3.659
30	0.256	0.683	1.310	1.697	2.042	2.457	2.750	3.030	3.385	3.646
40	0.255	0.681	1.303	1.684	2.021	2.423	2.704	2.971	3.307	3.551
60	0.254	0.679	1.296	1.671	2.000	2.390	2.660	2.915	3.232	3.460
120	0.254	0.677	1.289	1.658	1.980	2.358	2.617	2.860	3.160	3.373
∞	0.253	0.674	1.282	1.645	1.960	2.326	2.576	2.807	3.090	3.291

Table D. Random Numbers.

Each digit in this table of computer-generated pseudo-random numbers is an independent sample from a population where each of the digits 0 to 9 has a probability of occurrence of 0.1.

65 23	68 00	77 82	58 14	10 85	11 85	57 11	73 74	45 25	60 46
06 56	76 51	04 73	94 30	16 74	69 59	04 38	83 98	30 20	87 85
55 99	98 60	01 33	06 93	85 13	23 17	25 51	92 04	52 31	38 70
72 82	45 44	09 53	04 83	03 83	98 41	67 41	01 38	66 83	11 99
04 21	28 72	73 25	02 74	35 81	78 49	52 67	61 40	60 50	47 50
87 01	80 59	89 36	41 59	60 27	64 89	47 45	18 21	69 84	76 06
31 62	46 53	84 40	56 31	74 96	52 23	72 95	96 06	58 83	85 22
29 81	57 94	35 91	90 70	94 24	19 35	50 22	23 72	87 34	83 15
39 98	74 22	77 19	12 81	29 42	04 50	62 34	36 81	43 07	97 92
56 14	80 10	76 52	38 54	84 13	99 90	22 55	41 04	72 37	89 33
29 56	62 74	12 67	09 35	89 33	04 28	44 75	01 57	87 45	52 21
93 32	57 38	39 36	87 42	72 55	73 97	98 36	57 41	76 09	11 68
95 69	51 54	43 19	20 49	57 25	90 55	26 20	70 98	43 73	56 45
65 71	32 43	64 67	22 55	65 65	48 86	10 88	20 12	40 18	49 25
90 27	33 43	97 84	20 57	49 91	41 20	17 64	29 60	66 87	55 97
95 29	42 45	61 34	30 13	30 39	21 52	59 28	64 98	08 76	09 27
99 74	06 29	20 55	72 70	11 43	95 82	75 37	90 24	77 43	63 21
87 87	56 91	16 97	51 50	61 36	96 47	76 68	49 11	50 56	51 06
46 24	17 74	97 37	39 03	54 83	34 00	74 61	77 51	43 33	15 67
66 79	81 43	40 92	84 72	88 32	83 24	67 01	41 34	70 19	26 93
36 42	94 58	83 30	92 39	18 40	03 00	12 90	32 27	91 65	48 15
07 66	25 08	99 27	69 48	85 32	16 46	19 31	85 02	86 36	22 96
93 10	05 72	18 26	36 67	68 48	31 69	68 58	93 49	45 86	99 29
49 50	63 99	26 71	47 94	32 71	72 91	34 18	74 06	32 14	40 80
20 75	58 89	39 04	42 73	37 93	11 07	28 77	91 36	60 47	82 62
02 40	62 09	00 71	09 37	80 44	50 37	32 70	20 38	71 86	75 34
59 87	21 38	29 78	72 67	42 83	65 21	54 79	66 42	47 86	31 15
48 08	99 66	43 38	28 13	50 25	47 93	11 15	07 84	28 30	19 07
54 26	86 75	44 15	20 39	20 03	58 54	80 29	62 53	09 67	71 51
35 35	58 45	23 58	63 66	09 62	80 92	14 55	81 41	21 48	87 34
73 84	90 49	01 21	90 29	57 06	68 73	51 10	51 95	63 08	57 99
34 64	78 00	92 59	67 74	58 48	92 09	42 20	40 37	63 80	58 93
68 56	87 47	63 06	24 71	41 98	79 06	07 18	58 29	16 49	67 37
72 47	05 52	88 07	27 55	58 74	82 08	42 28	26 48	25 32	00 31
44 44	96 75	89 57	12 60	42 38	77 36	45 69	21 68	32 70	04 96
28 11	57 47	61 57	89 88	62 18	93 67	57 32	96 72	21 17	13 54
87 22	38 88	91 99	16 08	17 76	27 47	52 14	98 86	35 68	23 85
44 93	14 59	67 40	24 10	11 63	40 47	07 56	14 22	62 74	93 39
81 84	37 25	90 43	58 62	94 58	49 03	84 22	57 22	47 98	86 37
09 75	35 21	04 47	54 08	98 44	08 16	44 86	69 71	20 52	64 94
77 65	05 04	22 18	20 10	81 87	05 69	43 70	96 76	42 05	21 10
19 06	51 61	34 03	61 55	98 58	83 50	01 48	99 85	08 67	15 91
52 91	87 07	19 62	32 28	04 91	42 48	66 24	86 09	87 68	55 51
52 47	25 14	93 91	75 51	49 26	49 41	20 83	30 30	43 22	69 08
52 67	87 40	63 41	91 86	10 47	80 70	56 87	25 86	89 94	21 42
65 25	71 73	78 60	50 62	91 04	95 97	64 16	71 31	32 80	19 61
29 97	56 42	56 90	16 75	74 95	99 26	01 63	25 16	54 18	54 46
15 25	03 68	92 45	53 00	06 29	46 43	46 66	27 12	85 05	22 44
82 08	65 67	64 13	51 14	38 28	24 30	39 62	20 35	23 90	57 36
81 35	03 25	87 24	83 59	04 67	51 52	26 21	69 75	87 28	61 50

Table D. Random Numbers—*continued*

67 00	76 07	06 04	17 26	85 10	29 42	93 48	93 46	52 72	77 53		
37 41	48 98	99 14	86 78	56 14	20 12	28 86	70 70	66 62	99 86		
54 85	60 58	43 58	36 74	44 33	96 38	13 52	98 74	01 27	52 08		
82 78	21 26	47 21	31 66	50 67	34 87	78 86	26 32	35 38	94 63		
72 32	72 25	83 98	34 31	63 44	31 47	09 57	26 23	89 88	16 10		
86 73	37 38	09 68	16 67	81 32	03 42	28 56	09 92	75 20	50 35		
54 67	40 72	97 91	06 61	98 95	38 02	94 57	65 32	75 34	64 33		
80 86	35 17	08 51	17 12	07 87	75 39	83 43	77 04	66 02	13 46		
08 32	44 20	01 13	17 22	42 71	76 76	33 56	94 22	02 67	70 98		
96 84	83 43	36 80	18 75	16 54	53 48	71 77	34 88	43 51	41 76		
48 67	84 20	48 23	50 47	15 85	24 65	78 93	01 84	02 04	41 31		
35 99	47 15	37 62	62 27	35 41	55 57	03 12	74 45	83 25	14 57		
13 07	22 58	68 80	91 93	64 68	59 55	19 45	72 83	08 01	28 93		
73 15	83 78	75 46	76 36	65 56	34 75	92 58	99 38	51 64	98 42		
18 92	29 56	47 99	74 31	42 88	52 71	90 84	23 56	75 22	62 08		
50 07	11 21	26 62	94 01	89 32	51 14	17 11	30 31	12 01	18 58		
59 50	53 71	99 35	15 56	41 95	71 78	53 15	10 51	86 17	53 81		
45 55	85 24	55 08	49 43	00 21	31 67	73 35	42 10	71 12	46 37		
90 80	65 04	38 06	30 57	56 62	21 88	30 85	56 89	02 21	43 40		
84 51	93 90	28 31	22 31	48 44	45 97	48 85	79 68	78 78	05 18		
07 66	01 78	75 25	68 67	31 08	85 38	37 76	01 94	22 20	03 04		
19 41	96 21	21 48	53 68	46 91	11 40	98 12	50 26	58 52	74 39		
01 38	53 01	20 30	43 53	83 34	87 15	63 52	17 89	43 19	31 11		
12 95	21 94	99 72	76 51	69 20	66 93	80 83	88 97	35 52	23 76		
25 88	63 69	99 41	89 27	18 92	52 49	56 75	99 20	68 13	04 50		
95 89	07 45	38 96	63 61	11 49	98 72	50 67	30 94	93 01	20 20		
49 69	36 31	40 43	65 22	63 59	43 94	43 18	76 48	00 90	10 65		
47 52	59 03	71 19	04 67	42 38	98 78	36 75	12 62	10 27	23 83		
41 89	34 25	98 99	14 49	65 61	20 09	71 32	63 20	88 92	25 40		
41 89	18 07	02 57	18 44	53 64	89 51	56 63	63 37	25 64	17 23		
46 58	12 07	61 94	29 39	90 76	24 23	64 84	38 61	35 84	78 95		
98 42	17 61	53 32	62 34	19 38	05 03	07 09	45 01	61 01	81 34		
09 44	61 42	84 40	80 09	25 36	73 61	09 53	51 95	76 09	13 64		
41 97	74 05	94 04	57 50	28 49	26 54	91 50	26 20	75 12	91 39		
70 42	82 33	21 08	41 30	67 58	46 55	84 19	40 76	47 37	85 59		
05 18	96 66	53 07	84 44	17 62	70 43	76 28	64 80	98 32	21 11		
69 44	33 07	09 02	87 76	98 50	65 99	36 27	77 23	93 92	15 72		
71 95	73 70	09 66	69 55	73 19	20 59	12 95	01 99	75 88	31 13		
99 59	52 07	54 56	90 44	75 85	84 35	17 08	97 87	56 04	61 52		
97 07	78 13	46 90	10 48	53 29	43 92	58 51	39 39	18 38	47 35		
85 04	86 52	92 49	65 46	99 78	99 66	82 34	22 86	79 10	85 96		
11 68	36 63	15 84	92 56	31 78	47 49	14 51	34 78	76 47	87 47		
12 69	35 64	97 00	63 69	41 06	75 10	94 21	70 74	06 08	90 56		
62 72	73 45	26 19	35 75	15 23	75 26	98 66	97 45	31 86	44 80		
78 63	02 76	61 95	57 00	30 05	18 52	19 86	40 08	83 32	17 42		
65 40	31 04	87 02	46 38	43 16	63 83	76 95	23 06	76 48	54 60		
42 68	22 96	29 30	39 32	75 36	64 03	70 64	83 51	61 81	15 96		
40 15	54 28	80 30	30 07	53 91	62 62	26 31	75 25	10 23	43 84		
51 19	95 91	95 98	92 53	98 08	55 70	68 78	21 13	95 15	87 36		
77 55	25 60	17 30	53 23	98 29	52 71	92 10	71 72	52 21	06 21		

Appendix 2

Computer Packages
for Statistical Analysis

This appendix gives brief details of some of the most widely available computer packages for statistical analysis; more extensive information is available in Richards and Ryan (1985, chapter 7). There is no attempt to cover the enormous range of packages now available for microcomputers, although several of those listed below now have microcomputer versions. Similarly, with the exception of cluster analysis, there is no attempt to list the many sets of programs which have been written for particular purposes; except for CLUSTAN all the rest are general-purpose packages for statistical analysis.

In general they are straightforward to learn and use but it is worth remembering that at the initial stage they often involve what can be a considerable amount of time and effort learning your way around them, especially if you're a beginner. Although introductory manuals are available for some, the sheer bulk of the documentation of the major packages can be daunting and not all of it is as clear as it might be (to say the least!).

The execution of particular tasks is controlled by keywords, which call up relevant procedures. These procedures generally have standard options for routine analysis and are therefore extremely easy to use, while non-standard options can be called up by providing extra information; thus, a considerable amount of flexibility is possible.

The big danger with these programs is that in general they do not tell you when you are using techniques inappropriately. The fact that a package will carry out an instruction doesn't necessarily mean that the instruction is statistically appropriate: ability to run the packages, and not much is required, can easily outstrip statistical expertise. This is a point you should always bear in mind.

MINITAB
(Minitab Inc., 215 Pond Laboratory,
University Park, PA 16802, USA)

The MINITAB statistical package provides a comprehensive set of procedures for carrying out statistical analyses up to the level of multiple regression. It includes many techniques not described in this book, including comparisons of means and analysis of variance. It also includes a useful set of procedures for matrix manipulation, including eigenvectors and eigenvalues.

Perhaps the best feature of MINITAB, especially at an introductory level, is its ease of use. It is interactive (results of instructions come straight back to the screen for the user to look at) in a flexible and straightforward way and provides excellent help facilities which can be requested if you're stuck or you've forgotten something. Furthermore, the MINITAB Handbook (Ryan *et al.* 1985) is easy to use and includes details of the statistical methods as well as of the relevant MINITAB procedures.

A microcomputer version is available.

SPSS–X
(SPSS Inc., Suite 3300, 444 North Michigan Avenue,
Chicago, Illinois 60611, USA)

This is the successor to SPSS, a long-standing and very widely used general statistical data analysis package, and has extensive file handling, data modification and report preparation facilities in addition to statistical analysis. It covers virtually all the methods described in this text, including frequency distributions and descriptive statistics, cross-tabulations, regression and correlation, as well as factor analysis and log-linear models, in addition to many other techniques not covered here.

Documentation is extensive, with simplified versions for beginners, and includes descriptions of statistical techniques as well as details of SPSS–X procedures.

A microcomputer version is available.

SAS
(SAS Institute Inc., Box 8000, Cary,
North Carolina 27511–8000, USA)

The SAS System is a comprehensive system for data analysis. It provides facilities for information storage and retrieval, for data modification, for file handling and report writing, in addition to statistical analysis. As well as basic descriptive statistics it includes methods for significance testing, regression, log-linear modelling, cluster analysis and multivariate analysis, including methods which this text has not covered. Extensive documentation is available. In Britain it does not have the popularity of some of the other packages but elsewhere, especially in the United States, it is very widely used.

BMDP
(BMDP Statistical Software, 1964 Westwood Blvd,
Suite 202, Los Angeles, CA 90025, USA)

This is another general statistical package very similar to SPSS and SAS, although it does not include the non-statistical report writing facilities included in the other two; nor does it have their introductory level documentation. There is simply one large manual, which looks rather forbidding at first sight. In fact, it's not as bad as it looks. What it says in the manual (Dixon 1983, 15) is not too far from the truth: BMDP programs are easy to use if you ignore what you don't need to know. For a beginner, however, what you don't need to know is not necessarily obvious.

The range of techniques covered is very extensive, particularly at the more complex end of the range.

GENSTAT
The Statistical Package Co-ordinator,
Numerical Algorithms Group Limited,
NAG Central Office, Mayfield House,
256 Banbury Road, Oxford OX2 7DE, UK)

GENSTAT is another general purpose statistical package but it is unlike the others listed in this appendix in that it is in some ways more like an ordinary high-level computer language, such as FORTRAN, than a package. This gives it a great deal of flexibility while at the same time making it rather more difficult to use. It is probably true to say that it is less easy to misuse GENSTAT than the other packages because it requires more knowledge and expertise to use it in the first place. In some circles GENSTAT has acquired something of a cachet as the expert's statistics package! It covers an enormous range of techniques, including correspondence analysis.

The GENSTAT manual is not particularly easy reading but an introduction to the package appeared a few years ago (Alvey *et al.* 1982), which makes coming to grips with it rather easier.

GENSTAT does not seem to be especially popular in North America, at least in archaeological circles, in the light of lack of reference to it in the literature.

From the same general stable as GENSTAT, and thus very similar to it, is the generalised linear modelling package GLIM (Baker and Nelder 1978).

CLUSTAN
(Dr D. Wishart, c/o Dept. of Computational Science,
University of St Andrews, North Haugh,
St Andrews KY16 9SX, UK)

This is an extremely comprehensive set of programs for cluster analysis. In addition to all the clustering procedures described in this text and many others, CLUSTAN has facilities for the production of similarity and distance matrices using a very wide range of coefficients. It also now includes some of the cluster validation procedures described in chapter 12.

A weakness is the lack of facilities for data modification and manipulation, but the package does provide the possibility of links with BMDP, and with SPSS in particular, which help to overcome this. An associated program called CLUSCOM allows interactive input of CLUSTAN instructions, but it is not available everywhere and without it instruction input can be rather tedious and mistake-prone.

Beginners tend to find the manual rather difficult to follow.

References

Aldenderfer, M. (1981) Creating assemblages by computer simulation: the development and uses of ABSIM, in J. A. Sabloff (ed.) *Simulations in Archaeology*, 67-117. Albuquerque: University of New Mexico Press.

Aldenderfer, M. (1982) Methods of cluster validation for archaeology. *World Archaeology 14*, 61-72.

Alvey, N., N. Galwey, & P. Lane, (1982) *An Introduction to GENSTAT*. London: Academic Press.

Baker, R. J. & J. A. Nelder, (1978) *The GLIM System, Release 3: Generalised Linear Interactive Modelling*. London: Royal Statistical Society.

Barnett, V. (1974) *Elements of Sampling Theory*. London: English University Press.

Barth, F. (1966) *Models of Social Organisation*. Royal Anthropological Institute Occasional Paper No. 23. London: Royal Anthropological Institute

Bellhouse, D. (1980) Sampling studies in archaeology. *Archaeometry 22*, 123-32.

Bellhouse, D. & W. D. Finlayson (1979) An empirical study of probability sampling designs: preliminary results from the Draper Site. *Canadian J. Archaeology 3*, 105-23.

Berry, K. J., P. W. Mielke & K. L. Kvamme (1984) Efficient permutation procedures for analysis of artefact distributions, in H. Hietala (ed.) *Intrasite Spatial Analysis in Archaeology*, 54-74. Cambridge: Cambridge University Press.

Bettinger, R. L. (1979) Multivariate statistical analysis of a regional subsistence-settlement model for Owens Valley. *American Antiquity 44*, 455-70.

Binford, L. R. (1964) A consideration of archaeological research design. *American Antiquity 29*, 425-41.

Binford, L. R. (1981) *Bones: Ancient Men and Modern Myths*. New York: Academic Press.

Binford, L. R. (1983) *In Pursuit of the Past*. London: Thames & Hudson.

Blalock, H. M. (1972) *Social Statistics*. Tokyo: McGraw-Hill–Kogakusha.

Bølviken, E., E. Helskog, K. Helskog, I. M. Holm-Olsen, L. Solheim & R. Bertelsen (1982) Correspondence analysis:

an alternative to principal components. *World Archaeology 14*, 41-60.

Bow, Sing-Tze (1984) *Pattern Recognition*. New York and Basel: Marcel Dekker.

Boyle, K. (1983) *The Hunters Nobody Knows*. Unpublished M sc dissertation, University of Southampton.

Bradley, R. & C. Small (1985) Looking for circular structures in post-hole distributions: quantitative analysis of two settlements from bronze age England. *J. Archaeological Science 12*, 285-97.

Brainerd, G. W. (1951) The place of chronological ordering in archaeological analysis. *American Antiquity 16*, 301-13.

Brumfiel, E. (1976) Regional growth in the eastern Valley of Mexico: a test of the 'population pressure' hypothesis, in K. V. Flannery (ed.) *The Early Mesoamerican Village*, 234-49. New York: Academic Press.

Buchvaldek, M. & D. Koutecky (1970) Vikletice: ein schnurkeramisches Gräberfeld. Praha: Universita Karlová.

Cable, C (1984) *Economy and Technology in the Late Stone Age of Southern Natal*. Cambridge Monographs in African Archaeology 9, B A R International Series 201. Oxford: British Archaeological Reports.

Carothers, J. & W. A. McDonald (1979) Size and distribution of the population in Late Bronze Age Messenia: some statistical approaches. *J. Field Archaeology 6*, 433-54.

Chatterjee, S. & B. Price (1977) *Regression Analysis by Example* New York: John Wiley & Sons.

Cherry, J. F. (1977) Investigating the political geography of an early state by multidimensional scaling of Linear B tablet data, in J. L. Bintliff (ed.) *Mycenaean Geography*, 76-83. Cambridge: British Associatiion for Mycenaean Studies.

Clark, G. A. (1976) More on contingency table analysis, decision-making criteria, and the use of log-linear models. *American Antiquity 41*, 259-73.

Clark, G. A. (1982) Quantifying archaeological research, in M. Schiffer (ed.) *Advances in Archaeological Method and Theory 5*, 217-73. New York: Academic Press.

Clarke, D. L. (1962) Matrix analysis and archaeology with particular reference to British Beaker pottery. *Proc. Prehistoric Society 28*, 371-82.

Clarke, D. L. (1966) A tentative reclassification of British Beaker pottery in the light of recent research. *Palaeohistoria 12*, 179-98.

Clarke, D. L. (1968) *Analytical Archaeology*. London: Methuen.

Clarke, D. L. (1970) *Beaker Pottery of Great Britain and Ireland*. Cambridge: Cambridge University Press.

Cochran, W. G. (1977) *Sampling Techniques* (3rd ed.). New York: John Wiley & Sons.

Constantine, A. G. & J. C. Gower (1978) Graphical representation of asymmetric matrices. *Applied Statistics 27*, 297-304.

Cormack, R. M. (1971) A review of classification. *J. Royal Statistical Society A, 134*, 321-67.

Cowgill, G. L. (1970) Some sampling and reliability problems in archaeology, in J. C. Gardin (ed.) *Archéologie et Calculateurs*, 161-72. Paris: CNRS.

Cowgill, G. L. (1972) Models, methods and techniques for seriation, in D. L. Clarke (ed.) *Models in Archaeology*, 381-424. London: Methuen.

Cowgill, G. L. (1977) The trouble with significance tests and what we can do about it. *American Antiquity 42*, 350-68.

Davis, J. C. (1973) *Statistics and Data Analysis in Geology*. New York: John Wiley & Sons.

Dixon, C. & B. Leach (1977) *Sampling Methods for Geographical Research*. Concepts and Techniques in Modern Geography 17. Norwich: University of East Anglia, Geo. Abstracts.

Dixon, W. J. ed. (1983) *BMDP Statistical Software*. Berkeley: University of California Press.

Djinjian, F. (1980) *Construction de Systèmes d' Aide à la Connaissance en Archéologie Préhistorique. Structuration et Affectation*. Thèse de Doctorat de 3ᵉ Cycle, Université Paris 1, UER d'Art et d' Archéologie.

Doran, J. & F. Hodson (1975) *Mathematics and Computers in Archaeology*. Edinburgh: Edinburgh University Press.

Ester, M. (1981) A column-wise approach to seriation. *American Antiquity 46*, 496-512.

Everitt, B. (1980) *Cluster Analysis* (2nd ed.). London: Heinemann Educational Books.

Everitt, B. & G. Dunn (1983) *Advanced Methods of Data Exploration and Modelling*. London: Heinemann Educational Books.

Fieller, N. R. J. & A. Turner (1982) Number Estimation in vertebrate samples. *J. Archaeological Science 9*, 49-62.

Fienberg, S. E. (1980) *The Analysis of Cross-Classified Categorical Data* (2nd ed.). Cambridge, Mass: MIT Press.

Forsberg, L. (1985) *An Analysis of the Hunter-Gatherer Settlement Systems in the Lule River Valley, 1500-BC/AD*. Umea: Dept of Archaeology, University of Umea.

Gabriel, K. R. (1981) Biplot display of multivariate matrices for inspection of data and diagnosis, in V. Barnett (ed.) *Interpreting Multivariate Data*, 147-73. London: John Wiley & Sons.

Gaines, S., ed. (1981) *Databank Applications in Archaeology*.

Tucson: University of Arizona Press.

Gamble, C. S. (1982) Leadership and 'surplus' production, in C. Renfrew & S. J. Shennan (eds) *Ranking, Resource and Exchange*, 100-5. Cambridge: Cambridge University Press.

Gardin, J. (1980) *Archaeological Constructs*. Cambridge: Cambridge University Press.

GENSTAT, A General Statistical Program (release 4.04), 1983. Oxford: Numerical Algorithms Group Ltd.

Gero, J. & J. Mazzullo (1984) Analysis of artefact shape using Fourier series in closed form. *J. Field Archaeology* 315-22.

Gordon, A. D. (1981) *Classification: methods for the exploratory analysis of multivariate data*. London: Chapman & Hall.

Gower, J. C. (1971) A general coefficient of similarity and some of its properties. *Biometrics 27*, 857-72.

Gower, J. C. (1977) The analysis of asymmetry and orthogonality, in J. R. Barra (ed.) *Recent Developments in Statistics*, 109-23. Amsterdam: North-Holland Publishing Co.

Haggett, P., A. D. Cliff & A. Frey (1977) *Locational Analysis in Human Geography* (2nd ed.). London: Edward Arnold.

Hartwig, F. & B. E. Dearing (1979) *Exploratory Data Analysis*. Sage University paper series on Quantitative Applications in the Social Sciences, series no. 07-016. Beverley Hills & London: Sage Publications.

Hawkes, J. (1968) The proper study of mankind. *Antiquity 42*, 255-62.

Hietala, H. (1984) Variations on a categorical data theme: local and global considerations with Near Eastern paleolithic applications, in H. Hietala (ed.) *Intrasite Spatial Analysis in Archaeology*, 44-53. Cambridge: University Press.

Hill, M. O. (1973) Reciprocal averaging: an eigenvector method for ordination. *J. Ecology 61*, 237-49.

Hodder, I. (1978) *Simulation Studies in Archaeology*. Cambridge: Cambridge University Press.

Hodder, I. (1982) Theoretical archaeology: a reactionary view, in I. Hodder (ed.) *Structural and Symbolic Archaeology*, 1-16. Cambridge: Cambridge University Press.

Hodder, I. & C. Orton (1976) *Spatial Analysis in Archaeology*. Cambridge: Cambridge University Press.

Hodson, F. R. (1977) Quantifying Hallstatt: some initial results. *American Antiquity 42*, 394-412.

Hole, B. L. (1980) Sampling in archaeology: a critique. *Annual Review of Anthropology 9*, 217-34.

Hosler, D., J. Sabloff & D. Runge (1977) Situation model development: a case study of the Classic Maya collapse, in N. Hammond (ed.) *Social Processes in Maya Prehistory*, 553-90. New York: Academic Press.

References 351

Huggett, J. (1985) Expert systems in archaeology, in M. A. Cooper & J. D. Richards (eds) *Current Issues in Archaeological Computing*, 123-42. BAR International Series 271. Oxford: British Archaeological Reports.

Ihm, P. (1978) *Statistik in der Archäologie*. Archaeo-Physika 9. Köln: Rheinland Verlag.

Jardine, N. & R. Sibson (1971) *Mathematical Taxonomy*. London: John Wiley & Sons.

Johnson, G. A. (1973) *Local Exchange and Early State Development in Southwestern Iran*. University of Michigan Museum of Anthropology, Anthropological Papers No 51. Ann Arbor: University of Michigan.

Johnston, R. J. (1978) *Multivariate Statistical Analysis in Geography*. London: Longman.

Kampffmeyer, U. & W. R. Teegen (1986) Untersuchungen zur rechnergestützten Klassifikation von Gefässformen am Beispiel der eisenzeitlichen Keramik des Gräberfeldes von Veis, Quattro Fontanili. *Die Kunde 37*, 1-84.

Kemp, B. (1982) Automatic analysis of Predynastic cemeteries: a new method for an old problem. *J. Egyptian Archaeology 68*, 5-15.

Kendall, D. (1977) Computer techniques and the archival map-reconstruction of Mycenaean Messenia, in J. L. Bintliff (ed.) *Mycenaean Geography*, 83-87. Cambridge: British Association for Mycenaean Studies.

Kintigh, K. W. & A. J. Ammerman (1982) Heuristic approaches to spatial analysis in archaeology. *American Antiquity 47*, 31-63.

Kruskal, J. B. & M. Wish (1978) *Multidimensional Scaling*. Sage University Paper series on Quantitative Applications in the Social Sciences, series no. 07-011. Beverley Hills & London: Sage Publications.

Leese, M. N. & S. P. Needham (1986) Frequency table analysis: examples from early bronze age axe decoration. *J. Archaeological Science 13*, 1-12.

Levy, J. (1982) *Social and Religious Organisation in Bronze Age Denmark*. BAR International Series 124. Oxford: British Archaeological Reports.

Lewis, R. B. (1986) The analysis of contingency tables in archaeology, in M. Schiffer (ed.) *Advances in Archaeological Method and Theory 9*, 277-310. New York: Academic Press.

Lovis, W. A. (1976) Quarter sections and forests: an example of probability sampling in the northeastern woodlands. *American Antiquity 43*, 364-72.

McDonald, J. & G. D. Snooks (1985) The determinants of manorial income in Domesday England: evidence from Essex. *J. Economic History 45*, 541-6.

MacIntosh, S. K. & R. J. MacIntosh (1980) *Prehistoric Investigations at Jenne, Mali.* BAR International Series 89. Oxford: British Archaeological Reports.

McManamon, F. P. (1981) Prehistoric land use on outer Cape Cod. *J. Field Archaeology 9,* 1-20.

Marquardt, W. (1978) Advances in archaeological seriation, in M. Schiffer (ed.) *Advances in Archaeological Method and Theory 1,* 257-314. New York: Academic Press.

Mather, P. M. (1976) *Computational Methods of Multivariate Analysis in Physical Geography.* London: John Wiley & Sons.

Mathiesen, P., I. M. Holm-Olsen, T. Sobstad & H. D. Bratrein (1981) The Helgøy Project: an interdisciplinary study of past eco-ethno processes in the Helgøy region, northern Troms, Norway. *Norwegian Archaeological Review 14,* 77-117.

Mellars, P. A. & M. R. Wilkinson (1980) with an appendix by N. R. J. Fieller. Fish otoliths as indicators of seasonality in prehistoric shell middens: the evidence from Oronsay (Inner Hebrides). *Proc. Prehistoric Society 46,* 19-44.

Mojena, R. (1977) Hierarchical grouping methods and stopping rules: an evaluation. *Computer Journal 20,* 359-63.

Morrison, D. F. (1967) *Multivariate Statistical Methods.* New York: McGraw-Hill.

Morwood, M. J. (1980) Time, space and prehistoric art: a principal components analysis. *Archaeology and Physical Anthropology in Oceania 15,* 98-109.

Mosteller, F. & J. W. Tukey (1977) *Data Analysis and Regression.* Reading, Mass: Addison-Wesley.

Nance, J. (1981) Statistical fact and archaeological faith: two models in small-sites sampling. *J. Field Archaeology 8,* 151-65.

Nance, J. (1983) Regional sampling in archaeological survey: the statistical perspective, in M. Schiffer (ed.) *Advances in Archaeological Method and Theory,* 6, 289-356. New York: Academic Press.

Nance, J. & B. F. Ball (1986) No surprises? The reliability and validity of test pit sampling. *American Antiquity 51,* 457-83.

Norusis, M. J. (1983) *SPSS-X: Introductory Statistics Guide.* New York: McGraw-Hill.

Norusis, M. J. (1985) *SPSS-X: Advanced Statistics Guide.* New York: McGraw-Hill.

Orton, C. (1980) *Mathematics in Archaeology.* London: Collins.

Orton, C. (1982) Computer simulation experiments to assess the performance of measures of quantity of pottery. *World Archaeology 14,* 1-20.

Ottaway, B. (1973) Dispersion diagrams: a new approach to the display of carbon-14 dates. *Archaeometry 15*, 5-12.

Peacock, D. P. S. (1971) Petrography of certain coarse pottery, in B. W. Cunliffe (ed.) *Excavations at Fishbourne*, 2, 255-9. Report of the Research Committee of the Society of Antiquaries 27. London: Society of Antiquaries.

Peebles, C. S. (1972) Monothetic-divisive analysis of the Moundville burials – an initial report. *Newsletter of Computer Archaeology 8*, 1-13.

Petrie, W. M. F. (1901) *Diospolis Parva*. London.

Plog, F. T. (1974) Settlement patterns and social history, in M. Leaf (ed.), *Frontiers of Anthropology*, 68-92. New York: Van Nostrand.

Plog, S. (1976) Relative efficiencies of sampling techniques for archaeological surveys, in K. V. Flannery (ed.) *The early Mesoamerican Village*, 136-58. New York: Academic Press.

Plog, S. (1980) *Stylistic Variation in Prehistoric Ceramics*. Cambridge: Cambridge University Press.

Read, D. W. (1982) Towards a theory of archaeological classification, in R. Whallon & J. A. Brown (eds) *Essays in Archaeological Typology*, 56-92. Evanston, Illinois: Center for American Archaeology Press.

Redman, C. (1974) *Archaeological Sampling Strategies*. Addison-Wesley Modular Publications in Anthropology No. 55. Reading, Mass: Addison-Wesley.

Renfrew, C. (1977) Alternative models for exchange and spatial distribution, in T. Earle & J. E. Ericson (eds) *Exchange Systems in Prehistory*, 71-90. New York: Academic Press.

Renfrew, C. & K. L. Cooke, eds (1979) *Transformations: Mathematical Approaches to Culture Change*. New York: Academic Press.

Renfrew, C. & G. Sterud (1969) Close-proximity analysis: a rapid method for the ordering of archaeological materials. *American Antiquity 34*, 265-77.

Richards, J. D. & N. S. Ryan (1985) *Data Processing in Archaeology*. Cambridge: Cambridge University Press.

Robinson, W. S. (1951) A method for chronologically ordering archaeological deposits. *American Antiquity 16*, 293-301.

Rogge, A. E. & S. L. Fuller (1977) Probability survey sampling: making parameter estimates, in M. B. Schiffer and G. J. Gumerman (eds) *Conservation Archaeology*, 227-38. New York: Academic Press.

Ryan, B. F., B. L. Joiner & T. A. Ryan (1985) *The MINITAB Student Handbook* (2nd ed.). Boston: Duxbury Press.

Sabloff, J. A., ed. (1981) *Simulations in Archaeology*. Albuquerque: University of New Mexico Press.

Schoknecht, U., ed. (1980) *Typentafeln zur Ur-und Frühgeschichte der DDR*. Weimar: Kulturbund der DDR.

Scollar, I. W. (1969) Some techniques for the evaluation of archaeological magnetometer surveys. *World Archaeology 1*, 77-89.

Service, E. R. (1962) *Primitive Social Organisation*. New York: Random House.

Shanks, M. & C. Tilley (1982) Ideology, symbolic power and ritual communication: a reinterpretation of neolithic mortuary practices, in I. Hodder (ed.) *Structural and Symbolic Archaeology*, 129-54. Cambridge: Cambridge University Press.

Shennan, S. J. (1977) *Bell Beakers and their context in Central Europe: a New Approach*. Unpublished Ph D dissertation, University of Cambridge.

Shennan, S. J. (1983) Disentangling data, in G. Howson & R. McLone (eds) *Maths at Work*, 109-26. London: Heinemann Educational Books.

Shennan, S. J. (1985) *Experiments in the Collection and Analysis of Archaeological Survey Data*. Sheffield: Department of Prehistory and Archaeology, University of Sheffield.

Shennan, S. J. & J. D. Wilcock (1975) Shape and style variation in Central German Bell Beakers: a computer-assisted study. *Science and Archaeology 15*, 17-31.

Shott, M. (1985) Shovel-test sampling as a site discovery technique: a case-study from Michigan. *J. Field Archaeology 12*, 457-68.

Sidrys, R. (1977) Mass-distance measures for the Maya obsidian trade, in T. Earle and J. E. Ericson (eds) *Exchange Systems in Prehistory*, 91-107. New York: Academic Press.

Simek, J. F. (1984) Integrating pattern and context in spatial archaeology. *J. Archaeological Science 11*, 405-20.

Sneath, P. & R. Sokal (1973) *Numerical Taxonomy*. San Francisco: Freeman.

Sokal, R. & P. Sneath (1963) *Principles of Numerical Taxonomy*. San Francisco: Freeman.

Späth H. (1980) *Cluster Analysis Algorithms*. Chichester: Ellis Horwood.

Spaulding, A. C. (1953) Statistical techniques for the discovery of artefact types. *American Antiquity 18*, 305-13.

Spaulding, A. C. (1977) On growth and form in archaeology: multivariate analysis. *J. Anthropological Research 33*, 1-15.

Speth, J. & G. Johnson (1976) Problems in the use of correlation for the investigation of tool kits and activity areas, in C. E. Cleland (ed.) *Cultural Change and Continuity: Essays in Honour of James Bennett Griffin*, 35-57.

References   355

Tainter, J. A. (1975) Social inferences and mortuary practices: an experiment in numerical classification. *World Archaeology* 7, 1-15.

Thomas, D. H. (1975) Non-site sampling in archaeology: up the creek without a site?, in J. W. Mueller (ed.) *Sampling in Archaeology*, 61-81. Tucson: University of Arizona Press.

Thomas, D. H. (1976) *Figuring Anthropology*. New York: Holt, Rinehart and Winston.

Thomas, D. H. (1978) The awful truth about statistics in archaeology. *American Antiquity 43*, 231-44.

Tilley, C. (1984) Ideology and the legitimation of power in the Middle Neolithic of southern Sweden, in D. Miller and C. Tilley (eds) *Ideology, Power and Prehistory*, 111-46. Cambridge: Cambridge University Press.

Tufte, E. R. (1983) *The Visual Display of Quantitative Information*. Cheshire, Connecticut: Graphics Press.

Tukey, J. W. (1977) *Exploratory Data Analysis*. Reading, Mass: Addison-Wesley.

Tukey, J. W. (1980) We need both exploratory and confirmatory. *American Statistician 34*, 23-5.

Turner, A. & N. R. J. Fieller (1985) Consideration of minimum numbers: a response to Horton. *J. Archaeological Science 12*, 477-83.

Van der Veen, M. (1985) Carbonised seeds, sample size and on-site sampling, in N. R. J. Fieller, D. D. Gilbertson & N. G. A. Ralph (eds) *Paleoenvironmental Investigations: Research Design Methods and Data Analysis*, 165-74. Symposium 5 (ii) of the Association for Environmental Archaeology. BAR International Series 258. Oxford: British Archaeological Reports.

Van der Veen, M. & N. Fieller (1982) Sampling seeds. *J. Archaeological Science, 9*, 287-98.

Vescelius, G. S. (1960) Archaeological sampling: a problem of statistical inference, in G. E. Dole & R. L. Carneiro (eds) *Essays in the Science of Culture, in Honour of Leslie A. White*, 457-70. New York: Thomas Y. Crowell.

Vierra, R. (1982) Typology, classification and theory building, in R. Whallon and J. Brown (eds) *Essays in Archaeological Typology*, 162-75. Evanston, Illinois: Centre for American Archaeology Press.

Vierra, R. K. & D. L. Carlson (1981) Factor analysis, random data and patterned results. *American Antiquity 46*, 272-83.

Wainwright, G. J. (1979) *Mount Pleasant, Dorset: Excavations 1970-71*. Society of Antiquaries Research Report 37. London: Thames & Hudson.

Whallon, R. (1982) Variables and dimensions: the critical step in quantitative typology, in R. Whallon and J. A. Brown (eds) *Essays in Archaeological Typology,* 127-61. Evanston, Illinois: Centre for American Archaeology Press.

Whallon, R. (1984) Unconstrained clustering for the analysis of spatial distributions in archaeology, in H. Hietala (ed.) *Intra-site Spatial Analysis in Archaeology,* 242-77. Cambridge: Cambridge University Press.

Whallon, R. & J. A. Brown, eds (1982) *Essays in Archaeological Typology.* Evanston, Illinois: Centre for American Archaeology Press.

White, J., A. Yeats & G. Skipworth (1979) *Tables for Statisticians.* Stanley Thornes (Publishers) Ltd.

Wilson, A. G. & M. J. Kirkby (1980) *Mathematics for Geographers and Planners* (2nd ed.). Oxford: Clarendon Press.

Winham, P. (1978) Sampling populations of sites: a case-study from Shetland, in J. F. Cherry, C. S. Gamble & S. J. Shennan (eds) *Sampling in Contemporary British Archaeology,* 105-20. BAR British Series 50. Oxford: British Archaeological Reports.

Winter, M. (1976) Excavating a shallow community by random sampling quadrats, in K. V. Flannery (ed.) *The Early Mesoamerican Village,* 62-7. New York: Academic Press.

Wishart, D. (1978) *CLUSTAN User Manual* (3rd ed.) with 1982 supplement. Inter-University/Research Council Series Report No 47. Edinburgh: Program Library Unit.

Wobst, M. (1983) We can't see the forest for the trees: sampling and the shapes of archaeological distributions, in J. A. Moore & A. Keene (eds) *Archaeological Hammers and Theories,* 37-85. New York: Academic Press.

Zubrow, E. & J. Harbaugh (1978) Archaeological prospecting: kriging and simulation, in I. Hodder (ed.) *Simulation Studies in Archaeology,* 109-22. Cambridge: Cambridge University Press.

Index

accumulation effect, 156
aggregation, 321, 324
Aldenderfer, M., 229, 230
archaeological culture, concept of, 190
arithmetic probability paper, 108-9
artefact types in archaeology, 193
association, 81, 93, 94, 98
  and causation, 82-3
  coefficients of, 88
  measures of, 81-99
association analysis, *see* cluster analysis
attributes, 193
autocorrelation, 151, 154-9, 160
average-link cluster analysis, *see* cluster analysis

bar charts, *see* graphs and charts
Barth, F., 60
BMDP (computer package), 345
Bellhouse, D., 317, 322, 326
beta weights, *see* coefficients, beta; *see also* partial regression
Bettinger, R. L., 275, 276, 277, 283
bimodal, *see* mode
Binford, L., 8
Blalock, H. M., 81, 99, 132, 183, 184, 331
Bølviken, E. *et al.*, 283, 284
box-and-whisker plots, *see* graphs and charts
Brainerd, G. W., 191, 193
  see also Robinson and Brainerd
Buchvaldek, M. and Koutecky, D., 15

calculus, 331
Carothers, J. and McDonald, W. A., 154
causation, dangers of inferring from association, 82-3
central tendency, measures of, 35-40, 47
  arithmetic mean, *see* mean
  deviations from mean, 41
  median, 38-9, 40, 44, 108, 160
  mode, 34, 39-40
charts, *see* graphs and charts
Chatterjee, S. and Price, B., 154
Cherry, J. F., 283
Childe, V. G., 190-1
chi-squared test, 65-74, 90, 93, 97, 191

for cross-classified data, 70-4
formula for, 67
limitations of, 74, 77, 78, 92-3
one-sample test, 65-70, 71
statistic, 92, 222-4
tables, 68, 69, 336-7
city-block metric, *see* coefficient
Clarke, D. L., 192, 212
classification, 11, 190, 196-7, 241, 286
  biological, 212
  numerical, 190-232
  numerical versus traditional typological, 229
close-proximity analysis, 209-11, 233, 234
clumping, *see* aggregation
CLUSCOM (cluster analysis computer package), 346
CLUSTAN (cluster analysis computer package), 221, 225, 228, 229, 230, 343, 346
cluster(s), 195-6, 217, 225, 242, 323, 327
  discrete, 270
cluster analysis, 196, 197-8, 207, 212, 235, 237, 241, 242, 243, 244, 269, 288, 289, 295, 332, 343, 345, 346
  evaluation of, 228-31, 346: cophenetic correlation coefficient, 230, 231; discriminant analysis, 229; Jardine and Sibson's Δ, 230; principal components analysis, 229 (*see also* ordination, methods of); scatterplots, 229; stopping rule, 229; Wilk's lambda statistic, 229, 230
  methods of: association analysis, 221-4; average link, *see* group average; complete linkage, *see* furthest neighbour; furthest neighbour, 214-15; group average, 215-17; hierarchical, 197; hierarchical agglomerative, 197, 212-20; hierarchical divisive, 197, 212, 220-5; information statistic, 225; iterative relocation, 226-8; nearest neighbour, 213-14, 218, 230, 324; partitioning, 197, 225-8; single link, *see* nearest neighbour; Ward's method, 217-20, 226, 289, 295

357